27 50

GENDER AND CULTURE

Lynne Huffer

Mad for Foucault

Rethinking the Foundations of Queer Theory

Columbia University Press   New York

Columbia University Press
Publishers Since 1893
New York Chichester, West Sussex
Copyright © 2010 Columbia University Press

Library of Congress Cataloging-in-Publication Data
Huffer, Lynne, 1960–
Mad for Foucault: rethinking the foundations of queer
theory / Lynne Huffer.
p. cm. — (Gender and culture series)
Includes bibliographical references and index.
ISBN 978-0-231-14918-1 (cloth: alk. paper)—
ISBN 978-0-231-14919-8 (pbk.: alk. paper)—
ISBN 978-0-231-52051-5 (e-book)
1. Foucault, Michel, 1926–1984.   2. Homosexuality.
3. Postmodernism.   4. Queer theory.   I. Title.

HQ76.25.H843   2009
306.76′601—dc22
2009012554

Casebound editions of Columbia University Press books are
printed on permanent and durable acid-free paper.

Printed in the United States of America
c 10 9 8 7 6 5 4 3 2
p 10 9 8 7 6 5 4

For Tamara

Contents

Preface

To shake off philosophy necessarily implies a . . . casual abandon. . . . It's to counter [philosophy] with a kind of surprised and joyful foolishness, a sort of incomprehensible burst of laughter which, in the end, comprehends or, in any case, breaks. Yes . . . it breaks more than it comprehends.

—Michel Foucault, 1975

The flashes and sparklings, the statements that tore themselves away from words, even Foucault's laughter was a statement.

—Gilles Deleuze, 1990

This intensive way of reading, in contact with what's outside the book, as a flow meeting other flows, one machine among others, as a series of experiments for each reader in the midst of events that have nothing to do with books, as tearing the book into pieces, getting it to interact with other things, absolutely anything . . . is reading with love.

—Gilles Deleuze, 1973

This book is a story about reading Michel Foucault, with love. When I started this project, I had been studying and teaching Foucault for a number of years, but had never committed myself to writing about him. This half-hearted commitment was due, in part, to my intense ambivalence about his work. Like many feminists, I admired Foucault's brilliance, but felt uneasy about his seeming indifference to feminist concerns. Then, in September 2006, I spent a month in the Foucault archives in Normandy. That experience of what Deleuze calls a "contact with what's outside the book" not only shifted much of what I thought I knew about Foucault but also transformed my hot-and-cold feelings. Suddenly I burned with passion. My archival encounter was nothing less than an experience of rupture: I was, like Deleuze's book, torn to pieces. Returning home to Atlanta, I gathered the pieces and found the shape of a different Foucault, a different feminism, and a different queer theory than what I had known.

Finding a different Foucault "outside the book" brought me, paradoxically, back to a book: Foucault's first major work,[1] *History of Madness*, published in French in 1961 but only fully translated into English in

2006.[2] In unpublished remarks I discovered in the archives, Foucault insists, again and again, on *Madness*'s importance to his oeuvre. Like most feminists with an interest in queer theory, I had not paid much attention to *Madness*, focusing instead on the first volume of the *History of Sexuality* (1976) for an understanding of sex and sexuality in Foucault.[3]

Rediscovering *Madness* now, almost two decades after the emergence of queer theory, I insist on *Madness*'s importance for our present, postqueer age. This is not to erect *Madness* as a monument to Foucault, but rather to bear witness to its capacity to move us. Both the archival material and *History of Madness* tell a story of transformation grounded in a specifically Foucauldian eros. This singular, life-affirming eros offers us resources for an ethics of living in the biopolitical world of the twenty-first century.

My own singularly strange, intensive encounter with *Madness* is strikingly similar to what Foucault describes as the explosive contact that occurs between a book and a reader. In his marvelous, self-ironizing preface to the 1972 French revised edition of *Madness*, Foucault describes his book as an object-event. The voice of the preface is a humble one: The event is "minuscule," "almost imperceptible among so many others," "an object that fits into the hand" (*M* xxxvii). As humble object, the book must take care to avoid speaking with the weight or solemnity of a "text." Rather, it should have the *désinvolture*—the lightness, the attitude of disengagement or abandon—to present itself as discourse, releasing itself from literary and philosophical traditions alike. Rejecting the *belles lettres* book as text—the already coded, received, and ordered canonical tradition of books solidly implanted in libraries, fields of criticism, and pedagogical systems—Foucault chooses instead the book as discourse—the object-event that, like a weapon, ruptures tradition with the force of an opening in history.

Paradoxically, it is precisely in its lightness—in its refusal to be weighed down by a tradition of *explications de texte,* which would confer on it some official status—that the book as discourse and as object-event carries the explosive force of a dramatic, even violent unsettling. It functions, Foucault writes, as "both battle and weapon, strategy and shock, struggle and trophy or wound, conjuncture and vestige, strange meeting and repeatable scene" (*M*xxxviii). For Foucault, the book is a confluence of forces—causes and effects, contexts and consequences, acts and their traces, the sharp thrust of the present and the percussive repetitions of a past remembered. It is also, ultimately, a small explosion, one of many object-events destined to disappear: "I think of my books as mines, explosives. . . . The book should disappear by its own effect."[4] If the book has a voice, it is only the repeated one that, with true humility, performs again the work's disappearance in the Nietzschean cry of the mad philosopher: "I am dynamite."

There is much to be unpacked in this constellation that brings together book as object-event, discourse, repetition, and explosive disappearance. In the pages of this book, I will unpack these concepts and use them to guide my thinking on Foucault, queer theory, and the ethics of sex. Taking seriously the status of Foucault's writings as object-events, I focus primarily on *Madness* as one of the great unread texts of queer theory. My major aim is to read *Madness*, retrospectively, in light of its absence from the only academic field that takes as its primary focus the study of sexuality. I read this absence against the backdrop of the more widely read Foucauldian works that ground queer theory, especially *Sexuality One*. I also include in my considerations the last two published volumes of *History of Sexuality, The Use of Pleasure* and *The Care of the Self*—both published in French in 1984—as well as some of the published and unpublished materials that have come to light in the years since Foucault's death in 1984, including interviews, public lectures, radio debates, roundtables, political pamphlets, and transcriptions of his courses at the Collège de France. In engaging *Madness* and these other more peripheral writings and interviews, I hope to productively unravel some of the blind spots and dogmas of contemporary queer theory.

Foucault's description of the book as an object-event serves to situate my reading of him within a larger conceptualization of historical writing that Foucault called eventialization (*événementialisation*). For Foucault, the concept of the *event* crystallized history as discontinuity and rupture, rather than as a progressive narrative based on the logic of cause and effect. In his reflections on *Madness*, Foucault's teacher, Georges Canguilhem, reminds us that Foucault defined eventialization as "the bringing to light of 'ruptures of evidence.'"[5] This notion of eventialization as an approach to writing history reinforces the text-discourse distinction mentioned above, where the traditional view of human history as a seamless past waiting to be read functions like the falsely solidified text of the belles lettres tradition. Eventialization—the disruptive bringing to light of that which is plain or clear to sight or understanding—functions, like discourse, as the illuminating but fragmenting force through which the discontinuous multiplicity of history becomes an object of sight and, paradoxically, in that moment of visibility disappears from view. In this sense, the book as object-event takes its place within a larger conceptualization of history as eventialization.

"Foucault," Deleuze writes, "is haunted by the double and its essential otherness."[6] Eventialization links history with philosophy through the concept of the double, and doubling brings out the political dimension of the book as object-event. As just one moment in a repetitive "bringing to light of 'ruptures of evidence,'" the book as event "takes its place in an incessant game of repetitions" (M xxxvii). These doublings, in turn, form part of what Foucault will always refer to as games of truth. As an event inevitably caught in a movement of repetition, fragmentation, copying, reflection, and simulation, the book disappears in this other sense, into the infinite proliferation of its doubles as truth. What remains of the book are these truth-effects in the world. The book as discourse—as the repeated rupture of truth-effects—occurs with the force of dynamite. That force is felt in the world, in "the series of events to which [the book] belongs" (M xxxviii)—its readers, its commentators, the multiple interlocutors who constitute its various discursive contexts. In this way, the book's truth-effects ripple through the world like rings on water, as the light-bringing rupture of an expansive doubling.

These concepts of event and doubling, gleaned from the 1972 preface, have opened a passage, belatedly and retrospectively, into my reinterpretation of *History of Madness* in the context of queer theory. Foucault's picture of the explosive doubling of the book-event points to the complexity of a book's reception and its impact in the world. The "doubling" of a book-event occurs in very specific ways, including translation, commentary, interpretation, retranslation, and reinterpretation. This is how a book both appears and "disappears . . . into the series of events to which it belongs" (M xxxviii). In the case of *History of Madness*, its status as a nonevent in queer theory is, at least in part, a consequence of the story of its nontranslation into English. Let me briefly recount that history.

The first English translation of the book occurred in 1965, four years after its first appearance in French. Originally published in 1961 as *Folie et déraison: Histoire de la folie à l'âge classique*, the book was soon reissued in a truncated inexpensive French paperback version for "train station waiting rooms,"[7] as Foucault put it. Although pleased with a popular edition of *Madness*, Foucault was disappointed that this abridged version became the standard edition of the book. Not only was the French public likely to read an incomplete book but, with the exception of the Italian version, all the foreign language translations of *Madness* were based on this shortened popular edition. This explains the severely abridged English translation by Richard Howard, entitled *Madness and Civilization: A History of Insanity in the Age of Reason,* that was published in 1965. At 230 pages, the book was about one-third the length of Foucault's original version. *Madness and Civilization* was widely distributed to an American audience that had, for the most part, never heard Foucault's name before. And, although the book had a considerable impact on American readers, it was not subsequently engaged by queer theorists.[8]

Forty-five years after the book's initial publication in French, a complete English translation of *Madness* finally appeared in 2006. This unabridged translation by Jonathan Murphy and Jean Khalfa includes both the 1961 and 1972 prefaces; a foreword by Ian Hacking; an introduction by Jean Khalfa; two appendixes from the 1972 French edition, "Madness, the Absence of an Oeuvre" and "My Body, This Paper, This Fire"; an additional appendix, "Reply to Derrida," from a 1972 Tokyo lecture; and four critical annexes with supporting historical documents and bibliographic material.[9]

There is no denying the importance of this translation-event; for the first time, English speakers have access to the pivotal arguments that established the groundwork for Foucault's thinking during the remaining twenty-three years of his life. It is not yet clear, however, whether or not this new translation—still poorly marketed in the U.S.—will have any impact on American queer theory and the study of sexuality or on the American reception of Foucault's thought more generally. Whatever that impact might be, it is Ian Hacking's astute comments in the foreword that I follow. Describing the difference between the original and its translation, he writes: "Doublings: I suggest that you hold in your hands two distinct books. . . . Despite the words being the same, so much has happened that the meaning is different" (*M* xii). This book focuses on how that difference in meaning emerges, post–queer theory, in my own doubling return to sexuality in *Madness*.

Queer theorists should care deeply about *History of Madness*. The impact of Foucault's thought on queer theory is undeniable, and yet, because *Madness* has only recently been fully translated into English, queer theory's uptake of this work has been truncated and therefore distorted. This is especially significant given that *History of Madness* is not only Foucault's first major book but also the one Foucault himself favored over all the others. Additionally, although there is great disagreement among Foucauldians about the continuity of Foucault's ideas over the course of his life, *Madness* clearly lays the foundations for certain constants in Foucault's thinking. These include, most importantly, Foucault's sustained critique of moral and political exclusion and his lifelong challenge to the despotic power of philosophical reason: to "shake off philosophy," as he puts it in this book's first epigraph. Finally, as Didier Eribon notes in *Insult and the Making of the Gay Self* (2003), *Madness*'s dissection of the structures of madness and unreason in the Age of Reason constitutes an analysis of sexuality a full fifteen years before the publication of the first of three volumes explicitly dedicated to that subject. Not only is *Madness* an earlier consideration of sexuality, but, historically, analytically, and stylistically, it gives a thicker, experiential texture to its subject than *Sexuality One*. Significantly, Foucault's "archeology" (*M* 80) of a vast field of unreason uncovers an array of figures of sexual alterity, including not only homosexuals, but hysterics, onanists, libertines, prostitutes, debauchers, nymphomaniacs, and other sexual "abnormals." *Madness* therefore directly engages the question of sexuality as an experience by incorporating it within the frame of madness. By contrast, Foucault's purely discursive definition of sexuality in *Sexuality One* drains it of any possible experiential meanings. To read Foucault on sexuality without reading *History of Madness* is to miss a crucial dimension of sexuality in Foucault.

Finally, and more specifically, if we ignore *Madness*, we miss Foucault's early, radical thinking about ethics. And a queer ethics is something that we, queer theorists and activists, desperately need to help us shape our increasingly confusing intellectual and political positions. When we don't read *Madness*, we miss an important story about sexuality that links the apotheosis of reason and the objectifying gaze of science with what Foucault called bourgeois structures of moral exclusion. We also miss the grounding of Foucault's devastating critique of psychoanalysis in that structure which links reason and science to moral exclusion. And, finally, we miss a crucial element—namely, experience—in Foucault's thinking about morality and ethics, one that both deepens and complicates Foucault's later work on ethics in *Sexuality Two* and *Three*. These three dimensions of ethics in *Madness* can be linked to the more explicitly ethical and political language of Foucault's later work, in what Michel Feher calls Foucault's interest in "the potential for moral innovation and a politics of resistance."[10]

Mad for Foucault reads *History of Madness* belatedly, through the lens of a queer theoretical project that missed it the first time around. This queer reading of *Madness* builds on the work begun by Eribon, but moves in a slightly different direction. Eribon's attention to homosexuality's exclusion in the world of unreason and his emphasis on Foucault's critique of psychoanalysis in *Madness* clearly make the case for a more sustained engagement with the book, especially in a queer context. My analysis of *Madness* begins where Eribon ends, by looking more closely at the critique of psychoanalysis and asking, more specifically, about the question of ethics as it relates to sexual experience. Providing an alternative to the psychoanalytic language that purportedly allows the madness of sexuality to "speak," *Madness* offers an alternative ethical language of eros for engaging the difference of sexual unreason.

Toward the end of his life, in his lectures, courses, and the second and third volumes of *History of Sexuality,* Foucault returned to his earlier interest in the problem of sexuality as a problem of experience. He did this, primarily, in his minute dissection of the technologies of the self that, in the Greco-Roman and early Christian worlds, constituted sexuality as an ethical experience whose condition of possibility was freedom. That project was his attempt to release sexuality as an ethical experience from its suturing to bourgeois categories of morality. In that context, *Madness* both explores how that suturing occurred and forges an opening toward alternative ethical perspectives for living in the present. Looking through the lens of Foucault's final work on an ethics of experience, we can thus return to ethics in *Madness* through the back door, as it were, by asking the question Foucault posed in 1984 not long before his death, "why [have] we made sexuality into a moral experience?"[11]

There are many possible responses to that question, including: it was Christianity that turned the erotic relation into something to be judged according to a rigid system of moral norms. This is, in fact, what Foucault saw after writing the still unpublished fourth volume of *History of Sexuality, Confessions of the Flesh,* about the Christian period, the practices of confession, and the beginnings of the discursive proliferation of sexuality that culminated in the modern production of perversions. If Christianity was at least partially responsible for turning sexuality into a moral experience in the Western world, how do we get out from under it? Most Foucault readers, when faced with that question, turn to his work on the Greco-Roman world and the ethics of the self as self-fashioning. Foucault ultimately saw, the story goes, that one way to get out from under morality as we know it in the West was to return to the ancient world in order to unearth pre-Christian corporeal practices that were not coded according to Christian moral conceptions of the body and desire. Only in this pre-Christian petri dish could an experiment occur where ethical self-fashioning in relation to others might take place in a context that Foucault calls freedom.

This familiar reading of a Foucauldian ethics of self-fashioning is a worthy one. But I propose reading Foucault from a different angle and under a different light. Specifically, in order to grapple with the difficult question of why we've made sexuality into a moral experience, we must also examine *History of Madness* and the great division between reason and unreason. If returning to the Greeks was Foucault's way of getting out from under Christian morality, returning to the moment of splitting in the Age of Reason was Foucault's way of getting out from under philosophy's despotic moralizing power. This is not to deny the suggestive value of Foucault's pre-Christian approach to ethics in *Sexuality Two* and *Three*. Rather, it is to offer a way of proceeding that takes seriously the secular, rationalist production of a normative ethics through which the erotic bonds of bodies are coded as moral experience. This approach to Foucault will tease out, in *Madness*, his ethical alternative to the philosophical production of moral norms by a sovereign secular reason. That ethical alternative to rationalist morality—something we might imagine as sexual experience released from its moral frame—is what I call Foucault's ethics of eros.

This ethics of eros is situated in a trajectory of thought that confronts the Cartesian mind-body dualism with an insistence on the role the body plays in intersubjective relations. As a site of pleasure but also of death, of erotic connection but also of pain, the body reactivates the tragic dimension of subjectivity, the fact of our life and our annihilation in the body's eventual death. In its premodern form, madness as unreason stood in for that bodily dimension of human experience: the cosmic, tragic presence of life and death—Eros and Thanatos—at the heart of all subjectivity. By the late eighteenth century, that tragic subjectivity had been masked by science in the capture of madness as mental illness.

Within that conception of modern subjectivity as a mask that hides our tragic corporeality, Foucault celebrates an erotic, desubjectivating subjectivity that embraces the body in its life and death. Paradoxically, however, to reclaim tragic eros is also to negate it as already captured by the gaze of scientific reason. As Foucault puts it in the 1961 preface: "Any perception that aims to apprehend [those insane words] in their wild state necessarily belongs to a world that has captured them already" (*M* xxxii). Thus the historical objectification by the Age of Reason of our bodily selves as a repudiated madness makes Foucault's reclamation of eros not only tragic but also ironic, since it can only be grasped through the hindsight of its undoing.

Foucault's eros is not a redemptive cure for that which ails us; it does not provide us with an essential plenitude to which we can cling for solace in these modern, science-dominated, seemingly loveless times. Foucault's conception of history as a series of doublings refuses the comfort of a nostalgic return to the tragic subjectivity we have lost. Rather, in its ironic mode, historical doubling always includes a force of destruction, unhappiness, and pain. As the constitutive element of Foucault's ethics, eros is driven not only by the force of an intersubjective generosity but by a force of ironic undoing as well. Eros indeed contains its opposite, Thanatos, just as reason, for Foucault, is inhabited by its opposite, unreason. As the point of that division, Foucault's ethics of eros describes a force of both connection and dissolution: It is both tragic and ironic, lyrical and ludic, the site of utopian promise and aporetic cynicism. If erotic generosity makes us want to cling to its promise of transformative connection, the violent force of erotic irony reminds us that the thing we're clinging to is a stick of dynamite.

This explosive force of ironic generosity repeats the description of the explosive force of the book-event in the 1972 preface. Reading this alternative ethics in Foucault brings together, then, Foucault's final question about sexual morality—Why have we made sexuality into a moral experience?—and his earlier reflections on sexuality and madness. Bringing them together allows us to reengage the question of a possible queer ethics in Foucault as an erotic response to secular philosophy's unquestioned reliance on reason. Approached in this way, thinking queerly becomes not just a way of responding, from within Christianity, to the murderous exclusions of religious morality. It becomes a way of rethinking the despotic rationalism of a secular order whose effects are equally murderous. The queer as an experience sits on the threshhold that I am naming the erotic. Eros names a nonself-identical force that resists the exclusions of moral rationalism, but that also moves beyond the pure negativity of ethical rupture. Although never fully articulated here as a political theory, *Madness* offers the elements of an ethics that can speak to our queer political present.

A Postscript on Prefaces

And why, one might ask, do I begin with a preface, when in 1972 Foucault so adamantly denounces the form as "a declaration of tyranny"

(*M* xxxviii) that allows the author to impose her own image on the book's reception? "'I am the author'" (*M* xxxviii), the sovereign preface declares: "'Look at my face'" (*M* xxxviii) to see "my intention. . . . When I speak of the limits of my enterprise, I mean to set a boundary for your freedom" (*M* xxxviii).

Foucault is right, of course, when he writes these lines in the "non-preface" he supplies in 1972. But it's difficult to let go, to avoid imposing an intention on the book one has written. Foucault faces this difficulty when he is asked to write a new preface for the 1972 French revised edition of *Madness*. "I really ought to write a new preface for this book," Foucault begins. But he finds the idea to be "unattractive" (*M* xxxvii), even repugnant, as the original French *j'y répugne* (*F* 9) suggests. Nonetheless, Foucault cannot dispense with a new preface altogether, even if its only real purpose is to say, as it does: "Then remove the old one [*l'ancienne*]" (*M* xxxviii, *F* 10, translation modified). Alas, even the liberating act that would remove the declaration of tyranny leaves another, more despotic declaration to take its place.

No one is more aware of this irony than Foucault himself in the 1972 preface, a mere two-page affair whose conclusion splits and doubles the singularity of the narrative "I." Suddenly, at the end, two voices emerge to mock the entire enterprise:

> When I was asked to write a new preface for this book . . . I could only answer: Then remove the old one. That will be the honest course.
>
> . . .
>
> "But you've just written a preface."
> "At least it's short." (*M* xxxix/*F* 10; translation modified)

I love that split voice of 1972, just as I love the doubling of that split in the 2006 English translation, where we can read both the suppressed 1961 preface and the new 1972 version side by side. To me, the emergence of the two prefaces together in 2006 mirrors the doubled voice that emerged at the end of the 1972 preface. But it is a "distorting mirror [*trouble miroir*]" (*M* 354–355/*F* 374), as Foucault later puts it in *Madness*, one that destabilizes the certainty of the self-identical authorial subject's declaration of freedom from an ancien régime: "Then remove the old one [*l'ancienne*]" (*M* xxxix/*F* 10; translation modified).

As we will see later in my analysis, the ancien régime to be suppressed—the 1961 preface—is the overly poetic, "lyrical" voice of a young Foucault. That voice will dissolve into the ironic discourse of the

1970s. But even in the 1960s—and despite his later reservations about what he retrospectively saw in *Madness* as "a lingering Hegelianism"[12]— Foucault knew that irony was not a simple matter of dialectical reversal along the linear timeline of a story: "*Homo dialecticus*," he wrote in 1964, "is already dying in us" (*M* 543). Today, in the marvelous 2006 English translation, there is no neat narrative sublation of the 1961 lyricism into the mastering irony of 1972. The two prefaces coexist in an aporetic relation that refuses to erase, in some happy resolution, the contradictory traces of their doubled construction.

I've written this preface, then, to signal a postmodern, aporetic irony at the heart of Foucault's project. But if aporia—from the Greek *aporos*— suggests in its etymology that there will be "no passage" to something other, that is where Foucault has a different tale to tell than the familiar deconstructive story. The passage through the rupture of the ironic split may not be dialectical, but that doesn't mean there's no passage at all. Indeed, finding a passage—"giving the mad a language"[13]—is Foucault's declared purpose in writing *Madness*. And finding a passage—a way through the thicket, a breach in the wall—describes this book's purpose as well.

Acknowledgments

This book, unexpected, came from many places. It unfolded in ways I had never imagined, and even after the process of writing had ended I felt I was being pulled by a tide of others. There was something fierce in that pull. I want to acknowledge here some of those who gave the pull its energy, assisting the transformation of a gut feeling into a book: an object to be released, as Foucault would put it, into the series of events to which it belongs.

First and foremost, I want to thank my dear friends Jonathan Goldberg and Michael Moon, both of whom read much of the manuscript in its multiple versions. It was Jonathan and Michael, more than any others, who first helped me to see that the passion I felt *was* a book. I also want to thank Didier Eribon for stimulating conversations at the Café Beaubourg, assistance with references and biographical details, and access to Foucault's letters to Jean Barraqué. Cindy Willett read many of these pages and helped me work through the most philosophically knotted places. Jill Robbins helped me explore the ins and outs of dialectical thinking; I am especially grateful for conversations during our frequent walks around the lake at Lullwater. Another friend and Foucault afficionado, James Faubion, provided me with advice and much-needed encouragement. Thanks to Debarati Sanyal for our week together on a lake in Texas, for her intelligent interventions and ongoing inspiration. I am grateful to Michel Achard for help on the nuances of

French-English translation and to my research assistants Kelly Ball, Kathryn Wilchens, and Lizzy Venell for their tireless and impeccably executed work on this project. Many thanks to my doctoral student, Brooke Campbell, for her helpful thinking about gender and sexuality in Foucault. I am also grateful to my friend and colleague, Paul Kelleher, for his interest in my project and a shared, always happy, obsession with Foucault.

Much of the first draft of this book was written in a house I rented during the winter and early spring of 2007 in Milledgeville, Georgia. Many thanks to my friend and writing companion, Leslie Harris, for encouragement, humor, long walks on country roads, and writerly in- spiration. I am grateful to Marcelina Martin for making her home avail- able to us and to Tashi, Ravi, Savannah, and the cats for the uncondi- tional affection only animals can give.

The writing of later drafts of the manuscript was undertaken during three residencies at the Hambidge Center in the north Georgia moun- tains during the summers of 2007 and 2008 and for a short week in December 2007. I am grateful for the creative spark and intense focus these residencies provided and offer a special thanks to Bob Thomas, the residency director. I also want to thank the staff at the Institut Mé- moires de l'Edition Contemporaine (IMEC) at the Abbaye d'Ardenne near Caen, France, where I spent some of the most blissful weeks of my life in September 2006 and again in August 2008. I owe a special debt of gratitude to José Ruiz-Funes, the Foucault archivist, and to Philippe Artières, the director of the Centre Foucault. A heartfelt thanks goes to Rose-Marie Janzen for her generosity in giving me full access to Fou- cault's letters to Jean Barraqué.

Much of the thinking behind chapter 5 developed during a graduate seminar on Foucault I cotaught with Mark Jordan during the fall semes- ter of 2007. I am grateful to every student in the course and especially to Mark for what I will always remember as a singular event that took us far beyond the bounds of the seminar genre into an experience I can only describe as poetic. I know it taught me to think *and feel* differently than I had before. I am also grateful to members of my two writing groups, one "academic," the other "creative"—Pamela Hall, Liz Bounds, Cindy Willett (again), and Ruby Lal, Laurie Patton, and Leslie Harris (again)—their attentive readings and exquisite writing kept me going.

I want to express my appreciation to Emory University, and especially Dean Robert Paul, for providing the leave time and research funds nec- essary for travel and writing during the 2006–2007 academic year. I am grateful to my colleagues and students in the Women's Studies Department at Emory, who inspire me in more ways than I can count. Many thanks to Judith Butler, Elizabeth Weed, Larry Schehr, and Zahi Zalloua for their support of this project through publishing some of its parts. I also want to thank Cecelia Cancellaro, my agent, for being my champion and using her skills and talents to help me find a home for this book. The home it has found is a good one. I am grateful to Wendy Lochner for her consistent support of the book and to Nancy K. Miller and Victoria Rosner for including me in the Gender and Culture Series.

Although my family is physically distant much of the time, I have felt their encouragement throughout the sometimes tumultuous process of writing. They have been through this book-writing business with me twice before, and I continue to be grateful for their unremitting support of my writing life. Thanks to Smudge and Zora, my furry, purring companions who spent as many hours in my study—in my lap, on my keyboard—as I did. And finally, to Tamara, I want to offer arms-wide-open thanks for loving me madly through every page; each word holds the light of your yes-saying living. It is to you that I dedicate this book.

Mad for Foucault

Introduction

MAD FOR FOUCAULT

*Why did Western culture expel to its extremities the very thing in
which it might just as easily have recognised itself—where it had in
fact recognised itself in an oblique fashion?*

—Michel Foucault, 1964

*Tell all the Truth but tell it slant
Success in Circuit lies*

—Emily Dickinson, 1890

Splitting: A Love Story

The story of queerness—as a story about madness—begins with the
story of a split: the great division between reason and unreason. That
split organizes Foucault's *histoire*—his history and his story—about
forms of subjectivity tossed into a dustbin called madness. Queerness
is a name we have given to one of those forms. Since the early 1990s,
we—queer theorists and loving perverts—have tried to rescue the queer
from the dustbin of madness and make her our own. Theory calls this
gesture resignification: we have dusted her off, turned her around, and
made her into something beautiful.

But somehow, over the years, the queer has become a figure who has
lost her generative promise. She turned in on herself and became frozen into a new, very American identity. And if the transformation itself
is to be celebrated, the final freezing is not. Getting stuck in identities
that are often politically or medically engineered, the queer is drained of
her transformative, contestatory power. This is where *History of Madness* can help us, as the story of a split that produced the queer. Not only
a diagnosis of the great division between reason and unreason, *Madness*
is also a contestation of that division's despotic "structure of refusal . . .
on the basis of which a discourse is denounced as not being a language
[and] as having no rightful place in history. This structure is constitutive
of what is sense and nonsense" (*M* xxxii).

Just as reason excludes nonsense from itself, so, too, it excludes the queer. But as both a diagnosis and a contestation, Foucault's story about splitting offers a new way to tap into the generative promise of the queer. From the Middle High German *quer*, queer means oblique, as in the Foucault epigraph cited at the beginning of this introduction—from the Latin *obliquus*, slanting: a new way of speaking. "Tell all the Truth but tell it slant / Success in Circuit lies," a queer Emily Dickinson reminds us. *Quer* also means adverse—from the Latin *versus*, a turning, the root that gives us perverse, perverted, pervert. The danger of the queer is that it can easily be re-turned against us: we can be recaptured and pinned down again in our perversions and our genders. So if the etymological circuit—*quer, obliquus, versus*—threatens to bring us right back to where we started, the trick is to keep things turning into something other. *History of Madness* has much to teach us about that resistant, transformative turning: about turning adversity into new ways of thinking, feeling, and acting in the world.

Like Foucault, I begin my book here with a story about splitting—about writing a book as a split subject. To some, this abstract language about split subjectivity will sound nonsensical or, even worse, Lacanian. If it sounds like nonsense, we might do well to remember that nonsense is just the unruly child of despotic reason. Regarding her as such, we may be persuaded to loosen the reins of nonsense-hating judgments, at least for a while. And if it sounds Lacanian, we might do well to just keep reading. Like Freud, Lacan does not belong here, except as a movement out the door, and this book explains why that is so. Indeed, one of my goals in my encounter with *Madness* is to rethink splitting—and split subjectivity—from a nonpsychoanalytic perspective.

I have circled around the subject of splitting, the split subject, for many years, often heading off in strange directions trying to find my way through the thicket. Many days, even now as I'm writing, I'm convinced there's no book here at all. I try to console myself, as I would a friend. I look at the Ziggy cartoon tacked to my bulletin board (figure 0.1). It's one I have offered to others in their moments of sheer panic at the seeming emptiness of their own writing endeavors.

"See, there's a book in there," I cheerily tell them. "You may not see it, but it's there."

This familiar scene of self-doubt is one I've decided to place at the beginning, as a way of starting, because self-negation resides at the heart of any project which, for better or worse, becomes a book. Faced with their own nothingness, my book-writing friends have told me that

FIGURE 0.1 Ziggy cartoon

the cartoon brings them solace. But here's the truth: I don't actually believe there's a book in there. Don't get me wrong: I believe in the book, but it's not *in there*. Yes, we talk about our insides all the time; it's a fiction we live as something real. It helps us see ourselves as containers that can be full. But we don't have insides. Not really. I'll develop this critique of psychic interiority in the chapters that follow. For the moment, I want simply to note this opening connection between a belief in our insides and the problem of splitting.

This introduction gestures toward the splits that fracture the surface of this fairly contained reinterpretation of Foucault's first major book. In that gesture, I'm inspired by Foucault, whose basic focus in *History of Madness* is the reverberating impact of the great historical split between reason and unreason. But "unreason," Ian Hacking reminds us, "is no longer part of daily language" (*M* xii). And from the very start, Hacking continues, "you will have been wondering what it means. Rightly so" (*M* xii). I'm afraid we can only keep on wondering. It's the problem and the promise of nonsense again. We can only know what unreason is in relation to the reason from which it splits. In itself, it is nothing.

Since in itself unreason is nothing, I make my entrée into this difficult material through the act of splitting itself. Splitting is complex, as the fraught relation between reason and unreason shows us. Splitting is both a unity and a division into something other in which the unity is lost. It is both the moment of that division and its result. And one can only apprehend it retrospectively, after the fact, as it were. For example, if I say, "she's crazy," I have retrospectively apprehended the historical split that separates reason from unreason.

As someone who speaks mostly with a voice of reason, I accept the ironic terms of this project: that is, my own place in a grid of historical contingencies that separate reason from unreason, and reason's reliance on its difference from unreason in order to stake its claims. I don't have to look far to find myself on the shifting line of demarcation that separates the two. In seventeenth-century Europe, for example—or even in twentieth-century Milledgeville, Georgia, where the world's largest asylum stood (and where, strangely, I ended up renting a house in 2007 and drafting this book about madness)—my queerness would have been reason enough to lock me up in the madhouse down the road. And yet today, as a feminist scholar—and despite my queerness—I can't help but lay claim to a voice that speaks in the language of reason.

The irony suggests that the split must be interrogated. I do this here by starting with a story about feeling divided: wanting to take sides, and then, in a stubborn refusal, negotiating the uncomfortable space of the in-between. This in-between is the space and time of the division itself: the subject in the act of splitting.

Specifically, the splits emerge here around a configuration of terms, including queer and feminist, theorist and activist, French and American, hate and love. Oddly, perhaps, I get at these splits—try to work through them nonpsychoanalytically—by using Foucault and his great story about the split that creates unreason and eventually madness. Ultimately Foucault is the split figure that, for me, helps explain all the others. Inspired by Susan Howe who, in *My Emily Dickinson* (1985), makes the poet her own without possessing her, I've found myself receiving Foucault through personal channels, in a mode I had not expected. "My voice formed from my life belongs to no one else," Howe writes. "What I put into words is no longer my possession."[1] Like Howe with Dickinson, I've made this Foucault *my* Foucault, the one I found after years of splitting and getting lost in the thicket.

I had been working on Foucault for a number of years in a quiet, relatively invisible way. I taught him in seminars, read most of his work, and even used him in some of my own thinking about feminism and nostalgia in a previous book, although not explicitly. It's hard keeping up with the ever-proliferating Foucault-machine: if it's not another thick volume of course lectures, then it's yet another brilliant interpretation of his work. I admire all this discursive production, but it also overwhelms me.

More problematically, like many feminists, for many years I was in a love-hate relationship with Foucault. Yes, his theories of disciplinary subjection as a modern form of productive power have been important for understanding the complex ways in which marginalized people, including women, are caught in mechanisms of subjection and subjectivation (*assujettissement*), where their lack of freedom is both already imposed and self-perpetuating. But I also have heard and analyzed many of the ways in which Foucault seemed not to notice women: "It was literally as if I wasn't there," one of my graduate school professors told me when recounting a time she had met him in Paris. Very early on, in reading him, I noticed the strange deviation through which Foucault refused to acknowledge the gendered specificity of rape, both in his famous description of the bucolic pleasures of a nineteenth-century French village idiot, Jouy, in *Sexuality One* and *Abnormal*, and in his infamous comments before the 1977 French commission on rape, recounted by Monique Plaza in her angry article, "Our Damages and Their Compensation: Rape: The Will Not to Know of Michel Foucault" (1981).[2] As Plaza tells us, that was the time he asserted, "Whether one punches his fist in someone's face, or his penis in the sexual organ makes no difference."[3]

In my Franco-American encounter with Foucault, I also took seriously Angela Davis's critique of him as a thinker of imprisonment who does not acknowledge the role of race in what critics call the prison-industrial complex.[4] To be sure, as a founding member of the French antiprison movement, Groupe d'Information sur les Prisons (GIP, 1970–72), Foucault was part of a transnational movement against modern structures of imprisonment. As a GIP member, Foucault participated in writing and distributing French materials about antiprison campaigns in the U.S. For example, GIP publicly denounced the 1971 murder of George Jackson in the San Quentin prison in one of their pamphlets, "Intolérable 3: L'Assasinat de George Jackson," which included a preface by Jean Genet. In September 1971, GIP published a text, "Le Prisonnier Affronte Chaque Jour la Ségrégation," which exposed the racism that led to the Attica revolt and massacre a few days earlier and compared American racism to the anti-immigrant repression that characterizes the French prison system. GIP also helped bring the writings of Eldridge Cleaver and other activists in the American Black Power movement to the attention of the French public.[5]

Despite the racial dimension of GIP's analysis of the prison system, in the book Foucault wrote following the group's dissolution in 1972, *Discipline and Punish* (1975), the traces of that analysis disappear.[6] Davis is right to note that, if *Discipline and Punish* is "arguably the most influential text in contemporary studies of the prison system . . . gender and race are virtually absent"[7] from the book. And while the influence of European carceral models on the American prison system is a topic that has yet to be adequately explored, Davis highlights what Foucault ignores: namely, the specificity of American slavery as part of the history of the U.S. prison system. "A more expansive analysis of U.S. historical specificities," Davis writes, "might serve as the basis for a genealogy of imprisonment that would differ significantly from Foucault's."[8]

Given this context, it was hard for me to put my feminist and antiracist worries aside and embrace Foucault. And yet, despite the problems, over the course of my own process of becoming queer, getting to know Foucault better became more and more important to me. Grounded and formed both in the world of French belles lettres and in the world of women's studies and feminist theory, over the years I became increasingly interested in the overlapping but very different realm of queer theory. This shifting interest was partially due to my own coming out process in the early 1990s, which corresponded with the early development of queer theory in the U.S. If I was going to be queer, I thought, I'd better know something about it. And so I started teaching courses in lesbian and gay studies, sexual identities in literary texts, the history of sexuality, and queer theory. Still an antiracist feminist but also queer, I have remained there ever since, in that threshold space where those positions come together but also split.

The splitting gets worse. For within each of these categories, other splits appear. A big one for me—a crack as deep as the San Andreas fault—is the split between my political activist self and the academic self that speaks the strange language of high French theory. And that split holds true both for the feminist and queer parts of me—the reader of Luce Irigaray who has also participated in Take Back the Night marches and worked on feminist antiracist projects in New York City; the reader of Foucault who has also organized to oppose antigay legislation, hosted a queer radio show, worked to help elect a progressive African American activist to Houston City Council, and rode the Atlanta light rail registering voters during the Obama campaign for the U.S. presidency.

Although some of my friends have trouble reconciling these different parts of me, Foucault helps me to understand them as related, existing in a tension with each other that I hope can continue to be productive. The language I use to interrogate queer theory may not be accessible to the "woman on the street." But that doesn't mean what I have to say in my theory voice has nothing to do with her either. Nor does it mean that I'm not accountable to her, called by her presence to acknowledge what Foucault describes as "a certain common difficulty in bearing what happens"[9] and to develop strategies for transforming that difficulty into possibilities for human flourishing. For Foucault, in both his intellectual and activist work, "neither cultural or moral affinities, nor a community of interests, nor a similarity of experiences, nor a congruence of political projects . . . assures the coherence or legitimacy of a resistance,"[10] although any of these elements can have a role to play. Ultimately, what drives Foucault-the-intellectual and Foucault-the-activist is what Michel Feher calls "a shared intolerance with regard to a particular situation."[11]

So already Foucault helps with these splits within splits: the theorist-activist within the feminist-queer. But things are never simple. For Foucault himself has contributed to the feminist-queer split with which my own splittings started. Further, his role in that split in relation to me—his role as *my* Foucault—has a dimension that is at once personal, intellectual, and affective. As I mentioned earlier, I call that dimension my love-hate relation to Foucault. The love part stems from the aspects of Foucault's work that are admired by many: his capacity to shake up the boundaries that define our thinking, to reshape thought itself, and to engage in that disruptive reconceptualization through considerations of concrete historical events. That tenuous but powerful straddling of philosophical and historical modes of thinking defines the split Foucault I love.

The hate part comes in through the familiar story about Foucault's purported exclusion of women, what feminists have called Foucault's will not to know us. The more I read him, the more I saw it, not just in the bucolic rape passage in *Sexuality One,* or the infamous scene before the rape commission, but also in his final volumes on the history of sexuality, where the Greco-Roman world is reduced primarily to a universe occupied by elite men and where the reality of the lives of women and slaves is given little attention. I didn't much like those final volumes—for the most part, I thought they were boring—but the relative absence of women there gave me more ammunition for my feminist critique of Foucault.

Nonetheless, I decided that I needed to understand Foucault's work more fully. My favorite Foucault was the middle Foucault, the one who has been most acknowledged in the Anglo-American context I inhabit. Although trained in French departments, I didn't get to know Foucault there. The French spaces I occupied were imbued with the heady prose of Sévigné and Proust, the dazzling poetry of Scève, Baudelaire, and Mallarmé, and the theoretical pirouettes of Lacan, Barthes, and Derrida. For reasons that, I believe, remain to be explored, Foucault was scarcely read in most American French departments during the twenty-year period I spent within them, between 1985 and 2005. However, in the U.S. he was being taught in history, English, and women's studies programs.

My own access to Foucault came through Gayle Rubin's essay, "Thinking Sex," in a graduate women's studies seminar in 1987, taught by Sherry Ortner. Three years later, I found him again, in the work of Judith Butler and Eve Kosofsky Sedgwick. Ironically, given my subsequent feminist misgivings about his work, I met Foucault through the American channels of women's studies. And although I didn't know it at the time (reading Rubin, Butler, and Sedgwick, as I did, virtually hot off the press), looking back I can see, as others have, that these three thinkers formed part of what today we can call the feminist beginnings of queer theory. These three writers used the Foucault of the middle period—the Foucault of *Discipline and Punish* (1975) and especially *Sexuality One*—to articulate ways of thinking about gender and sexuality together and in the process changed American academic conceptions of identity, politics, and marginalization. That chronological moment, around 1990, was a crucial time for the paradoxical coming together as splitting that we might retrospectively call the feminist birth of queer theory.

It is worth noting here another split emerging just below the surface of this story. It's the Franco-American one, and it forms an important strand in this story of splittings. The specification of "American" in the story I just told about the feminist birth of queer theory is weighted and deliberate. The French intellectual community of which Foucault and his work are a part has been slow to take up seriously any of the theorists, especially the queer and feminist ones, who have so profoundly transformed the American intellectual context, and for whom Foucault's work has been so crucial. Butler's most widely read book, *Gender Trouble* (1990), was only translated into French in 2005.[12] A French translation of Sedgwick's paradigm-shifting *Epistemology of the Closet* (1990) appeared even later, in 2008, almost twenty years after its original publication in English.[13] Rubin's two most widely read essays, "The Traffic in Women" (1974) and "Thinking Sex" (1984) have been translated, but are not widely cited or acknowledged in the French context.[14] Books like *Queer Critics* (2002) and *French Theory* (2003) by François Cusset take glee in ridiculing the American uptake of what has been called, from an American perspective, "French theory," a perspective that mixes together thinkers as diverse as the psychoanalytic Lacan, the deconstructive Derrida, and the genealogical Foucault into an odd American stew. While the stew seems outrageous from the perspective of those raised on French haute cuisine, that Franco-American difference or disconnection deserves an exploration that goes deeper than the Francocentric mockery of writers like Cusset.

In 2006, faced with a long overdue sabbatical, I decided to go to France and get to know Foucault better. Mired as I was, at that moment in my life, in my split self—the one caught between France and America, feminist and queer, hate and love and, perhaps most significantly for someone on sabbatical, the one who both "had a book in there" and had nothing to say at all—I intuitively felt that Foucault would help me to work through these tangled webs of splittings, which, like spidery cracks across a broken windshield, seemed only to proliferate the more I pursued them. Perhaps I really had crashed without knowing it at the time of the collision. In my professional life, I had recently left French departments altogether and claimed, once and for all, my women's studies self as a full-time member of a doctorate-granting women's studies department. Having taken that step away from things French, I returned to France after a thirteen-year hiatus. Unexpectedly, when I returned, I experienced myself not as reconciled, but as a fully split subject. I went, uncomfortably split, to the archives in Normandy, to read Foucault through the marginalia which had not yet been published: some radio debates and roundtables from the 1970s, some still unpublished courses, and, most important, the four-hundred-page typescript of an unpublished 1975 interview with Roger-Pol Droit. What I ended up finding was something I never expected: the capacity to embrace my split, my own contradictions, my queerness—what Foucault might have called my madness.

Approaching the archive represented a significant methodological step for me. Up until that time, I had not experienced the archive fever that had long afflicted so many of my friends and colleagues, to say nothing of Foucault himself. My former disinclination to work in the archives mostly reflects my training as a literary scholar educated in the 1980s. Archives, as the unpublished detritus of lives spent writing, seemed peripheral to me, and they stayed that way for many years. As texts, archival materials were potentially interesting, but chances were against someone's scribbled letters or off-the-cuff remarks measuring up, textually speaking, to the perfection of *Madame Bovary*. Besides, time was limited, and those meticulous close readings were difficult enough without spending untold hours in dusty archives. The *text* was the main event in most French literature departments in the 1980s. And to study a text was to engage in a process of interpretation that was open only to those initiated into *reading*. This italicized approach to knowledge—the close reading of texts—combined the traditional French explication de texte with the incisive, meticulous unraveling of a passage that became deconstructive rhetorical reading. To be sure, during the same period, women's studies taught me to take seriously the sociopolitical context of a text and my feminist commitments kept me anchored in the world of activism even as I moved ever more deeply into the world of French high culture.

During my sabbatical-year trip to France, I met Foucault in a kind of repetition of my initial encounter with him in women's studies decades earlier, a reacquaintance with someone I felt I had known for quite some time. Strangely, the encounter bore all the marks of the *coup de foudre*, the lightning flash of a beginning. It was as if I'd never met him before: a first love. And then I had it: archive fever.

Interlude: Coup de Foudre

Today I've been rereading Didier Eribon's book, *Insult and the Making of the Gay Self*, the last third of which is devoted to Michel Foucault's "Heterotopias." I met Didier at the Café Beaubourg in Paris in September, after my two-week stint with Foucault in the archives. Didier graciously agreed to spend an evening with me, to clear up some biographical questions I had, and to give me his insights into the reasons for the suppression of some of Foucault's work, most notably "Confessions of the Flesh," the unpublished fourth volume of *History of Sexuality*, which explores the Christian period.

During our café encounter, Didier and I talked about Daniel Defert, Foucault's lover and longtime companion, the executor of his estate and papers. For reasons that are not mine to know, and that Didier could not explain either, today, over twenty years after Foucault's death, Defert will not allow researchers to consult "Confessions of the Flesh," written by Foucault in the 1970s but never published. It's hard not to see the suppression of the volume as anything other than a withholding that repeats the structure of a secret, and a specifically sexual one at that. We have access only to a title whose words literally signal a promised revelation of flesh. Defert's stubborn gesture of withholding the volume itself gives the entire relationship between author, executor-lover, and archive the contours of a desire forever thwarted, a striptease forever deferred. We, Foucault's readers, can only sit and wait for that far-off moment of future titillation. Still, I thought, as I said goodbye to Didier and left the café, there's something poignant in Defert's resistance, his refusal to let go. I've never met him, but I choose to read this maddening grip on Foucault's papers over two decades after his death, in the midst of the ever-accelerating Foucault production machine, as a lover's stubborn insistence that something between them as friends and lovers—like "a lump in the throat" (*M* xxxi)—remain unshared, unread, like an "obstinate murmur" (*M* xxxi), and not be offered up for public consumption. I choose to read this—this withholding, this suppression, this unarticulated lump in the throat—as a story about love.

Another story emerges fleetingly, this one about a beginning, in Eribon's book. It is the story of the dodecaphonic composer Jean Barraqué, whom Eribon describes as another of the great loves of Foucault's life. Foucault and Barraqué met in the early 1950s after a period in which Foucault had made two suicide attempts. As Eribon presents him, Barraqué may accurately be described as a first love, and one that allowed Foucault to go on living. In an undated letter quoted by Eribon, Foucault compares himself to Proust's Swann forever devoted to his *cocotte* lover, Odette. Is it a coincidence that Barraqué is a musician, and that Swann and Odette find in music—for Proust, the highest of art forms—the proper expression of the love that binds them? "I would like," Foucault writes in his letter to Barraqué, "like Swann, to stand guard at the entrance to the Verdurin palace until the first rays of dawn appear."[15] Eribon describes the relationship between Foucault and Barraqué, which lasted from 1952 to 1956, as one that produced in Foucault a transformation and a growing acceptance of his own homosexuality.

I had the chance to flesh out this brief story by reading Foucault's original letters to Barraqué in August 2008.[16] Not available for public scrutiny, the forty-seven letters sit on a shelf in a private Paris apartment under the auspices of the Association Jean Barraqué. The first thing I noticed when I arrived at the apartment building in the sixth arrondissement was the historic plaque above the door: Blaise Pascal lived here. Funny, I thought, Foucault opens *Madness* with an epigraph from Pascal: "Men are so necessarily mad, that not being mad would be being mad through another trick [*tour*] that madness played." How, I wondered as I pushed the buzzer, did Foucault's love letters manage to find their perfect resting place here, in Paris, chez Pascal? Two thinkers of the limit—the infinitely small and the infinitely large—Foucault and Pascal both liked to play on the edge of reason and unreason. How fitting, I mused as I mounted the stairs, that the epistolary traces of Foucault's first coup de foudre, his *fol amour*, should settle here.

After I entered the apartment, the keeper of the correspondence graciously gave me access to the contents of a red looseleaf binder where the letters live, tucked away in a series of cellophane sleeves. I spent the better part of a day reading the correspondence: a guilty pleasure, I must admit. These letters, after all, were not written for me. And yet, I rationalized, shouldn't we, Foucault's readers, know about them? My guilt soon dissipated, and I greedily devoured every word, frantically typing notes into my computer.

Per the requirements of Foucault's estate, I promised not to cite any of the letters directly. But I must describe them: they are part of the fabric that forms *History of Madness* and part of the story of my own coup de foudre—my own mad plunge into Foucault. The correspondence begins with a postcard from Venice, September 1954, on the front of which is a reproduction of the mosaic ceiling of the baptistry in Ravenna depicting the baptism of Jesus by St. John the Baptist (figure 0.2). Foucault's scrawled message to Barraqué tells him he's been swimming during his stay in Italy—he uses the expression *faire trempette*— just like Jesus. *Faire trempette*: to go for a swim or take a dip, but also, more commonly, to soak bread in a liquid before eating it. Foucault tells Barraqué that taking a dip has made him think of him: another baptizing Jean. And in the postcard image, Foucault-Jesus's naked body is submerged in a milky liquid with which his lover, a leopard-skin clad

FIGURE 0.2. Ceiling mosaic, Ravenna baptistry (fifth century)

Jean, has been baptizing him; that same body, we must assume, will then be lovingly eaten in an erotic transmutation of bread into spirit. The entire scene in the mosaic is witnessed by a naked pagan god: the personification of the Jordan River, the source of the milky liquid. Most visibly, at the center of the mosaic, the Holy Spirit descends in the form of a dove who (there's no denying it) is ejaculating liquid over the naked Jesus.

After the titillating postcard come the first letters, from late 1954 through early 1955, mailed from Italy, Corsica, Vendeuvre, Poitiers. These early letters are dazzling imitations of Proust. Addressing Barraqué as Madame, for example, Foucault solemnly regrets not having a chauffeur who might drive him around Paris for the sole purpose of letting Monsieur know he's thinking of him. Later (it's clear things aren't going well), Foucault becomes Eurydice, languishing in the void of Barraqué's absence, brought to life again only by the arrival of new letters from his lover, letters which become increasingly infrequent and then cease altogether. I am, Foucault writes to Barraqué, like a red thread, forever knotted into the fabric of your life. My sole wish is your happiness, your freedom, your pleasure. As your letters cease I too disappear, becoming a myth. Sometimes, at night, in my narrow bed pushed up against the wall, I find you again: I enter that space, deliciously contracted, of body against body. I am pressed by you like a flower against paper. Hearing only your silence, I slip quietly beneath your sleep, feel only your breath. You are my most faithful madness.

Madness, silence, love's little deaths. The correspondence forms the arc of a story, from the Ravenna postcard to Foucault's last letter dated May 1956. By the fall of 1955, Barraqué had stopped responding to Foucault's letters from Sweden; it appears that Barraqué chose his work over what he saw as the trap of passion.[17] Foucault promises to leave quietly, tiptoeing out the door. In the final letters from late 1955 and 1956, written from Sweden (where Foucault held a post at the university in Uppsala), what remains, most palpably, is Foucault's distress. But this suffocating sadness, although obvious, is surprisingly munificent, nonpossessive, unselfish: Foucault wants to make way for the breath of the other. And so, as I read what amounts to an epistolary novel written by a lovelorn, romantic Foucault, I am struck, most of all, by Foucault's generosity. If life has come to matter, as it has for a once suicidal Foucault, what matters most is the life—the breath—of the other.

For this Foucault of the 1950s, Barraqué means more than the silence of a little death. Barraqué marks a shift—an opening, a transformation—not only in Foucault's life, but in his thinking: a shift he compares to his reading of Nietzsche during the same period in the mid-1950s. Foucault told his friend, Paul Veyne, that it was Barraqué who taught him to think differently about form and to contest the Hegelian notion of the spirit of an age.[18] Similarly, in 1967 Foucault told an interviewer that his "first great cultural shock" came from his exposure to "French serial and dodecaphonic musicians—like Boulez and Barraqué," to whom he was connected "through relations of friendship."[19] The Barraqué coup de foudre represented for Foucault the "first 'snag' in [his] dialectical universe."[20] This dedialectizing transformation—this shock, this snag—allowed Foucault to acknowledge both the dark and the light, both the self-negation of attempted suicide and the Nietzschean *Ja-*

sagen of life: "the revelation, at the doors of time, of a tragic structure" (*M* xxix).

It was this rediscovery of the "tragic structure" of light and dark that took the form of Foucault's first major book, *History of Madness*, written in the late 1950s. Placing the Barraqué correspondence in dialogue with Foucault's published work, I read this massive volume—943 pages, we are told, when Foucault first turned it in to his teacher, Georges Canguilhem—as the deferred flickering of the coup de foudre that was Foucault's "baptism"—his first experience of love. Foucault himself admits, years later, that he wrote *Madness* a bit blindly, "in a kind of lyricism that came out of personal experience."[21] It was an experience he compared, in one of his letters to Barraqué, to an emerging philosophical landscape: pale, unreal, and as uncertain as a dawn which holds both the promise of sunrise and the finality of an executioner's death. Indeed, another of Foucault's teachers, Louis Althusser, described *Madness* as a matutinal work "with elements of night and flashes of dawn, a twilight book, like Nietzsche, yet as luminous as an equation."[22] It was a book that—like a first love, like a baptizing coup de foudre—came into the world as a fragment of night formed by a flash of lightning.

Dossiers of Madness

An interlude appears in the midst of a story as a moment of rupture, as an interruption in the narrative flow. To allow for rupture in the flow of a story is to allow for the "obstinate murmur" of something other to come to the surface, to attempt to speak. My own structure here—where story is fractured by interlude—playfully reflects Foucault's intervention into a seamless tale that reason tells about itself. In *History of Madness*, madness repeatedly punctures—as reason's rupture or limit—that self-perpetuating history or story (*histoire*) called reason. Interludes function like those limits or ruptures that Foucault describes, again in the 1961 preface, as "those obscure gestures, necessarily forgotten as soon as they are accomplished, through which a culture rejects something which for it will be the Exterior" (*M* xxix). The interludes reactivate, within a coherent history of Foucault's published work, the "dull sound from beneath history, the obstinate murmur of a language talking to itself—without any speaking subject and without an interlocutor, wrapped up in itself, with a lump in its throat, collapsing before it ever reaches any formulation and returning without a fuss to the silence that it never shook off. The charred root of meaning" (*M* xxxi–xxxii).

The "lump in the throat" of this Foucault, the one I am calling mine, is the messy tangle of unpublished writings and unedited encounters that help to form a doubled love story, one that becomes my own story of love. In order to tell that story, I need the suppressed and unpublished marginalia of the Foucault writing machine. These marginalia take many forms: the extratextual details of biographical encounters in the margins of Foucault's life such as my meeting with his biographer, Eribon, in a café; the letters to Barraqué; the few unedited, unpublished papers and recordings still to be found in the archives; the suppressed 1961 preface to *History of Madness*. Thus the "charred root of meaning" I'm calling love makes itself known, somewhat ironically, precisely in those places the Foucault machine has consigned to the silence of the margins.

Inspired by my encounter with the unpublished Foucault archive, the interludes trace a "personal" story about Foucault and *Madness* that, interwoven with the more academic discourse, constitutes an important part of the discursive fabric of my engagement with Foucault. This is not to privilege one discourse over the other, but rather to put them in dialogue with each other. As will become clear, my academic voice continually threatens to overwhelm my more personal, experiential one: my Cartesian mind wants to take over, to make sense of the bodily realm of heart and passion: reason wants to overtake unreason. So, with its interludes, this book performs my own personal, post-Cartesian drama in a way that repeats a similar struggle Foucault describes in *History of Madness*.

A word to those readers whose preferences run counter to my taste for these queer interruptions: skipping over the interludes is always an option, although, in my humble opinion, to miss them is to miss the most "enlightening," lightninglike parts of the story. The purpose of the interludes is not to distract or annoy those who prefer the clean line of an airtight philosophical argument. My goal in the interludes is to allow the personal voice—one that both "belongs to no one else" and is "no longer my possession"[23]—to become part of the fabric of Foucault's queer madness. Indeed, the juxtaposition of philosophical, historical, and personal voices in this book reflects the polyphonic play of the materials themselves—both archival and published, personal and not—that inform my engagement with Foucault. The interludes remind us that history is not History, with a capital *H*. The past cannot be captured as a singular narrative line: "History," as Elsa Barkley Brown puts it, "is everybody talking at once."[24] The interludes also remind us of Foucault's philosophical project to rupture Philosophy: to "shake it off." So I like to think of them as those metaphorical firecrackers Foucault loved so much, tiny object-events whose casual abandon both punctures and lightens the ink-heavy atmosphere of theory. I offer them, then, as a "surprised and joyful foolishness" that, like Foucault's "incomprehensive burst of laughter," is more interested in breaking than understanding.

Before moving forward, let me signal, along with Foucault, the limits of Hegelian dialectical thinking for any attempt to make sense of this "charred root of meaning" that I'm implicitly linking with Foucault's "personal" story. Earlier I cited Foucault's 1964 essay, "Madness, the Absence of an Oeuvre," where he reminds us: "That which will not be long in dying, that which is already dying in us (and whose death bears our current language) is *homo dialecticus*" (*M* 543). The doubled structure of flow and interruption I have been describing cannot lead to the neat resolution of a dialectical sublation where, as Simone de Beauvoir sarcastically puts it, "one can thus repose in a marvelous optimism."[25] Indeed, to produce such a resolution would be to repeat the psychologizing gesture through which madness is mastered by a discourse of reason. In the 1961 preface, Foucault writes, "Having mastered his madness, and having freed it by capturing it in the gaols of his gaze and his morality, having disarmed it by pushing it into a corner of himself finally allowed man to establish that sort of relation to the self that is known as 'psychology'" (*M* xxxiv).

I read this as a warning. I must take care to avoid repeating that optimistic gesture of dialectical capture by the moralizing gaze of science, where "Foucault" becomes "the animal that loses its truth and finds it again illuminated, a stranger to himself who becomes familiar once more" (*M* 543). This means not reducing *my* Foucault to a narrative about the biographical subtext that would explain the work. Not to give in to the psychologizing gesture of mastery means allowing the voice and the lump in the throat to enter into dialogue with each other. In that dialogue between the work and its rupture, I can refuse the mastering gesture of the dialectic. And in that refusal, an opening is forged in a language other than that of science.

In my reading, then, the Foucault archive symbolizes that part of "Foucault" which "Foucault" himself rejected as the biographical Exterior of his own published writing. For indeed, in the relationship between the written "Foucault"—the Foucault that can be traced across the entirety of his published work—and the unedited, unpublished, or suppressed "Foucault" of the margins, there is an uneasy resistance—that lump in the throat which one might read as a stubborn refusal to speak. Just as the language of reason expels from itself all the traces of the unreason from which it came, so too "Foucault" (in 1961) expels from himself in the form of suppression "the memory of all those imperfect words, of no fixed syntax, spoken falteringly" (M xxviii) of his own madness: his suicide attempts in the 1950s, his coups de foudre, his homosexuality, his coming out, his first love, his early obsession with literature, and the excessively lyrical prose of his first preface. The trick, in reading this unedited, suppressed Foucault—against Foucault, as it were—is to avoid the psychologizing gesture of mastery that would turn the biographical Exterior that is the unpublished writing into an originary cause or explanation of all that follows. Instead, I want to read these pieces of Foucault as the precious, cast-off remains of Foucault the philosopher, the one who speaks in the voice of reason. These are his own "dossiers of indecipherable delirium, juxtaposed by chance to the words of reason" (M xxxi). In naming the Foucault of the archives as such—as dossiers of delirium in a relation, not of cause and effect, but of juxtaposition, to reason—I hope to forge an opening, however small, for a passage to something other.

That opening of a path points, paradoxically, to what Foucault in 1961 called "a passage refused by the future, a thing in becoming which is irreparably less than history" (M xxxi). This enigmatic phrase suggests that, in our habitual, retrospective reading of history as a teleological story, we imbue the events of the past with meanings that shut down other, nonteleological possibilities for apprehending ourselves in history. This teleological production of the past, and of ourselves, as meaningful and coherent unities denies existence, as part of history, to the nonsensical, the inchoate, the obscure murmurings of the mad "thing in becoming." This denial takes place in the very gesture by which reason constitutes itself against unreason, the repudiated "thing in becoming" that haunts it. In this way, the mad "thing in becoming" is "irreparably" lost to history. It becomes "less than history" through the retrospective process of History making that happens, structurally, as the future. The future—as a retrospective, teleological act of meaning making that distances itself from nonmeaning—is the stance reason takes, in History, as separate from unreason. To interrogate its own History making gesture as an exclusionary activity of reason would mean to interrogate itself as reason. And to do this would be to claim the future as mad, to occupy a place of unreason whose renunciation grounds History itself. In that sense, the opening of a passage produced by the mad "thing in becoming" is inevitably an opening "refused by the future" because that future—the act by which the present makes sense of itself—depends on the sense making of reason and History.

Thus to occupy that historical future, as we do, and, at the same time, to commit to opening a passage foreclosed by the very future we occupy is, indeed, to take up an impossible position: to be mad. But that impossible, queer position—the position of madness—is also, politically, the one we must hold. It is a position that refuses many of the terms according to which our own present has been constructed by a totalizing history, a Sartrean sense of History with a capital *H* vehemently critiqued by Foucault. As he says in the 1975 interview with Roger-Pol Droit, Sartre associates the practice of historians with a totalizing *"grand feeling"* of history oriented and articulated by a human consciousness which is both the product and reflection of that history.[26] That is, if our commitment to the "thing in becoming" Foucault describes as "less than history" is real, we *must* occupy that place of resistance to History.[27] This, I believe, was Foucault's most important contribution to the question of how to think about the past: he understood the philosophical work of history making as a fraught negotiation between the present and the future whose purpose is to bring that which is "irreparably less than history" into view. Doing so, he made a commitment to a different future.

The ironic structure of impossibility that governs this commitment to the "thing in becoming" repeats what we can now see as the ironic structure of splitting with which I opened this introduction, the structure that says: it's there but it's not. To try to make sense of it, once and for all, would be to mire myself, again, in the great swamp that is the division of reason and unreason. The impossible structure points, in fact, to an unsettling contradiction that underlies Foucault's entire project, which is never more obvious than in the writing of his book, *History of Madness*. For indeed, in writing a history to be read and understood, Foucault uses not the language of "indecipherable delirium," but rather the rhetoric, syntax, grammar, and argumentative structures of reason. In the 1961 preface, Foucault himself is fully aware of the ironic impossibility of his project:

> We need to strain our ears, and bend down towards this murmuring of the world, and try to perceive so many images that have never been poetry, so

many fantasies that have never attained the colours of day. But it is, no doubt, a doubly impossible task, as it would require us to reconstitute the dust of this concrete pain, and those insane words that nothing anchors in time; and above all because that pain and those words only exist, and are only apparent to themselves and to others in the act of division that already denounces and masters them. . . . Any perception that aims to apprehend them in their wild state necessarily belongs to a world that has captured them already. The liberty of madness can only be heard from the heights of the fortress in which it is imprisoned. (*M* xxxii)

Confronted with this irony of mastering madness, Foucault eventually rejects the 1961 preface in which he attempts to govern madness's meanings. As I pointed out in the preface to this book, later, in Foucault's 1972 preface, he also renounces the gesture through which the "monarchy of the author" establishes itself in "a declaration of tyranny" and an act of "eminent sovereignty" over the meaning of a book (*M* xxxviii). Letting go of mastery, he adopts, instead, the position of irony. But that irony cannot be the "final word," since to stop there would be to construct another position of mastery. Thus the force that animates my reading of a split Foucault can best be described as the generative but fragile movement of a dialogic voice caught between lyricism and irony, tragedy and comedy. I do not make a claim for either per se as *the* voice of transgression or transformation. Rather, I bring out Foucault's lyricism, along with his irony, in order to produce a new encounter—a happening, to borrow a term from Linda Hutcheon—to unsettle the object-event we call Foucault.

Both lyricism and irony "happen" in my engagement with Foucault. And they happen most powerfully and specifically in his thinking about sexuality. I perceive the tension between them—most forcefully, undoubtedly, in the passage from the 1960s to the 1970s, from *Madness* to *Sexuality One*—through the grid of this first aporia, the one underlying the impossible gesture of writing a reasonable book about madness. Aporia, not mastery, ultimately governs Foucault's manipulations of the language of reason, where the rhetorical "turns" of metaphorical troping are revealed as the "tricks" or "turns" of madness, what Pascal calls the *tours de la folie*. This Pascalian turning—placed, as it is, at the beginning of the beginning, as an epigraph to the first preface of Foucault's first book—constitutes the vertiginous opening to the rest of Foucault's work: "Men are so necessarily mad, that not being mad would be being mad through another trick [*tour*] that madness played."

Although it makes my head spin, this place of aporetic turning is the place I have chosen to meet Foucault, the one I am calling mine. I allow the tensions between lyricism and irony to guide my readings of the oppositions that emerge in my approach to Foucault through the lens of *History of Madness*: the opposition between the 1961 and 1972 prefaces, the redoubling of *Madness*'s exploration of sexuality in *Sexuality One*, and the play between the published and suppressed or unpublished versions of Foucault.

All this forms the context for my narrative about meeting Foucault, over and over, in a vertiginous movement of eternal return. I met him again, in 2006, in that liminal space that marks the split between the work and its unpublished remains, a split that is itself in a constant process of transformation with the ongoing production of published volumes of previously unpublished material. In the archives, I focused especially on the 1975 Foucault interview with Roger-Pol Droit. Foucault had consented to engage in a fifteen-hour conversation with Droit over the course of several sessions, the culmination of which would be its publication as a book. It appears that Foucault was dissatisfied with the results, refusing publication and returning the money he had received as an advance. Droit subsequently published small parts of the interview in *Le Monde* (1986) and *Le Point* (2004), after Foucault's death, and republished both excerpts in a 2004 collection of Foucault interviews, *Michel Foucault, entretiens*.[28] The rest of the interview remains, in unedited and unpublished form, as four hundred typed manuscript pages available for consultation at the Institut Mémoires de l'Edition Contemporaine (IMEC) in Normandy, where the Foucault archives are housed. It was there, specifically, in those archives, that I reexperienced my relationship to Foucault as a coup de foudre and a turning or *tour* of my love-hate into something like the madness of transformation. The result of this Pascalian *tour de folie* was a Foucault that I couldn't help but love and a return to the beginnings of his work in *History of Madness*.

Interlude: Archive Fever

While in Normandy at the archives I spent most of my time retyping parts of the fifteen-hour 1975 interview with Droit that Foucault had disliked so much. The interview fascinated me precisely because Foucault didn't like it and because—I can't help it, I've always been rebellious—it has NO written all over it. The note that accompanies the sheaf of pages says: "Ne pas copier des extraits" (Do not copy excerpts) and, even more dramatically, "inpubliable donc embarras" (unpublishable, therefore a nuisance, a burden).

Why the judgment and condemnation: *inpubliable* and *embarras?* Why this enforcement of the *droits d'auteur* when Foucault famously refused the category of author altogether? And why this refusal, in light of the current massive publication of all his courses at the Collège de France, to say nothing of his interviews, radio addresses, and other lectures? Indeed, in his famous "What Is an Author?" (1969), Foucault asks about the limits of an author's "work":

> Even when an individual has been accepted as an author, we must still ask whether everything that he wrote, said, or left behind is part of his work. The problem is both theoretical and technical. When undertaking the publication of Nietzsche's works, for example, where should one stop? Surely everything must be published, but what is "everything"? Everything that Nietzsche himself published, certainly. And what about the rough drafts for his works? Obviously. The plans for his aphorisms? Yes. The deleted passages and the notes at the bottom of the page? Yes. What if, within a workbook filled with aphorisms, one finds a reference, the notation of a meeting or of an address, or a laundry list: is it a work, or not? Why not? And so on, ad infinitum. How can one define a work amid the millions of traces left by someone after his death?[29]

The contradiction between statements like these and the severe directive—"inpubliable donc embarras"—stirred up a resistance in me. They made me want to dig deeper, to salvage something from this piece of rejected, unpublished Foucault marginalia. But mostly, as I read further into the four-hundred-page typescript, the interview whispered *pay attention to me and reread Madness.*

I suspect that one of the reasons Foucault disliked this interview so much was its insistent tilt toward the biographical. Over and over Foucault remarks on his recourse to biography in his attempts to answer Droit's questions. Toward the end of the interview, as things unravel and Foucault respectfully declares that he isn't satisfied with the result of their work together (he generously blames himself as much as Droit), he describes an experience of "suffocation." Foucault complains that these suffocating questions "to me and about me"[30] forced him to resort to biographical answers.

I understand the discomfort and the gasping for breath. For, although in other interviews Foucault asserts that his thinking is clearly shaped by autobiography, context is everything. Perhaps because of the sheer length of the Droit interview, it ends up feeling more insistent, more despotic, in its attempts to pin down this *moi*, "Foucault," than most of the shorter interviews. And given Foucault's lifelong effort to undo the *moi*—to interrogate the humanist illusion of an unsplit, self-identical, coherent "I"—his discomfort with the insistence makes sense.

Still, what emerges out of all this discomfort, and all these attempts by Droit to pin him down, is a personal confession that, in speaking the "I," unravels itself in the very moment of its self-disclosure. As the conversation turns to the topic of madness and Foucault's famous first book, Foucault reminds Droit that, although *Madness* marks the beginning of his writing efforts, his interest in madness has never left him: "for twenty years now I've been worrying about my little mad ones, my little excluded ones, my little abnormals": "mes petits fous, mes petits exclus, mes petits anormaux."[31] But why, exactly, Droit wants to know, did Foucault insist on writing *History of Madness*? Foucault responds:

> In my personal life, from the moment of my sexual awakening, I felt excluded, not so much rejected, but belonging to society's shadow. It's all the more a problem when you discover it for yourself. All of this was very quickly transformed into a kind of psychiatric threat: if you're not like everyone else, it's because you're abnormal, if you're abnormal, it's because you're sick.[32]

Given Foucault's well-known reticence to talk about his own sexual experience, his "coming out," or his personal negotiation of the homophobic French culture to which he belonged, this "confession" is dramatic, at least for me. Most of us have thought, as Butler does in *Gender Trouble*, that Foucault "always resisted the confessional moment."[33] But here in his description of his sexual "awakening," his feelings of "exclusion," and the shock of a "psychiatric threat" that would label him as "abnormal" and "sick," Foucault declares his solidarity with those who belong to "society's shadow," those he calls the "excluded ones": "my little mad ones, my little abnormals." And in that solidarity he is, like them, an unraveled self, a self that cannot be pinned down.

When I came across this passage, I was immediately thrilled to have discovered such a "confession." Later that evening, I mentioned the passage to my companions at the archives who were working on other writers. They stared at me blankly. Yeah, they responded, so what? Not only were they unimpressed, but they left me feeling a bit silly about my excitement. Then I wrote to my American queer friends, Michael and Jonathan, who via email received the passage with the same kind of passion that I had felt. "We're on the edge of our seats," they said. Without that shared passion, I probably would have let the whole thing drop. But they encouraged me to stay with the feeling, my oh-so-American coup de foudre. And that marks the moment when the ground of my understanding of Foucault and sexuality shifted.

I know that my insistence on citing an unpublished interview Foucault disliked will be seen by some as disloyal or, at the very least, in bad taste. But I see it differently. Although mostly unpublished, the interview has become a book of sorts, four hundred pages available for reading to those with the time, resources, and inclination to travel to a refurbished medieval monastery in Normandy. As a book, the interview takes its place as an object-event that, as Foucault insisted in his 1972 preface, must evade the grip of "the person who wrote it" (*M* xxxviii) or, in this case, spoke it in conversation. Rather than being shut away as a shameful secret never to be uncovered, this book-event must finally "disappear" (*M* xxxviii) into "the series of events to which it belongs" (*M* xxxviii): events, Foucault reminds us, which "are far from being over" (*M* xxxviii). So perhaps this coup de foudre that sparked a fever in me— an archive fever I'd never caught before, and from which I have yet to recover—can be perceived as the most loyal kind of disloyalty to Foucault. Perhaps it can be received as an event of discovery that engendered what Deleuze calls a resistant thinking: "a thought of resistance"[34] to the despotic readings that refuse to see Foucault's queer madness.

Requeering Foucault

This book can be conceived as a queer intervention into Foucault studies through a sustained reengagement with *History of Madness*. The intervention takes place within a vast critical context that includes myriad responses to Foucault. My purpose here is not to reproduce an exhaustive overview of those responses to *Madness*. Others have done so, and interested readers can consult those works which are listed in the bibliography.[35] My goal is different. I want to show that what has been missed, by admirers and critics alike, has been the importance of *History of Madness* as part of Foucault's lifelong project to rethink sexuality as a category of moral and political exclusion. So while Jean Khalfa's comment, in his introduction to the 2006 English translation of Foucault's work, that the *"History of Madness* has yet to be read" (*M* xiii) seems a bit overstated, it is true that something crucial has been elided in critical responses both to the book and to Foucault in general. Specifically, with the exception of Eribon, those readers of Foucault who have paid attention to *Madness* have completely missed the significance of its sexual dimension. Conversely, those readers of Foucault who have paid attention to sexuality in his work have missed *Madness* altogether. My goal is to address that gap.

Generally speaking, historians have been sharply critical of *History of Madness*, arguing that the book suffers from oversimplification or even flies in the face of empirical evidence regarding the management of madness in seventeenth- and eighteenth-century Europe. Others have argued that, while Foucault's historical description is broadly accurate with regard to France and Germany, the history of confinement in England differs dramatically from the picture he painted. Even those who admire the quality of Foucault's writing in the book—Andrew Scull calls *History of Madness* "a provocative and dazzlingly written prose poem"[36]—criticize the book on factual grounds.[37] Others assert that it is not history at all.[38] For example, Allen Megill argues that Foucault "is *anti*disciplinary, standing outside all disciplines and drawing from them only in the hope of undoing them."[39] Foucault surely would have welcomed this assessment.

To be sure, some historians have praised the work, including Fernand Braudel and Robert Mandrou of the French *Annales* school, Jan Goldstein, Colin Gordon, Gary Gutting, and others.[40] But to argue the book's merits or lack thereof according to the criteria of the discipline of history is to miss the book's point entirely. "I am not a professional historian," Foucault said at a University of Vermont lecture, adding wryly, "nobody is perfect."[41] Most tellingly, in the Droit interview, Foucault responds sharply to Sartre's famous criticism that he has no sense of History. Foucault responds that "to have a sense of history," for Sartre, "means to be capable of making a totalization, at the level of a society or a culture or a consciousness."[42] It means to construct a history whose "crowning" achievement will be the apotheosis of the subject and human consciousness. And "it's true," Foucault says, "I have no sense of *that* history."[43]

Given Foucault's rejection here and elsewhere of what he sees as the totalizing frames of professional historians, others have gauged his work from the perspective of philosophy. But if the reactions of historians to *History of Madness* have been mixed at best, philosophers have been no less polarized. Generally speaking, philosophers have objected to what they perceive as the nihilism of Foucault's critique of the Enlightenment.[44] By showing only the negative aspects of the Age of Reason, they argue, Foucault denies the value of the genuine freedoms and advances that came about with Enlightenment thinking. Others have rejected what they see as an apology for an irrationalism that categorically rejects the virtues of reasoning. Still others have responded to *Madness* through the lens of its reception by the British antipsychiatry movement, critiquing it on the grounds that it denies the reality of mental illness.[45]

The most famous philosophical critique of Foucault has come from an equally famous critic of Enlightenment thinking, Jacques Derrida, who, especially in the American mainstream highbrow press, is often lumped together with Foucault. In postmodern philosophical circles, Derrida's dispute with Foucault over his interpretation of Descartes's exclusion of madness from the *cogito* in the *Meditations* has become legendary.[46] As Edward Said and others have pointed out in their analyses of the Derrida-Foucault dispute over Descartes, the disagreement hinges on their differing conceptions of textuality, language, and dialectical thinking. For Derrida, Descartes lends himself to an internal reading of a metaphysical structure that establishes the conditions of possibility of all thought. Rather than excluding madness, Derrida argues, Descartes radically universalizes it by comparing it with the sensory illusions of dreams. For Derrida, the structure of madness is allied with the structure of language in its *différance* (with an *a*), its feeble capacity to perform a gesture of protection and enclosure against the terrifying specter of meaninglessness. Shannon Winnubst points out that *différance*—"the undecidability of endless differing and deferring"—"operates within the same system of lack initiated by the Hegelian dialectics of desire and recognition."[47] Foucault himself, in his scathing response to Derrida, "This Body, This Paper, This Fire"—written in 1964 and included as an appendix to the 1972 French reedition of *History of Madness*—slams Derrida for reducing "discursive practices" to "textual traces" for his "little pedagogy, a pedagogy which teaches the pupil that there is nothing outside the text" (*M* 573). For Foucault, Derrida's self-enclosed textual *différance* is problematic because it leaves out those effects that cannot be traced to linguistic forces. Descartes's text, for example, has the force of an "event" within a network of sociopolitical relations that Foucault dramatizes through the institutional practice of confinement of the mad in seventeenth-century Europe. Thus the rationale and practices of exclusion and confinement he describes in *Madness* are not simply textual or linguistic structures but the result of institutional, political, and historical forces as well. These forces inhabit what Winnubst calls a Foucauldian "space of endless contestation": "the site in which discourses shape themselves, a site of conflict, violence, disruption, discontinuity, struggle, contest, and endless movements."[48]

Other philosophically oriented interpretations of *Madness* read it as the beginning of a progress narrative over the course of which Foucault will overcome some of the problems of this early work. Dreyfus and Rabinow, in their influential *Beyond Structuralism and Hermeneutics*, liken Foucault's conception of madness to "the Word of God" and criticize what they call "his flirtation with hermeneutic depth" in *Madness*.[49] Along the same lines, in his foreword to Foucault's *Mental Illness and Psychology* (1964), Dreyfus links what he sees as *Madness*'s problems to a Heideggerian "hermeneutics of suspicion," to use Paul Ricoeur's words, that requires the uncovering of the everyday cover-up of *Dasein*'s nothingness, its "strangeness."[50] Dreyfus views both *Madness* and *Mental Illness* as making "the claim that madness has been silenced and must be allowed to speak its truth."[51] Only with *The Birth of the Clinic* (1963) and *The Order of Things* (1966), Dreyfus asserts, does Foucault reject hermeneutics along with Freud, Marx, and early Heidegger.[52]

Similarly, Lois McNay's otherwise lucid feminist reading of Foucault too easily dismisses *Madness* for its "tendency to essentialize a certain experience of alterity."[53] Agreeing with Habermas, McNay asserts that "it is impossible to attribute an *a priori* revolutionary force to any form of knowledge" (40), including those which are subjugated or disqualified by dominant forms of knowledge. "After *Madness and Civilization*," McNay continues, "Foucault abandoned the attempt to recover an authentic experience of madness and acknowledged the philosophical impossibility of such a project" (40). McNay argues that only after *Madness* does Foucault mature beyond a romantic conception of insanity as an essential locus of transgressive speech. "Madness in itself is no longer the esoteric source of an experience of transgression" (46), McNay writes. Foucault's later "redefinition of transgression as an endless task or permanent process of contestation and experimentation signals the end of the phenomenological quest for an essential experience that characterizes *Madness and Civilization*. The mad are no longer romantically celebrated as the bearers of an ineffable source of otherness" (46).

I view these critiques of *Madness* as either seriously missing the point of the book or simply not reading what it actually says. The reasons for my disagreement will become abundantly clear over the course of my more detailed engagement with *Madness* and the archival marginalia that informs it in the chapters to follow. Here I want to simply emphasize the facts about what Foucault actually writes in *Madness*. Nowhere in *Madness* does Foucault claim to "recover an authentic experience of madness," as McNay asserts, nor does he posit, as Dreyfus suggests, that a silenced madness "must be allowed to speak its truth." Indeed, in the 1961 preface to the book, he insists precisely on what McNay calls "the philosophical impossibility" of capturing madness and speaking its truth: to capture that experience, Foucault writes, "is, no doubt, a doubly impossible task" (*M* xxxii). He continues: "that pain and those words" cannot be spoken because they "are only apparent to themselves and to others in the act of division that already denounces and masters them" (*M* xxxii). All one can do is describe what Foucault calls the historical "structure of the experience of madness" (*M* xxxii), precisely the kind of genealogical approach which critics of *Madness* attribute to Foucault in his later works.

In contrast to these readings of Foucault's *Madness* as essentialist, romantic, or stuck in a phenomenological structure of hermeneutic depth, I frame my engagement with *Madness* through the lens provided by Gilles Deleuze, whose controversial book on Foucault Eleanor Kaufman describes "as a more concise, exhaustive, and thorough doubling of Foucault than Foucault himself."[54] Indeed, in *Foucault* (1986), published two years after Foucault's death, Deleuze brilliantly condenses all of Foucault's work around the familiar themes of doubling, foldings, and repetition. And although Deleuze's *Foucault* only directly engages *History of Madness* in a few key passages, as a "sketch" of Foucault or as his "mask," "double," or "overlay,"[55] Deleuze's book both maps a trajectory of changes over the course of Foucault's thinking and, at the same time, traces the doubling effect wherein each of Foucault's books doubles or repeats another. Within that context, I am particularly interested in the Deleuzian theme of doubling as a frame for thinking about *Sexuality One* as the doubling of sexuality in *Madness*. More specifically, I view that doubling of sexuality as a lens for reconceptualizing Foucault's lifelong interest in subjectivity as subjectivation. Conceived in this way, all of Foucault's work on sexuality—from *Madness* to *Sexuality One* to the final two volumes of *History of Sexuality*—can be treated as different approaches to the problematization of ethics within a conception of subjectivity as subjectivation.

In *Foucault*, Deleuze emphasizes the complex relation between history and philosophy Foucault stages in a conception of subjectivity I call coextensive. Understanding coextension in *Madness* is crucial to my argument that Foucault's early conception of subjectivity cannot be regarded solely or even primarily as a project to uncover that which is buried, either as the "truth" of madness or as the politically "repressed" object of exclusion. *Madness* is not, as John Caputo claims, only "a vertical plumbing of the dark sedimented depths from which *homo psychologicus* emerges" (239), the relentless disclosure of a "great motionless structure lying beneath the surface" (239). Nor is *Madness* only keyed to the early Nietzsche of *The Birth of Tragedy*, disregarding, as Caputo asserts, later Nietzschean writings like *The Genealogy of Morals*. Indeed, Nietzsche's *Genealogy* is crucial to Foucault's critique of *homo psychologicus* as the product of a bourgeois moral order, as I show more fully in chapter 2. Engaging *Madness* through a Deleuzian lens brings into view the critique of morality in Nietzsche's later works as an important philosophical source for Foucault's thinking about subjectivity and ethics in *Madness*.

Most crucially, the concept of the double, so central for Deleuze in his description of doubling as a function of the fold, allows us to see what other readers of *Madness* have missed, namely, that depth itself is the result of an operation of thinking where, as Deleuze puts it in a passage that alludes to the ship of fools, Foucault sees "an inside which is merely the fold of the outside, as if the ship were a folding of the sea."[56] In Deleuze's reading of Foucault, hermeneutic depth is a dimension of the "folds and foldings that together make up an inside: they are not something other than the outside, but precisely the inside *of* the outside."[57]

We can see this abstract formulation of the Deleuzian fold at work more concretely in the imagery and rhetoric of *Madness*. Every depth is doubled by a corresponding surface, and every tragic articulation is put into question by the ludic rupture of tragedy's depths. We can only read the lyrical language of tragedy in *Madness* in its doubled reflection as shattering irony, just as the depths of repressive power are mirrored by a surface network of productive power. The tension between the two—lyricism and irony, repression and production, depth and surface—is precisely the tension of madness itself, what Foucault refers to as the great split between reason and unreason. *Madness* exposes what we take for granted when we think of depth as something stable or real, revealing the illusion of a sedimented verticality as a self-doubling conceptual and historical movement that puts into question the opposition between depth and surface itself. Those readers of Foucault who have only seen the tragic, deep, repressive dimension of *Madness* are missing Foucault's intervention into that binary logic. It is only by considering Foucault's interrogation of depth and interiority that we can grasp the significance of his early conception of subjectivity within an ethical frame.

This brings us back to the Deleuzian approach to Foucault as a thinker of subjectivity as coextension. Why this is important specifically with regard to sexuality in *Madness* will be spelled out more fully in my Nietzschean reading of "Queer Moralities" in chapter 2. Here I want to highlight, in general terms, how Deleuze can guide us in approaching *Madness* not as an early, excessively phenomenological or hermeneutic moment in Foucault, but rather as a book that contains the binary tensions—between depth and surface, repression and production—that characterize all of Foucault's work, from its beginnings in *Madness* to its end in sexuality in the Greco-Roman and early Christian worlds. Specifically, the Deleuzian rethinking of the subject in Foucault involves a radical intervention into the logic of inside and outside—me and not-me, subject and object—that normally guides us in our conception of ourselves as entities in a world. The coextensive subject is the exposure of the "I" as the result of an inward folding. Coextensivity is a concept that unfolds the "I" to reveal the illusory nature of subjectivity conceived as a separate, coherent, stable form of individuation. The coextensive subject is an "inside" unfolded to bring into view the inseparability of the subject with its "outside." In that sense, the inside of the subject doesn't exist as such; the subject is coincident—in space, time, and scope—with an outside that is both a function of thinking and the condition of possibility of thinking itself. This view of subjectivity is more radically unstable than what we tend to think of as the "socially constructed" subject, a sociological view where the subject is located within an outside we call its geographical, historical, or political "context." Coextension suggests that the subject *is* the outside, *is* its context; the subject is never *in* a context, because both the subject and the context depend on a form of thinking whose origin by necessity escapes us. Like the chicken and the egg, we cannot dissociate the subject from the outside from which it purportedly arose; both the chicken and the egg—

the subject and its context—are functions of a movement that Deleuze calls an "unformed element of forces."[58]

Less abstractly, if *extension* refers to the ensemble of concrete or abstract subjects or objects to which a concept, proposition, or relation applies, *coextension* describes two or more ensembles that share the same extension. In Foucault, the coextension of two or more becomes the bounded multiplicity of a cartography that encompasses the complex relations among social, historical, political, linguistic, and conceptual fields. With regard to the subject, this multiplicity of coextension demonstrates, again, that what we think of as the subject is not an "inside" that faces an "outside," nor is it a "depth" within a horizontal "surface." The subject is coterminous, contingent, or contiguous with an outside that is in a continual process of transformation and expansion. In this way, the social, historical, political, linguistic, and conceptual borders—the edges we tend to think of as defining the boundaries of the contextual containers that hold the subject—are continually contested and reconfigured. Coextension understands those borders as part of a relational grid of forces always in a process of becoming form. The subject is the emergence-as-movement of one of those forms out of the bounded multiplicity of that map of forces, part of "the area of concrete assemblages where relations between forces are realized."[59]

Those assemblages or diagrams are what Deleuze calls a machine, a machine that is paradoxically concrete and abstract. It is both human and social—the machine-asylum, the machine-prison, the machine-school, the machine-hospital. And it is both technical and abstract—the informal "diagram," to use an important Deleuzian term, that is a "spatio-temporal multiplicity" (34): a "map of relations between forces" (36) that "proceeds by primary non-localizable relations" (36). But if the diagram is abstract, it is always also social and specific, and "there are as many diagrams as there are social fields in history" (34). The coextensive subject is neither "inside" the machine or diagram nor "outside" it, but part of the spatiotemporal play of forces that is the machine. In that sense the subject is both social and technical, concrete and abstract, human and not-human. And, unlike the structuralists with whom Foucault is often confused, Foucault does not regard the subject as simply a grammatical figure to be found inside an institutionally circumscribed order that is purely linguistic. Rather, like Blanchot, who obliquely but powerfully informs Foucault's thinking about the subject, Foucault repudiates "all linguistic personology" (7) and situates the subject within

an "anonymous murmur . . . without beginning or end" (7) who confronts what Foucault calls in "The Thought of the Outside" (1966)
"this anonymity of language liberated and opened to its own
boundlessness."[60]

This insistence on Foucault as a writer who works in the interstitial
space between inside and outside, depth and surface, philosophy and
history, technology and human society, conceptual abstraction and concrete institutions, addresses the critiques of historians and philosophers alike. Further, the Deleuzian conception of subjectivity in Foucault—what I am calling coextensive—responds to those critics of
Madness who fault it for relying on an ontotheological model of hermeneutic depth. For, if *Madness* may contain traces of Foucault's philosophical formation in phenomenology, the book clearly demolishes
both the sovereign subject and its corollary of inner depth. The problematization of the subject as a container within which we can discover
that depth also responds to charges of essentialism, for without a conception of the unknown as depth, there can be no essence to be extracted from it. As Peter Hallward puts it, "madness itself . . . simply
interrupts, contests, and despecifies."[61]

As for the "revolutionary" dimension of the essentialism McNay attributes to *Madness*, for Foucault the word *revolution* itself is fraught at
best. Foucault's attention to madness in the Age of Reason implicitly
challenges a purely celebratory view of a French Revolution that was as
irrational in its violence as it was despotic. More immediately for Foucault himself, the term *revolution* corresponds to a cultural moment in
modern France—from the end of the Second World War to the mid-
1970s—of which he was deeply critical even as early as 1961 when *Madness* was published. As Michel Feher explains, that moment was dominated by a crossing of Marxist and psychoanalytic fields of thought
represented, on the one hand, by Herbert Marcuse and, on the other, by
Louis Althusser. Foucault's turn away from a revolutionary ideology to
which he himself briefly ascribed in the early 1950s was also, in part, a
reaction to problems within the French Marxist party. Further, Foucault's 1958–59 experience in Poland brought him face-to-face with the
devastating results of Communist revolution in eastern Europe; in the
1961 preface to *Madness*, his sarcastic reference to "the stubborn, bright
sun of Polish liberty" (*M* xxxv) leaves no doubt about his critical attitude
toward revolutionary politics. Finally, Foucault explicitly criticizes the
notion of linguistic "revolution" and a concomitant sacralization of subversive writing favored by *Tel Quel* writers and others during the 1960s

and seventies. In the excerpt of the 1975 Droit interview published in *Le Monde* in 1986, Foucault complains about a certain "exaltation" of literature itself, mocking those theorists (probably Sollers and Kristeva, among others, although he doesn't name them) who proclaim that "the writer has, even in the gesture of writing, an inalienable right to subversion!"[62] All these critiques of "revolution" underline what I see, at the heart of *Madness*, as an ethical critique that can be linked to the book's political perspective. That perspective views social and political change as the result of successive, strategic contestatory practices, not as the result of the massive, totalized overturning of entire societies contained in the concept of revolution. Foucault's political perspective might be better described as a politics of resistance, to use Feher's term. This specifically Foucauldian politics of resistance requires the linking of an ethical transformation of the self with interventions into larger structures of power.[63]

Most important, what is missing from virtually every reading of *Madness* to date—including Deleuze's—is an attention to the queerness that both sparks and shapes the entire project. This is obviously not to say that historians and other thinkers of queer sexuality have ignored sexuality in Foucault. Quite the contrary. But it is to say that almost without exception queer attention has gone to those books by Foucault that contain the word *sexuality* in their title, namely, the three volumes that constitute *The History of Sexuality*, with the huge preponderance of attention falling on the first of these volumes. Indeed, queer theorists agree that without Foucault's *Sexuality One* queer theory as we know it would not have developed.

The one exception to this critical erasure of sexuality in *Madness* is, as I've mentioned, Eribon's *Insult and the Making of the Gay Self*.[64] Not surprisingly, Eribon writes from a French perspective and as one with a deep and long-standing knowledge of the life and work of Foucault. *Insult* is important for bringing *Madness* to our queer attention and for linking Foucault's work to other homophile traditions, including those associated with John Addington Symonds and the Oxford Hellenists, Oscar Wilde, and André Gide.

In *Insult*, Eribon is primarily interested in demonstrating the importance of Foucault's thinking about gay culture and new modes of life and placing that theme within the larger context of Foucault's life and work in order to release homosexuality from the shame-ridden structures that bind it. Linking Foucault to other examples of gay subjectivity and culture, Eribon performs an analysis of "the contemporary mechanisms of gay subjectivation" (xv) that produce both positive forms of "cultural affiliation" (xv) and negative structures of "inferiorization" (xvi) linking homosexuality with shame. More positively, those mechanisms constitute, for Eribon, "the launching pad for a process (again both individual and collective) of resubjectivation or of the reconstruction of personal identity" (xv). Ending with an addendum on Hannah Arendt's concepts of a "common world" and her denunciation of "worldlessness" as the condition of Jewish exclusion from participation in the world, Eribon argues for a similar thinking about homosexuality. The exclusion of groups, like homosexuals and Jews, thus becomes "the origin of a kind of political action in which the members of these groups intervene in public space in order to propound their own vision of the world and their own culture" (349).

My book is indebted to Eribon's work and is very much in solidarity with the project he undertakes. But our projects are extremely different in their conceptual orientation and theoretical frames. First, while Eribon insists that Foucault's story is ultimately the history of gay men, I argue explicitly against such specifications: as forms of madness, sexual abnormalities shift over time and cannot be pinned down as lasting continuities. Second, like many queer theorists, Eribon does not engage the question of ethics. I, by contrast, build my argument around the central question of a postmoral queer political ethic. Third, like many contemporary queer theorists, Eribon distances himself from feminist thought—in fact, he does not mention it. *Mad for Foucault*, on the other hand, explicitly addresses the feminist origins of queer theory in order to link Foucault's ethical thinking about sexuality to a long tradition of feminist ethics. And finally, unlike Eribon and most other Foucault scholars, I pay close attention to the literary and rhetorical dimensions of Foucault's writings as essential to an understanding of his project not only in *History of Madness* but in his oeuvre as a whole.

Most crucially, my objectives in rereading *Madness* are different than Eribon's, a difference that is reflected in my sustained focus on *Madness* itself over the course of the entirety of this book. Some will interpret my analyses as a series of "close readings," although in my loyalty to Foucault I prefer to think of them otherwise and to give them a different name. For Foucault rejects in numerous interviews the belletristic sacralization of texts associated with the practice of poststructuralist close reading. Remembering Foucault's more explosive or utilitarian metaphors—firecracker, dynamite, toolbox—for the contact that occurs between books and their users, I call my approach a close encounter with *Madness* that takes seriously the historical, conceptual, institutional, *and* rhetorical dimensions of Foucault's writing.

Further, unlike Eribon, I inhabit an explicitly American theoretical field that has long been concerned about feminist and queer ethical divisions around the question of sexuality. In that context, my primary interest is to unravel a complex theoretical knot in *Madness* that I identify as its ethical dimension: specifically, Foucault's critique of the structures of moral and rationalist exclusion through which sexual otherness is created and reproduced. Again and again, as I move deeper into *Madness*, I will return to Foucault's 1984 question: "Why [have] we made sexuality into a moral experience?" *Madness* has much to offer in answering that question. It is my contention that we cannot understand what Foucault is doing in *Sexuality One* (or volumes 2 and 3)—indeed we cannot understand sexuality *tout court* in Foucault—without understanding this ethical dimension of *Madness*.

My insistence on ethics in *Madness* leads directly to my engagement with psychoanalysis in its relation to queer theory. I see Foucault's devastating critique of Freud in *Madness* as the culmination of his critique of morality. In *Insult,* Eribon asserts, somewhat polemically, that "it is urgent and necessary to think outside the limits of psychoanalysis" (xix) since it is, in his view, "nothing other than a long heterosexual discourse on homosexuality" (xviii). Generally speaking, I agree with this assessment of the institution of psychoanalysis, although the statement denies the complexity and nuances of psychoanalytic thought and writing. I do agree with Eribon that "the Foucauldian conception of relationality, as well as his theory of power, are elaborated in the movement of an intransigeant challenge [*mise en question*] to the analytical theory of drives, 'sexuality,' and psychism."[65] Unlike Eribon, I focus specifically on the ethical dimension of Foucault's critique of Freud in *Madness* to bring out, somewhat counterintuitively, the despotic rationalism on which the oedipal structures of psychoanalysis are founded.

In light of Foucault's critique of psychoanalysis, Eribon argues that queer theory and psychoanalysis are fundamentally incompatible. Given the fundamental heterosexism of psychoanalysis, Eribon writes, "I wonder if it is really possible—and desirable—to engage in a project to join queer theory or, in a more general way, radical thought . . . with psychoanalysis?"[66] Although I am sympathetic with the negative conclusion this question implies, I want to understand *why* queer theory has increasingly turned toward psychoanalysis in the way it has. Rather than simply condemning queer theory's psychoanalytic propensities out of hand, I address the question: if Foucault and Freud represent intellectual trajectories that are fundamentally incompatible, why do they both hold a foundational place for queer theory?

In my view, this strangely American twinning of Freud and Foucault has produced the odd, distorted, infamously ungraspable conception of sexuality that has become the common fare of queer theory. As I will argue at greater length in later chapters, the erasure of *Madness* from queer theory produces, out of *Sexuality One*, a sexuality from which the complexity of *experience* has been drained away. Sapped of what we might call the messy thickness of erotic life, *Sexuality One* gives us only the thin abstractions of a *dispositif*—the webs of power-knowledge that have no contact with the living, breathing world of eros. Ironically, queer theory rediscovers that which is lost—what I'm calling eros—in the seductive depths and imagistic vocabulary of psychoanalysis. But, as I will show in chapter 3, Foucault's critique of psychoanalysis in *Madness* is categorical; it undermines its potential as a source of insight into the realities of lived erotic experience. Further, Foucault condemns psychoanalysis's oedipal structure as patriarchal, thereby aligning his critique with a critical approach we might call feminist. Finally, there is a direct connection between the critique of psychoanalysis in *History of Madness* and the great ironic redeployment of Freudian sexuality that constitutes *Sexuality One*. It is only from the perspective we have on Freud in *Madness* that we can "get" the irony of Foucault's reengagement of him in *Sexuality One*.

Interlude: Close Encounters

In reading and rereading *Madness* for this project, I've been repeatedly drawn back to Foucault's "confession" in the Droit interview about his reasons for writing the book: "for personal reasons . . . from the moment of my sexual awakening . . . when you discover it for yourself . . . if you're not like everyone else, it's because you're abnormal . . . it's because you're sick."[67] And I continue, as I read, to wonder about the reasons for Foucault's suppression of these remarks in 1975, fourteen years after the publication of the book he discusses with his interlocutor. To be sure, the comments are autobiographical and, therefore, nonphilosophical, although Foucault did on occasion describe each of his published philosophical works as an "autobiographical fragment."[68] To publish the comments would inevitably open the door to psychological readings of the author, "Foucault," in the discursive establishment of a psychic truth revealed to be the inner motor—and a sexual one, at that—which would come to constitute both the "origin" and the final "telos" of an otherwise inchoate "Foucault." Indeed, that kind of reductive psychological reading is all too familiar, epitomized by the irresponsible but widely reviewed James Miller biography of Foucault.[69]

Despite these clear dangers, I nonetheless want to return to the autobiographical confession in the Droit interview because, quite frankly, as I mentioned before, when I read it I *experienced* it as nothing less than a coup de foudre. (Did the fact that I read it in the divine surroundings of a twelfth-century Premonstratensian abbey have something to do with this excessive, almost mystical reaction?) Coming upon it, as I did, purely by accident, I was changed by it—both in my understanding of my own sexuality and in my understanding of "Foucault." In that sense, this piece of rejected detritus of the Foucault writing machine had, for me, the explosive force of the object-event Foucault describes in his 1972 preface to Madness. Its force was all the more impressive because it had been rejected and suppressed by the complex juridical and editorial *dispositif* that determines precisely which Foucault will be made available for public consumption.

But why, exactly, is the remark so important? To highlight the comment is not necessarily to ascribe a psychological motive to the writing of Madness; not only would Foucault vehemently reject such a gesture, but such an ascription would reproduce the very scientific, psychologizing logic of normality and abnormality the book sets out to unravel. Receiving the remark as I did—as a coup de foudre—I experienced Foucault, for the very first time in over twenty years of reading him, as a force of rupture within the tight machinery of philosophical reason. That experience of rupture was of a different order than the intellectual understanding I had developed over the years of the well-known Foucauldian concept of rupture. To intellectually conceive rupture is one thing; to experience it is quite another.

In retrospect, I interpret that rupturing experience of reading—reading as a coup de foudre—as an erotic countercoup to what Foucault terms in Madness a despotic *coup de force* (F 56) or "takeover" (M 44) by Cartesian rationalism and the equally despotic Freudian coup that captures the psyche in a patriarchal system. As an autobiographical remark that Foucault himself wanted stricken from the public record, its transformative status in my own St.-Theresa-like reading of him is nothing if not ironic. Upon reflection, I have come to see the irony as appropriate to what, with all humility, I regard as a desire I share with Foucault: to get out from under the thumb of rationalist philosophy. In that sense, my highlighting of his autobiographical, nonphilosophical remark is a kind of doubling of which Foucault himself might approve. To put it bluntly, my nonphilosophical, personal interlude interrupts—however slightly—the potential philosophical despotism of "Foucault."

On a more thematic level, the comment also provides a clue—an explicitly nonpsychological one—a kind of key for reading the multivalent meanings of madness in *History of Madness*. For indeed, the remark brings out precisely the category of sexual experience that figures so prominently in the story I want to tell about Foucault and queer theory. First, the comment clearly articulates a connection between an experience of sexuality and the renaming of that experience by medical science as abnormal and ill. In that sense, it speaks to one of the fundamental gestures of *History of Madness*: to interrupt the knowingness that would confine inarticulable experience within diagnostic categories. Second, Foucault's sexual experience comes into a relation with my experience of sexuality in a strangely inchoate experience of reading. That complex overlapping of inchoate experiences produces a new experience that I am calling a close encounter. The new experience is structured by the sameness of identification: experience 1 (Foucault's sexuality) = experience 2 (the reader's sexuality) = experience 3 (close encounter). But this identificatory structure is repeatedly interrupted by the limits of knowing that the overlapping structure implicitly exposes. I cannot know what Foucault's sexuality really is; I cannot really even know my own. Yet we both have experiences we call sexual: what Foucault calls the "awakening" of his sexuality finds its counterpart in what I, in 1994, called my "coming out" as a lesbian. But both experiences are reduced, in their naming, to distortions of the experience itself: sexuality emerges as unknowable and unnameable. In the context of *Madness*, that is precisely the position occupied by unreason: it is the interruption of the knowingness of reason. And it is precisely that rupture of reason that characterizes the third experience—that of an erotic, nonphilosophical, coup de foudre encounter that is lyrical and ironic: an experience of knowing that fails to know, but which, nonetheless, carries with it a powerful force of transformation.

Encountering *Madness*

This book stages a close encounter with *History of Madness* in the light of queer theory. It asks the question: What is at stake in thinking queerly about *Madness*? The answer to that seemingly simple question is the work of the chapters and interludes that follow. In moving toward that answer, I separate my inquiry into five main chapters: 1. "How We Became Queer," about the production of sexual deviance as a form of madness; 2. "Queer Moralities," about the framing of sexual deviance within a Nietzschean internalizing grid of moral exclusion; 3. "Unraveling the Queer Psyche," about the critique of the inner psyche and the psychoanalytic capture of sexuality in the unconscious; 4. "A Queer Nephew," about an alternative, nonpsychic reframing of sexuality as eros; and 5. "A Political Ethic of Eros," about an artful, literary Foucault who reengages sexuality in order to articulate an erotic ethics of experience. Within the breaks that separate the chapters are narrative interludes similar to those that are woven throughout this introduction, which serve to playfully offset the heavier theoretical apparatus of the detailed explication of *Madness* contained within the chapters. In their disposition between the chapters, the interludes also mimic those lighter, sometimes ludic intermediary dramas introduced between the acts of traditional morality plays to offset the weight of what might otherwise be an overly serious affair.

The sequence of the book's chapters, along with the interludes, is governed by my commitment to stay close to the material, whether it be *History of Madness* or the archival marginalia in which Foucault refers to the genesis and reception of the book. To be sure, there are crucial questions that come from "outside" of the *Madness* material informing my investigation here. For example, each chapter engages with the question of the American reception of Foucault's work generally, as well as the more specific question of the queer uptake of his thought. But rather than beginning with those external questions to frame my argument, I have allowed the Foucault material—book and archive—to guide the structure and elaboration of my inquiry. The result is a close encounter with *Madness* whose motivation is both erotic and politically strategic: to articulate an ethics of sexual experience that can inform a radical politics of tranformation, especially in a U.S. context. In that approach, I try to remain faithful to Foucault's instrumentalist understanding of the book as tool: "I write for users [*utilisateurs*]," he says, "not for readers."[70]

Let me describe here more fully how I use Foucault in my close encounter with *History of Madness*. Following Didier Eribon and, to a lesser
extent, Eric Fassin in their work on Foucauldian sexuality in an American context, I view my elaboration of sexuality in *Madness* not as an
"application" of Foucault to a scene which would otherwise remain foreign to it, "a social space that he would not have encountered."[71] Rather,
my approach to *Madness* deepens an engagement whose history goes
back at least to the late 1970s, when American scholars like Gayle Rubin
and David Halperin read the Foucault of *Sexuality One* and were forever
changed.[72] I see *Madness*, retrospectively, as now taking its place within
a specifically American intellectual movement that was sparked, in
large part, by the excitement generated by *Sexuality One*, when it was
published in English in 1978. During that period, Foucault also began
traveling more and more frequently to the U.S. to give lectures at col-
leges and universities and, most influentially, to teach courses at Berkeley during the early 1980s. Together with the publication of volumes 2
and 3 of *History of Sexuality* in English, in 1985 and 1986, respectively,
this series of exchanges helped to consolidate what we might call a specifically American Foucault. Foucault's thinking about sexuality has
thus remained a consistent presence on the American intellectual scene
since the late 1970s and has become even more pronounced in the last
several years with the interest generated by the transcription, translation, and publication of his courses at the Collège de France.

To reencounter Foucault's thought about sexuality in *Madness* is
therefore, as Fassin puts it in a slightly different context, "to make it
work precisely where it already plays an important social role, at once
intellectual and political."[73] The stage is set for the encounter to occur;
the purpose of this book is to make it happen. More particularly, here is
the story the following chapters tell:

1. "How We Became Queer": In telling the story of madness in the
classical age, Foucault is also telling a story about the production of
nonnormative sexualities, categories of abnormality that are, from the
moment of division between reason and its others, included in the categories of reason's exclusions. The production of sexuality—like the
production of unreason more broadly—is a story about the production
of subjectivity through structures of moral exclusion. That story about
the production of normative subjectivity is a familiar one for American
readers of the "middle Foucault" of the mid-1970s, for it is the story
Foucault tells in both *Discipline and Punish* (1975) and *Sexuality One*
(1976). In a close encounter with one of the most oft-quoted passages in

Foucault's oeuvre, I challenge the ubiquitous interpretations of Foucault that claim him as a historian who locates the emergence of homosexual identity in 1870. So doing, I insist on the ethical questions about subjectivity that are taken up and condensed in *Sexuality One* after their more sustained narrative treatment in *History of Madness*.

2. "Queer Moralities": I argue in this chapter that we miss a crucial component of Foucault's critique of morality when we only read the Foucault of the 1970s and eighties. Specifically, what we miss when we read about productive power only through the lens of the middle and late Foucault is the story he tells about moral exclusion as the normative and normalizing production of interiority. This tale of interiority is a Nietzschean story that today we might describe, following Deleuze, as a critical one about subjectivity as coextensive. *Madness* tells a story about the production of norms through the practice of confinement, which is also, ultimately, a practice of moral exclusion. That moral practice creates the appearance of human interiority in the form of conscience and guilt. In other words, woven through Foucault's early argument about locking up the mad is a story about the production of interiority. Psychic interiority, in this view, is the result of moral exclusions generated by reason's self-separation from its other, unreason. The Age of Reason is thus the age of rationalism's production of the guilty conscience as a means of enforcing social norms. The guilty conscience will become, in the nineteenth century, the psyche of psychology, psychiatry, and, eventually, psychoanalysis. Drawing on this reading of *History of Madness*, I contrast Foucauldian subjectivation as part of the production of moral interiority with the concept of performative identities made famous by Judith Butler. Performativity reveals an investment in subjectivity and an inner psyche that Foucault's work consistently challenges. And the differences between these two conceptions of subjectivity have serious implications for queer and feminist theory, particularly debates about the ethics of sex.

3. "Unraveling the Queer Psyche": Moving more deeply into Foucault's critique of the psyche, I argue in this chapter that the critique of psychoanalysis we find in *Sexuality One* redeploys and reduces *Madness*'s much deeper and more devastating critique of psychoanalysis as the offspring of a despotic philosophical reason. Foucault's Nietzschean critique of the production of interiority through structures of moral exclusion has vast implications both for our understanding of sexuality generally and, more specifically, for an assessment of the increasingly psychoanalytic turn taken by queer theory. Although many have recog-

nized *Sexuality One* as a critical genealogy of psychoanalysis, most American queer theorists have not taken Foucault's critique of psycho-analysis to mean that a psychoanalytic conception of sexuality should be rejected out of hand. In this chapter I challenge queer theory's often uncritical reliance on psychoanalysis by bringing out Foucault's argument against it in *Madness* and comparing it with queer theory's claims about Foucault, with a particular focus on Butler's *Psychic Life of Power* (1997). While the more widely read *Sexuality One* ironizes psychoanalysis as the product of a bourgeois order in which discourses of sexuality proliferate, *Madness* suggests that psychoanalytic thinking itself is the product of a deeper divide between reason and unreason through which interiority is produced. That production of interiority effaces sexual experience as coextension, as a nonself-identical movement of forces toward their limit.

4. "A Queer Nephew": Following on the critique of Freud, I read *Madness* as a critique of the Hegelian self-reflective structures of reason and the consequences of that self-reflective machinery. Engaging *Rameau's Nephew* in *Madness*, I reopen Foucault's critique of self-reflection to move us constructively toward an ethics that would allow unreason to speak. The implications of that critique and that reopening are far-reaching not only for queer theory but also more generally for an ethics of sex conceived as a nonpsychic redeployment of eros with a framing of subjectivity as radically coextensive. Thus *Madness*'s negative, critical intervention into a history of reason and moral exclusion also posits, in a constructive mode, an alternative logic of nonself-reflection which can be read as a call for a different ethics of sexual experience. In the convergence between *Madness*'s embrace of nonself-reflection and queer theory's similarly insistent critique of self-identity, a path is reopened for a dialogue between them.

5. "A Political Ethic of Eros": Finally, I argue that it is precisely in an erotic mode that the political ethic which refuses the moral exclusions of reason can be practiced. Trapped by the philosophical voice of reason, Foucault looks to other models of subjectivity to find a philosophical practice that would puncture reason's false self-sufficiency. The two places to which antirationalist philosophers like Lyotard and Derrida have turned are psychoanalysis and literature. But, whereas psychoanalysis offers a system and a vocabulary that speaks the irrational, for Foucault psychoanalysis is the product of the bad interiority of moral exclusion, and thus the bad creation of despotic reason itself. So too with literary texts: if literature seems to speak that which reason cannot

speak, for Foucault literature's tendency to speak the unspeakable marks its complicity with a rationalist system that manages life as bio-power. Rather than looking to distinct corporeal practices or discursive sites as models for a modern erotic ethics, I argue that Foucault is a philosopher who, in his work on the archives, engages in an erotic practice of thinking and feeling. Eros informs Foucault's relation to his own histories of the present, to which he gains access through the alterity of the archives. And this is precisely where, as a subject in a relation to truth, Foucault is himself transformed. As a transformative practice whose condition of possibility is freedom, Foucault's ethical *ars erotica* is explicitly political.

That political ethic of eros names a different Foucault than the one I had known for many years in my feminist love-hate engagement with his work. It is also a different ethics than the explicit self-fashioning of the Greco-Roman model, an ethics that some have read as radically new, others as participating in a tradition of virtue ethics, and still others as nothing more than narcissistic aestheticism. Reading Foucault as contributing to the articulation of an ethics of eros reads him differently, in a different light or through a different lens, as a slightly different object-event. It is, in part, the result of my own belated response to him, after all those years of love-hate reading, as a coup de foudre in the archives. The interludes tell the story of that coup de foudre, where I was responding, in part, to the fleshy, material generosity of a different Foucault, a Foucault of the margins, an unedited, unpublished, suppressed Foucault. The material generosity I found in the archives opened a passage in me that I can only name as itself animated by an erotic impulse as unsettling as it is transformative. This postulation of the ethical possibilities of eros is not sentimental or romantic. Rather, the eros of generosity always acknowledges and remains in tension with the possibility of erotic dissolution. The tension between the two is not resolved, redeemed, or sublated; it is nondialectical; it is what Jean-Luc Nancy calls "the disturbance of violent relatedness."[74] Foucault's eros articulates an ideal of freedom that hovers in the moment before its separation into pain and pleasure, dissolution and connection, the forces of undoing and merging. From that perspective, this book as a whole—in its back-and-forth movement between chapters and interludes—reflects in its structure both the disturbance and the promise of a transformative erotic practice.

1 / How We Became Queer

One day, perhaps, we will no longer know what madness was.
—Michel Foucault, 1964

Foucault's Queer Prodigals

In *Split Decisions: How and Why to Take a Break from Feminism* (2006), queer legal scholar Janet Halley tells a personal, theoretical, and political story about feminism's wayward offspring, those "prodigal sons and daughters who have wandered off to do other things."[1] She herself is one of those children—son or daughter is not quite clear: "if I could click my heels and become a 'gay man' or a 'straight white male middle-class radical,' I would do it in an instant—wouldn't you?"[2] As it turns out, those children are more rebellious than wayward, not "wandering off" but running away from a "governance feminism" (32) they regard as unjust. Halley is referring specifically to feminist legal reforms such as sexual harassment legislation when she writes: "any force as powerful as feminism must find itself occasionally looking down at its own bloody hands. . . . Prodigal theory often emerges to represent sexual subjects, sexual possibilities, sexual realities, acts, bodies, relationships onto which feminism has been willing to shift the sometimes very acute costs of feminist victories in governance" (33).

To buttress her argument that "feminism . . . is running things" (20), Halley divides all of feminism into its two legal versions: power feminism, represented by Catherine MacKinnon, and cultural feminism, epitomized by Robin West. And if she continues to be filled "with awe" (60) by the dazzling power analyses of early MacKinnon, such is not the case with regard to the "bad faith" (60) of an "intensely moralistic" (76)

Robin West who tries to combine an ethics of justice with an ethics of care. Halley complains: "The distinctive cultural-feminist character of West's project . . . is the pervasive *moral* character of patriarchy and feminism" (61). Cultural feminists see a male-dominated world in which "female values have been depressed and male values elevated in a profound *moral error* that can be corrected only by feminism" (61; emphasis added). Her own position as a Harvard law professor notwithstanding, Halley asserts that she cannot follow either MacKinnon or West into the corridors of legal and institutional power where their "governance feminism" has taken them. And if she continues to admire MacKinnon and profess an allegiance to the epistemological focus of her early work, this is not the case with Robin West. The vehemence of Halley's rejection of cultural feminism and, with it, her former self, takes on the force of a religious conversion:

> I was a cultural feminist for years, a fact that I confess with considerable shame. Somehow, now, cultural feminism is a deep embarrassment to me. . . . It was a time of intense misery in my life—misery I then attributed to patriarchy but that I now attribute to my cultural feminism. And it was a wrenching and painful—also liberating and joyful—process to move into a different metaphysics, a different epistemology, a different politics, and *a different ethics*. (59–60; emphasis added)

I begin with this sketch of Halley's opening arguments and confessions as a context for my project on Foucault, madness, and queer theory. Specifically, I want to situate *my* Foucault within a queer theory formed, from the start, within a feminist matrix whose primary analytical focus was the sex/gender system.[3] And although it is tempting to engage Halley in the detail of her arguments, that is not my purpose here. Rather, I use her image of prodigal children in their rebellion against an "intensely moralistic" (76) feminist mother, to situate my work within a contemporary queer feminism that continues to interrogate, long after queer theory's feminist birth, gender's translations into ever-new contexts and fields of study. My specific focus is the complex result of a series of divergences—figured by Halley as "split decisions"— within a configuration of terms—specifically, sex, sexuality, and gender—that have now been institutionalized and theoretically established as that inchoate project we call queer theory.

I am especially interested in the ethical dimensions of those split decisions and view Halley's work as but the latest moment in a string of events that might well be described as a queer resistance to an age-old figure: the scolding feminist prude. In her figuration within queer "prodigal theory," that sex-phobic nag is both overly victimized and overly powerful: always "about to be raped,"[4] as MacKinnon puts it, and, at the same time, as Halley complains, always "running things"[5] in order to ensure her own protection. As a result of the feminist movement, the scolding prude now "walk[s] the halls of power,"[6] using the state to do violence to sexual "others"—those loving perverts we have come to call queer—in the name of feminism's superior moral values.

But how, exactly, did this feminist-queer split come about? In the complex play of translations and interpretations that solidify as theoretical and political positions, no one is more important for the establishment of queer theory as distinct from feminism than Foucault. Most prominently, Gayle Rubin's aegis-creating article, "Thinking Sex" (1984), draws heavily on Foucault to make the case for "an autonomous theory and politics specific to sexuality" (34), distinct from a feminist "theory of gender oppression."[7] And if, as I argued in the introduction, the founding thinkers of the queer come out of feminism, its institutional and theoretical distinctiveness has, to a great extent, been defined in terms of its *difference* from feminism and gender.[8] In that process, Foucault has taken his place as the radically poststructuralist, foreign father of a host of queer children bent on rejecting a feminist, Anglo-American mother whose normative governance projects are threatening to them. This is what Halley has come to call "taking a break," and she lists Foucault first in her genealogy of "some classics" (38) in that antifeminist project.

Significantly, when Halley and other queer theorists—including feminist ones—refer to Foucault, they mean the very limited, specific Foucault I mentioned in the introduction: the Foucault of the massively read *Sexuality One*. In her brief chapter on Foucault, Halley is typical of queer theorists generally in her attention to Foucault's familiar theories about sexuality as power-knowledge: power appears as relational (120) and productive (119), subjectivity emerges as subjectivation or *assujettissement* (121), and sexuality, not gender, becomes the "primum mobile" (123) of modern subjectivation.

Halley's typical queer privileging of sexuality over gender as the "prime mover" of subjectivation in Foucault exposes a terminological knot worth unraveling, especially with regard to the ethical incommensurabilities outlined above. My critique of Halley's reading here is not directed at her alone and could be applied to Rubin and others as well. It follows a path already laid out by Judith Butler in "Against Proper Objects" and Elizabeth Weed in "The More Things Change" in *Femi-*

nism Meets Queer Theory (1997).[9] In using Halley as my initial lens for focusing on Foucault and queer theory, I want to open a queer-feminist, Franco-American question about some incipient linguistic and conceptual problems that swirl around the terms *sex, sexuality,* and *gender.* Most fundamentally, there is a problem of translation: like Rubin before her, Halley imputes to Foucault a semantic distinction between sexuality and gender that cannot be supported by the original French vocabulary that would designate such a difference.[10] Broadly speaking, *Sexuality One* is about sex: *le sexe.* Foucault describes *le sexe* as "a fictitious unity"[11] produced from within the *dispositif* of sexuality. As its linguistic ambiguity in French suggests, the "dense transfer point of power"[12] Foucault calls *le sexe* includes within it all the meanings English speakers differentiate into sex-as-organs, sex-as-biological-reproduction, sex-as-individual-gender-roles, sex-as-gendered-group-affiliation, sex-as-erotic-acts, and sex-as-lust. And if *le sexe* is produced by the dispositif of sexuality, this hardly means it supersedes or reverses the primacy of gender, as many queer theorists would like to claim. Sex, sexuality, and gender are inseparable and coextensive.[13]

The queer overreading of sexuality in Foucault through a causal logic that makes gender secondary or "epiphenomenal"[14] produces a messy tangle of problems that will directly inform my engagement with Foucault in *History of Madness.* To begin, Foucault is not a causal thinker, either historically or conceptually speaking: Foucauldian genealogical events and concepts have no origin, but repeat themselves in complex doublings and feedback loops. Second, the queer emphasis on sexuality's primacy in Foucault reinterprets him within a non-Foucauldian identitarian logic that yields an Anglo-American division between "sexuality" and "gender." This problem is compounded by queer theory's almost exclusive focus on the Foucault of *Sexuality One. Sexuality One's* "archeology of psychoanalysis"[15] has been read as a critique of sexual "identity" as it emerged in the nineteenth century. In a chiastic twisting of the standard reading of Foucault, where sexuality is primary and gender is secondary, early queer theory used Foucault's critique of *sexuality* to resignify *gender* as nonidentitarian and, in so doing, to trouble the stability of sexual identities as well. That radical interrogation of identity itself has been the most salient and distinctive of queer theory's claims.

But for all the value of that anti-identitarian critique, queer theory has been less successful in articulating, beyond morality, an ethics of lived erotic experience. The result has been the kind of ethical split we see in Halley, between feminist moralists and sex-positive queers. And if Foucault has provided queer theory with an arsenal of weapons for unraveling the moralism of governance feminism, his work has been less useful for articulating sexuality within a constructive ethical frame that can actually be used as a map for living. Beyond his elliptical gestures toward the "resistances" of "bodies and pleasures" at the end of *Sexuality One* or his descriptions of erotic subjectivities in the ancient world in the final two volumes of *History of Sexuality*, Foucault seemingly gives us little to work with for constructing an ethics that would speak to the political dilemmas of contemporary experiences of *le sexe*.

This is where my close encounter with *History of Madness* hopes to reengage Foucault as a theoretical resource for a constructive ethical project that can speak to queers and feminists alike. To read sexuality in Foucault as Halley and so many "prodigal theorists" do—through the lens of sexuality as the *primum mobile* of subjectivation in *Sexuality One*—is to read only the middle of a longer Foucauldian story about sex, sexuality, and gender. In *Insult and the Making of the Gay Self* (2004), Eribon insists on the importance of *Madness* as part of Foucault's thinking about the production of nonnormative sexualities. In his chapter, "Homosexuality and Unreason," Eribon asks: "Would it be possible to read Foucault's *Madness and Civilization* as a history of *homosexuality* that dared not speak its name?"[16] The question is both necessary and difficult to answer. Eribon is especially keen to warn his readers against a psychological interpretation of *Madness* that Foucault himself would reject, one in which homosexuality would become its hidden meaning or inner truth. That said, the centrality of sexuality to Foucault's study of madness is undeniable. Eribon focuses specifically on homosexuality as a category of unreason in the Age of Reason and interprets Foucault to be laying the groundwork for his later critique of psychoanalysis in *Sexuality One*. As Eribon explains, the seventeenth-century exclusion of homosexuality in the domain of unreason takes place within bourgeois structures of moral exclusion that attach shame and scandal to "abnormality" and thereby silence its expression. This ultimately moral experience of unreason leads to the establishment of scientific and medical knowledge about madness in the form of psychology, psychiatry and, eventually, psychoanalysis.

Eribon's remarks on homosexuality in *Madness* help me to link the queer-feminist divisions outlined above with Foucault's archeology of what will later become specifically sexual forms of exclusion in *History of Madness*. In this way they also open up a terrain for this chapter's exploration of sexuality's imbrication in a structure that separates reason and unreason. I focus here on the story Foucault tells in *Madness* about the structures of moral exclusion that use repression to produce not only homosexuality but also "abnormal" sexual subjectivities more generally—modes of being that today we might call queer. I begin with a careful reading of the geographical metaphors Foucault outlines in *Madness* in order to describe the repressive production of unreason in the Age of Reason. In this focus on repression and production, I distance myself from those who read Foucault as progressing from an early Reichian notion of sexual repression in *Madness* to an explicit rejection of Freudo-Marxist repression in his later theories of productive power.[17] Careful attention to the central theme of subjectivity in *Madness* reveals that a conception of productivity is already at work fourteen years before *Discipline and Punish* (1975), the book that immediately preceded *Sexuality One* that many view as marking the turning point in Foucault's thinking about power.[18] To be sure, in its early articulation in *Madness*, productivity is not yet developed into the more sustained exposition of disciplinary power, biopower, and governmentality that we find in Foucault's later work. Nonetheless, a conception of forms of subjection through which subjects are created—what Foucault calls *assujettissement* in *Discipline and Punish* —is clearly present in *Madness*. This productive conception of sexual subjectivity coexists, in an uneasy tension, with a conception of sexual subjectivity as politically repressed.

After tracing the story *Madness* tells about the repressive production of sexual subjectivity and its others, I then compare *Madness* to the "fable" of sexuality presented in *Sexuality One*. Specifically, I use *Madness* as a queer ethical lens through which to reread Foucault's later assertions about sexuality and to challenge some of queer theory's most dogmatic and inaccurate interpretations of what Foucault writes in *Sexuality One*. In linking sexual subjectivity in *Madness* to its reemergence in *Sexuality One*, I challenge the now legendary story of a Foucault who tells us that the "homosexual" emerged as an "identity" in 1870 out of a past that had only perceived him as a series of "acts." Reading *Sexuality One* in light of *Madness* clearly shows that Foucault's primary concern in thinking about sexuality—from *Madness* through *Sexuality One* to the final two volumes of *History of Sexuality*—is its relationship to morality.

The *Cogito's* Ghosts

As a story about madness, *History of Madness* is a tale about forms of subjectivity that have come to be labeled as normal or deviant, reasonable or irrational, straight or queer. This split within conceptions of subjectivity emerges from its earliest chapters in the form of the Cartesian *cogito*. Foucault's central argument in the early chapters is that the production of unreason in the Age of Reason is the result not only of institutional practices of confinement in the seventeenth century but also and, more importantly, of the philosophical despotism of Cartesianism. Indeed, Foucault opens the second chapter of *Madness*, "The Great Confinement," not with a reading of practices of confinement, but rather with a critique of Descartes, the "father of modern philosophy."[19] As Maurice Blanchot puts it, the Great Confinement "answers to the banishment pronounced by Descartes."[20] This focus on Descartes—the philosopher par excellence of the subject, the "I" of the cogito—highlights the centrality of subjectivity as a category of analysis for a history of madness. With Descartes and the rise of reason, it is the conception of the "I" that dramatically changes.

By beginning his story of the split between reason and unreason as a story about a split subject, Foucault highlights the relationship between deviant or irrational subjects and what we might call, after Luce Irigaray, the structures of "othering"[21]—including, importantly, the sexual ones that will produce the queer—through which the modern subject constitutes himself in relation to those whom he both desperately needs and insistently rejects. In *Madness*, this queer figure or character will variously appear—sometimes anonymously, sometimes with names—as the leper, the fool, the pauper, the vagrant, the sodomite, the libertine (Sade), the prostitute, the homosexual, the hysteric, the poet (Nerval), the mad philosopher (Nietzsche), the crazy painter (Van Gogh), the suicidal writer (Roussel), or the antitheatrical playwright (Artaud). All these characters, along with others—onanists, *précieuses*, melancholics, hypochondriacs, nymphomaniacs, ad infinitum—will emerge and disappear over the course of the book as figures of the othering structure that simultaneously produces and excludes sexual subjects and their others. They are what Foucault calls, in the 1975 Droit interview, "mes petits fous": my little mad ones.[22]

Behind these figures of the sexual subject and its others lies a historicoethical question that will continue to reverberate throughout Foucault's life work: what persists? How is it that a medieval sodomite becomes a nineteenth-century invert? How does an eighteenth-century onanist become, in the twentieth century, the liberated woman celebrated by Betty Dodson in her masturbation workshops? What persists in those temporal transmutations? What is lost when we give them a name—an act of reason—and tell their history, their story? Do we know what a sodomite was, or even a homosexual? Or are they mere figures like those Gothic symbols Foucault describes whose meanings are lost in subsequent periods? "The forms remain familiar," Foucault writes, "but all understanding is lost, leaving nothing but a fantastical presence" (*M* 16–17; translation modified).

At stake in Foucault's tracing of these figures in their historical appearance and disappearance are ethical questions about subjectivity and alterity within a modern rationalist moral order. Faced with an objectifying language of reason for the telling of history, *History of Madness* refigures those sexual subjects transformed by science into objects of intelligibility—as homosexuals, onanists, perverts, and so on—by allowing them to hover as "fantastical" ghosts. They haunt our present, but we can't quite grasp them. These ghosts of *Madness* prefigure, as elusive characters in a story, Foucault's later conceptual articulation of history as genealogy, where shifts in rationality produce a series of temporal discontinuities whose epistemic breaks go all the way down to the limits of thinking. These breaches of intelligibility are marked by divisions such as the one Foucault identifies at the end of the eighteenth century as the split between unreason and madness. Unreason is the name Foucault gives to the thing from the past, now called madness, that remains, in our historical present, radically unassimilable and untranslatable. As an inchoate ensemble of experiences of madness from the premodern past, what Foucault calls unreason persists as forms; hovering over the present, they "occasionally intersect with our pathological analyses" (*M* 132), but they "could never coincide with them in any coherent manner" (*M* 132). In *Madness*, these forms appear as figures or characters: less the fleshy, well-rounded creations of realist fiction than the thin silhouettes of a *nouveau roman*. And because we can capture them only in the disappearance of their meaning, like those Gothic symbols, over the horizon of history, we can only perceive them as the thin shadow cast by something as it is leaving.

This focus on characters and figures highlights the representational framing of subjectivity in *Madness*: not only does Foucault draw on literary, artistic, and symbolic sources to set up his historical and philosophical investigation of the splits around which rationalist othering occurs, but he himself engages in a kind of writing that draws on literary devices. Indeed, *Madness* has been called a "prose poem,"[23] a work that revels in "a love of ambiguity,"[24] a narrative that takes the mythical form of "a struggle between monsters and heroes"[25] and, by Foucault himself in the 1961 preface, simply as "these flickering simulacra" (*M* xxvii). So if *Madness* is not quite a fiction or fable, it is not a traditional history either. Foucault uses both literary images and philosophical concepts to give a form to the archival traces he consults—"ruptures of evidence" about the mad—in order to weave a narrative about reason and unreason at a crucial juncture in Western history. In that sense, *History of Madness* occupies the generative, ambiguous space of an untranslatable French *histoire*: the *in-between* of a history or story that refuses the article—*une histoire* or *l'histoire*—that would pin it down and define it as either fiction or documentary history.

Foucault's symbolic rendering of this spatiotemporal othering structure as the historical shadow cast by something that is leaving is made clear from the very first pages of *Madness*. He begins the book with a story about the disappearance of leprosy from medieval Europe and its eventual replacement with madness in the Renaissance figure of the ship of fools. From the book's opening paragraph, lepers are dead. But, throughout the pages of *Madness*, they will silently and invisibly haunt the arid landscape of a world that repeatedly rejects them. Like the mad, lepers are created by a brutal "game of exclusion" (*M* 6) that will "be played again, often in the same places" (*M* 6)—in places like Charenton, St-Germain, and St-Lazarre (*M* 3)—"and in an oddly similar fashion two or three centuries later" (*M* 6) in the confinements and asylums of the Age of Reason. Indeed, the leper is the "ghost" (*M* 3) who hovers at the margins of the inhabitable social world that rejects him, a figure of the "inhuman" (*M* 3) who will continue to haunt the sun-filled spaces of a Western humanism Foucault spent his life critiquing.

In that context, it is significant that Foucault opens his book with a geographical metaphor for a structure of exclusion that, in the form of the leper's ghost, will *not* disappear: "At the end of the Middle Ages, leprosy disappeared from the Western world. At the edges of the community, at town gates, large, barren, uninhabitable areas appeared, where the disease no longer reigned but its ghost hovered. For centuries, these spaces would belong to the domain of the inhuman" (*M* 3).

The images of the edges and gates at the threshold of inhuman spaces devoid of life form a backdrop for the subsequent image of the watery mobility of the ship of fools. For if lepers themselves were perceived as coextensive with the uninhabitable spaces they occupied, their necessity as figures of moral and social alterity remained. As ghosts, the lepers bring attention to the paradoxical spaces of *Madness* Foucault describes in the 1961 preface as "both empty and peopled at the same time" (*M* xxxi). Against that backdrop of an inhabited void that contains but swallows up the other, the symbolic movement of the ship of fools represents a certain cultural struggle and disquieting uncertainty about the place and the role of alterity; as Foucault puts it, "the ship is a symbol of the sudden unease [*inquiétude*] that appears on the horizon of European culture towards the end of the Middle Ages" (*M* 12/*F* 24).

It is important to emphasize the symbolic dimension of Foucault's geographical rendering of his story here. In this opening chapter, "*Stultifera Navis*," the Renaissance ship of fools symbolizes a transitional moment between the medieval exclusion of lepers outside the gates of the city and the classical exclusion of the mad within the social body. As Foucault tells us later in the book, by the end of the eighteenth century "the great image of medieval horror rose up once again, leading to a new panic among the metaphors of terror (*M* 355). Internment shifts from an exclusion of lepers outside the city to what Mercier called "a terrible ulcer on the political body" (*M* 355). In this "geography of evil" (*M* 357), the forms of unreason which "had taken the place of leprosy, and had been banished to the extreme margins of society, have become now a visible form of leprosy [*lèpre visible*], offering their corrosive wounds to the promiscuity of men" (*M* 357/*F* 377; translation modified). The fear of the other—of unreason itself—becomes the fear within, marked by "the imaginary mark of an illness" (*M* 358/*F* 377; translation modified) to which everyone is susceptible. The suppurating wounds on the social body of a medicalized eighteenth-century imaginary will serve as a reminder—in a ghostly reactivation of the medieval figure of the leper— of the dangers of unreason's contagious effects on positivist reason.

In this context, the Renaissance ship of fools becomes a symbol "heavily loaded with meaning" (*M* 10): neither an image of absolute freedom nor of absolute containment, the ship is a figure of an agonistic struggle whose stakes are defined by reason's grappling with its own limits as unreason. If, as Foucault puts it, "water brings its own dark symbolic charge, carrying away, but purifying too" (*M* 11/*F* 22; translation modified), the navigation it requires represents a different subjectivity and a different thinking that we might, as shorthand, call a Renaissance humanism, which contrasts with the humanism of the Age of Reason. This engagement with the limits of reason and unreason— the human and the inhuman, life and death—doesn't confine itself, as Enlightenment reason confidently does, to an absolute, categorical division between a human reason and a vast realm of unreason where those deemed to be less than human—the queer, racial others, the mad—reside. In the "liminal situation" of the Renaissance fool, Foucault finds a figure for a questioning of the limits of reason that re-mains undecided. Unlike the cogito who considers "the other world" (*M* 11) of madness and definitively excludes it from himself, in the Re-naissance we find a back and forth movement between reason and madness: "the madman on his crazy boat sets sail for the other world, and it is from the other world that he comes when he disembarks" (*M* 11). In that exploration, reason is repeatedly disarmed by an unreason it touches: the stern expression of the philosopher is continually shat-tered by the "laugh of madness" (*M* 15), just as all life's projects dissolve into the laugh that is death: "the laugh of madness is an anticipation of the rictus grin of death" (*M* 15). Unreason, like death, is the unsettling force that puts the subject into question: the "dark, disordered, shifting chaos, the germ and death of all things" (*M* 12). And while unreason is a threat to life and "the luminous, adult stability of the mind" (*M* 12), it is not completely expelled from the subject's realm.

It is in this symbolic sense that the Renaissance ship of fools consti-tutes a cultural acknowledgement of what Foucault calls the "tragic" di-mension of subjectivity. Like the medieval leper's ghost, that tragic con-sciousness haunts the subject, right up to the present, as a spectral "consciousness of madness, which has never really gone away" (*M* 27). It reemerges, in the plurality of unreason's many forms, in "the last words of Nietzsche and the last visions of Van Gogh" (*M* 28), in "the work of Antonin Artaud" (*M* 28), and even, momentarily, in the Freud-ian "mythological struggle between the libido and the death instinct" (*M* 28). As the Age of Reason unfolds and tragedy goes underground, reason will undertake "a more perilous masking" (*M* 28) of that tragic dimension of subjectivity by rejecting and excluding it as other. This masked repudiation of the subject's alterity culminates in the positivist "analysis of madness as a form of mental illness" (*M* 28/*F* 40; transla-tion modified) that transforms the tragic fool into an object of scientific knowledge. Even Freud, for all his brilliant insights into the coexistence of Eros and Thanatos, will ultimately participate in the despotic coup that will confine and objectify the unraveled subject as an excluded other: a madman, a hysteric, a pervert, a queer.

So how, exactly, does the ship of fools call into question a stable con-ception of rational subjectivity? It is important to emphasize here that Foucault's famous rendering of the Renaissance ship of fools in the opening chapter of *Madness* is at once a historical description of the social management of the excluded, an aesthetic encounter with forms of representation, and a philosophical investigation of what Foucault calls games of truth. It is difficult to grasp this multilayered aspect of Foucault's histoire, which is both symbolic and real. Geography is the metaphor Foucault uses in *Madness* to tell a story about the subject's split across the great divide of reason and unreason. As Foucault will tell us again and again, this geography is itself "half-real, half-imaginary" (*M* 11/*F* 22; translation modified). The ship of fools negotiates that geography; in so doing, it represents a certain kind of freedom. It is "clearly a literary composition" (*M* 8/*F* 18–19; translation modified), a "literary commonplace" that draws on the "ancient cycle of the Argonauts" (*M* 8) and other morally coded symbolic ships: a Ship of Health, a Ship of Virtuous Ladies, a Ship of Princes and Battles of the Nobility (*M* 8). But of all these "satirical and novelistic ships" (*M* 9), Foucault asserts that only the ship of fools—the *Narrenschiff*—"had a genuine existence" (*M* 9). Sociologically and historically speaking, "they really did exist, these boats that drifted from one town to another with their senseless cargo. An easily errant existence was often the lot of the mad" (*M* 9/*F* 19; translation modified). Finally, the ship of fools is also a philosophical device: "with a crew of imaginary heroes, moral models or carefully defined social types" (*M* 8), the ship is "the figure of their destiny or of their truth" (*M* 8). As a figure of the subject's search for truth, the ship of fools forms a contrast with the other figures of the quest for truth, metaphorically rendered in *Madness* as images of containment and therefore of unfreedom. From the "games of exclusion" that define the leper to the back-and-forth movement of the ship of fools to the confinement of truth within the gaze of science, *Madness* narrates a story about subjectivity that Thomas Flynn describes as Foucault's "spatialization of reason"[26] and Deleuze calls a "map of relations of force."[27] In all three dimensions—literary, historicosociological, and philosophical—the ship of fools opens a story about subjectivity rendered as a geographical navigation of the split between reason and unreason: "an oceanic line that passes through all points of resistance."[28]

This insistence on geography allows us to understand *Madness*'s opening opposition between mobility and confinement as a spatial metaphor that dramatically conveys the devastating effects of the Cartesian coup of reason in the seventeenth century. The Renaissance provides a panoply of geographical images of "Madness [*Folie*] at work at the heart of reason and truth" (*M* 13/*F* 25; translation modified): in the paintings of Van Oestvoern (*Blauwe Schute*, 1413) and Hieronymus Bosch (*The Ship of Fools*, 1490–1500, figure 1.1); in the allegorical verses of Sebastian Brant (*Das Narrenschiff*, 1494) enhanced by a famous set of Dürer woodcuts (figure 1.2); in other humanist texts like Erasmus's *Praise of Folly* (1509); and in erotic poetry like Louise Labé's *Débat de folie et d'amour* (1555), where Love (*Amour*) and Madness (*Folie*) debate each other, but neither emerges as the clear victor. Against this literary and imagistic backdrop of reason struggling, back and forth from city to city, with forms of unreason that call into question the very definition of reason and the limits of the subject, the seventeenth-century confinement of society's excluded others—the "asocial" (*asociaux*) (M 80/F 94) and the "misrecognized strangers" (*étrangers méconnus*) (M 80/F 94; translation modified)—constitutes an image of reason's coup in a game of truth that rejects and imprisons the excluded other.

Over the course of *Madness*, Foucault will redeploy these contrasting figures of movement and stasis to articulate subjectivity as a function of the historical and conceptual relation between reason and unreason. For if the Renaissance "liberated" the voices of unreason in the mad subjectivity of the ship of fools, those voices are silenced in the classical age—a period that extends roughly from 1650 to 1800—by that "strange coup" (M 44/F 56; translation modified) which gave rise to the cogito. That coup is not only a shift in practices—from the ship of fools to confinement in hospitals—but also and, more importantly, a shift in philosophical thinking about the subject. Reason itself (*ratio*) becomes an "event" that not only divides the Renaissance from the classical age but also divides the thinking from the nonthinking subject. This event is a coup, epitomized by Descartes, in the establishment of the sovereignty of the thinking subject who abolishes madness as alien to truth: "*I*, who think, I cannot be mad" ("Moi qui pense, je ne peux pas être fou") (M 45/F 57; translation modified). Madness becomes the "condition of impossibility of thought" (M 57/F 45; translation modified), and the mad, as a result, are excluded from thinking. In this system that confers sovereignty on the thinking subject—*I think therefore I am*—to be excluded from thinking is to be excluded from being. The logic is clear: the thinking subject's use of reason to abolish madness from himself exiles the mad into the category of nonexistence.

That place of exile is like a Deleuzian machine: both a conceptual space produced by philosophy and a concrete space of imprisonment within the city that arose in France and elsewhere in Europe over the course of the seventeenth century. Indeed, by mid-century, a full 1 percent of the Parisian population was confined in "hospitals." Foucault's chapter on this "Great Confinement" describes the juridical and institutional practices that resulted in the confinement of those consigned by reason to

FIGURE 1.1 Hieronymus Bosch, *The Ship of Fools,* 1490–1500

FIGURE 1.2 Sebastian Brandt, *Das Narrenschiff,* 1494

that place of exile within. In this juxtaposition of Cartesian subjectivity with institutional practices of confinement, Foucault exposes the moral stakes of systems of social control carried out in the name of reason. Confinement becomes, for Foucault, the most visible structure of a classical experience of madness that includes both the rise of exclusionary philosophical reason and, concomitantly, an "upheaval" (*bouleversement*) within an "ethical experience" (*M* 83/*F* 97; translation modified) marked by the triumph of the work ethic and bourgeois values.

Foucault clearly articulates here the way in which the Cartesian exile of the mad is also the result of an ethical choice. Those consigned to the realm of unreason—the nonexistent exiles of rationalist thinking—are produced against the social, economic, and ethical horizon of a bourgeois order whose norms are those of family morality. Lumped together into the great space of unreason, reason's exiles within become, increasingly, an undifferentiated mass of others: the poor, the infirm, libertines, prostitutes, magicians, alchemists, beggars, debauchers, *précieuses*, sodomites, nymphomaniacs, homosexuals. They live together, within reason and within the city, as the bourgeois subject's repudiated shadow: "the negative [*le négatif*] of this city of morals" (*M* 74/*F* 87; translation modified).[29]

The language Foucault uses to describe this experience of unreason in the classical age reflects a double vision of repressive and productive forces that, together, remove mad subjectivity from its prior experience of freedom in the ship of fools. Specifically, the unfreedom of the mad is the result of repressive gestures of exclusion as well as productive forces of reorganization. The word *repression* occurs throughout Foucault's description of the bourgeois, juridical, and monarchical authority that locks up and silences the mad in the seventeenth century.[30] Even with the great medical, juridical, and political "reforms" of the eighteenth and nineteenth centuries, that repressive power of subjugation, exclusion, and confinement continues.

At the same time, from the earliest moments of the great confinement, productive forces are at work as well. Indeed, acknowledging this productive conception of subjectivity in Foucault's description of the Age of Reason is crucial to understanding his fundamental argument about madness itself. Unlike the modern psychiatrist who looks for an essential object called madness whose truth can be grasped by science, Foucault argues that there is no prior category of madness to be isolated and dissected. Rather, madness is produced as a "form of exteriority,"[31] as the alienated exile of rational subjectivity and a bourgeois moral order. Rationalism and bourgeois morality work together to produce a "reorganization of the ethical world" (M 82) masked by a language of objective truth. This system finds its apotheosis in nineteenth-century positivism and the triumph of scientific knowledge; it continues today as what Foucault calls simply "our knowledge" (*savoir*) (M 273/F 291; translation modified).[32]

Foucault's "archaeology of alienation" (M 80) in *Madness* insists on the double gesture of negative exclusion and positive reorganization through which fools in a ship become specimens of mental illness. Repression and productivity work in tandem: the repressive gesture of confinement produces madness. The rejected figure of asociality that science will eventually label as mad "was produced [*suscité*] by the gesture of segregation itself" (M 79/F 94). In the seventeenth century, Paris did not lock up its exiles in order to free itself of the "asocials" and the "misrecognized strangers" who had been there all along, waiting to be confined. Paris created them: "Il en créait" (F 94).[33] In doing so, repressive power transformed once recognizable faces within the city into "bizarre figures that nobody recognized. It produced [*suscitait*] the Stranger even in places where he had not been previously suspected" (M 80/F 94; translation modified). In other words, both reason and the moral city created the stranger within bourgeois subjectivity itself: "the gesture of confinement" also "created alienation" (M 80).

This double conception of mad subjectivity in the Age of Reason is crucial for an understanding of sexuality in Foucault, especially after the advent of queer theory. Most readers of *Madness* only see the repressive dimension of power in Foucault's history of unreason in the classical age; this pervasive view of *Madness* is supposedly reinforced by Foucault himself in later comments about the book.[34] Critics use these comments, along with their own reading of *Madness*, to reinforce an understanding of Foucault in which his conception of power moves from early repression to later production, just as his conception of the subject and its truth purportedly moves from archeological depth to genealogical surface. Most critics argue that it was only later, in his investigations of sexuality, that Foucault came "to see another mechanism of power, the productive one,"[35] just as they argue that Foucauldian subjectivity moves from a phenomenological subject to an individuation as subjectivation (*assujettissement*) that puts the subject itself into question.[36]

But, *pace* the author, "Foucault" himself, to whom we can, in all good conscience, happily deny total sovereignty over the meaning of his books, power in *Madness*, like subjectivity itself, is more complex than most critics have allowed. Indeed, John Caputo's comments about Foucauldian power generally can be taken to apply not only to Foucault's later work but to *Madness* as well. Caputo argues, rightly in my view: "The fact of the matter is that unless power has a univocal essence, unless power means just one thing, it is impossible to sustain the idea that power is only or essentially or primarily 'productive' and not also repressive."[37] Or vice versa, I can't help but add. Caputo continues: "Power is only a descriptive category for Foucault and it means many things, in keeping with the plurality of historical situations in which it is deployed. There is no power as such; we can only describe the 'how' of power relations. Power is now repressive, now productive, and now something else that Foucault had not noticed, and later on something else that perhaps has not yet come about."[38]

These comments are not only right with regard to Foucault; they become especially relevant when we read *Madness* for the story it tells about modern sexuality. Tracing the emergence of sexuality within the larger history of reason and unreason throws into question the neat trajectory from the repression of madness in early Foucault to the production of sexuality in his later work. Indeed, in *Madness*, Foucault gives numerous examples of the various figures of sexual deviance that inhabit the world of unreason: the libertines, debauchers, prostitutes, sodomites, nymphomaniacs, and homosexuals mentioned earlier. I want to highlight here not only their presence in this shadowy world but also the specifically sexual logic through which their consignment to the realm of unreason occurs. First, like the "mad" more generally, sexual abnormals are the result of both repressive and productive forces that Foucault locates, spatially and temporally, in seventeenth-century Europe. Second, if madness marks the threshold that separates reason from its own potential error, delirium, or passion, sexuality sits on that threshold. This second point is crucial. Foucault's narrative about madness is not simply a historical recounting of social and institutional practices of confinement at a particular time and place; more crucially, it is a philosophical critique of Cartesian rationalism in its explicit repudiation of the body. *Madness*'s description of the great confinement is not just a recounting of "what happened" to sexual deviants in Paris in the seventeenth century; it is also an analysis of the costs of rationalism's conceptual exclusions. This bringing together of sins of the flesh with infractions against reason into the same space of institutional and philosophical othering constitutes, for Foucault, "the imaginary geometry of morality" (*M* 86) that will define sexual experience "on the threshold of the modern world" (*M* 86/*F* 100; translation modified).

This invented, specifically modern imaginary geometry, which excludes in the same gesture both the "passions" and "free thought," is complex. Because the new geometry redefines morality within a new geographical landscape of confinement, it implicates sexuality in what Foucault will call an ethical reorganization of the relationship between love and unreason. Specifically, in the gesture that imprisons, within the same space, the "sins of the flesh and faults committed against reason" (*M* 86), the Age of Reason binds together erotic love and unreason in a figure of guilt and criminality. So doing, it invents what Foucault calls a strange modern "kinship" (*parenté*) (*M* 86/*F* 100; translation modified) that "the alienated of today still experience as their destiny" (*M* 86/*F* 100; translation modified) and that "doctors discover as a truth of nature" (*M* 86). In a strange twist of morality that binds eros to error—or passion to free thought, love to unreason—sin and madness come to inhabit the same figure of alterity as the sexually deviant. Right up to the present day, the sexual deviant—a dangerously mad lover—experiences his condition of otherness as inalterable—"as destiny"—because reason defines that condition not as the result of contingent forces but as an immutable truth of nature. Unlike that other figure of destiny, the Renaissance ship of fools, the deviant subject of this new moral geometry is trapped and pinned down as an object to be dissected and explained. In the Renaissance, by contrast, the mad subjectivity of the ship of fools zigzagged toward and away from that "other world" where erotic love touches madness; it staged a dialogue, as in Labé's famous verse, between Love and Madness: back and forth, this "communal odyssey" (*M* 13) of the Renaissance put "all mankind aboard the foolish ship" (*M* 13). In the Age of Reason, such a dangerous "kinship" between love and unreason cannot embrace an entire culture in a collective erotic journey. It can only ever be the justification for an absolute exclusion.

Erotic Experience

As a new form of subjectivity within a modern moral geometry, the sexual deviant is both the victim of repression and an invention of power conceived in its productive dimension. However, in *Madness* there is no simple, one-to-one correspondence between the repression of sexual practices and the production of sexually deviant subjects. Nor is there an inverse relationship between repression and production (as we see in the case of punishment in *Discipline and Punish*), where easing up on repression would correspond to a tightening of the disciplinary screws of productive power. In the case of sexual deviancy and homosexuality in particular, Foucault argues that the forms of repression and productivity change over the course of the seventeenth and eighteenth centuries. Noting that one of the last capital punishments for sodomy in France occurred in 1726, Foucault brings into view what might appear to be a new indulgence toward sodomitical acts. "The period when sodomites are being burned for the last time is also the period when 'erudite libertinage,' and an entire homosexual lyricism [*tout un lyrisme homosexuel*] tolerated unquestioningly in the Renaissance, begins to disappear" (*M* 88/*F* 102; translation modified). Like the leper in the opening paragraph of *Madness*, "homosexual lyricism" can only be glimpsed as the shadow of something disappearing over history's horizon.

This suppression of "homosexual lyricism" is double-edged. Its relation to subjectivity within the new morality is both repressive and productive: it both silences the homosexual lyrical subject who had previously spoken and, at the same time, creates a new homosexual subject as a figure of muteness. "The homosexuality to which the Renaissance had accorded a liberty of expression now passes into silence" (*M* 102–103/*F* 88; translation modified). By suppressing homosexual lyrical expression, the Age of Reason both effaces an old form of erotic subjectivity and produces a new one as a figure of silence: homosexual subjectivity as the secret sexual love that dare not speak its name.

Put somewhat differently, and in terms that will resonate with queer theorists, the Age of Reason simultaneously creates sexual deviants as homosexuals and puts them in the closet by suppressing the mad erotic love of their lyrical expression. That suppression takes the form of modern guilt and crime. Although Foucault does not pursue the idea of closeting here, the picture he paints of sexual silencing in the Age of Reason introduces a structure that will eventually take on the contours of the modern closet that Eve Kosofsky Sedgwick famously locates at the turn of the twentieth century. But here, even in the seventeenth century, this closeting structure is "already close to modern forms of guilt" (*M* 88). Significantly, again in terms that queer theory has adopted, in this historical and conceptual moment of splitting, the closeted deviant consigned to the silent realm of unreason is neither an identity nor a set of sexual practices. He is, rather, as Foucault describes him, a "lyrical voice" and a "homosexual sensibility" out of sync with the moral strictures of a rationalist bourgeois order.

This silenced lyricism signals the existence of a world of expression, sensation, and feeling that Foucault calls, quite simply, *amour* or love. In Foucault's rendering of it, the voice and sensibility associated with this *amour* recall Platonic eros, a sublime form of love always related "either to a blind madness of the body, or to the great intoxication of the soul" (*M* 88/*F* 103; translation modified). And, if the Renaissance rediscovers and celebrates that love, in the seventeenth century eros goes underground into the closet of homosexual expression. Thus the emergence of the closeted homosexual in the Age of Reason reveals a larger change in the contours that delineate erotic subjectivity more generally: a choice must be made between a "reasoned" love and a love "governed by unreason" (*M* 88). Sexual deviants belong, by definition, to the second category: they exemplify mad eros as the modern sexual love that dare not speak its name; they must, if discovered, be excluded and confined. Not only that, but the new moral geometry redefines sexuality for an entire culture. Erotic subjectivity in general is changed by the closeting of mad forms of sexual love. Just as the movement that defined the Renaissance constituted a "communal odyssey" (*M* 13), so too the new structures of rigid confinement in the Age of Reason reorganize the relationships of an entire society.

It is important to emphasize here that Foucault's professed aim in writing *Madness* was to describe the "experience" of madness which, in the context of queer theory, means also the "experience" of sexuality.[39] *Madness*'s exposure of the shift from lyricism to silence and from movement to stasis traces, more than anything, an experience of alienation in the modern world. But as a description of experience, Foucault's story is odd. Philosophically speaking, *Madness* does not, as Caputo claims, "perfectly parallel the phenomenological goal of finding a realm of pure 'prepredicative' experience, prior to its being carved out by the categories of logical grammar."[40] As I have already shown, there is more going on in *Madness* than the simple uncovering of a hermeneutic depth within which we will find the (mad) truth of a subject. Neither does Foucault's history of experience make sense in traditional historiographical terms. Unlike the personal testimonies, private journals, letters, or other documents historians tend to use to get at the "truth" of an experience in the past, Foucault's materials—artistic and literary representations, individual cases documented by doctors, anonymous brochures, royal edicts, hospital regulations and rules of order, medical treatises, architectural plans, statistical inventories, and proposals for reform—are strangely impersonal. And yet he insists, over and over, that his book recounts the experience of madness.

The oddness of the relationship, between the experiential claim and the lack of documents or philosophical approach which would support that claim in traditional terms, suggests something about the difficulty of accessing experiences in history. Indeed, as Joan Scott argues in "The Evidence of Experience" (1991), the difficulty of that access might lead us to think differently about experience itself. Quoting Gayatri Spivak, Scott writes: "It ought to be possible . . . to 'make visible the assignment of subject-positions,' not in the sense of capturing the reality of the objects seen, but of trying to understand the operations of the complex and changing discursive processes by which identities are ascribed, resisted, or embraced, and which processes themselves are unremarked and indeed achieve their effect because they are not noticed."[41]

This astute comment by a feminist historian about the complexity of using "experience" to get at the truth of the past is especially germane to what Foucault is doing in describing the "experience" of madness and, by extension, to what it means in different diagrammatic moments to be queer. To "captur[e] the reality of the objects seen," as Scott puts it, would be to repeat the despotic gesture of a positivist science that pins down and names sexual deviants. That gesture of capture not only turns the subject into an object but also misses the erotic experience altogether. In addition, because the voices of the mad have, for the most part, been lost to us—we have very few documents in which they speak for themselves and in their own words—the problem of accessing the "reality" of their experience is compounded.

As the project of a traditional historian or philosopher, then, the task of rendering the "experience" of madness, including its specifically sexual forms, is, as Foucault puts it in the 1961 preface, "doubly impossible" (*M* xxxii), both because the rendering captures and objectifies the subject, and because "those insane words that nothing anchors in time" (*M* xxxii) are lost to us. But in another, antihistorical or antiphilosophical sense, Foucault does render something like the experience of madness and sexual deviance. He does so by uncovering the "structure" and the "rudimentary *movements* of an *experience* . . . before it is captured by knowledge" (*M* xxxii; emphasis added). This is not a move, as Caputo claims, to find a pure truth that would precede knowledge—Foucault is hardly as naive as that, as his nonlinear conception of the interdependence of history and knowledge demonstrates. Rather, Foucault is working from the perspective of the present, from *within* a knowledge that knows too much and therefore misses experience itself: "In our time," Foucault writes, "the experience of madness is made in the calm of a knowledge which, through *knowing it too much, passes it over*" (*M* xxxiv; emphasis added). He is thus, as Scott puts it, both "trying to understand the operations of the complex and changing discursive processes" by which mad sexuality is formed and trying to get at those processes which are "unremarked and indeed achieve their effect because they are not noticed" (408). In that project, Foucault tries "to allow these words and texts"—the documented cases that form his corpus and "which came from beneath the surface of language" (*M* xxxiv)—"to speak of themselves" (*M* xxxiv–v), so that those words and texts might "find their place without being betrayed" (*M* xxxv).

Again, one might be tempted to linger here, as so many Foucault critics have done, over the language of depth that figures madness "beneath [a] surface." But as I've argued earlier, the images of depth are only one part of the picture. Foucault knows better than anyone that if the project to bring words from beneath a surface is the attempt to avoid a betrayal, that project is doomed from the moment of its inception. For of course the betrayal is there, from the start, as the constitutive irony of the project itself: the experience of madness cannot be captured, and, even if we could capture it, to do so would be to betray it. Foucault knows this well and states it repeatedly in the pages of *Madness*. Given the irony of this inevitable betrayal, "it is tempting," Scott writes, "to abandon [experience] altogether" (412). And yet, as Scott puts it, and as surely Foucault would concur: "experience is not a word we can do without" (412). Nowhere does this hold more true than in Foucault's project to trace the "rudimentary movements of an experience" (*M* xxxii) of madness. Especially with madness, "what counts as an experience is neither self-evident nor straight-forward; it is always contested, and always therefore political" (Scott 412). The documents are thin, written most often with the words of others and never those of the mad subjects themselves. Indeed, as Foucault's 1964 essay "Madness, the Absence of an Oeuvre" makes abundantly clear, when the mad actually "speak"—as in the empirical cases of Nerval, Nietzsche, and Roussel—their "work" disappears. Their experience becomes, then, the opening of a question, an approach that "interrogates the processes of [a subject's] creation" and, in so doing, "refigures history and opens new ways for thinking about change" (Scott 412).

I have emphasized this problem of experience in order to contrast Foucault's project in *Madness* with the project he undertakes in *Sexuality One*. Specifically, in recounting the suppression of homosexual lyricism in the Age of Reason, Foucault is tracing "the rudimentary movements of an experience" by, paradoxically, describing its disappearance: it is the shadow cast by something as it's leaving. Neither the lyricism nor its silencing "captures" the historical experience of homosexuality itself, either as a historical truth or as the result of a phenomenological epoché. But this hardly means that sexual experience has no relevance for the story Foucault wants to tell. The image of a disappearance—as the shadow of "homosexual lyricism" sinking over the edge of the horizon of reason—ultimately renders something that had not been noticed before. And that something is what Foucault describes as a world of expression, sensation, and sensibility "whose wild state" (*M* xxxiii), like madness, "can never be reconstituted" (*M* xxxiii) but that we can, nonetheless, "strain our ears" to hear.

The result is a certain thickness and stylistic flourish in the written qualities of *Madness* itself: a descriptive density, rhetorical texture, imagistic play, and—why not say it?—a certain "lyricism" that produces not only a cognitive effect but also importantly translates as affect in the manner of a "literary" text. Indeed, Foucault's rendering of a movement of alienation—the experience of being queer—that stretches from the age of lepers to the age of Freud is both conceptually antiphilosophical as well as stylistically so. And this signals a writerly quality apparent to all who read Foucault and, further, as Deleuze puts it, "a style of life, not anything at all personal, but inventing a possibility of life, a way of existing."[42] Nowhere is this stylistic quality as a style of life—what we might call a writerly eros—more visible than in *History of Madness*. Again Deleuze, in his comments on Foucault, must surely have been thinking of *Madness* when he described Foucault as "a great stylist. Concepts take on with him the rhythmic quality, or, as in the strange dialogues with himself with which he closes some of his books, a contrapuntal one. His syntax builds up the shimmerings and scintillations of the visible but also twists like a whip, folding and unfolding, or cracking to the rhythm of its utterances."[43]

But if *Madness* is marked by the lyrical thickness of a stylistic flair that uses the texture of writing to transmit the erotic qualities of an experience we now call sexual—what Deleuze calls "style . . . [as] a way of existing"—that sense of a "possibility of life"[44] is entirely missing from Foucault's rendering of sexuality in the first volume of *History of Sexual-*

ity fifteen years later. In *Sexuality One*, sexuality is thin—as Nietzsche might put it: "as thin as if it were stretched between two membranes."[45] No longer articulated in terms of the "rudimentary movements" of a subject's experience as "scintillations of the visible" or twists of a whip, sexuality in *Sexuality One* reflects Foucault's turn in the early 1970s toward what he calls a microphysics of power and away from the rhetoric and imagery of "representations"—precisely those aspects of *Madness* that make it thick. As the French title of *Sexuality One*, *La Volonté de savoir*, insists, modern sexuality in that volume is nothing more than the discursive result of a "will to knowledge" that has developed over time to specify sexual "individuals"[46] as a tantalizing array of perversions within a dispositif or cultural grid of intelligibility. And if the dispositif is complex, it is also thin: "a great surface network."[47] It is a skeleton that has no flesh, no passion, no eros. And if it has style— which I think it does—the style is as thin as the sexuality it describes. As a "style of life," *Sexuality One* offers us the aporetic rhetoric and anorectic imagery of an erotic experience whose possibility is no longer even a shadow. Even its ghost, it seems, has disappeared altogether under the objectifying gaze of science.

Queer Acts and Identities in *Sexuality One*

I insist on the thinness of the dispositif not only to contrast an experiential *Madness* with a discursive *Sexuality One* but also to demonstrate what will be missed when readers engage Foucauldian sexuality only through the lens of his middle and later work. Reencountering Foucault, in *Sexuality One*, through the lens of a *Madness* that most of his queer readers have missed altogether allows me to resituate his thinking about sexuality as a consistent engagement, from start to finish, with ethics. The concepts and frames for thinking about sex that emerge out of that process of reengagement and revision challenge some of the most dogmatically reiterated *idées reçues* about sexuality in Foucault.

Specifically, in highlighting sexuality as an ethics of experience, I want to contest the ubiquitous readings of Foucault that interpret him primarily as a historian who rearranges sexual acts and identities on a linear time line. It would be easy to fill a book with the numerous examples, from historians and nonhistorians alike, of scholarship that captures sexuality in Foucault in this way. Especially problematic are those introductions that present Foucault to an uninitiated audience of virgin readers. Let me give just a few examples. Tamsin Spargo asserts, in *Foucault and Queer Theory* (1999), that Foucault "insisted that the category of the homosexual grew out of a particular context in the 1870s."[48] Along the same lines, in *Queer Theory: An Introduction* (1996), Annemarie Jagose is impressed by a Foucault who is "confident" enough to furnish "an exact date for the invention of homosexuality."[49] More recently, in their introduction to the interdisciplinary anthology *Queer Studies* (2003), Robert Corber and Steven Valocchi state that "Foucault traced the transformation of sexuality in modern societies from a set of *practices* and relations governed by religious and secular law into a set of *identities* regulated by norms."[50] The examples of these assertions about Foucault's purported specification of the invention of homosexual identity in the nineteenth century are as pervasive as they are repetitive. As I've mentioned elsewhere, virtually every reader of Foucault with an interest in queer sexuality begins with *Sexuality One*, often with two preconceptions already, like perversions, "implanted" in their heads: first, that Foucault contrasts earlier sexual *acts* with later sexual *identities* and, second, that Foucault locates the moment of the shift from one to the other at a precise point in the nineteenth century.

In order to buttress and build on those assertions, queer Foucauldians typically cite the following passage, which I quote at length both in French and English. I will spend some time on the passage in order to tease out the larger conceptual assertions I want to make, countering what I view as queer theory's repeated misreadings of Foucault. For reasons that will become clear, I italicize those words and phrases in both the French and English versions, where the English translation will produce a significant distortion of the French meaning. After citing the passage in French, I include in brackets within the English translation a more precise rendering of the terms in question:

Cette chasse nouvelle aux sexualités périphériques entraîne une incorporation des perversions et une spécification nouvelle des individus. La sodomie—celle des anciens droits civil ou canonique—était un type d'actes interdits; *leur auteur* n'en était que le sujet juridique. L'homosexuel du XIXe siècle est devenu *un personnage:* un passé, une histoire et une enfance, un caractère, une forme de vie; une morphologie aussi, avec une anatomie indiscrète et peut-être une physiologie mystérieuse. Rien de ce qu'il *est* au total n'*échappe* à sa sexualité. Partout en lui, elle *est* présente: sous-jacente à toutes ses conduites parce qu'elle en *est* le principe insidieux et indéfiniment actif; inscrite sans pudeur sur son visage et sur son corps parce qu'elle *est* un secret qui se trahit toujours. Elle lui *est* consubstantielle, moins comme un péché d'habitude que comme une nature singulière. Il ne faut pas oublier que la catégorie psychologique, psychiatrique, médicale de l'homosexualité s'est constituée du jour où on l'a caractérisée—le *fameux* article de Westphal en 1870, sur les "sensations sexuelles contraires" peut valoir comme date de naissance—moins par un type de relations sexuelles que par une certaine qualité de la sensibilité sexuelle, une certaine manière d'intervertir en soi-même le masculin et le féminin. L'homosexualité est apparue comme une des *figures* de la sexualité lorsqu'elle *a été rabattue* de la pratique de la sodomie sur une sorte d'androgynie intérieure, un hermaphrodisme de l'âme. Le sodomite *était un relaps*, l'homosexuel *est* maintenant une espèce.[31]

This new persecution of the peripheral sexualities entailed an incorporation of perversions and a new specification of individuals. As defined by the ancient civil or canonical codes, sodomy was a category of forbidden acts; *their perpetrator* [their author] was nothing more than the juridical subject of them. The nineteenth-century homosexual became *a personage* [a character]: a past, a case history, and a childhood, in addition to being a type of life, a life form, and a morphology, with an indiscreet anatomy and possibly a mysterious physiology. *Nothing that went into his total composition was unaffected by* [Nothing of what he is, in total, escapes] his sexuality. It *was* [is] everywhere present in him: at the root of all his actions because it *was* [is] their insidious and indefinitely active principle; written immodestly on his face and body because it *was* [is] a secret that always *gave itself away* [gives itself away]. It *was* [is] consubstantial with him, less as a habitual sin than as a singular nature. We must not forget that the psychological, psychiatric, medical category of homosexuality was constituted from the moment it was characterized— Westphal's *famous* [notorious (with strong irony)] article of 1870 on "contrary sexual sensations" can stand as its date of birth—less by a type of sexual relations than by a certain quality of sexual sensibility, a certain way of inverting the masculine and feminine in oneself. Homosexuality appeared as one of the *forms* [figures] of sexuality when it was *transposed* [cut away] from the practice of sodomy [and reattached] onto a kind of interior androgyny, a hermaphrodism of the soul. The sodomite *had been* [was] a *temporary aberration* [a fall back into heresy]; the homosexual *was* [is] now a species.

This passage from *Sexuality One* is undoubtedly one of the most frequently quoted passages of Foucault's corpus. The three feminist founding thinkers of queer theory I mentioned in the introduction to this book—Rubin, Sedgwick, and Butler—either cite or refer to it in

"Thinking Sex" (16), *Epistemology of the Closet* (83), and *Gender Trouble* (106), respectively. It has been quoted and requoted, again and again—not only by queer theorists but also by historians, literary critics, and legal scholars—to fashion arguments about the relative merits, or lack thereof, of conceptualizing sexuality as either acts or identities in particular contexts or historical moments. This proliferation of citations, often from a not-quite-precise English translation, has had a number of consequences, not least of which is a drastic simplification of what Foucault is actually saying in the paragraph. My intent is not to be pedantic by indulging in obscure etymologies or hairsplitting differences of definition. Rather, because of the considerable importance of the passage in question for an entire generation of thinking about sexuality, I linger on what I see as some key distortions of interpretation in order to challenge what have long been considered to be some basic Foucauldian queer "truths." Indeed, since Foucault insisted on the instability of "games of truth," it seems appropriate to question those truths that have somehow solidified into a kind of queer dogma.

When we read the passage closely, both with *Madness* in mind and with an attention to the nuances of Foucault's French terminology, we may be surprised that it has been so widely read as a definitive statement about sodomitical acts becoming homosexual identity in the nineteenth century. That commonly accepted reading of Foucault is questionable for a number of reasons. First, from the start we see quite clearly that nowhere in the passage does the word *identity* appear. In fact, it is a word that Foucault uses infrequently, usually ironically or in its arithmetical meaning: identity as equality.[52] Like most of his French compatriots, Foucault saw identity, in its personal or political meanings, as a specifically American obsession. In the passage, he uses the words *individus* (individuals), *personnage* (character), and *figure* (figure) to name a phenomenon of emergence that Anglo-American readers have interpreted, again and again, as identity. And while an *individual*—a single human being—could have the personality or specific traits that, together, we sometimes call an identity, this is not necessarily the case. Particularly in queer theory, *identity* means not only a general sense of identification or sameness (from the Latin *idem*) in one's relation to oneself or to others; it also includes, more importantly, the connotations of group belonging or affiliation associated with American identity politics. Identity in this political sense is what the French tend to call the *communautarisme* of American politics, as opposed to a French *universalisme* that grows out of their republican political tradition. In fact, more often than not, from a French perspective the "individual" is viewed as exemplifying the free choices and freedoms of a French republicanism that stands *in opposition* to an "identity" that grows out of an American *communautarisme*. Indeed, as Eric Fassin points out, since the 1990s French philosophers like Alain Finkielkraut and Frédéric Martel have reclaimed, "recycled," and repatriated Foucault as "a titular figure of French republicanism"[53] and as a philosophical force of "individual" French resistance against what is viewed, sometimes homophobically, as the scourge of American identity politics: the "communitarian wind that blows in the U.S.," as sociologist Irène Théry so derisively puts it.[54]

This initial suspicion about an assumed equivalence between Foucault's *individual* and an Americanized *identity*, in either the political or personal sense of the word, is confirmed by the other terms. Both *personnage* and *figure* (officially translated as "personage" and "form," respectively) highlight an understanding of sexuality as the fictive or metaphorical product of a representational order, like a character in a play or the protagonist of a novel or even the "face" acquired through a rhetorical troping. In addition, the seemingly minor matter of punctuation becomes important here. In the French version, *personnage* is not one of a long series of attributes separated by commas—"a personage, a past, a case history, a childhood," and so forth—thus constituting "personage" as one of the elements that, taken together, might form an identity. In fact, a colon separates the "character" from the attributes with which it is endowed; those attributes are deposited within the character that simply provides a container for them. In that sense, the *personnage* is not so different from the social types one might find in a medieval morality play or a Renaissance allegory like Bosch's painting or Brandt's narrative verses about the *Ship of Fools* that Foucault invokes at the beginning of *Madness*.

However, a familiarity with *Madness* provides a clue to one important difference between the Renaissance *personnage* and its modern version. It is *not* the distinction between acts and identities that matters, as so many readers have asserted, but rather the difference between the ethical universes each set of characters represents. As we saw earlier, the ship of fools symbolizes a moving social microcosm in its struggle with complex ethical questions about love and the body, one's relations with others, life's destiny in death, and how reason and unreason determine the limits of subjectivity. The individual "character" who emerges in *Sexuality One*, by contrast, is an isolated, objectified puppetlike figure whose insides—its past, its childhood, its inner life—is merely the reversal of what the gaze of science sees on the outside: "written immodestly," as Foucault puts it, "on his face and body." This structure of reversal is only an identity to the extent that identity names a subject deprived of the complexity of lived experience. It is not an identity in either the political or personal sense—in the fullness of its lived, experiential meanings—but rather the draining away of erotic life into a discursive category Foucault calls sexuality.

Read through the lens of the moral reorganization that *Madness* describes, this ethical shift from the ship of fools to a modern scientific morality play provides a key for reinterpreting the relationship between acts and the characters who perform them. In *Sexuality One*, modern "characters" act, but only as the medicalized, psychiatric doubles of premodern juridical subjects; as specifically "homosexual" characters, they are what Foucault calls in *Abnormals* the "ethico-moral doubles" of premodern sodomites.[55] In the passage I have cited from *Sexuality One*, this psychiatric doubling and objectification of the modern homosexual *character* is reinforced by its opposition, lost in the English translation, to the earlier term that is its binary complement: the *author* of sodomitical acts. Further, the "character" in question is not "socially constructed," as many have implied, by some interchangeable, generalizable array of juridical, pedagogical, literary, or political dispositifs. Rather, he is specifically constructed by psychological science. The combined structures of rationalist exclusion and bourgeois morality which led to the apotheosis of that science is precisely what the six hundred pages of *History of Madness* so meticulously describes. Here, in *Sexuality One*, Foucault insists on the fictional construction of the ontological essence that results from the apotheosis of the psyche as sexual: "what he *is, in total*" is the creation of a *"psychological, psychiatric, medical category"* (emphasis added).

So if the ancient "juridical" subject was still the "author" or agent of the acts for which he was then judged according to a moral code, here the modern medical subject faces a different kind of moral control with the psychiatric depositing of guilt and shame into the heart of his inner life: an alienated, monstrous sexual interiority. As I will demonstrate in the next two chapters, *Madness* describes how that internalization of bourgeois morality occurs, from the moment of the great confinement to its culmination in the creation of the Freudian unconscious. With the rise of positivism, that inner life has been frozen into the attributes of a character to be viewed under a microscope and dissected into the elements that constitute a "case history." This ethical alteration describes not so much the constitution of the modern "identity" of identity politics—again, Foucault does not use the word here—than it does a process of rationalist, positivist objectification through the production of an ethico-moral double. The premodern juridical subject who was the "author" of his acts comes out of the Age of Reason as the object, puppet, or character of the psychiatric author or agent who created him.

In that sense he is not simply neutrally "transposed," as the English translation of *rabattue* suggests at the end of the passage. Rather, psychological knowledge cuts out or abstracts "homosexuality" from a thicker set of experiences called sodomitical practice that involve not only the singular body of a sodomite but also a form of social organization that Foucault calls "a type of sexual relations." Knowledge diminishes that complex, erotic, relational experience of what will become sexuality by capturing it and pinning it down as a "figure" it can use. The verb *rabattre*, from the Latin *abattere*, insists on this sense of a weakening, a diminishment, or even a fall from what came before: the practice of sodomy within a perhaps brutal system of moral codes, but within which the juridical subject was the "author" of his acts. The diminishment of *rabattre* also reinforces a sense of the repetition of an earlier "fall" back into a condition designated by the specifically religious meaning of the word *relaps* in the final sentence. Not a "temporary aberration," as the English translation would have it, "the sodomite was a *relaps*": a fall back into a *heresy* that had been previously abjured.

But if the fall into heresy—produced as the repeated acts of "habitual sin"—marks a position of resistance, however tenuous or unsuccessful, to the dogma of the age, such is not the case for the modern equivalent of that religious fall. With the fall of modern homosexuality into "a singular nature" that cannot be changed, the possibilities contained in the agency and resistance of the heretical sodomite disappear. As science rises, the homosexual falls into his modern condition as naturalized object: "the homosexual is now a species." Thus an ethical experience—the judgment, choices, acts, feelings, sensations, sensibilities, and forms of relation of resisting, heretical subjects together—is degraded and reversed as a singular essence or "sensibility" within. The subject-turned-object can have no experience—resistant or otherwise, relational or not—that would constitute an ethical life of freedom. Although as a "character" he acts *like* a subject engaged in practices of freedom, as a medicalized double he can only act as a puppet. The condition of possibility of an ethics of experience—the freedom to be the author of one's acts, to form relationships, to make judgments, and to resist—have been taken away from the now subjugated (*assujetti*) subject-as-object captured by the rationalizing gaze of science.

I insist on this detailed attention to the French and English versions of *Sexuality One* in order to make a larger point about queer theoretical readings of Foucault. Reengaging *Sexuality One* through the ethical lens of *Madness* both challenges and complicates categorical interpretations of a taxonomic Foucault who would simply slot sexualities into acts or identities at a precise moment in history. As *Madness* demonstrates, the objectifying act of the rationalist puppeteer does not occur only once or as a singular event in time; it happens over and over, taking different shapes during different periods. Indeed, even in *Sexuality One*, which lacks the detail and nuance of *Madness*, one can see that the objectification of sexual alterity is ongoing, as the repeated French verbs in the present tense insist: "It *is* everywhere present in him," "it *is* a secret that always betrays itself," "it *is* consubstantial with him," and "the homosexual *is* now a species." This sense of the ongoing nature of subjectivation also marks sexuality in the past, reinforced here by the imperfect tense of the verb *être* in the final sentence: "The sodomite was a fall back into heresy." Oddly rendered as "had been" in the English version, the better translation of *était* as "was" conveys a past whose beginning and end cannot be specified; the *imparfait* signals the past as a condition or state of being that not only happens again and again, but cannot be definitively separated from the time of the present. Thus the time of the sodomite and the time of the homosexual are coextensive. And yet, if we take seriously the historic breach between reason and unreason after the Renaissance, they are also radically incommensurable with each other. In that sense, the historical, epistemic movement that links the ancient sodomite to the modern homosexual makes them, paradoxically, both temporally coextensive and conceptually untranslatable.

As *Madness* shows us, the modern epistemic breach that divides the sodomite from the homosexual begins with the Cartesian coup of the cogito and the great confinement of the seventeenth century; this coup will be repeated by different actors over the course of the centuries—by Tuke and Pinel in the eighteenth century, by Charcot in the nineteenth, and by Freud in the twentieth. Those with a taste for the acclaim and career-making precision of a positivist discovery will proclaim, as Foucault parodically does in the famous passage from *Sexuality One*, that we can objectively pin down the exact date of birth of a new scientifically designated "species." And so, the story goes, Foucault declares the birth of homosexual identity in 1870.

But given all that we know about genealogy, rupture, and a Foucauldian conception of the past that refuses to posit an origin of *anything*, these "straight" readings of Foucault seem flat-footed and naive. We can only read this inaccurate declaration—the actual date of Westphal's article is 1869—of the "notorious" scientific birthday of "the homosexual" as highly ironic, in the same way that "identity" can only be ironically American from a French perspective.[56] We can only hear Foucault's "confident dating," as Jagose puts it, of homosexuality's birth as the parodic repetition of what a serious scientist might confidently assert.[57] And in case we didn't get it, that irony is underscored by the French *fameux* which describes the scientific paper where the birthday declaration is so notoriously made; unlike *célèbre*, which carries the "straight" meaning of famous, *fameux* is almost always tinged—again, like *identity*—with a slightly derisive irony. Indeed, to read the date 1870 as other than ironic is to buy into the psychological, psychiatric, and medical authority that Foucault goes to great pains to dismantle.

Thus rather than opposing acts and identities along the linear time line of Sartrean history, as so many identity-obsessed readers are wont to do, Foucault describes here an ethical shift with regard to erotic subjectivity that is perfectly clear if we read the passage through the lens of *Madness*. "Juridical" morality before the advent of modern psychology translates certain "acts" into a mode of subjectivity we might describe as practices or ways of living. Another modern form of bourgeois morality—what we might call, following Nietzsche, the morality of interiority—creates a "character" (*personnage*) and doubles the juridical subject with the psychiatric illusion of an inner life: the modern soul. That new subjectivity is the product of a rationalism that creates a psyche and, along with it, psychology, psychiatry, and psychoanalysis. Not only that but, with the advent of the psyche, exteriority is transformed and captured: science manages the horizontal complexity of "sexual relations" and "the masculine and the feminine" by "inverting" that complexity through a play of mirrors which makes it appear as an inner depth. And if the psychic management of sexual alterity is no less despotic than the ancient juridical codes through which sodomitical acts were judged, it masks that despotism through the inverting process.

If we haven't read *Madness* in its unabridged form, we will miss the nuances of those ethical meanings that flicker across the surface of *Sexu-*

ality One; we will read it, instead, as so many have, as a categorical claim about acts and identities in history. For indeed, what we don't get in *Sexuality One* is the complex scaffolding that explains how those shifts occur in relation to rationalist structures of exclusion, the shifts Foucault describes in *Madness* as the ethical reorganization of love and unreason. I will go into more detail about Foucault's critique of the bourgeois production of morality as interiority in the following chapter, where I link *Madness* to Nietzsche's critique of "bad conscience" in *Genealogy of Morals*. *Madness* will show us that Foucault's story is not about an absolute historical shift from sexuality as acts to sexuality as identities; rather, it is about the internalization of bourgeois morality which produces, eventually, the "fable" of an inner psyche, soul, or conscience.[58] Only in this way does the "thin" homosexual "thing" of modern science acquire the illusory "thickness"—a self-doubling trick of mirrors—of what so many have called an identity. It may be more accurate, like Foucault with his fable, to call that thickness the fiction of the psyche. That psyche is a "character" that inverts the magnificent exterior diversity of the world—the proliferating gender trouble of homosexuals, androgynes, hermaphrodites, and all they will become as modern gender-queers—and stuffs it "inside." That inside, of course, doesn't really exist in what is merely the flat space of a scientific fiction. But if the inner "secret" of sexuality is ultimately no secret at all, it is nonetheless "indispensable" as the "fable" that is "written immodestly" all over a queer object which rationalism and morality want to contain.[59]

Generally speaking, then, the interest of sexuality in Foucault is not to plot acts versus identities on a historical time line. Foucault reminds us, again and again, that he is not a historian. Rather, he "uses" history in a particular way, to locate those moments of rupture that Deleuze would describe, along with Blanchot, as the confinement of the outside.[60] The seventeenth century is one of those moments for several reasons including, most pertinently in the case of *Madness*, the advent of Cartesian rationalism and the great confinement of the mad in the hospitals of Paris. The classical age is obviously not the only moment of rupture in the story of what will become sexuality; neither is it the first. There is nothing in Foucault's analysis that excludes the possibility of medieval sodomites as "personages" or Renaissance tribades as "characters." But as Foucault insists numerous times in *History of Madness*, the historical "geography" within which those characters appear is "half-real, half-imaginary" (*M* 11/*F* 22; translation modified). They are spatiotemporal diagrams or assemblages, continual processes of folding and unfolding that describe Foucault's histories as repeated but changing stories. In that conception, acts and identities cannot emerge just once, because history itself is an ongoing process of emergence. As Deleuze puts it: "That everything is always said in every age is perhaps Foucault's greatest historical principle."[61]

If we understand this strongly anti-Historical (with a capital *H*) dimension of Foucault's histories, we can make some headway into the endless debates about acts versus identities and how they emerge in history. It would be difficult to overstate how strongly Foucault rejects a Sartrean "totalizing" sense of history that would pin *anything* down—sexual or otherwise—as an object of knowledge fully available to "human consciousness," as he puts it in his unpublished 1975 interview with Roger-Pol Droit. Even more important, the insistent focus on a binary choice between acts and identities—a choice that effaces Foucault's reference to "sexual sensibility" in *Sexuality One* as the inverted thing pinned down by science—disregards entirely the affective dimension of erotic experience.[62] We are more than the fables we tell about ourselves—that aspect of sexuality that readers of Foucault have called our modern Western identities. We are also more than the juridical interpretation of what our bodies do—that dimension of sexuality the famous passage from *Sexuality One* calls our acts. To miss the nuance of what Foucault is saying, and limit ourselves merely to a choice between acts and identities, in fact reinscribes the Cartesian coup—splitting the mind from the body—that was so effective in rationalizing the great confinement.

My purpose in challenging a pervasive understanding of homosexuality in Foucault is ultimately not negative but constructive: to expand Foucauldian conceptions of sexuality to encompass the problems of lived experience in relation to our historical and political present. Such an expansion can occur on the far side of a critique that challenges acts versus identities in *Sexuality One* through the retrospective lens of *Madness*. So what specifically does the acts-versus-identities critique bring us, constructively speaking?

First, it allows us to shift the terms of historical scholarship on sexuality, displacing arguments about acts versus identities toward other, more interesting questions about the specific configurations of bodies, sensibilities, sensations, feelings, acts, and relations in different times and places, without being trapped in a rigid binary frame for thinking about those configurations. Second, within Foucault scholarship itself, we can resolve what Eribon sees as the "contradictory presentations"[63] of the historical "invention" of homosexuality in *Madness* and *Sexuality*

One, in the seventeenth and nineteenth centuries, respectively. As we have established, a linear time line is beside the point, and contradiction doesn't end with the seventeenth century, as we can clearly see with the disappearance of a "homosexual lyricism" Foucault associates with the European Renaissance. Third, in conceptual terms, we can alter our focus away from the Anglo-American concept of identity toward a more capacious understanding of erotic experience—as lyrical or silenced, relational or confined—that includes, beyond acts and identities, the thick residue of sensations and sensibilities that constitutes an ever-expanding "archive of feelings," to borrow from Ann Cvetkovich's evocative title.[64] This shift toward experience promises to be a more fruitful approach to sexuality in Foucault than the search for an "identity" that Foucault himself does not directly invoke. It will allow us to open up new questions for queer and feminist scholarship, moving our inquiry away from the identity versus nonidentity binarism on which, to a large extent, the concept of queerness was founded—with the "queer" constituting the nonidentitarian, slightly Frenchified alternative to a flat-footed American feminist (or LGBTQI) identitarian position. Reading the passage through the lens of *Madness* as I have done turns the queer toward the question of sexuality and ethics where it has needed to turn for far too long. We can let go of the need to pin Foucault down on a historical time line and turn to ethical questions about sexuality that can speak to our political present.

In more general terms, this initial reading of *Sexuality One* in the light of *Madness* shows more clearly the salient conceptual figures in Foucault that have worked to define what we mean by queer theory. The thin, de-eroticized model of sexuality we find in *Sexuality One* has significantly shaped the discursive terms within which queer theory has been framed. Put simply, it has produced a queer theory that, in many of its manifestations, is drained of the experience of life and love, of eros. *Madness*, by contrast, engages sexuality as a field of sensibility, sensation, and forms of relation that cannot be reduced to a binary choice between acts and identities or the "singular nature" of modern science described in *Sexuality One*. Further, *Madness*'s coding of sexuality as "lyrical" links this repressed sensibility to a literary history of sexuality that Foucault will swerve away from in his later work. The loss of the affective, literary expression of erotic experience produces, in *Sexuality One*, a theory of sexuality that, in pinning down "sexual sensibility" as simple inversion, actually cuts eros off from the world of sensibility and lived experience where an ethics may be shaped.

So what ultimately is at stake for queer theory in this reading of *Madness* as a story about sexuality? How does Foucault's tracing of the "rudimentary movements" of an experience of madness tell us something about how we became queer? In *Madness*, what is now sexuality emerges out of an experience of love as eros, only to be targeted as the site of ethical condemnation in the Age of Reason. This perspective on love provides a piece of the answer to Foucault's 1984 riddle—why have we made sexuality into a moral experience? We have done so, we might say, because erotic love was repudiated by the Cartesian splitting of the mind from the body and forced underground in the great confinement. The object of this repudiation and confinement was not simply a set of bodily acts or identities at a specific moment in history, although acts, identities, and history constitute a few of the elements of a more complex movement of confinement Foucault describes in *Madness*. That complexity shows that confinement cannot be reduced to acts and identities in a linear history. Blanchot saw this complexity in Foucault better than anyone, as Deleuze reminds us: "confinement refers to an outside, and what is confined is precisely the outside. It is by excluding or placing outside that the assemblages confine something."[65]

From that perspective, what I'm calling erotic love might describe an ethical attitude or sensibility that remains unconfined and unexcluded; its condition of possibility is figured as the navigation of the ship of fools: as freedom. Diagrammatic examples of this freedom can be found, historically, not only in the Renaissance figure of the ship of fools or the tragic lyricism of its poets but also in the Platonic eros of ancient Greece. Even after its containment in the great confinement, eros emerges as glimmers of freedom in the amorous literary experimentation of the *précieuses* (M 89–90); in the libertine writings of Sade (M 104; M 533–535); and throughout *Madness*, in the mad rebirth of lyricism in Nietzsche, Nerval, Artaud, Hölderlin, and Roussel. In this way the diagram is always becoming something other as it bumps up against the limits of thinking. It both speaks to the specificity of an event in history and, at the same time, signals the ongoing possibility of transformation in a conception of history as nonlinear. "The diagram," Deleuze writes, "stems from the outside but the outside does not merge with any diagram, and continues instead to 'draw' new ones. In this way the outside is always an opening on to a future; nothing ends, since nothing has begun, but everything is transformed."[66]

This conception of an open future traces the outline of an erotic alterity whose presence is crucial in Foucault. The glimmers of eros that episodically burst through the pages of *History of Madness,* and Foucault's writings as a whole, point to what I will call an erotic other as the figure for an ethical love conceived as freedom. She corresponds to what Caputo calls, in the later Foucault, "the murmurings of a capacity to be otherwise."[67] I argue here that this murmuring of otherness is there, from the start, as a consistent presence in all of Foucault's writing, as "scintillations of the visible" and a "style of life."[68] For, if that otherness is silenced in the great confinement, that closeting is never total. If it were, we would never know that the erotic other had ever been there at all. In her emergence as ghost—as the persistent shadow of something leaving—she is both there and not there, as images and murmurings that both reactivate the monstrous imaginary of earlier ages and transform themselves into new forms of monstrosity. Ironically, because she is closeted, eros is as muted in Foucault as she is in the philosophical and historical discourses he contests. Nonetheless, her stuttering voice is not only *Madness*'s most important one, but a voice that signals, over and over in Foucault's writings, interviews, and lectures, the persistence of an ethical resistance to "the great confiscation of sexual ethics by family morality" (*M* 89).

That stuttering voice of resistance is one that can be useful to queers and feminists alike. It is a lyrical and ironic voice that both ruptures and amplifies those dominant voices of rationalism and bourgeois values. It is easy to mishear it, emerging as it does in the gaps of the pervert's silence or the hysteric's delirious babble. It is a voice that links the tragic madness of the Renaissance, the ironic dialogic splitting of *Rameau's Nephew,* and the suicidal tropisms of Roussel. As the result of an erotic *asujettissement,* the voice is both old and new, trapped and free: both "all that was foreign in man . . . snuffed out and reduced to silence" (*M* 431/*F* 451; translation modified) and a defiant, living strangeness. Like the heretic closeted in the word *relaps* in *Sexuality One,* she never disappears altogether. If we had to give her a modern name, we would have to call her queer.

Toward a Prodigal Queer Feminism

Let me return, like the prodigal son, to the place where I began this chapter, with Janet Halley's image of queers as rebellious children who, unlike the biblical character, seem unlikely to come back to the fold from which they emerged. I want to "put my cards on the table," to use one of Halley's favorite phrases.[69] As a queer feminist, I object to the "taking a break" project and would make a bid to disqualify Foucault as one of its progenitors. As I mentioned in the introduction, Foucault's capacity to raise feminist eyebrows is undeniable. Nonetheless, I want to argue for a Foucault who provides us, in *Madness*, with a valuable, still untapped store of conceptual resources for dealing with the sexual dilemmas that continue to fracture us into "split decisions."

I recognize that in my desire to remain a "queer feminist" and, more generally, to keep feminists and queers together, Halley would see me as a "convergentist," a position that she, as a clear "divergentist," ultimately eschews. She doubts that the "convergentist ambitions of feminism" will "bring the prodigals back home" (34). And even though she admits that "prodigal theories . . . have their own will to power" and are, like feminists, likely to "get blood on their hands," in Halley's view they will only do so if they become convergentist, a political position she equates with being "prescriptive" and "wield[ing] power while denying it" (34–35). But the divergentist Halley—"a sex-positive postmodernist, only rarely and intermittently feminist" (15)—could herself be accused of convergentism in her prescriptive performance of a judicial decision to "take a break" from a feminism she repudiates. And if the "rarely and intermittently feminist" quotation vitiates that accusation, the phrase rings false in the context of a book whose rhetorical force is that of a how-to" manual designed to teach its readers "how and why" to split up with feminism completely. Given how generative even intermittent queer-feminist affinities can be, I wish Halley's "break" were less categorical. What are the ethical terms within which the rare or not so rare conjunctions between sex-positivism and feminism might—do, in fact—occur? What are the conditions of possibility for a more constructive and more visible realization of that intriguing conjunction? Or should the terms themselves be subjected to scrutiny?—not just *feminism,* as a limiting form of personal and political self-positioning, but also *sex-positivism,* as a term that epitomizes the modern, scientistic, positivist "sex" project that Foucault spent his life critiquing.

Foucault's story about sexuality in *History of Madness* uses the great split between reason and unreason to reframe the binary oppositions that function, like Halley's, to split sexuality across an ethical divide. For if *Madness* brings together, along convergentist lines, all those categories of otherness labeled as unreason, it also, divergently, speaks to those differences that Halley celebrates as the specifically queer—and *not femi-nist*—"revelations of the strangeness and unknowability of social and sexual life" (15). But as Foucault, Irigaray, and other thinkers of differ-ence have been arguing since the 1960s, the divergentist move is the move of alterity: both the result of exclusion and the reclaiming of one's otherness as a stance of resistance to the processes of othering through which the exclusion occurred. To remain stuck in that stance—what Hal-ley calls convergentism—is hardly the sin of feminists alone, nor does it define all feminism. As just one example, a queer Irigaray—whom Hal-ley unfairly recuperates under the cultural feminist banner—powerfully demonstrates that processes of othering endlessly reproduce a hege-monic structure of the Other of the Same. It is not unlike the structure that Foucault calls the great split between reason and unreason. Stuck-ness is the problem, and that can be true for queers as well as feminists, for a project about sexuality as well as one that focuses on gender.

So let me end by retelling this story about queerness not as Halley tells it, but in a madly Foucauldian rewriting. The story of queerness—as a story about madness—begins with the story of a split: the great di-vision between reason and unreason. That split generates a story about the Western subject as an othering process that produces madness. Queer is one of the names we have found to describe that historical other of the modern rationalist Western subject. And although we've tried to make her beautiful by dusting her off and spinning her around, the queer has tended, like the feminist before her, to get stuck in rigid categorical positions. This is where *History of Madness* can help us, as the story of a split that produced the queer not as a break away from feminism, but as one of *reason's* prodigal children.

The queer prodigal child is not "going out in this world"—as the Roll-ing Stones sing it in "Prodigal Son" (1968)[70]—only to return to reason. For if we tend to think of "prodigal" within a lost-and-found biblical family structure, the word's actual "extravagant" meanings point to an excess that reorganizes love into new forms of relation. Both feminists and queers are to be counted among those extravagant prodigals of rea-son who can't or don't want to go home again; we are the ever-changing subjects of the exclusions of rationalism and family morality. Pinned down, as we are, as reason's others, we have resignified ourselves as forces of resistance. The danger of resignification is that we can get stuck in ourselves, to our own detriment: we can be recaptured and pinned down again, like dead butterflies, in our perversions and our genders. So if resignification threatens to bring us right back, like the prodigal son, to that place of patriarchy where we started, the trick is to keep things turning into something other. *History of Madness* has much to teach us about that resistant, transformative turning: about turning the adversity of "split decisions" into new ways of thinking, feeling, and acting in the world.

First Interlude

NIETZSCHE'S DREADFUL ATTENDANT

When in spite of that fearful pressure of "morality of custom" under which all the communities of mankind have lived . . . new and deviate ideas, evaluations, drives again and again broke out, they did so accompanied by a dreadful attendant: almost everywhere it was madness which prepared the way for the new idea.
— Friedrich Nietzsche, 1881

Did Nietzsche's madness, that "dreadful attendant,"[1] give birth to Foucault's *Madness*? Or is Nietzsche a "dead man in the game of writing":[2] a stuttering ghost, a "murmur of dark insects" (*M* xxxiii) on "a sterile beach of words" (*M* xxxi)?

In late 1888 or early 1889 Nietzsche went mad. An incident often recounted to describe the first signs of Nietzsche's illness occurred in January 1889, when Nietzsche caused a public disturbance at a piazza in Turin after witnessing the whipping of a horse. Nietzsche ran to the horse, threw his arms around its neck, then collapsed to the ground. Following the Turin incident, Nietzsche sent *Wahnbriefe*, or "madness letters," to some of his friends. Alarmed by the letters, his friends and then his mother sent him to psychiatric clinics—first in Basel, then in Jena. The Jena clinic was directed by Otto Binswanger, the uncle of the existentialist psychoanalyst Ludwig Binswanger, for whom Foucault wrote the introduction to *Dream and Existence* in 1954. According to notes from the three-day medical examination at Jena, Nietzsche's face was flushed, his tongue furred, and the pupil of his right eye wider than the left. During his stay at the clinic, he often seemed confused about his identity, calling himself the Kaiser, the Duke of Cumberland, or Friedrich Wilhelm IV. During the summer he smashed windowpanes and a drinking glass, wanting "to protect his approaches with glass splinters."[3] In March 1890 he was released from the asylum and went to live with his mother, who devoted virtually all her time to taking care of him until the end of her life. Her greatest fear was "losing him to Binswanger again" (Hayman 346).

In September 1895, Nietzsche's oldest friend, Franz Overbeck, recorded Nietzsche's condition in a letter:

> I saw him only in his room, half-crouching like a wild animal mortally wounded and wanting only to be left in peace. He made literally not one sound while I was there. He did not appear to be suffering or in pain, except perhaps for the expression of profound distaste visible in his lifeless eyes. . . . He had been living for weeks in a state of alternation between days of dreadful excitability, rising to a pitch of roaring and shouting, and days of complete prostration. (348)

After the death of Nietzsche's mother in 1897, Nietzsche's opportunistic sister, Elisabeth, moved with Nietzsche and his archive, over which she had gained full legal control, to a villa on the outskirts of Weimar. One of the investors in Elisabeth's lucrative Nietzsche project, Count Harry Kessler, recorded in his diary after visiting the Nietzsches in August 1897:

> He was asleep on the sofa. His mighty head had sunk half-way down to the right as if it were too heavy for his neck. His forehead was truly colossal; his manelike hair is still dark brown, like his shaggy, protruding moustache. . . . In the lifeless, flabby face one can still see deep wrinkles dug by thought and willpower, but softened, as it were, and getting smoothed out. There is infinite weariness in his expression. His hands are waxen, with green and violet veins, and slightly swollen, as on a dead body. A table and a high-backed chair had been positioned at the edge of the sofa to prevent the heavy body from slipping down. . . . He looked less like a sick man or a lunatic than like a corpse. (349)

Following Nietzsche's death from a stroke in August 1900, his sister laid out the corpse in the room that housed the Nietzsche archive. The body was displayed on white linen and damask in a heavy oak coffin framed by potted plants and flowers. After a lengthy funeral oration by an eminent art historian, one observer remarked: "The same sterile scholasticism Nietzsche had always fought followed him to his grave. If he could have arisen, he would have thrown the lecturer out of the window and chased the rest of us out of his temple" (350).

In *Daybreak* (1881) Nietzsche asks why it had to be madness that "prepared the way for the new idea."[4] Is it "something in the voice and bearing as uncanny and incalculable as the demonic moods of the weather and the sea and therefore worthy of similar awe and observation"? Or is it "something that bore so visibly the sign of total unfreedom as the convulsions and froth of the epileptic, that seemed to mark the madman as the mask and speaking-trumpet of a divinity"?[5] Or is it, perhaps, something a bit more troubling? "Let us go a step further," Nietzsche suggests. "All superior men who were irresistibly drawn to throw off the yoke of any kind of morality and to frame new laws had, *if they were not actually mad*, no alternative but to make themselves or pretend to be mad— . . . even the innovator of poetical metre had to establish his credentials by madness."[6]

And so we find Overbeck writing in 1890: "I cannot escape the ghastly suspicion . . . that [Nietzsche's] madness is simulated. This impression can be explained only by the experiences I have had of Nietzsche's self-concealments, of his spiritual masks."[7] Another friend, Gast, saw Nietzsche's insanity as "no more than a heightening of [his] humorous antics."[8]

In that impasse between Nietzsche slumped over and his humorous antics—between "actual" madness and "pretending" to be mad—we encounter Nietzsche's "dreadful attendant." In that impasse we also find Foucault, a poet, establishing his credentials. "We have no choice," Nietzsche's biographer writes, "but to follow him into [that] impasse. . . . He has left us to find our own way out."[9]

Take Foucault himself: you weren't aware of him as a person exactly.
Even in trivial situations, say when he came into a room, it was
more like a changed atmosphere, a sort of event, an electric or mag-
netic field.

—Gilles Deleuze, 1986

Nietzsche's *Madness*

Critics have recognized the obvious presence of Nietzsche throughout
the pages of *History of Madness*, from the celebration of the "tragic" in
the 1961 preface to *Madness*'s Dionysian, lyrical style, to the explicit flirtation in its final pages with the possibility of philosophy's own fall into
madness. References to the early Nietzsche—especially *The Birth of
Tragedy*'s (1872) evocation of Dionysian intoxication and nonrationality
as a creative force—are common in readings of *Madness*. However, critics have paid less attention to the traces *Madness* bears of the later
Nietzschean critique of morality that begins with *Daybreak* (1881), continues with *Beyond Good and Evil* (1886), and culminates with *On the
Genealogy of Morals* (1887). In this chapter I perform a shift in this critical reading of Nietzsche in Foucault. Specifically, in rethinking *Madness*
I move away from an early to a later Nietzsche to throw into question
the standard reading of a Nietzschean chronology in Foucault, where an
early Nietzsche corresponds with an early Foucault and where the later
"genealogical" Nietzsche doesn't appear until the 1970s with "Nietzsche,
Genealogy, History" (1971).[1] In its explicit thematization of both genealogy and ethics, *Madness* unsettles this Nietzschean patterning in Foucault and thus also scrambles the categories typically used to classify
Foucault's oeuvre as a whole. If critics tend to neatly divide Foucault
into the archeological (1960s), genealogical (1970s), and ethical (1980s)

phases of his thinking, the late Nietzschean (ethical, genealogical) dimension of *Madness* throws into question (in true Nietzschean, Foucauldian fashion) the clean continuities this periodization assumes. The fact that Foucault himself (in a moment of consolidation of his authorship and his name) suggested such a tripartite, linear framing of his own work hardly constitutes a defense against a Nietzschean scrambling of his own continuity as a discursive subject. Indeed, such self-scrambling is something Foucault surely would have welcomed.

Nietzsche's madness stands as an emblem of *Madness* caught between the tragic and the comic, grief and laughter: a "dreadful attendant"[2] with "humorous antics."[3] For, if the cogito's rationalism and moralism go hand-in-hand, then the spectacle of a "mad Nietzsche"—crying over a whipped horse, breaking window panes, crouching like an animal, roaring and shouting—demonstrates in starkly experiential terms the enormous costs revealed by such antirationalist, antimoralist critiques of the Cartesian subject. This hardly constitutes a romantic celebration of Nietzsche's insanity as creative or transgressive, as most readers of *Madness* have disapprovingly asserted, but rather an exposure of the price exacted by rationalist moralism from those who resist its despotic order. As Nietzsche put it: "even the innovator of poetical metre had to establish his credentials by madness."[4] Foucault makes clear the dangers of romanticism, as well as the later psychoanalytic talking cure that merely inverts romantic madness. As he warns in the closing pages of *Madness*: "we must be wary of the emotional appeal of the accursed artist, or the inverse and symmetrical danger of psychoanalysis" (*M* 537).

I am not making a claim here about any one of the much-debated theories regarding the cause of Nietzsche's madness: Was it syphilis? Was it philosophy itself? Indeed, to assert a single *cause* of insanity misses the point of *Madness*. The point of unreason is this: what begins, in Nietzsche, with a critique of rationalism and morality cannot be sustained within the terms that philosophy can understand. Philosophy's terms are the terms of our language and our thinking, and the critique of those foundations can only end, as it does with Nietzsche, with the cessation of a thinking and a speaking we can hear: "Nietzsche's madness," Foucault writes, is "the collapse of his thought" (*M* 537). And if Foucault finds in that crumbling of thought a certain Nietzschean pregnancy[5] for a different future—"that thought opens onto the modern world" (*M* 537)—the thinking which might be born from that collapse comes at the expense of a life that Nietzsche's "sane" writings never ceased to affirm. Like the inhabitants of the hospitals and asylums of the classical age, Nietzsche in his experience of madness becomes lost to himself and to us, transformed into a figure of rupture. This Nietzschean figure—the living dead man with a corpselike body and waxen hands[6]—prepares the way for what Foucault describes in his 1964 lecture, "Nietzsche, Freud, Marx," as the unfinished business of a Blanchotian "book-to-come" (*livre à venir*): "the point of rupture of interpretation" where thought transgresses its own limits "toward a point that renders it impossible."[7] At the edge of thought is "Nietzsche, going mad, proclaim[ing] . . . that he [is] the truth" (*M* 549).

The Moral Subject of Madness

History of Madness describes the convergence of historical and social forces that result in the emergence of sexual deviance, first as unreason and then as madness. In Foucault's diagnosis of unreason in the classical age, the simultaneous production and repression of sexual alterity is directly linked to a "great confiscation of sexual ethics by family morality" (*M* 104) that persists today. And if Foucault locates the beginnings of that great moral confiscation in the seventeenth and eighteenth centuries in Europe, his gesture of geographical and historical specification should not be understood as a traditional historian's assertion of factual truth. Rather, *Madness* constitutes an archeological description of historical structures that continue to determine our present sexual condition. Like Nietzsche, Foucault understands his philosophical task to be the diagnosis of the present: "Nietzsche discovered that philosophy's distinct activity consists in the work of diagnosis: what are we today? What is this 'today' in which we live?"[8] With regard to the specifically moral structures that define our sexuality, the question of who and what we are is explicitly linked to the larger ethical world in which we live. In this sense, *Madness*'s diagnosis of our sexual present responds, in ethical terms, to Nietzsche's call for a historical critique of present values: "Finally a new demand becomes audible. Let us articulate this new demand: we need a critique of moral values, the values of these values themselves must first be called in question—and for that there is needed a knowledge of the conditions and circumstances in which they grew."[9]

This chapter explores the use Foucault makes of Nietzsche in *Madness*'s critique of sexual morality. Although the question of Foucault's various philosophical influences continues to be the subject of ongoing debate, I will not engage here in an argument about influence at all. Drawing as it does on a strange combination of astrology—"influence" in its etymology as astral power—and traditional "great men and their works" theories of history, the causality-driven concept of influence seems particularly ill-suited to a Foucauldian conception of the quasi-random and ever-changing series of explosions he calls book-events. Indeed, for Foucault the question of influence—"where does that come from?"[10]—is the product of modern juridical power: "an identity question, a policing question."[11] Rather than constituting a philosophical identity to be matched with another identified as "Foucault," "Nietzsche" names an appearance in the book-event we call *History of Madness*. To exercise a metaphor Foucault deploys to describe his own books, Foucault's use of Nietzsche can be usefully compared to a game that involves both skill and chance: Nietzsche's books are "like marbles that roll. You capture them, you take them, you throw them again. And if it works, so much the better."[12]

To be sure, Foucauldians will continue to ask those seductive but misleading policing questions about that great chain of thinkers known as Philosophy: who influenced Foucault more, Nietzsche or Heidegger? Merleau-Ponty, Bachelard, Cavaillès, or Canguilhem?[13] But if using Nietzsche is like a game of marbles, those "influence" questions can be put aside. In their place I propose engaging in a critical interpretive practice that is closer to literary reading than it is to either philosophical argumentation or historical narration. In his *Genealogy*, Nietzsche called for "reading as an art" (23): something, he adds, "that has been unlearned most thoroughly" (23) and "for which one has almost to be a cow and in any case not a 'modern man'" (23). Foucault's lyrical reading of the metaphors we call madness can serve as a guide for this practice. Perhaps Foucault, especially in this and his other "literary" work of the 1960s, is that future Nietzschean reader who has finally learned to "ruminate" (23) like a cow: to make those "mad" writings "readable" (23).

The dangerous specter of identity I just evoked in my dismissal of "influence" theories of intellectual history cannot be separated from what Nietzsche diagnosed, more generally, as the danger of morality and its historical relation to the emergence of the modern, normative subject against whom the exclusions of deviance are produced. More pointedly, the identity of what Nietzsche calls "that little changeling, the 'subject'" (45) can be traced, in *Genealogy*, to the production of "bad conscience" as the historical result of a process of internalization whose beginnings are "soaked in blood" (65). In *Madness*, Foucault takes up

again—as in a game of marbles—that Nietzschean trope of moral interiority in order to launch a critique of the subject in its medicalized,
modern form, not only in nineteenth-century positivist psychology but
also, eventually, in psychology's apotheosis as psychoanalysis.

In this philosophical game of marbles, the other book-event whose
effects will be felt across the surface of my reading of Nietzsche in *Madness* is Deleuze's 1986 book on Foucault. Although I am hardly a "Deleuzian" (a label that smells—"Bad air! Bad air!"—of the influence theory of texts and readers), the Deleuzian concept of the fold is useful for
my engagement with *Madness*'s geographical metaphors of navigation
and confinement. As a number of Foucault's interpreters have argued,
these metaphors function as figures for abstract conceptual functions:
the "spatialization of reason,"[14] the "conditions of freedom,"[15] the "mapping of the present,"[16] or "spatial nomadism."[17] With Deleuze's focus on
the limit in Foucault, I connect *Madness*'s spatial figures of movement
and stasis to something Foucault explores more explicitly in essays on
Bataille (1963) and Blanchot (1966): thinking's movement, as "transgression" toward its own undoing as "the thought of the outside." In his
essay on Bataille, "Preface to Transgression," Foucault explicitly links
the undoing of thinking at its limit with sexuality. Using an image that
anticipates the famous disappearance of "man's" face at the edge of the
shore in *The Order of Things* (*Les Mots et les choses*, 1966), Foucault describes sexuality as "that line of foam showing just how far language [*le
langage*] may advance upon the sands of silence."[18] And that undoing of
thinking at its limit is associated, for Deleuze, with the function of the
fold in Foucault. With regard to the moral questions *Madness* engages, I
redeploy the fold—"that fold that allows us to unfurl that which has
been curled up for centuries" (*M* 544)—as a tool for rethinking Nietzschean interiority across the historical structure of separation and exclusion *Madness* describes. Using Deleuze, I "unfurl" the interiority of
Nietzschean "bad conscience" in *Madness* to expose the historical emergence of the "*moral subject*" (*M* 60, original emphasis) as the mystified
result of forces of exclusion. This unfolding of the interiority of a seemingly self-contained subject with an "inside," a "psyche," or a "soul" allows me to link the production of sexuality as an "inner" essence to the
rationalizing moral structures that Foucault traces across the classical
age. In that sense, the resistance to "thinking the outside" would also
constitute a resistance to a Nietzschean critique of moral values.

My engagement with Nietzschean interiority and the Deleuzian fold
through a reading of *Madness* sets up a series of questions in the last
part of this chapter about sexual subjectivity, ethics, and queer theory. I

use the structure of the fold to interrogate performativity as a name queer theory gives to a conception of subjectivity that would challenge both psychic interiority and the morality from which it is constituted. But what ethical work does performativity in fact do in contemporary queer theory? I question the extent to which performativity actually challenges the concept of the psyche, a concept Nietzsche links to modern morality. Indeed, as I argue more extensively in chapter 3, many versions of queer theory are deeply invested in the psyche and its twentieth-century science, psychoanalysis. The Nietzschean dimension of Foucault's moral critique exposes a theoretical ruse at the heart of psychoanalytic queer theory, where the subject with a psyche is partially dismantled but ultimately reconfigured within predetermined philosophical structures. The result is the replacement of a conservative, moralizing sexual discourse of "family values" with a queer political discourse that at times bears the traces of a new moralism.

Ultimately, this chapter about queer performativity, the sexual psyche, and the rise of family morality that *Madness* describes reengages the philosophical question of the subject that arose in France in the 1960s. From today's twenty-first-century theoretical perspective, reports of that subject's death seem to have been greatly exaggerated.[19] Nietzsche helps us to see the theme of the death of the subject in specifically moral terms. Indeed, in his critique of moral values—"of the values of these values" (19)—Nietzsche was the philosopher who allowed Foucault, beginning in the 1950s, to think differently about the sovereignty of the subject as a historical question. That different thinking meant a rejection of the Hegelian, phenomenological idealizations of subjectivity that had hitherto defined his philosophical universe. More specifically, with Nietzsche, Foucault began interrogating the subject as a phenomenon of historical emergence rather than as a timeless truth. In that context, *History of Madness* can be seen as the first story Foucault tells about both the historical emergence of the subject and its cost: madness. In historical terms, as Foucault puts it, by the end of the eighteenth century, "madness was clearly inscribed in the temporal destiny of man; it was even the consequence and the ransom [*la rançon*] paid for the fact that men, unlike animals, had a history" (*M* 377/*F* 397; translation modified). Madness is the "ransom" paid by the "other" for the historical rise of the rational moral subject.

But what is a subject? Or, more specifically, what is a subject today? Like Nietzsche in his time or Foucault in his, I ask this question again, from the perspective of the present, in order to mine the complex story

Madness tells about the "imaginary moral geometry" (*M* 86/ *F* 22; translation modified) that gives rise to a subject and a sexual order still with us. That moral geometry has much to teach us about the distance that separates a violent order of sexual subjectivity from the life-affirming possibilities of an erotic ethics. If the spectacle of a dying subject seems now to be safely behind us, what does that mean for us, today, about the ethical concerns that gave rise to the antihumanist critique of the subject in the first place?

To refine my question about the subject even further: what is a subject, in *History of Madness*, from today's postqueer perspective? Deleuze reminds us that the subject in Foucault is not so much a person as a "personal or collective individuation," "a sort of event."[20] *Madness* describes one such subjectivating event, the rise of the Cartesian "I," as a philosophical coup that excludes unreason from the subject of reason. The "subject" of reason and its "other" are the result of that event. As the consequences of an "othering" event, the rise of the subject includes the production of an interiority that Nietzsche will call the soul and that Freud will call the psyche. In general terms, subjectivation may or may not be an event that produces a subject; in and of itself subjectivation is a process and, as such, has no properties: no psyche, no soul, no identity. As Deleuze puts it: "A process of subjectivation cannot be confused with a subject, unless it is to discharge the latter from all interiority and even from all identity."[21]

Reading Foucault through Nietzsche and Deleuze allows me to interpret *Madness* as the story of the specifically rationalist, moralizing, subjectivating event that produced a modern Western subject with a psyche, an identity, and a soul. As an exposé of a historical process, *Madness* participates in a familiar project of denaturalization where the taken-for-grantedness of subjective interiority is radically undermined by its careful historical and conceptual unraveling. In that sense, Foucault could be said to "discharge" the subject "from all interiority and even from all identity" by demystifying the ruse of interiority's construction.

But what is at stake in that demystification? It is one thing to disrupt the subject by performatively redeploying the acts that constitute her in a now familiar queer gesture of resignification. There is something playful, ludic, and optimistically subversive about such identity-rupturing gestures, a bit like Nietzsche's humorous antics. But what does it mean to name the evacuation of the subject's identity and interiority as "actual" madness? If the "subject" in Foucault is not so much a person as a rationalist, moralizing event, this hardly means that reason's "other" isn't real, in all the experience—sometimes documented, often not—of her pain and marginalization.

This is where the stylistic, *erotic* difference between *Madness* and Foucault's later, more well-known work on sexuality becomes important. As I argued in chapter 1, in its almost unilateral attention to the dispositif of subjectivation (*asujettissement*) in *Sexuality One*, queer theory has missed sexuality as an experience. Here we can see why that missed experience is crucial in the context of a Nietzschean critique of moral values. "Present experience," Nietzsche writes in *On the Genealogy of Morals*, "has, I am afraid, always found us 'absent-minded'" (15). From the perspective of the present we all inhabit "in our time" (*M* xxxiv), we work from within a knowledge that, "knowing it too much" (*M* xxxiv), misses the experience of eros that has been captured by science as "sexuality." As Nietzsche puts it, we have come to believe that "*our* treasure is where the beehives of knowledge are" (15), what Foucault calls "our knowledge" [*notre savoir*] (*M* 73/ *F* 291; translation modified): the accumulated baggage of the subject of reason as "the visible presence of the truth" (*M* 277).²² But what knowledge misses is what we, in our reason, cannot feel and cannot hear: our present erotic, lived experience (*M* 15). As Nietzsche puts it: "we cannot give our hearts to it—not even our ears!" (15).

If we "absent-minded" professors of the now recentered, performative subject have missed the experience of sexual subjectivity, as well as its costs, it is because we have "given" our heads to it, but not our hearts, to say nothing of our ears. We haven't heard the other, except as the thoughts in our own heads. We are, in a sense, the same bodiless subjects that Foucault diagnoses as the de-eroticized result of the Cartesian cogito, mesmerized by our own subjectivation. As Foucault puts it in his Bataille essay, modern sexuality is "cast into an *empty* space where it only encounters the *thin* form of the limit."²³

History of Madness gets us back to the thickness of our bodies, our feelings, our eros—the "hearts" and "ears" of our "sexual" experience—by demystifying the moral, emptying experience of subjectivation that both gives rise to the subject and produces madness. The subjectivation most of us know in Foucault—from *Discipline and Punish* and *Sexuality One*—has little to do with our hearts or our ears or the life-affirming ethics of experience. Indeed, with the rise of biopower, life is managed and thereby drained of eros. As Foucault puts it at the end of *Sexuality One*: "Sex is worth death. ["Le sexe vaut bien la mort"]. It is in this, strictly historical sense, that sex is indeed *traversed* [*traversé*] by the death instinct."[24] And yet, for all its historical negation of life as eros, queer readers of Foucault have tended to embrace sexual subjectivation as a condition that defines us all: we are trapped in our prisons and panopticons, choked by the noose of governmentality. Biopolitical subjectivation has come to define us-as-everyone, now and always, as universally subjected and unfree. But now, as with all definitions, it is time to be suspicious of the ways we have come to know subjectivation in Foucault and to unravel the histories that have been obscured by its semiotic concentrations: "only that which has no history is definable," Nietzsche reminds us (80). *Madness* unravels our knowingness about subjectivation as something definable; it gives us back our hearts and our ears by, paradoxically, putting the subject into question again: now, queerly, for us.

What are the theoretical consequences of this unraveling? This chapter continues the work begun in the previous chapter by showing how the historical unpeeling that *Madness* performs offers a way out of the deathly theoretical bind of *Sexuality One*: Foucault's famous exposure of the ruse of sexuality as something "buried within." In *Sexuality One*'s demystification of the "repressive hypothesis," Foucault tells a story about sexual subjectivation with no way out, except, perhaps, through a tiny escape hatch at the very end of the book where he hints, quite elliptically, at other possibilities called "bodies and pleasures."[25] With the debunking of the repressive hypothesis, any resistance to the *moral* norms that have been used against us reinforces our sexual subjectivation since we are, in that resistance, simply adding to the discursive store of sex talk that *is* the repressive hypothesis. Even when we replace psychoanalytic desire with "bodies and pleasures," we hardly dismantle the discursive moral universe that imagines sexuality as a kind of Jack-in-the-box: a libidinal force which, once unleashed, will free us (like death!) from those norms. *Sexuality One*'s message is clear: as sexual beings, we can never be free. Our speech and gestures are like the "convulsions and froth" of Nietzsche's mad epileptic: "sign[s] of [our] total unfreedom."[26] In our politics, our writing, and our lovemaking we can only discursively reproduce the structures that have been used to marginalize us as sexual deviants in the first place. Not surprisingly, ever since *Sexuality One* we've been trying to get out from under the hold of the ruse of the "repressive hypothesis," to escape our sexual subjectivation. Indeed, that attempt to escape the specifically sexual ruse of identity that the repressive hypothesis describes has, to a large extent, been queer theory's purpose.

Like Eve Kosofsky Sedgwick and Adam Frank over a decade ago in *Shame and Its Sisters* (1995), I remain skeptical of the claims made thus far in contemporary criticism and theory "to have mastered the techniques for putting the ruses of the repressive hypothesis firmly out of bounds."[27] Those techniques are various but, as Sedgwick and Frank suggest, can be collectively characterized as adopting a "bipolar analytic framework"[28] that alternates between claims for hegemony and subversion. And despite a clear rejection of what Foucault calls bourgeois morality, contemporary theory—and especially queer theory—is afflicted, as Sedgwick and Frank put it, by a "moralistic hygiene"[29] that fails to think the alterity of the past—especially the recent past—except in the mode of condescension. Sedgwick and Frank's question is a paradigmatically Foucauldian one: "What was it possible to think or do at a certain moment of the past, that it no longer is?" The "highly moralistic allegories"[30] of many versions of contemporary queer theory fail to shake us up, ethically speaking, because of their failure to engage historical alterity in the context of a critique of "the values of . . . values."[31] Again, Nietzsche teaches us that the critique of morality cannot simply lead to another morality, one that would emerge, like a photographic negative, as the mere underside of the moral norms we have submitted to critique. In fact, a diagnosis of the present which takes seriously the alterity of the past requires that we venture again into that enemy territory of "family values": the land of morality. As Nietzsche puts it: "The project is to *traverse* with quite novel questions, and as though with new eyes, the enormous, distant, and so well hidden land of morality—of morality that has actually existed, actually been lived" (21; emphasis added). The verb *to traverse* is important here, and recalls the word Foucault uses in *Sexuality One* to describe sexuality's historical "traversal" by death: "sex is indeed *traversed* [*traversé*] by the death instinct."[32] To unravel that history of sex-as-death requires a *re*traversal, a retracing of historical steps. *History of Madness* offers a path for retraversing the life-ordering morality of sex.

Let me offer one more preliminary observation about the theoretical stakes of my reading in this chapter. In the U.S. context that frames this book, the last several decades have given rise to concrete successes resulting from the intellectual and political work that can be slotted under the heading "sex and gender." Those successes include the institutionalization of women's studies, gender studies, and sexuality studies; the establishment of feminist and queer theory as distinct and legitimate fields of scholarship; the adoption of measures, both formal and informal, to redress the harms of gender violence, sexual harassment, and other forms of "sex and gender" discrimination both large and small; the conferral of individual rights ranging from abortion (*Roe v. Wade* 1971) to sodomy (*Lawrence v. Texas* 2003) through legislation and legal decisions; and, most importantly, the gradual adoption of a "sex and gender" culture that sees itself as having won the battles of inequality: now, people say, we live in an era where feminism and queer activism are no longer necessary. And, because so many of these successes have come as victories that have meaning for individual, rights-bearing citizen-subjects, the sovereignty of those subjects seems so firmly established and morally just that to question such sovereignty seems downright reactionary.

Still, I argue, it is worth raising the question of the subject again. Given the renewed sovereignty of the subject that comes with a present sexual condition characterized, more or less, as better than it was before the rise of feminist and queer movements, the concept of a "morality that has actually existed, actually been lived"[33] takes on a new, specifically "postfeminist" and "postqueer" resonance. In the current political context I just described, the exuberantly anti-identitarian queer performances of the 1990s may seem, from the perspective of feminist and queer juridical reforms, quaintly trivial or simply irrelevant. To the extent that some of us still consume, if only through our teaching, the subversive claims of those theoretical leftovers from the 1990s, there is no doubt that in the present our tastes have changed; many of those dishes seem to have lost, as leftovers do, both their heat and their flavor. This has meant also a postfeminist, postqueer shift toward a different Foucault than the one we were obsessed with in the 1980s and nineties. If we still use him, it is usually for purposes other than sex: the rethinking of race, sovereignty, religion, and nation. Indeed, we seem to be echoing Foucault himself, who, toward the end of his life, famously complained that "sex is boring."[34]

To be sure, the contradiction between our sexual subjectivation and our "sex and gender" successes is glaring. Except, of course, that the contradiction is not a contradiction at all. The cost of our purported successes as sovereign subjects is, precisely, our subjectivation, as the Foucauldian concept of governmentality makes clear. Not only do our successes mean "more governmentality" in the Foucauldian disciplinary and biopolitical sense but, in ethical terms, "our" sexual successes come at the cost of others. Often those costs are difficult to see. But if we scratch the surface of sovereign successes, what do we find? Those successes are not free, as Nietzsche never ceases to remind us. This is as true today as it was in Nietzsche's time or as it was in the antihumanist philosophical period that constitutes the diagnostic present of *History of Madness*. As an early contribution to an antihumanist project we would do well to consider again, *Madness* offers a way to make those layers beneath the surface of sovereign subjectivity "readable."[35]

History of Madness scratches the historical surface of the sovereign subject to uncover the structures that weld rationalism to morality; that welding produces the sexual subject as historically normal or deviant. Because it explicitly interrogates the process through which morality as subjective interiority is produced, *Madness* allows for an interrogation of ethical questions in the context of subjectivation in ways that *Sexuality One* does not. It does so by framing subjectivation and morality as a question about madness, including, most radically, the possibility that reason itself is mad. It is this specter of the mad philosopher—the decentered subject, the subject undone—that continues to haunt readers of *Madness* as well as those who have ignored its call. Invested, as we are, in our need to be both "right" and "good," the possibility of our own madness—of being "wrong" and "bad" or, even worse, of being reason's anonymous "other"—is more than our theoretical systems can stomach.

Queer Foldings

In his book on Foucault, Deleuze devotes a chapter—"Foldings, or the Inside of Thought"—to the theme of interiority as a function of the fold. It is one of the few places in *Foucault* where Deleuze cites *Madness* at length, making reference to the ship of fools as a figure for an operation of thought:

> The inside as an operation of the outside: in all his work Foucault seems haunted by this theme of an inside which is merely the fold of the outside, as if the ship were a folding of the sea. On the subject of the Renaissance madman who is put to sea in his boat, Foucault wrote
>
>> he is put in the interior of the exterior, and inversely [. . .] a prisoner in the midst of what is the freest, the openest of routes: bound fast at the infinite crossroads. He is the Passenger par excellence: that is, the prisoner of the passage.
>
> Thought has no other being than this madman himself.[36]

In *Madness*, Descartes functions as the founding father of a philosophical tradition that refuses the specter of the mad philosopher. The ship of fools, on the other hand, symbolizes the philosophical possibility that the act of thinking itself pushes thought toward madness. In the passage I've just quoted, Deleuze reads the ship of fools to name the impossibility of thinking at the very heart of thought as madness. Specifically, Deleuze describes madness as a thinking of the limit: a thinking that addresses itself to an outside, "the empty form of the limit as such."[37] But that outside, or madness, is also paradoxically "inside" thought as the result of thinking. This inside/outside paradox of thinking the limit as void is what Deleuze calls the operation of the fold. In *History of Madness*, the ship of fools becomes a figure for a circular movement of thinking as it negotiates the possibility of its own madness: thinking's own impossibility. The paradoxical possibility of thinking's impossibility, or madness, is thus the result of thinking itself: the fold of the outside or thinking the limit.

But what of the watery element that constitutes the ship, "as if the ship were a folding of the sea"? In figural terms, thinking's impossibility—the ship of fools—is, again paradoxically, also its condition of possibility as freedom, figured here as the sea. This means that "thought," the result of thinking, "has no other being than this madman himself": thought is nothing other than the result of the movement of an "inside" that confronts the empty form of an "outside" and vice versa. This freedom is both the condition of possibility of thinking and its disintegration: its creative movement ("thinking outside the box") and its limit as madness. In this sense the formless outside ("madness") is also the inside form ("thought") and vice versa: the sea is also the ship. As thinking's result, thought is thus paradoxically "a prisoner in the midst of what is the freest, the openest of routes." Thought is "the prisoner of the passage" between thinking and madness: "A prisoner in the midst of the ultimate freedom, on the most open road of all" (*M* 11).

Deleuze's analysis, although abstract, adroitly reads the figure of the ship of fools to highlight *Madness*'s philosophical concerns. Clearly drawing on Foucault's later essay on Blanchot, "The Thought of the Outside" (1966), Deleuze shows that Foucault's "history" of madness is also a philosophical story about thought thinking itself; more specifically, *Madness* describes how thinking precipitates its own movement toward an "outer bound [*extrémité*] where it must continually contest itself,"[38] pushing thought toward its own madness as a failure of thinking in "the endless erosion of the outside."[39] Again, Nietzsche reminds us that "it was madness which prepared the way for the new idea."[40] Thinking's movement toward what we might call "genius" is thus also a movement toward "madness" or nonsensical, preposterous thinking:

FIGURE 2.1 Peanut butter and jelly cartoon

"Peanut butter and jelly? Preposterous! The line between genius and insanity is thinner than you think" (Figure 2.1).

Deleuze's interpretation of the ship of fools as thinking's movement across the "thin line" that divides "genius" from "insanity" or "success" from "failure" also describes what Foucault reads as the consequence of a historical coup: the rise of Cartesian reason and madness's exclusion from the thinking "I." To many, the idea that "the line between genius and insanity is thinner than you think" sounds romantic. (I can hear it now: "Do you know what it's *really* like to be *crazy?* There's nothing brilliant or beautiful about it.") But to level the charge of romanticism against Foucault is to seriously misunderstand him. In fact, Foucault never denies in any of his writing the lived reality of mental illness; indeed, in his own experiences of attempted suicide, repeated psychotherapies, alcoholic binging, and near hospitalizations Foucault "knew" that reality. Further, in his early clinical practice in the field of psychology, Foucault observed mentally and emotionally disturbed patients ranging from schizophrenics to anorectics to obsessional neurotics. His knowledge of such empirically verifiable disturbances is extensively documented in his 1954 book, *Mental Illness and Personality.*

History of Madness neither celebrates madness nor denies its reality; rather, it attempts to think madness historically. In philosophical terms, Foucault uses madness as a way to access the historicity of the emergence of a modern subject who can only be thought within historically shifting rational norms. This means, quite simply, that "crazy" in one period is not in another: the *historical* line between genius and insanity—reason and unreason—is thinner than you think. As just one example, we need only recall that until 1973—a breathtakingly recent date—homosexuality was medically codified in the U.S. as a mental disorder: a kind of madness. Not incidentally, within the historical terms of Foucault's own writing, *Madness* was produced *within* a scientific ethos sure of homosexuality's ontological status as mental illness. That scientific conception of homosexuality cannot be dismissed as one of the intellectual vectors interfacing with Foucault's lived experience to produce a sustained reflection on the historicity of such conceptions.

In his reading of Foucault, Deleuze helps us to see the historicity of the subject—the difference between then and now—as a function of a difference in thinking. Specifically, the edge-seeking thinking of the Renaissance, figured by the ship of fools, serves as a contrast to the imprisonment of thinking that comes with Descartes and the great confinement. In contrast to the movement of the ship of fools, the great confinement sets up a structure through which thinking divides itself into reason and unreason within the ontology of the cogito: I think therefore I am. To be sure, this historical shift from thinking's movement to stasis, from freedom to constraint, is not absolute. But in the Renaissance, "before" the cogito, the division between reason and unreason is less categorical than in the seventeenth century, a difference symbolized by the opposition between the ship of fools and the great hospitals of confinement, respectively. Both are important, then, not only as historical phenomena but also as philosophical symbols. Again Foucault reminds us of that doubled status: "They really did exist," Foucault writes of the ship of fools, "these boats that drifted from one town to another with their senseless cargo" (*M* 9). At the same time, they are "highly symbolic ships filled with the senseless in search of their reason" (*M* 10). Their navigation on the open seas, outside the city, traces "a half-real, half-imaginary geography" (*M* 11/*F* 22; translation modified) that highlights "the *liminal* situation of the mad" (*M* 11).

What Foucault describes as the "liminal situation of the mad" establishes *les petits fous* as figures to be used in a Nietzschean critique of reason and morality. From that perspective, we can now ask: what then are the ethical implications of the back-and-forth navigation of the ship of fools versus the stasis of the great confinement? Deleuze's conception of interiority as a function of the fold offers a way to think about ethical alterity as a result of thinking and, more specifically, the rise of reason. To be sure, thinking always resists the possibility of its own madness, even in the relative "freedom" of the Renaissance. In geographical terms, with the Renaissance ship of fools, madness is still symbolically detained at the threshold of the city: the madman is *"confined at the gates of the cities . . .* and if he has no *prison* other than the *threshold* itself he is still detained at this place of passage" (M 11/ F 22; translation modified). This description of the ship suggests a movement of division and confinement, with Foucault's italics insisting on the double nature of thinking's attempts to exclude madness from itself: *closed (enfermé)* at the *gates (portes)*, his *prison* is the *threshold (seuil)* that is the passage itself between reason and madness. But the Renaissance fool's exclusion is never final or absolute. Detained, as he is, "at the place of the passage," the madman is still free to come and go "in search of his reason" (M 10/ F 20; translation modified). Indeed, his "easily errant existence" *(existence facilement errante)* (M 9/ F 19; translation modified)[41] symbolizes the cosmic, tragic possibility of "madness" in everyone: madness is error, disorder, and death. The ship of fools is thus "the unreason of the world" (M 12/ F 23; translation modified); its navigation is the creative but shattering movement of thinking itself toward its own limit as unreason.

Ultimately, the Renaissance "passage" symbolizes a thinking that imagines, existentially, its own nonexistence or death: "the nothingness that is existence itself" (M 14/ F 26; translation modified). From this perspective, the madness of the ship of fools names the tragic irony of an existence inhabited by the void of nonexistence: "It is still the nothingness of existence that is at stake, but this nothingness is no longer experienced as a final and exterior end, a threat and a conclusion; it is felt from within, as the continuous and unchanging form of existence" (M 15/ F 26; translation modified). Again, as nonexistence, madness touches everyone: "the being-already-there of death" (M 14). It symbolizes the "rigorous division" (M 11) between reason and unreason, or existence and nonexistence, but also, inevitably, the porous, reversible passage between them: the "absolute Passage" (M 11).

This universalization of the possibility of madness, or death, in the Renaissance ship of fools explains Foucault's paradoxical insistence that the madman—here a figure for nothingness—"is placed on the inside of the outside, or vice versa" (M 11). This reversibility of inside and outside describes the Deleuzian fold of the outside or, in more concrete terms, the possibility of madness in everyone: life's inevitable implication in death. As John Caputo puts it, *Madness* shows us that the mad "are not truly 'other' than 'us.'"[42] But that common, shared alterity which constitutes the specificity of the ship of fools is rejected with the rise of reason. In the seventeenth century, the operation of the fold—thinking's movement toward the outside, its contestation of its own limits as void—is arrested and confined. This operation manifests itself both through the institutional practice of confining the mad in hospitals inside the city walls and through the philosophical gesture of exiling madness from within the reasoning cogito. Like the ship of fools, the hospital becomes both a figure of thought thinking itself and the manifestation of real social forces. As Deleuze puts it, for Foucault "hospitals and prisons are first and foremost places of visibility dispersed in a form of exteriority, which refer back to an extrinsic function, that of setting one apart and controlling."[43]

Both gestures—putting a fool in a ship or putting a madman in a hospital—are symbolic acts of internalization: operations of the fold. But for Foucault, between the Renaissance and the Age of Reason a crucial change occurs. If the ship of fools symbolized the possibility of thought's own madness, where madness, like death, happens to everyone, that is no longer the case in the seventeenth-century separation of reason and unreason. As Foucault puts it in the 1972 appendix to *History of Madness*, "Madness, the Absence of an Oeuvre" (written in 1964): "death at least says what *all* men will be. Madness, on the other hand, is that *rare* danger" (*M* 543; emphasis added). With Descartes and the great confinement, madness becomes the object of an act of division that is both exclusionary and irreversible. If the symbolic navigation of the ship of fools represented a collective longing for an elsewhere—abandonment to "the infinite sea of desires" (*M* 12), a shared inner chaos, and life's movement toward death—that ship was arrested at the gates of the city, but always ready to head off again: "a prisoner in the midst of what is the freest, the openest of routes." In the Age of Reason, the symbolic space of freedom, movement, and death—the sea—is methodically trapped and contained by systematic doubt. Isolated, silenced, and rendered invisible through an act of institutional and philosophical othering, the mad disappear *within* the city as the absolute negation of reason and bourgeois subjectivity. Irreversibly, the gesture of exclusion as internalization produces unreason as "something like a photographic negative [*le négatif*] of the city of morals [*la cité morale*]" (74).[44] We become, as Foucault puts it in 1967 in "Different Spaces," a "civilization[] without boats" whose "dreams dry up."[45]

This reading of *Madness* through the lens of the Deleuzian fold can now be linked to the Nietzschean critique of moral values in its revelation of the ethical significance of interiority. Specifically, the Foucauldian passage from the ship of fools to the great confinement retraces a Nietzschean genealogical story about the production of interiority as the result of "an act of violence" (86), what Foucault calls in "The Thought of the Outside" the Age of Reason's "interiorization of the law of history and the world."[46] For Nietzsche, the "bad conscience" (*Schlechtes Gewissen*) of a rationalist, moral order is the effect of this violence; "all those instincts of wild, free, prowling man" (85) are socialized and contained with an irreversible turn inward, much like an arrest of the Deleuzian fold. This "*internalization [Verinnerlichung] of man*" (84) is a turning of man against himself to produce the expansive depth of an "inner world" (84) or "soul" (38, 46, 84): "the entire inner world, originally as thin as if it were stretched between two membranes, expanded and extended itself, acquired depth, breadth, and height, in the same measure as outward discharge was *inhibited*" (84).

The result of this movement of internalization is a moral order that relies on an illusion of psychic interiority to police itself as conscience. Like a sock turned inside out, the "outside" "act of violence" (86) by the state—"some pack of blond beasts of prey" (86)—becomes an "inner" moral conscience. Unlike the "state" of political theory, this "state" in Nietzsche is neither specifically political nor social; as he reminds us, the state appears in its oldest form "as a fearful tyranny, as an oppressive and remorseless machine" (86); its purpose is "the welding of a hitherto unchecked and shapeless populace" (86)—something in mutation, like Foucault's ship of fools—"into a firm form" (86): the new geometry where the subject finds himself "enclosed within the walls of society" (84). The state masks the violence of its own conception with that Enlightenment "sentimentalism which would have it begin with a 'contract'" (86); that masking allows the new moral, juridical order to appear as nonviolent and just. But rather than taming the state's founding violence, those norms internalize that violence—"hostility, cruelty, joy in persecuting" (84)—to produce the modern subject "with a conscience." And if the "sting of conscience" (*morsus conscientiae*) (83) disciplines the sovereign, universal Enlightenment subject into governing himself, for Nietzsche that self-governing is nothing more than "man turned backward *against man himself*" (85).

Nietzsche is explicit in his description of the "serious illness" (84) of bad conscience as a rejection of the body through its internalization as shame. Nietzsche describes the sovereign subject turned specifically against a bodily instinct that is *life itself*: "man has evolved that queasy

stomach and coated tongue through which not only the joy and innocence of the animal but *life itself* has become repugnant to him—so that
he sometimes holds his nose in his own presence" (67; emphasis
added). This self-repugnance—what Nietzsche calls the "swamp" (67)
of shame—plays out the moral consequences of the Cartesian sacrifice
of the body for the mind. With the rise of reason and the internalization
of life as shame, the moral subject learns to "holds his nose" at his own
body: "impure begetting, disgusting means of nutrition in his mother's
womb, baseness of the matter out of which man evolves, hideous stink,
secretion of saliva, urine, and filth" (67).

In *Madness*, Foucault retells this story about the production of subjectivity as the internalization of man as shame. It is worth highlighting, in
this regard, that the period covered by *History of Madness*—the seventeenth and eighteenth centuries in Europe—corresponds precisely to
the period Nietzsche identifies as exhibiting the *ressentiment* that characterizes "bad conscience" (54). Further, in linking the rise of bourgeois
morality with reason, Foucault again follows Nietzsche as a genealogist
of morals. For Nietzsche, reason—"the whole somber thing called reflection" (62)—was purchased at a cost: the "blood and cruelty" that "lie
at the bottom of all 'good things'" (62). And reason corresponds, both
historically and conceptually, to "that other 'somber thing,' the consciousness of guilt, the 'bad conscience'" (62).

The establishment of "bad conscience" in the Age of Reason corresponds to what Foucault calls a bourgeois order. It is worth pausing
now over the word *bourgeois*, so popular in the French writings of the
1950s and sixties but used less and less since that time. In a Nietzschean
context, Foucault's repeated use of the term *bourgeois* throughout *Madness* can be understood as a way to identify the historical shift that Nietzsche critiques as the rise of the sovereign moral subject. In the context
of the Marxist Freudianism that dominated French intellectual life in
the fiftiess and sixties, Foucault's choice of the term *bourgeois* would
seem to align him with those who used Reich and Marcuse to reject
what was viewed as the capitalist "bourgeois" repression of the libido.
Once unleashed, this repressed libido would destroy the capitalist bour-
geoisie. But, if we read *Madness* through a Nietzschean lens, we can interpret *bourgeois* from the historical perspective that Nietzsche offers. In
that sense, *bourgeois* in Foucault points to the historical development of
the "city of morals" (74) and the rise of the private sphere as the privileged site for the production of moral norms. In other words, *bourgeois*
in *Madness* can be read to mean "family" in this historical and juridical

sense and can thus be directly linked to what today we might call the ethico-moral policing mechanisms of "family values."

From that perspective, in *Madness* the rise of the "city of morals" (*M* 74) corresponds to what Nietzsche describes as "that change which occurred when [man] found himself finally enclosed within the walls of society."[47] With that change, normalization occurs: men become "necessary, uniform, like among like, regular, and consequently calculable" (59). This constitutes what Nietzsche calls the "morality of mores" and the "social straitjacket" of the "sovereign individual" (59). For Foucault, the process of normalization that grounds the rise of the sovereign individual constitutes the victory of the moral family. In European historical terms, this corresponds to the rise of Enlightenment thinking and the defeat of the monarchy in the French Revolution. With the Revolution, the family takes over the governing function of the despotic sovereign—Nietzsche's blond beast—to create a system of internalized norms governed by the juridical authority of Foucault's bourgeois family. And although the family tribunals of the revolutionary period will not last long as institutions, the moral authority of the family will remain. That moral authority constitutes the foundation of social contract theory (whose deceptive "sentimentalism" Nietzsche decries); for Foucault, the juridical family gives the unwritten law the status of nature and private man the status of judge (*M* 447). This internalization of violence as self-policing produces norms enforced not with the external methods of execution and torture but, rather, with the more effective private, internal weapons of "family values": scandal, guilt, and shame.[48]

History of Madness repeats, over and over, this Nietzschean story about the birth of values in *ressentiment* (*M* 36) and the establishment of morality as "bad conscience." Foucault's historical narrative is also a philosophical story about the movement of thinking and how, together, history and thinking internalize "man" as a subject with a soul. In this sense Foucault's histoire is, like the ship of fools, both imaginary and real, both conceptual or generalizable and historically specific. Again Deleuze reminds us: "That everything is always said in every age is perhaps Foucault's greatest historical principle: behind every curtain there is nothing to see, but it was all the more important each time to describe the curtain, or the base, since there was nothing either behind or beneath it."[49] The Deleuzian "curtain" in *History of Madness* is the split within reason upon which rationalism is founded. That split generates a story—the curtain—which masks nonexistence: the "mad" idea that we're all just fools in a ship navigating toward a void, toward the fact

that "there is nothing to see." Thus Foucault "starts" at the place of the
snag in the curtain—the Cartesian moment of philosophical rupture—
where the wandering "bad" instincts of the ship of fools are suddenly
confined, as "bad conscience," within the walls of the hospital.

The Cartesian cogito and the great confinement are not the only "half-
real, half-imaginary" (*M* 11) doubling events Foucault could offer to
launch his Nietzschean story. Nor is the snag—the historic shift from
ship of fools to hospital—the "origin" of reason itself. For indeed, reason's story about itself—what we call philosophy—is also a curtain and
therefore both self-generating and infinitely doubled. It can have no origin in its impure other, the "unreason" that snags it from within, like a
snag within the snag. As Nietzsche reminds us in his opening to *Daybreak*: "All things that live long are gradually so saturated with reason
that their origin in unreason thereby becomes improbable."[50] Foucault's
snag—a moment in history where reason reveals its own unreason and
thereby attempts to excise that impurity from itself—leads him to un-
tangle some of the threads that form the fabric of rationalism's bourgeois order. In this way, he demonstrates how reason and the state work
together to produce moral conscience as a psychic inside. And again,
like all Foucault's histories, this story of madness is ultimately a history
of the present; the description of the curtain is a description of ourselves: "what was once the visible fortress of social order is *now* the
castle of *our* own conscience [*conscience*]" (*M* 11/*F* 22; translation modified, emphasis added).[51]

Significantly, Foucault's untangling of this particular historical snag
is also, as Nietzsche and Deleuze remind us, a description of a figure for
thinking whose strands form the fabric of our ethical and political life.
Foucault, Deleuze writes, is not interested in "the environments of enclosure as such;"[52] hospitals are important less as historical phenomena
than as figures that "refer back to an extrinsic function, that of setting
apart and controlling."[53] To be sure, Deleuze's absolute distinction between "enclosure as such" and the function "of setting apart and controlling" seems a bit overstated. Indeed, Foucault's antiprison activism
attests to his ongoing concern about "environments of enclosure as
such."[54] Nonetheless, Deleuze's insistence on the movement of exclusion—what Irigaray would call a process of othering—helps us to see
more clearly the Nietzschean dimension of Foucault's critique of a form
of power that, in "setting apart and controlling," also produces moral
and immoral subjects. Nietzsche's critique of moral systems and of
those who self-righteously preach morality forms an important part of

the philosophical logic that drives Foucault's story of madness. Nietzsche helps to explain why Foucault describes the rationalist management of madness as a transmutation of figures—from the ship of fools to the hospital—with a specifically ethical meaning: the Renaissance mad other who embodies the cultural "presence of imaginary transcendences" (M 72) becomes, in the Age of Reason, the bad other perceived through a grid of bourgeois moral condemnation. Finally, the specificity of confinement as an internalizing act of repression and production constitutes a crucial link between the Nietzschean critique of "bad conscience" and the Foucauldian challenge to an illusion of psychic depth that, as I argue in the following chapter, underpins the psychoanalytic conception of sexual subjectivity.

Becoming Anonymous

How does my insistence on Foucault's Nietzschean critique of morality contribute to this book's project to rethink queer theory in light of sexuality in *History of Madness*? In chapter 1, I demonstrated how sexuality is divided, after Descartes, across the line that separates reason from unreason, confining sexual deviants, as "mad," within the space of the hospital. In this chapter, I have used Deleuze and Nietzsche to interpret that sexual division not only as a political gesture of moral exclusion but also as an arresting of the movement of thinking toward its limit—a movement Foucault will later call freedom[55]—through the production of psychic interiority. Foucault's Nietzschean critique of "the castle of our own conscience" (M 11; translation modified) is also, then, a critique of any notion of sexual interiority—simultaneously scientific and moral—that would attempt to explain, eradicate, or cure "abnormal" erotic desires, acts, or relations. Any such attempt not only repeats the founding violence of morality itself but also replaces the cause (a founding act of violence) with its effect: a sexual subject with a shame-ridden psyche hidden "inside." Thus constructing "lightning" as the "subject" of an "action" (lightning's "flash") or "the doer" as the "fiction added to the deed,"[56] the Age of Reason produces an illusion of sexual subjectivity as the manifestation of "inner" drives.

Having clarified how *Madness* uses Nietzsche to expose the costs of modern subjectivity within a rationalist and moral logic, let me now return, within the context of queer theory, to the problem of subjectivation I introduced in the opening of this chapter. Performativity is the name queer theory gives to a conception of subjectivity that, along Nietzschean lines, questions the givenness of a coherent subject endowed with interiority. In terms that are useful for their resonance with the Foucauldian critique of Descartes, Vikki Bell describes the logic of performativity as part of a broader philosophical rebellion against the Cartesian cogito:

> The notion of performativity refuses to tie the fact that "there is thinking" to identity or ontology . . . Contra Descartes, "thinking" is only confirmation that an individual exists within a discursive world; indeed, no certainty arises from the fact of thinking. Rather, the state of doubt from which Descartes began his *Meditations* continues, since "the subject," in this rendering, is understood as co-extensive with his or her outside. There is no resolution of doubt, no passage into certainty, because the subject is itself the locus of effects of his or her surroundings. . . . This coextensivity is a radical critique of any originary notion of interiority.[57]

Like Foucault in his critique of the cogito, Bell questions the Cartesian "resolution" of systematic doubt that would produce a subject so certain of his own rationality that the very possibility of madness is rejected altogether. Drawing on the Deleuzian concept of coextensivity, Bell links the questioning of Cartesian reason to a Nietzschean critique of interiority as the "internalization of man" by highlighting the subject's existence "within a discursive world" and its status as "the locus of effects of his or her surroundings."[58] Bell's binding of performativity to a philosophical critique of rationalist interiority would seem to suggest, then, that Foucauldian and queer conceptions of subjectivity are aligned.

But from the Nietzschean-Deleuzian perspective I've developed in my reading of *Madness*, Foucauldian subjectivation and queer performativity actually become very different theoretical animals. The difference between them lies in the distinctive conceptions of coextensivity each implicitly espouses. Here my earlier discussions of Deleuzian coextensivity (in the introduction) and the Deleuzian fold (in this chapter) become useful again. Like the fold, coextensivity exposes the inseparability of the inside and the outside, not only in an abstracted description of thinking the limit but also in the concretized fiction of the subject who is the agent of that thinking. Importantly, however, in its Deleuzian conception, coextensivity is not simply the exposure of the subject's coincidence with the discursive or sociological environment that would contain her: the subject's *surroundings* or *discursive world,* to use Bell's terms. Although Deleuzian terms are still at play in performative conceptions of the subject, that subject is "discharged" of all interiority—her feelings and emotions, her libido, her psyche, her soul—only to the extent that her social and discursive surroundings produce her as a "locus of effects."[59] Deleuzian coextensivity goes beyond such understandings of subjectivity as sociologically and linguistically constructed to include subjectivation as a function of thinking.

Along these lines, in *History of Madness* Foucault's Nietzschean rejection of the cogito is more than a replacement of rationalist certainty with a healthy skepticism characterized by what would still be a kind of Cartesian doubt forever in search of a reason that would ground morality. In the context of *Madness*, if the coextensive subject never passes into certainty, it is not only because she is the effect of her surroundings, although, as a thinker of the specific, Foucault would not dispute this. But as a thinker of thinking (and not a sociologist), Foucault is interested in certainty and doubt less as indicators of the subject's social construction than as functions of the rationalist structures through which thinking itself has been defined to underwrite moral norms. Deleuze helps us to see that, with *Madness*, Foucault rethinks the subject in her coextension not only with her social, historical, and discursive environment but also, ultimately, with the act of thinking itself. Cartesian certainty, reason's goal, arrests the movement of thinking toward its limit; that movement is the freedom of thinking Deleuze uncovers in the Foucauldian image of the ship of fools as an "easily errant existence" (*M* 9/*F* 19; translation modified). But this movement toward the limit—the coextensive "outside" of thinking—also raises the specter of madness which, as I have shown, is both the failure of thinking "inside" thought and the limit of thinking's self-contestatory movement: its condition of possibility as freedom. In her coextension with the thought of the outside, the "subject" is therefore a consequence of the limits of our capacity to think her.[60]

Those limits have been determined, in the modern age, by the historically specific exclusionary structures of reason. Thus, for Foucault, the uncertainty of thinking is even more radical than Bell suggests; "the fact that 'there is thinking'"[61] does *not* confirm "that an individual exists within a discursive world."[62] Indeed, at its outer limit, thinking is madness: the disappearance of the subject into nonexistence, into an "experience of the outside . . . in which no existence can take root."[63]

From a post-Nietzschean, positivist, post-death-of-God perspective, that limit as void we call madness or death is also what we call sexuality.

As Foucault reminds us in "Preface to Transgression" (1963), an essay on Bataille that bears strong traces of Nietzsche:

> What characterizes modern sexuality from Sade to Freud is not its having found the language of its logic or of its nature, but, rather, through the violence done by such languages, its having been "denatured"—cast into an empty zone in which it achieves whatever meager form is bestowed upon it by the establishment of its limits, and in which it points to nothing beyond itself, no prolongation, except the frenzy that disrupts it.[64]

Hardly a liberation or a movement of freedom, modern sexuality is a void arrested at its limit—just as madness was in the seventeenth century—through the violent, "denaturalizing" languages of logic and nature wielded by science. If earlier practices in the Christian world allowed for experiences of the void as eros—"experiences . . . without interruption or limit" that led to "a divine love"[65]—with the rise of reason in a world "without God"[66] those same experiences, called sexuality, confront their own limits as the "meager form" that is the limit of ourselves: "the limit of our consciousness [conscience][67] . . . the limit of the law . . . the limit of language."[68] Thus, Foucault writes, "sexuality is a fissure—not one that surrounds us as the basis of our isolation or individuality but one that marks the limit within us and designates us as a limit."[69] Sexuality's designation of "us as a limit" thus anticipates Foucault's argument in *Sexuality One*: the modern subject is a sexual subject.

This conception of modern madness-as-sexuality as the limit of ourselves places us, Foucault says, in "an uncomfortable region" (*M* xxvii). If contesting sexuality is to contest ourselves, it is difficult, if not impossible, to know how to practice this "contestation that effaces"[70]—this thinking without a subject, this flash without lightning. Indeed, that is the irony of what Foucault calls "the merciless language of non-madness" (*M* xxvii) we are forced to use to talk about madness and the contestation of our rational selves. But it is also, more hopefully, the ironic impossibility of that contestation as the limit of our thinking that forces us, ethically, toward an encounter—again and again, in "our confused vocation as apostles and interpreters" (*M* 537)—with that outer bound where thought changes, becoming "afloat, foreign, exterior to our interiority."[71] To undo the subject—thinking madness as the limit— is thus to transform sexuality into something other when, like language, it "arrives at its own edge."[72] So perhaps the sexual subject will find, in

"I know not which future culture" (*M* 548), "not a positivity that contradicts it but the void that will efface it,"⁷³ allowing it "to be free for a new beginning . . . that is also a rebeginning."⁷⁴

In his thinking about Foucault, Deleuze boldly attempts to think that which it is so difficult for us to think. The sexual subject of thinking is not really a subject at all, but, as Deleuze puts it, an event of subjectivation: "a personal or collective individuation."⁷⁵ So if the modern sexual subject is an individuation that, in our time, characterizes the event of thinking, to question the subject as Foucault does is to transgress the limits of a sexuality that defines our historical thinking. As I have argued, that transgression—and again I am quietly guided here by Foucault's "Preface to Transgression" and "The Thought of the Outside"— is not the mere reversal, or turning inside out, of cause and effect, of the subject and his surroundings. It is not the confrontation between A (an inside) and B (an outside) in order to reverse and sublate them into a happy synthesis. "To negate dialectically," Foucault writes, "brings what one negates into the troubled interiority of the mind."⁷⁶ Foucault's transgression of the limits of thinking is explicitly nondialectical: rather than participating in a black-and-white logic of reversal, the relationship of transgression and the limit "takes the form of a spiral [*en vrille*] that no simple infraction can bring to an end."⁷⁷ Thus for Foucault the thinking of the limit is not a linguistically ordered act of negation; it is not that which philosophy attempts to think by discursively opposing what came before; rather, it is a "sideways" encounter with a language that speaks but that philosophy does not know: "In a language stripped of dialectics [*dédialectisé*] . . . the philosopher . . . discovers that there is, *beside him* [*à côté de lui*], a language that speaks and of which he is not the master."⁷⁸ And that thing "beside him" is madness, deprived "at every moment not only of what it has just said, but of the very ability to speak."⁷⁹ Thus "historical time imposes silence on a thing that we can no longer apprehend, other than by addressing it as void, vanity, nothingness" (*M* xxxi). The thing "beside him" becomes "less than history" (*M* xxxi), and "it is that 'less than' that we must investigate" (*M* xxxi) in historical, Nietzschean terms.

Performativity, on the other hand, remains invested in the philosophical act of negation and, consequently, undoes gender but not the subject itself. Drawing on an "outside" that is sociological and linguistic, performativity relies on a dialectical logic of reversal and sublation, what Beauvoir calls in her description of Hegelian thinking the "negation of the negation by which the positive is re-established."⁸⁰ Specifically, with performativity, reversal constitutes the "negation of the nega-tion" where the primacy of *cause* is reversed as *effect* to re-establish "the *interiority* of our philosophical reflection and the *positivity* of our knowl-edge"[81] for a new and better version of the subject. The most famous, indeed founding example of this performative logic is Judith Butler's reversal of the sex/gender distinction in *Gender Trouble* (1990). Drawing on Nietzsche's genealogical critique of a search for origins, Butler dis-mantles the interiority of sexual identity—"the inner truth of female desire"[82]—by revealing the "*origin* and *cause*"[83] of those inner identities to be the "*effects* of institutions, practices, discourses with multiple and diffuse points of origin."[84] In this way the primacy of sex-as-nature over gender-as-culture is dismantled and reversed, and gender becomes the "discursive/cultural means" for the production of "sex *as* the prediscur-sive."[85] Performativity's dialectical reversal of cause and effect reestab-lishes "the positive" as parodic resignification, the final or sublated term where the subject is reconstituted as a positive force of subversion who will "trouble gender" as we know it.

To describe performativity as dialectical is not to diminish it or to deny its tremendous power. Reversing nature-culture causality and re-configuring subjectivity beyond that reversal is no small feat; it is, in-deed, a radical gesture, as performativity's ongoing use as a theoretical tool attests. Performativity's popularity also bears witness to the stub-bornness of dialectical habits of thinking, habits that Foucault's breezy "dedialectizing" promises fail to acknowledge. As Butler quips in *Artfo-rum*: "It's hard to be queer all the time. And besides, I *do* like Hegel."[86] Importantly, performativity offers a means for questioning the given-ness of our "innate" sexual and gendered identities; in that way it would appear to be aligned with Foucault's project, in both *Madness* and *Sexu-ality One*, to demystify the ruse of interiority. And, from that perspective, performativity is successful as a project to denaturalize sex: it "dis-charges" interiority by unfolding it toward its outside in a reversal of cause and effect. But because the "outside" remains linguistic and so-ciological— the "institutions, practices, discourses"[87] that "created" sex and gender—it differs from the "outside" as a transgression *of thinking* that characterizes Foucauldian *de*subjectivation. Further, performativi-ty's dialectical logic reinforces the binaristic interpretations of acts ver-sus identities I challenged in the previous chapter's reading of *Sexuality One*. Seeing, as we have, how performativity deploys an apparatus of cause-effect reversal and sublation, we can now see a similar logic at work in the pervasive acts-versus-identities readings of *Sexuality One*.

Performativity *needs* the acts-versus-identities opposition in order to reverse and parodically resignify sex and gender.

The difference of thinking that distinguishes queer performativity from Foucauldian desubjectivation is ultimately linked to the problem of ethics and morality which frames this chapter. Desubjectivation explicitly "dedialectizes" language (or at least tries to do so) not to denaturalize "innate" sexual identities, but to do away with the subject altogether. Here Nietzsche becomes important again. Performativity draws on a slice of Nietzsche—*Genealogy*'s description of "the popular mind"[88] that separates the doer from the deed—to ground its nature-culture, identity-acts reversals. But performativity does not specifically address precisely that dimension of Nietzschean interiority which constitutes the heart of Foucault's ethical critique of the emergence of "man": the internalization of morality as the "serious illness" that is the psyche or the soul. In its earliest articulations, performativity has little to say about ethics and morality; as a conception of subjectivity linked to self-referential, first-person speech acts,[89] it does not explicitly thematize the ethical problem of the subject in relation to an other. As a destabilizing concept, performativity's critique of morality could be said to be *implicit* in the parodic undoing of gender norms: if "queer" is "bad," performativity repeats the "queer" in order to dismantle its moral meanings. Again, we can see a dialectical logic at work here with regard to moral norms, where performativity reverses the queer and the bad in order to reconstitute the queer as good. The queer becomes something to be celebrated and claimed: an intellectual moniker, a social calling card, a political passport. But rather than submitting morality itself to the Nietzschean historical critique it requires, performativity replaces "bad" family values with "good" queer ones, thereby engaging in a process of remoralization. This becomes explicit in Butler's later explorations of sex and gender; in *Undoing Gender* (2004), performativity does not mean, as some readers of *Gender Trouble* had claimed, "producing a new future for genders that do not yet exist."[90] Rather, performativity comes to mean fitting the genders that already exist into new forms of legitimation "within law, within psychiatry, within social and literary theory."[91] And if Butler continues to speak up for "those who understand their gender and their desire to be nonnormative,"[92] she also admits to a "*normative* aspiration" that "has to do with the ability to live and breathe and move."[93]

To be sure, no one would aspire to that kind of freedom for sexual "abnormals" more than Foucault. Nonetheless, to rebind such aspirations to legitimating norms skirts the problems of rationalist moralism that Foucault, with Nietzsche's help, systematically unravels in *History of Madness. Madness* suggests that the goal of moral critique should not be the expansion of moral norms to include a greater diversity of marginalized subjects. Rather, a Nietzschean critique of moral interiority ultimately renegotiates subjectivity itself. As we have seen, the modern sexual subject—"an animal soul turned against itself"—is *"pregnant with a future"*[94] not in his expansion of the norms produced by that inward turn, but rather in the undoing of those norms. That normative undoing is his own undoing: "as if man were not a goal but only a way, an episode, a bridge, a great promise."[95] Thus the promise lies in forms of self-transformation we might imagine not as expansions of the self but as self-unravelings. That unraveling opens a space for the invention of new desubjectivations we cannot now imagine.

Perhaps the greatest symptom of performativity's reliance on a conception of subjectivity that leaves unaddressed the historical rise of a moral subject is queer theory's investment in the psyche. What this means, more concretely, is that performativity leaves untouched the historically conjoined emergence of "man" and morality as the interiorization of violence "imperiously demanded by Western consciousness."[96] From a Nietzschean perspective, the subject *is* his moral values: "the man of *ressentiment*" whose "soul *squints*"[97] with the ingested cruelties of bad conscience. Those ingested cruelties gather as morality in the swamp of shame. And if, in our lived experience, queer subjects have been especially aware of the toxicity of that moral environment, it is not at all clear that performativity alone gets us out of the swamp that is morality. Yes, performativity has turned us "inside out," parodically unfolding our interiority as "sex." But as Butler puts it in "Imitation and Gender Insubordination": "to dispute the psyche as *inner depth*"—to performatively undo "sex"—"is not to refuse the psyche altogether."[98] This queer refusal to critique the psyche is particularly relevant to the psyche-driven "antisocial" thesis; in the work of Leo Bersani and Lee Edelman in particular, queer subjectivity performatively turns morality inside out by embracing and sublimating the psyche's "death drive" as shame.[99] In its embrace of figures of shame-driven finitude—the homosexual "sinthome" (Edelman) or the rectum-as-grave (Bersani)—antisocial performativity would appear to do away with the subject altogether. But what it takes away with one hand it gives back with the other, as it continues to assume the existence of a psyche as container of the subject's death. Precisely because queer performativity cannot let go of the "psyche" or "soul" which constitutes the rationalist modern subject, the moral violence of the swamp remains—even, and especially, in morality's dialectical negation as a resistance to sociality or a queer death drive. Indeed, from a Nietzschean perspective, the death drive of the queer antisocial thesis epitomizes the self-hating violence of the moral "I": "wild, free, prowling man turned backward against man himself."[100] In dialectical terms, negation alone does not undo the "I." As Beauvoir puts it pithily with regard to surrealism: "every assassination of painting is still a painting."[101] Every assassination of morality is still a morality.

In both its expansive legitimating aspiration and its seeming antithesis as antisociality, queer performativity dialectically unravels the subject's interiority as "sex," but leaves intact the internalizing violence that produces the moral soul. From a Foucauldian perspective, performativity fails to historicize its critique of the subject, thus leaving the historical problem of the normative internalization of violence unaddressed. As an approach to subjectivity that questions the subject's coherence within timeless social and linguistic structures, performativity's foundations in structuralist linguistics become clear. Whether in its Lévi-Straussian cultural version or its Lacanian psychoanalytic mode, structural linguistics freezes the subject within the atemporal, binary structures—nature/culture, signifier/signified, metaphor/metonymy— that allow us to rethink her from an antihumanist perspective. Not incidentally, Foucault admits in interviews to the importance of structuralism for his own antihumanist project. But this alone does not make him a structuralist. Indeed, that which differentiates Foucault from structuralism—his attention to thinking as a function of history— points precisely to that which differentiates Foucauldian desubjectivation from queer performativity.

In its inattention to the historical emergence of the moral subject, performativity inherits the ahistoricism of structural linguistics. As a field that describes itself as a science of language, structural linguistics bears many of the features of the positivist social sciences Foucault denounces over the course of *Madness* in his description of the rise of the sciences of the psyche. Unlike performativity, Foucauldian desubjectivation is explicitly historical, as this chapter's attention to Nietzsche and Deleuze makes clear. This differentiates Foucauldian desubjectivation from performativity both conceptually and methodologically.

Conceptually, to think subjectivation historically is to include within the concept far more than a subject conceived as sociological or as a grammatical position within a linguistic order. "Unlike those who are labeled 'structuralists,'" Foucault says in 1967, "I'm not really interested in the formal possibilities offered by a system such as language [*la langue*]."[102] For Foucault, as for Deleuze, subjectivation includes more than social or linguistic construction. Indeed, it includes more than the subject itself:

> Subjectivation as a process is a personal or collective individuation. . . . There are subject-type individuations ("that's you . . . ," "that's me . . . "), but there are also event-type individuations where there's no subject: a wind, an atmosphere, a time of the day, a battle. . . . One cannot assume that a life, or a work of art, is individuated as a subject; quite the reverse. Take Foucault himself: you weren't aware of him as a person exactly. Even in trivial situations, say when he came into a room, it was more like a changed atmosphere, a sort of event, an electric or magnetic field.[103]

What are the ethical implications of this difference between queer performativity and Foucauldian desubjectivation? What would it mean, in ethical terms, to think of the queer subject as an atmosphere? To begin, it would move the subject away from himself (or his dialectical negation) toward the place of anonymity that is the promise of the subject's undoing. This promise of anonymity is, again, a historical problem: "In the past, the problem for the one who wrote was to pull himself out of the anonymity of all; in our time, it is to erase one's own name, to come to lodge one's voice in that great anonymous murmur of discourses which are pronounced."[104] That move toward anonymity—the disappearance of the subject—constitutes for Foucault a move away from rationalist judgment toward the coextensive multiplication of forms of existence. As the anonymous speaker puts it in the "Masked Philosopher," an oft-cited 1980 "Foucault" interview published in *Le Monde*:

> I can't help but dream about a kind of criticism that would try not to judge but to bring an oeuvre, a book, a sentence, an idea to life; it would light fires, watch the grass grow, listen to the wind, and catch the sea foam in the breeze and scatter it. It would multiply not judgments but signs of existence; it would summon them, drag them from their sleep. Perhaps it would invent them sometimes—all the better. All the better . . . It would bear the lightning of possible storms.[105]

The ethical implications of such anonymity—the subject's transformation into an atmosphere or storm—can also be highlighted in methodological terms. One of the crucial differences between Foucault and the structuralists to whom he is often falsely compared is his attention to the archive. If Foucault's use of the archive upsets many historians, it is also what makes him a unique philosopher. Foucault is not only, conceptually speaking, a thinker of the limit but also a philosopher whose method entailed immersing himself in the material scraps, both celebrated and forgotten, that allowed him to hear and think the past, ethically and concretely. That immersion began, significantly, with *History of Madness*; Foucault's turn to the archive in the late 1950s with the writing of *Madness* not only differentiates him from his structuralist and budding poststructuralist contemporaries but also distinguishes the Foucault of the time of *Madness* from an earlier Foucault who had not yet engaged the subject as a specifically historical question. In ethical terms, Foucault's life-long attention to "the accumulated existence of discourses"[106] that is the archive—his commitment to the *petits fous* who existed in the past, exist today, and might exist in the future—points to a distinctively Foucauldian perspective on alterity that distinguishes him as an ethical thinker. For Foucault, the problem of the other is approached through the archive, in "the fact that speaking happened" (*des paroles ont eu lieu*) as events that "left traces behind them."[107] We might name that approach, embodied in the archival method, as a specifically Foucauldian kind of curiosity—not the objectifying curiosity of the scientist, but a habit of thinking Foucault describes as "the care one takes of what exists and what might exist."[108] As an ethical approach to alterity, this curiosity as care signals a willingness to be undone by another— even, and especially, by the other "beside him" who cannot be heard in the terms we know. This is not the historian's archive in the traditional sense. If history as a discipline is "the final refuge of the dialectical order,"[109] Foucault's dedialectizing approach to the archive will not yield a sublated truth about the past. Rather, Foucault's archive desubjectivates the knower. It is an archive that undoes, nondialectically, the researcher or the thinker as a bearer of truth: an archive that demands to be lent an ear, however impossible that hearing might be.

As an ethical model, this archival and conceptual undoing of the subject I'm calling desubjectivation is not only promising but deeply unsettling. Its face as the *petit fou* is not simply an other to be laughed at or cozied up to, but the terrifying disintegration of the face in madness: Nietzsche's lifeless eyes, his corpselike body. For it is one thing to celebrate, as we are wont to do, our own undoing by the ethical other. It is quite another to confront the lived experience of subjective undoing that madness names. To lose oneself completely in an absolute exile from one's culture and one's means of communication—to become "illegible," as Butler puts it in *Undoing Gender*—is neither freeing nor politically subversive. And yet, Foucault insists, we must confront it: this undoing of the subject that is reason's "other." Why must we confront it? Not to celebrate or romanticize all those examples of mad genius that Foucault names: Nerval, Van Gogh, Artaud, Hölderlin, Roussel, Nietzsche. To the extent that they dazzle us with their artistic flourish, and that we can celebrate them at all, *they are not mad*. When they "become" mad, we can no longer hear them. "Madness," Foucault writes in "Madness, the Absence of an Oeuvre," "neither demonstrates nor recounts the birth of an oeuvre . . . it designates the empty form from which such an oeuvre comes, i.e. the place from which it is unceasingly absent, where it will never be found because it has never been there" (*M* 548).

And how did those subjects "become" mad in the first place? That is precisely the historical question—the question of the subject—that *Madness* poses. As for the fact that "becoming" mad happens at all: that is what *Madness* attempts to grieve. But because, in its grief, *Madness* must rely on the rationalized forms of a given language—for grief, the form of the tragic—it both tries and fails to grieve. For even the tragic, for all its lyricism and poetic flight, requires the structures of reason that undergird the subject to make itself heard. As for the "others," they remain lost to tragedy and lost to history.

If *Madness* fails in its attempt to grieve that which has been lost to us, it distinguishes itself in naming that failure. Like the space that separates my first interlude about madness from this chapter's philosophical analysis of mad subjectivity, what *Madness* tells us about the actual disappearance of the subject can only be read between the lines, in that space of impasse that cannot be heard or read. Thus *History of Madness* ends with the image of the subject's disappearance in the spectacle of Nietzsche's madness. "Madness, the Absence of a Work" drives home the point that to transgress the "outside" where thought crumbles at the limit of thinking is not to parodically resignify conventional meanings, but, tragically, to disappear altogether "accompanied by a dreadful attendant."[110] Ironically, we only see that disappearance in the spectacle of madness's linguistic, narrative, tragic objectification: Nietzsche performing for his friends.

If *Madness* is marked by tragic grief, performativity's appearance was scaled, from the start, with a promise of political agency in the hyperbolic redeployment of gender norms that constitute the subject. With performativity, the subject is not undone but rebelliously remade: she is a joker, a trickster, a sassy artist who operates in the camp mode of ironic subversion. Foucault, of course, is a trickster too and, as such, no stranger to irony or the sassiness of camp, as we can see especially in the 1972 preface to *History of Madness* or throughout the pages of *Sexuality One*. But, particularly in its Nietzschean dimension, *Madness*'s rebellious irony cannot be dissociated from its recurring, unmistakably tragic theme and imagery. *Madness*'s distinctively lyrical style, its play with the familiar tragic imagery of light and dark, or its repeated evocation of romantic figures such as Nerval and Van Gogh, all signal the book's tragic dimensions. The tragic is also a pervasive theme inextricably linked to Foucault's philosophical preoccupations. As Foucault writes in the 1961 preface, with the age-old opposition between reason and unreason dialectical thinking confronts its rupture "with the revelation, at the doors of time, of a tragic structure" (*M* xxix). Further, it is Nietzsche who teaches us that the experience of madness "knots the tragic to the dialectic of history in the very refusal of tragedy by history" (*M* xxx): "these limit-experiences of the Western world" explode, at their center, "the tragic itself" (*M* xxx). Throughout *History of Madness*, Foucault is not only laughing at philosophical reason and its inflated subject; he is also grieving the loss of the other on whose back that subject is built.

So why must we confront the undoing of the subject that is reason's other? We must confront it for what it can tell us about a form of contestation that negotiates an opposition between tragedy and irony—grief and laughter, the sadness of acceptance and the exuberance of rebellion—to become a kind of resistance that is neither acceptance nor rebellion. It is not based on the reversal as negation of the dialectic. It is a nondialectical, or dedialectizing transgression of the limits of thinking. To "transgress" those limits of thinking itself—to put the subject "to death" or to become "mad"—is not, as Foucault explains in his essay on Bataille, "to deny existences or values"[111] in a gesture of moral and dialectical negation. Rather, it is to practice "this philosophy of nonpositive affirmation"[112] that is the experience of the limit. The experience of the limit is not its crossing but its illumination by thought as in a flash of lightning: this is what Foucault means by *transgression*. And this transgression-as-limit, Foucault says, makes possible what Blanchot calls contestation, a form of resistance to what is, where every value is brought back to its limits. And, brought back to its limits, each value reveals the limits of a thinking that constitutes the limit of ourselves. It is a long road from that contestation of limits to the freedom Foucault associates with self-undoing in *Sexuality Two* and *Three*. But, however long the road may be, contestation is a place to start. Contestation can produce what Foucault described toward the end of his life as "kinds of virtual fracture which open up the space of freedom understood as a space of concrete freedom, that is, of possible transformation."[113]

Starting yet again down that long road of contestation, let me end this chapter by recalling Foucault's haunting 1984 question about sexuality as an experience: why have we made sexuality into a moral experience? A part of an answer emerged in chapter 1. There we saw the repudiation of erotic love in the Cartesian splitting of the mind from the body and the imprisonment of eros in the great confinement. Here, in chapter 2, another piece of an answer comes to the surface. Sexuality becomes a moral experience because the repudiation and imprisonment of eros involves its reduction, as sexuality, to a form of psychic interiority. Sexuality attaches itself to morality through that violent Nietzschean process by which the erotic is reduced to an inner psyche as a swamp of killing shame.

Foucauldian desubjectivation raises, again, the question of eros and the subject as it negotiates the fold of inside and outside, reason and unreason, life and death. Conceived as such, desubjectivation thus names a reclaiming of erotic experience as a movement whose condition of possibility is freedom: a wind, an atmosphere, a time of day, a storm, an anonymous "inside which is merely the fold of the outside, as if the ship were a folding of the sea."[114] This picture of eros as a back-and-forth movement across the illuminated fold highlights the ambiguity of the erotic other as both thinking and feeling, act and actor, mind and body, reason and unreason, the subject and something other than a subject: "a changed atmosphere, a sort of event, an electric or magnetic field"[115] or perhaps, as the "masked philosopher" puts it, the Nietzschean "lightning of possible storms."[116] As a sensibility and a voice, eros emerges as a stuttering, suffocated, lyrical speaking: a muted call that we can't quite hear from our place in the prison of the modern psyche. At the same time, as an ethical force of desubjectivating rupture, eros lights fires and blasts open the door to thinking's "outside." In that opening lies the promise of a contestation that would summon unknown existences, drag them from their sleep, or even—all the better—invent them.

Second Interlude

WET DREAMS

Unless perhaps I think that I am like some of those mad people whose brains are so impaired by the strong vapour of black bile that they confidently claim to be kings when they are paupers, that they are dressed up in purple when they are naked, that they have an earthenware head, or that they are a totally hollowed-out shell or are made of glass. But those people are insane, and I would seem to be equally insane if I followed their example in any way.

—René Descartes, 1641

I've been trying to understand—really understand—what Foucauldian desubjectivation means, not a deadening assujettissement, but a life-affirming self-undoing Deleuze describes as becoming-other: becoming wind, atmosphere, lightning, storm. It sounds like psychosis to me. And isn't being psychotic different, after all, than being queer? Isn't there a difference between losing your mind and losing your sexed identity? Of course there is. That's the point of my ongoing comparison between desubjectivation and performativity, Foucault and Butler. People who call themselves queer generally still have their wits about them. And certainly it was possible to be both queer and sane even before 1973, the moment homosexuality was removed from the *DSM III*, a diagnostic manual which was, and still is, a list of all the ways people lose their minds. Surely there's more to it than the diagnosis, however brutalizing its uses might be.

From a historical perspective, the fabrication of categories of queer mental illness is hardly a thing of the past. After all, Gender Identity Disorders were added to the list, as Sedgwick points out, precisely at the moment homosexuality was removed. And if we look, simultaneously, at the evolution of queer theory as a field, we also find that the category of transgender has, to a large extent, as Robyn Wiegman suggests, displaced homosexuality as a truly queer topic of study. Maybe being on the list means more for queerness than we would like to admit.

To be sure, these things are not simple. We have to consider the complicated relationship between the list (*savoir*) and what Foucault calls institutions (*pouvoir*)—including anything from therapeutic practices to surgical interventions to mental hospitals to pharmaceutical treatments. If I'm queer (*savoir*), will I see a shrink, check into a hospital, take a pill, have top or bottom surgery (*pouvoir*)? Foucault points out in *Birth of the Clinic* that the medical technology of surgery constituted the body as "having insides" to be seen, diagnosed, and cured (*pouvoir-savoir*). Doesn't that perception of my body's insides and outsides affect how I think about what's going on inside my head? And if I'm "out" of my mind, the need to get back "in" seems irrefutable. It's the gray area condition of being queer (LGBTQQI—yet another kind of diagnostic listing) that trips us up, makes us hesitate, causes us to tentatively disagree with one another—should she take a pill, see a doctor, have top surgery? Psychosis, by contrast, doesn't give us pause. With the exception of a few antipsychiatry holdouts, we all readily agree it should be treated through medical intervention. Why is that?

Foucault asks the question: why is that? It's a difficult, disturbing, uncomfortable question. It makes people angry. Accusations start to fly: he's romanticizing madness. Madness is terrifying. Madness is suffering. Madness is real.

But if losing yourself completely is what it means to be stark raving mad—to think you're made of glass or have an earthenware head, as Descartes would put it—that is what desubjectivation as becoming-other means. A horrifying proposition for most of us and especially for those, like me, who have witnessed it in loved ones or have ourselves wandered over the edges of what looks like a very dark forest. But is the thing we fear actually out there or right here, in the self-shaming spectacle of our all-too-human faces? Do we fear becoming-other or becoming-more-human? Foucault dreams a world where entering the woods wouldn't be terrifying because the "human" and its "others" would have no meaning. In Foucault's wet dream, we all will have lost ourselves, becoming-forest: "we that were wood when that a wide wood was."[1] Emerging out of another past that no longer bears the imprint of the human, Foucault's future will hold neither madness—the other of the human—nor the othering selfhoods that prop themselves up, *as* human, by excluding the possibility of their own madness.

Here's a confession: I don't really know what desubjectivation as becoming-other means, *except* as a way to name madness. Maybe that's the point: the circuit that started with thinking—"I'm trying to really understand what it means"—and ends here with its limit—"I don't really know what it means"—is a thinking circuit attached to a subject. I in my knowing and confession of not-knowing become hypervisible as a thinking cogito. So, as much as I might want to claim otherwise, I *am* Descartes and I *have* rejected the possibility that I could be a shard of glass—or, for that matter, a wind, an atmosphere, a storm, a bolt of lightning, or a tree. (Unlike Deleuze, Foucault never talks about wanting to become a machine: a city, a garbage truck, or a microscope. His metaphors are all organic. As human-made objects, machines reek of the human.)

Janisse Ray writes, after witnessing severe mental illness in her grandfather and father that led to their hospitalization in Milledgeville, Georgia: "I search for vital knowledge of the land that my father could not teach me, as he was not taught, and guidance to know and honor it, as he was not guided, as if this will shield me from the errancies of the mind, or bring me back from that dark territory should I happen to wander there. I search as if there were a peace to be found."[2]

Madness is the absence of self, and knowledge is the sinecure of self-presence. Still, Ray admits to the *as if* quality of her search for peace through the cogito's honey-gathering activities. There's something illusory about our attempts to shield ourselves from the errancies of the mind. Those errancies are, after all, a kind of thinking. From the perspective of the Renaissance ship of fools, an errant existence doesn't have to be a source of fear. Sometimes thinking's edges look less like a dark forest and more like a glittering, folding sea or the spangled flight of astral bodies. Kay Jamison writes about losing something precious— a meteor shower or the great whirling fireworks of a Catherine wheel are images she uses.[3] She grieves its loss in the daily, repeated pharmaceutical cure of her bipolar disorder. And Janisse Ray, for all her misgivings, paints a mad father who is grateful for his madness. She cites a letter written by him thirty years after his nervous breakdown: "Mental illness, or nervous breakdown as some call it, is nothing to be afraid of. . . . I had what people call mental illness. I call it one of the greatest experiences of my life. I would not erase it from my past even if I could. I would not sell it for a million dollars. Its value cannot be measured."[4]

His letter is hard to take in. I hear myself saying: he must still be crazy to say something like that. Wanting his madness—not wanting to sell it for a million dollars—makes him different from most of us. We who cling to the cogito.

The cogito famously rejects madness. Descartes doesn't want it, and neither do I. Foucault touches that place of not-wanting: madness is the loss he grieves and the absence whose future he dreams. The moment of its rejection in the Cartesian *Meditations* is the seed out of which *History of Madness* sprouts. Still, Foucault only *dreams* of becoming-other, and dreaming is a different matter than madness. Descartes asks: "How often does the nocturnal quietness convince me of familiar things, for example, that I am here, dressed in my gown, sitting by the fire, when I am really undressed and asleep in my bed?"[5] Descartes, like most of us, doesn't reject dreams: they are, after all, a temporary, familiar, gentle kind of errancy. Our dreaming won't get us thrown into an asylum.

But if Descartes had dreams, were they ever wet ones? (You can't help but notice that he's "undressed" in his bed: a queer detail, especially coming from the father of modern rationalism.) Did Descartes have orgasms? Not a usual philosophical preoccupation, orgasm is a topic he fails to consider in his meditations on the self. But orgasm has something to do with what I've been doing throughout this book: hitching madness to sexuality, associating losing our minds with becoming queer.

In *Madness*, Foucault brushes up against orgasm in his discussion of Charcot and hysterical paroxysm, but never evokes it directly. He will, of course, famously talk about death-defying superorgasmic pleasures later in his life—pleasures so huge they transport him (supposedly) *beyond* orgasm, genitalia, sexuality, and selfhood. These are Foucault's heterotopias—little laboratories of pleasure where becoming-other can be tried out for a while, in ways that are more intense, more sustained, more shared perhaps, than dreaming or orgasms of the everyday variety.[6] Theorists of sexual subjection's "escape route" through "bodies and pleasures"—Halperin comes to mind (*Saint Foucault*)—have seized on that better-than-orgasmic heterotopia as the land of queer milk and honey.[7]

In *Madness*, Foucault's omission of the simple mind-blowing pleasure of everyday orgasm may simply be a function of the Cartesian blueprint from which he proceeds: "I am a thinking, non-extended thing," Descartes says, "distinct from my body."[8] In cutting off the body from the *res cogitans*, Descartes will not consider orgasms as possible forms of doubt, despite their obvious mind-bending qualities. But surely he had them, just like dreams? Where might orgasm fit into his schema? Isn't orgasm—*la petite mort*—a kind of momentary madness, a bit like dreaming?

We queer Cartesians love our orgasms because they allow us to flirt with those errancies of the mind that we touch, ever so gently, in *la petite mort*. Still, I've always been struck that although people tune in to the *mort* part of the metaphor, it's the *petite* dimension of it that's important. The *petite* makes it liveable, pleasurable, repeatable. We may fantasize about an endless orgasm—or even a fifteen-minute one. (My friend Zig once told a story about a kind of pig that can *come*—in a single orgasm—*for fifteen minutes straight*. I don't know if it's true, but we all envied the pig when we heard the story.) We toy with the idea of a *grande mort*, but we couldn't really live it. Why is that? Is that unliveability of total orgasm—the *grande mort* of real madness—purely a function of the split between reason and unreason? What *did* Descartes think about orgasm? Is it the same for him as believing you're earthenware, a shell, or glass? Probably not. He would no doubt put orgasm into the category of dreams—something from which you quickly recover to take up the continuity of your *self* in a *life* that is clearly *not* an orgasm and *not* a dream.

Or is it?

I may never know what becoming-other means. But sometimes I feel it, becoming-storm, when a summer sky opens and I'm no longer myself—just a woods' wet rhythm, a mounting beat of rain over tin.

3 / Unraveling the Queer Psyche

Children, you really shouldn't complain that you are not orphans,
that you always rediscover in your innermost selves your Object-
Mother or the sovereign sign of your Father: it is through them that
you gain access to desire.

—Michel Foucault, 1976

Queer Children

Toward the middle of *Sexuality One,* Foucault strikes the pose of Charcot, the paradigmatic analyst-doctor of the sexuality-saturated nineteenth century. In that pose, Foucault ironizes a doctor's response to the bourgeois anxieties that emerge when the public medicalization of private sexual secrets threatens to break up the family with its moral values. As Charcot, he offers advice that is reassuring to parents and children alike. "Parents," he says, "do not be afraid to bring your children to analysis: it will teach them that in any case it is you whom they love."[1] Children, for their part, require a different message. The doctor knows that, by design, rebellious children will seek to extricate themselves from the family love their parents so desperately want to preserve. Such rebellions give shape to desire, the outward thrust that propels children into individuation. In breaking with the family and thereby rubbing out the parental imprint within, children thus might find themselves symbolically orphaned. But, in a surprising twist to this classic story about leaving home, Foucault tells the children they are mistaken: "you are not orphans," he says. Not only that, but "you really shouldn't complain that you are not orphans, that you always rediscover in your innermost selves your Object-Mother or the sovereign sign of your Father: it is through them that you gain access to desire."[2]

In a campy repetition of Foucault's ventriloquism,[3] we might reframe his reassurances to children as a rhetoric directed at today's queer theorists who imagine themselves, if not as orphans, then at least, in Janet Halley's words, as "prodigal sons and daughters."[4] Foucault-Charcot's expert advice casts an ironic shadow over a theoretical field dazzled by its own queer spin on a family that stands at the origin of Freudian psychoanalysis. For, when it stops spinning, queer Oedipus looks much like the old-fashioned model. Like their nineteenth-century forebears, today's psychoanalytic queer children are not orphans or prodigals; their sexual extravagances have failed to spin them out of the family orbit. Nor should they complain about that fact. For as Foucault insists, the prodigal queer desire they claim in their "innermost selves"[5] can only be accessed through a psychoanalytic return to the family they thought they had left behind. What looks like a break from a heteronormative structure is in fact a turn inward toward the indelible stamp of the conjugal couple: "your Object-Mother or the sovereign sign of your Father."[6]

This rare moment of direct address by Foucault at the center of *Sexuality One* serves as a theatrical set piece—an almost Irigarayan mimicry of Charcot and his patients at the Salpêtrière—to dramatize the ironies of a contemporary queer project no less invested in psychoanalysis than it is in Foucault. Foucault mimes the speech act of scientific authority through which psychoanalysis forces the secret of sexuality and, at the same time, reinstalls sexuality at the heart of the chaste moral family. From this perspective, Foucault's well-known archeology of psychoanalysis in *Sexuality One* comes to function as an ironic allegory of the psychic entanglements in which queer theory finds itself when it attempts to give flesh to a sexuality it is also trying to escape.

Against this mimetic backdrop, I offer a reading of a different psychoanalytic scene in Foucault: the emergence of the psyche in *History of Madness*. Moving from the spinning tableau of *Sexuality One* to *Madness*'s longer narrative form feels a bit like stepping off a merry-go-round. In contrast to *Sexuality One*'s highly condensed, self-ironizing structure, *Madness* slowly unspools a seven-hundred-page story that stretches from the Middle Ages to the twentieth century. In the sweep of its narrative unfolding, *Madness* dramatizes the historical dimension of the psyche's gradual emergence over time, binding the logic of its conception to the Cartesian division between reason and unreason in the seventeenth century and tracing its transmutations into the present. In this chapter, I attend to the detail of that centuries-long narrative unfolding to support my conviction that queer theory's coupling of Freud with Foucault needs to be contested.

Specifically, this chapter demonstrates precisely why queer psychoanalytic approaches to sexuality are fundamentally at odds with Foucault's archival, historical project to rethink the emergence of the modern subject. Queer theory's pervasive investment in a timeless psyche betrays the ahistoricism of performative conceptions of subjectivity. Specifically, much of queer theory attaches itself to the concept of the unconscious as a disruptive force within the psyche that exceeds consciousness and subjectivity itself. Tim Dean and Christopher Lane's description of "the constitutive resistance of the unconscious to all norms" in their introduction to *Homosexuality and Psychoanalysis* (2001) typifies a queer investment in the antiheteronormative disruptions of psychic life.[7] Such readings of the psyche don't ignore Foucault completely, but are based on an incomplete engagement with his work. Dean and Lane's assertion that "Foucault rarely wrote directly about psychoanalysis" (8) could only be made from a perspective on Foucault that ignores *Madness* completely.

Dean and Lane's brief consideration of Foucault in their introduction is useful in its function as another kind of set piece that can bring into relief the ways in which queer theory's singular investment in *Sexuality One* can lead us astray, especially with regard to Foucault's treatment of psychoanalysis. Dean and Lane's analysis begins, in typical fashion, with a reprise of the famous "acts versus identities" passage I examined in chapter 1. But they add a twist to the usual interpretation of the paragraph. Honing in on Foucault's ironic sentence about Westphal's "famous" article of 1870 and the role of medical science in the invention of homosexuality, Dean and Lane argue that, in "his reference to 'the psychological, psychiatric, medical category of homosexuality'" (9), Foucault "pointedly omits psychoanalysis from this process of invention" (9).

Those who know *Madness*, or even just Foucault's interviews on the subject of psychoanalysis, will find this to be an astonishing claim about Foucault. As just one of numerous counterexamples, in a 1977 interview of Foucault by a group of his Parisian psychoanalytic colleagues— or perhaps more accurately, their interrogation of him as their analysand—Foucault speaks about the nineteenth-century "formidable mechanism, a machinery of confession, within which in fact psychoanalysis and Freud figure as one of the episodes."[8] In the interview, Foucault goes on to explain his reasons for "playing that game"—for to him it was a game—of writing *Sexuality One*: "the mere fact that I've played that game [*j'ai joué ce jeu-là*]," he says, "*excludes* for me the possibility of Freud figuring as the radical break, on the basis of which everything else has to be rethought."[9] He continues in the same vein by elaborating on a "general apparatus" (dispositif) of scientific technologies "in which Freud will come to have his place."[10] Foucault could not be clearer: Freud does not represent for him a radical rupture from the dispositif of the nineteenth-century medicalization of the psyche.

Let me pause here briefly in my engagement with Dean and Lane's introduction to comment on the seemingly minor matter of my counterexample's translation into English. As with the other moments of translation I've evoked in this book, the detail of a French event's rendering into another language brings out questions about linguistic differences that are not unrelated to the peculiar role played by *Sexuality One* in queer theory. In characterizing *Sexuality One* as a game in the 1977 interview, Foucault points to ludic aspects of the book that are widely acknowledged by his French readers. His Anglophone readers, on the other hand, tend to miss *Sexuality One*'s playful qualities. That French-English interpretive gap is in part due to infelicitous translations of Foucault. And if every translation is an approximation, some renderings are more successful than others. The less-than-successful translations of Foucault miss not only differences of vocabulary but also a range of rhetorical locutions, grammatical arrangements, and stylistic forms of doubling such as alliteration. These features of Foucault's distinctive turns of phrase point to his penchant for exploiting language's capacity not only to construct meanings but also to fracture them. This is not simply a stylistic tic, but part and parcel of Foucault's commitment to thinking history anti-Historically and to practicing an anti-Philosophical philosophy. Translations of his work that miss his self-rupturing ironies will also miss important dimensions of those qualities that distinguish Foucault as a thinker.

A small example of such an infelicitous translation from the 1977 interview clarifies this point. The English approximation of the moment in the interview where, not insignificantly, Foucault describes *Sexuality One*'s "gaming" qualities not only effaces the word *game*, but also flattens the rhetorical and grammatical play of Foucault's original locution. The French original—"le seul fait que j'ai joué ce jeu-là" (the mere fact that I played that game)—is rendered in English as "the mere fact that I've adopted this course." Unlike the translation, Foucault's French phrase goes out of its way, semantically speaking, to underscore his playful approach to *Sexuality One*'s sexual topic, particularly in Foucault's reinforcement of the noun "*ce jeu-là* (that game) with the verb *jouer* (to play) in *j'ai joué* (I played). Less obviously but equally important, in the context of a discussion about the costs of modern sexual subjectivity, it is not far-fetched to read Foucault's self-reflective toying with a *jeu* (game) as a self-ironizing play with the homophonous *je* (I) of his own sexuality-saturated subjectivity. Indeed, the alliterative repetition of *j'ai, joué*, and *jeu* invites such an interpretation. But no such reading can emerge in the phrase's smooth but inaccurate English rendering, where both the word *game* and the self-reflective linguistic structures disappear. Correspondingly, any guidance the interview might offer for a reading of *Sexuality One* that would be attuned to its ironies and playful self-doublings is also diminished, if not lost entirely.

These kinds of linguistic and conceptual nuances are missing in Dean and Lane's analysis as well, although their misrepresentation of Foucault's thinking goes beyond the strictly linguistic problem of translation. In a typically Freudo-Foucauldian argument, their introduction to homosexuality's relation to psychoanalysis misreads Foucault, dehistoricizes the psyche, and disconnects knowledge from power, *savoir* from *pouvoir*. Their conception of psychoanalysis insists on imposing a radical separation between theory and practice, between seemingly timeless ideas or concepts and the medical institutions or practices that both precede and follow Freud, but that somehow, in their view, do not include him. Building on their general claim about a Freudian rupture with medical science, Dean and Lane attempt to explain why "*Foucault's crucial distinction between Freudian ideas and psychoanalytic institutions has remained obscure to his Anglophone audience*" (10; emphasis added). Most crucially, they support their argument by correcting, ironically enough, a previously mistranslated passage from *Sexuality One*, replacing Robert Hurley's 1978 English translation of *psychanalyse* as "psychiatry" with its more accurate translation as "psychoanalysis":

> And the strange position of [psychoanalysis] at the end of the nineteenth century would be hard to comprehend if one did not see the rupture it brought about in the great system of degenerescence: it resumed the project of a medical technology appropriate for dealing with the sexual instinct; but it sought to free it [*l'affranchir*] from its ties with heredity, and hence from eugenics and the various racisms. It is very well to look back from our vantage point and remark upon the normalizing impulse in Freud; one can go on to denounce the role played for many years by the psychoanalytic institu-

tion; but the fact remains that[11] in the great family of technologies of sex, which goes so far back into the history of the Christian West, of all those institutions that set out in the nineteenth century to medicalize sex, it was the one that, up to the decade of the forties, rigorously opposed the political and institutional effects of the perversion-heredity-degenerescence system.[12]

At first glance, Dean and Lane's interpretation of this passage as positing a psychoanalytic rupture with nineteenth-century positivism seems understandable. Indeed, Foucault even uses the word *rupture* in the first sentence and seems to be genuinely conceding a separation of psychoanalysis from the complex of heredity-degeneration-racism. However, Foucault is not, thereby, exonerating the normalizing effects of psychoanalysis or its connection to the perverse implantation. Nor, as we shall see, is he actually positing a "rupture" between psychoanalysis and heredity-degeneration-racism. Dean and Lane's interpretation of the passage, and of *rupture* in particular, decontextualizes Foucault's typically ironic discourse about Freud in *Sexuality One*. Within the context of Foucault's thinking and assertions about psychoanalysis over the course of his work, this passage can be viewed as a rhetorical trap where Foucault holds out the tantalizing lure of a Freudian "rupture" that turns out to be no rupture at all.

Caught in the "yes and no" rhetoric of a back-and-forth grammar that structures the paragraph's doublespeak about Freud, Dean and Lane seize on this passage only for the positive assertions about Freud that emerge in the "but" clauses, ignoring the clauses that are more critical of Freud. They further extract those positive assertions from the larger context both of *Sexuality One* and of Foucault's work as a whole to argue that "Foucault viewed psychoanalytic concepts as conflicting not only with psychiatry, psychology, and medicine, but also with its own institutions and practices" (10). Again, this is a baffling assertion about Foucault that could only be made through a careful avoidance both of the details of the passage cited and of the larger context of Foucault's oeuvre. For both the cited passage and its larger Foucauldian context highlight precisely the antithesis of Dean and Lane's claim. Foucault insists, over and over, that psychoanalysis emerges at the end of the nineteenth century not as a break from positivist medicine, but as its culmination.

In an unremarked sentence from the passage, for example, Foucault writes: "[psychoanalysis] resumed the project of a medical technology appropriate for dealing with the sexual instinct."[13] In another cited but ignored sentence from the same passage, Foucault writes that psychoanalysis constitutes one of "the great family of technologies of sex," one of "all those institutions that set out in the nineteenth century to medicalize sex."[14] These unacknowledged sentences reinforce a more broad-based interpretation of Foucault that runs counter to Dean and Lane's conclusions. As the example from the 1977 interview suggests, Foucault asserts that psychoanalysis is an "episode"—indeed, a climactic season finale—of nineteenth-century medical science. Specifically, Foucault argues that Freud reestablishes, through its inversion as psyche, the scientific truth of a nineteenth-century organic conception of sexual instinct located in the organs or the brain: a sexual body already discovered and medicalized by Charcot, with whom Freud trained, and other nineteenth-century scientists. "Freud turned the theory of degenerescence inside out, like a glove," Foucault says in the same 1977 interview.[15] Significantly, the verb Foucault uses here to describe that conceptual and historical event of inversion and repetition is *retourner*, thereby playing on its double connotations as both a spatial turning inside out and a temporal return which will become crucial in *Madness*'s story of reason. As I will demonstrate, in describing psychoanalysis as "the sovereign violence" (M 339/F 360) of a Cartesian "return-as-*retour*," *Madness* will insist on Freud's place as the hinge that brings the Enlightenment's rationalist moral structures into the modern period.[16] This larger perspective on psychoanalysis in Foucault shows quite clearly that, in turning degenerescence inside out, Freud does not break "with psychiatry, psychology, and medicine" (10), as Dean and Lane claim, but constitutes their apotheosis. And, finally, Foucault's insistence on psychoanalysis as the inverted culmination of nineteenth-century medicine goes hand in hand—or better, glove in glove—with his signature framing of a psychoanalytic knowledge (*savoir*) whose power (*pouvoir*) is derived from the institutional practices that produce and sustain it. In the context of the specifically sexual technology of the psychoanalytic talking cure that constitutes Foucault's institutional object of critique, Dean and Lane's picture of a Foucault who would separate psychoanalytic theory from its institutional practice simply distorts him beyond recognition.

This queer set piece by Dean and Lane stages a typically straight reading of Foucauldian irony. Like a cat with its prey, *Sexuality One* toys with those who enter its spinning, self-mirroring maze. "It's a game!" Foucault repeats in the 1977 interview I cited earlier.[17] Not recognizing the game and its rhetorical duplicities, Dean and Lane's introduction flattens out Foucault. Further, their reading of him serves to legitimate their insistence on Freudian psychoanalysis as a unique theory disconnected both from its institutional practices and from its own history. Like other psychoanalytic queer theorists, Dean and Lane separate Freud from the truth-telling technologies of nineteenth-century positivism and from various homophobic medical appropriations of Freudianism, especially in the U.S., after Freud's death in 1939. Both the deinstitutionalizing and dehistoricizing investments exhibited by Dean and Lane are necessary for a queer use of the psyche and the antirationalist unconscious it holds to elaborate a project of resistance to sexual normalization. And, while the impulse to resist sexual normalization is one Foucault shares, queer theory's insistence on enlisting Freud along with Foucault to push forward an antiheteronormative project not only distorts Foucault but also dehistoricizes the concept of the psyche. For if Dean and Lane use Foucault to engage the history of nineteenth-century science, they do so only to reinscribe the psyche as the container of a "constitutive resistance . . . to all norms" (28) in all times and places.

Against this distorting backdrop, *Madness*'s condemnation of what it characterizes as the despotic coup of Freudian psychoanalysis is as relentless as it is unambiguous. In *Madness*, we find no "congruence between Foucauldian and psychoanalytic views of sexuality" (11), as Dean and Lane assert, either in their Freudian or Lacanian forms. What we find, instead, is a clear genealogy—or what Elden calls an *archiveology*[8]—of the psychoanalytic failure to hear or heal those modern forms of unreason we call madness. Indeed, rather than hearing or healing madness, psychoanalysis participates in the silencing structure of a rationalist, moralizing subjectivity that continues to produce madness as its unhealable wound.

From this perspective, *Madness*'s critique of Freud is significant for its links with Foucault's Nietzschean endeavor to historicize the emergence of the rational moral subject. By contrast, Dean and Lane's ahistorical extraction of a psychoanalytic theory of the unconscious separate from its practices leaves unaddressed the Nietzschean diagnosis of the psyche as the rationalist West's internalized moral soul. Historicizing the psyche requires a retraversal of its ground similar to the retraversal of a moral swamp which, in the Nietzschean conception, becomes the psyche and in turn props up the subject of modern humanism.

Unlike the snapshot quality of the ironic tableaux that form, in *Sexuality One*, a montage of *petits récits*, or "chronological reminders,"[19] chopped out of a longer story, *History of Madness*'s almost Proustian elaborations historicize, in an anti-Historical redeployment of the traditional *grand récit*, the emergence of the psyche as the engine that drives the machinery of modern sexual subjectivation. Queer theory's focus on *Sexuality One* reflects the formal and conceptual specificity of that volume, drawing on its highly condensed description of sexuality to reproduce a presentist conception of the psyche. Foucault's historicization of the psyche in *Madness* underscores his view that, rather than constituting a force of disruption, it serves to solidify our assujettissement. This Foucauldian understanding of the psyche, so obvious in *Madness*, challenges the common Freudian claim that psychoanalysis frees the queer subject through a psychic resistance—*from within*—to heteronormative subjectivation.

Before examining in detail the historical emergence of the psyche that *Madness* describes, let me clarify my own critique of psychoanalytic Foucauldianism in the historical terms that frame queer theory as a late twentieth-century phenomenon. To put it simply, my argument is impelled by my own recognition of the evolution of queer theory over time. Because queer theory now has a history—as a body of work, as an academic field, as an analytical focus, as a mode of thinking—the time has come to submit queer theory to the kind of historical, genealogical critique Foucault spent his life attempting to practice. From that perspective, the queer psyche can be situated in the context of queer theory's own temporal emergence. As I have intimated in earlier chapters, queer theory is born out of many places, some of them contiguous, some of them quite separate from one another. Those places include academic and political feminisms, especially lesbian feminism; the work of historians of sexuality such as Jonathan Katz, Jeffrey Weeks, Alan Bray, David Halperin, John D'Emilio, Jonathan Goldberg, and Martha Vicinus; various political activisms responding to the AIDS crisis and the oppression of sexual minorities; the discovery of Foucault with the 1978 English translation of *Sexuality One*; and, not insignificantly, the increasing use of psychoanalytic theory in the U.S. academy, primarily as an analytical tool for deciphering the sexual meanings of literary, cinematic, and other cultural objects.

Queer theory's psychoanalytic roots can be traced back, perhaps most importantly, to Leo Bersani's "Is the Rectum a Grave?" (1987), an essay whose dark anality, for all its resistance to reproductive futurity, rivals the most fecund of fertility figures in its continuing generation of queer meanings.[20] And if Gayle Rubin's "Thinking Sex" (1984), an essay almost contemporaneous with Bersani's, is more obviously Foucauldian than psychoanalytic, it explicitly calls for a positive reappraisal of the work of sexologists, including Freud, whose meticulous specifications of diverse sexual behaviors offer, in Rubin's view, a wealth of material from which contemporary scholars of sexuality might learn.[21] Along similar lines, Eve Kosofsky Sedgwick's *Between Men* (1985) and *Epistemology of the Closet* (1990) deftly weave together close literary readings and sociocultural analyses of the Victorian period within theoretical frameworks that include both Freud and Foucault.[22] And, in *Gender Trouble* (1990), Judith Butler accomplishes her critique of the stable "subject" of feminism by ingeniously combining, among other elements, Freud, Lacan, and Foucault.[23]

The progeny of those multiple points of emergence, today's queer children bear all the traces of its family's promiscuous beginnings. As a discursive formation that is not just a theory *of the queer* but that also *queers* theory, queer theory needed to arise, by definition, out of a promiscuous mingling of multiple methods and perspectives, a methodology Judith Halberstam calls a "scavenger methodology."[24] In that context, the common psychoanalytic picture of the psyche as normativity's other held out a promise to those who felt squeezed by the rationalist, heteronormative structures of a moral order that both produced and excluded the queer. Given the virtual dead end of sexual agency in *Sexuality One*, the psyche seemed to offer some wiggle room within a conception of subjectivity whose totalizing sexual dispositif was both disorienting and paralyzing.

This explains the basic conundrum of queer theory's ongoing reliance on both Foucauldian and Freudian descriptions of sexual subjectivity. For if queer theory is limited, as I've been arguing, by its deep investment in *Sexuality One*, that volume is precisely the place readily acknowledged to be the site of a critique of Freudian psychoanalysis. Rather than simply ignoring that critique, queer theory often acknowledges Foucault's unmasking of the ruse of repression that produces the psyche as the sexualized place of otherness within. At the same time, a significant number of contemporary queer theorists continue to deploy, alongside Foucauldian terminology, psychoanalytic concepts that only make sense if we bracket or distort Foucault's critique of the repressive hypothesis. This seeming contradiction begins to make sense if we consider the consequences of building a theoretical edifice on the spinning foundation that is *Sexuality One*. For within the pages of *Sexuality One*, the psychoanalytic couch and the psyche it cracks open offer a place where perverts are allowed to speak. And even if Foucault insists that the psyche's seeming hospitality toward queers is an illusion designed *not* to heal us from the pain of our exclusion—designed, in fact, to incessantly pin us down in our perversions—the invitation to speak and to explore the spaces of our previously muted "inner" life has been simply too strong to resist. Psychoanalysis has proven to be a gilded sexual cage too glittering to be dismantled. If we take away the psyche, what is left us? As Sedgwick reminds us in *Tendencies* (1993): "psychoanalytic thought, damaged at its origin, remains virtually the only heuristic available to Western interpreters for unfolding sexual meanings."[25]

Especially in the context of Foucault's demystification of our "insides" as sex, queer theory needs psychoanalysis to give us back the thickness of our own existence as sexual beings: what Foucault calls our truth. As I argued in chapter 1, queer theory uses *Sexuality One* to read into Foucault an Americanized sexual "identity" that is not really there; at the same time, it queers that "identity" by undoing it. But in the dialectical logic of identity's transformations—its making, unmaking, and remaking as nonself-identical performative agency—the ethical dimension of Foucault's Nietzschean critique of subjectivity disappears into the discursive play of the resignified queer subject. Because the ethical thickness of a lived experience of subjectivation is lost in the form of performative play, sexuality needs to acquire the thickness of a content or a complexity that the dazzling but thin dispositif has whisked away. This is where the thick language of psychoanalysis provides queer theory with precisely what it finds to be lacking in its reading of Foucault. For psychoanalysis is nothing if not a seemingly infinite store of stories about sexual experience; its tantalizing case histories and explanatory structures provide endless material for the project to put flesh on a skeletal sexuality from which eros has been drained. This explanation supports my claim that queer theory remains invested in psychoanalysis precisely *because* it has relied so heavily on *Sexuality One*. In fact, queer theory continues in its Freudo-Foucauldianism by *not* attending to the more explicitly historical Foucault volumes—and especially *History of Madness*—that would allow it to contextualize Foucault's conception of the psyche within a larger corpus.

But times have changed, both for queer theory and for the queer subject. Especially in the face of a new English translation of *History of Madness*, the generative coupling of Freud with Foucault that both constitutes and explains queer theory's beginnings needs to be contested from the perspective of today's historical present. Disimbricating Foucault from psychoanalysis in queer theory can help us to clarify both the historicity of the psyche as a function of our sexual subjectivation and the historicity of a theory that makes sexuality its object of knowledge. Indeed, the historicization of the psyche within a theory that would claim to know it is precisely the project Foucault undertook in writing *History of Madness*. *Madness* not only narrates the constitution of the psyche as concomitant with the rise of the moral subject. It also provides a structure for historically interpreting queer theory's reliance on psychoanalysis as symptom of its paradoxical position vis-à-vis sexuality as productive power. For, by definition, as a discursive formation whose primary purpose is to talk about sex, queer theory participates in a truth game that forces the secret of sexuality. But, if its distinctive focus on sexual subjects constitutes queer theory's prodigal status, it is not hard to see how that break from the family loops back as Freudian psychoanalysis to trap those queer prodigals in the oedipal fold. As children thus imprinted with the parental stamp of the moral family, psychoanalytic queer theory's "sex talk" ironically reproduces a nineteenth-century positivist discourse that objectifies alterity across the split between reason and madness. That objectification stems from the rationalizing moralities of internalized violence analyzed in the previous chapter.

This chapter unravels the next part of the story: the nineteenth-century rise of a science of the psyche that culminates in psychoanalysis. The result of the Freudian historical coup is a deep inner life whose deceptive promise is a resistance to those norms that imprison the subject within rationalist moralities. But, as my encounter with *Madness* will show, that coup will constitute reason's most devastating blow to the erotic possibilities of unreason symbolized, for example, by the Renaissance ship of fools. With psychoanalysis, those other-than-subjective forms of life will be swallowed up completely by the humanist machinery of a *psyche-logos* from which we have yet to emerge.

The Psyche in *History of Madness*

If Foucault's critique of Freud in *Sexuality One* is variously acknowledged, distorted, and ignored by queer Freudo-Foucauldians, that confusion also characterizes the larger field of thinkers writing about Foucault's relation to Freudian psychoanalysis and its concepts. At one extreme, Arnold Davidson corrects what he perceives to be a widespread *mis*interpretation of *Sexuality One* "as a full-scale rejection of psychoanalysis."[26] Citing out of context a carefully extracted selection of Foucault's assertions about Freud in the 1977 conversation mentioned earlier, Davidson claims that "Foucault wanted to divorce the psychoanalytic theory of the unconscious from the theory of sexuality" in order to use a Lacanian "logic of the unconscious" to undermine the humanist subject.[27] Inaccurately aligning Foucault with linguistic structuralism, Davidson levels the differences that distinguish thinkers—among them, Foucault and Lacan—whose similarities are limited to a general antihumanist negativity, shared by many of both Lacan's and Foucault's generations, toward the phenomenological intentionality of the existentialist humanist subject that dominated the Sartrean scene of French postwar philosophy. Arguing for a structuralist approach which, "in consonance with Lacan," would understand "the unconscious as a system of logico-linguistic structures," Davidson paints a misleading picture of a Foucault whose "search for linguistic structures" would work in tandem with his supposed embrace of a static Freudo-Lacanian concept of the unconscious.[28]

At the other extreme, Didier Eribon asserts again and again that Foucault's "attack on psychoanalysis"[29] is unrelenting, both in *Madness*'s "radical historicization"[30] of homosexuality as mental illness and in *Sexuality One*'s challenge to the Freudo-Marxism of the French sexual liberation movements of the 1970s inspired, among other things, by the writings of Reich and Marcuse. In *Echapper à la psychanalyse* ("Escape from Psychoanalysis"), Eribon also includes Lacan as one of Foucault's theoretical targets, arguing that Foucauldian and psychoanalytic thinking are fundamentally incompatible: "I think we must choose: Freud (Lacan) or Foucault. Foucault or psychoanalysis."[31]

Exemplifying a middle ground, both/and position is the Derridean deconstruction of any Freud-Foucault antagonism that would reductively pit one against the other in an either/or opposition. In a 1991 lecture marking the thirty-year anniversary of *History of Madness*, Jacques Derrida focuses on Freud as the ambiguous "border" figure whom Foucault "accepts and rejects, excludes and includes, disqualifies and legitimates, masters and liberates."[32] Here in Foucault's absence Derrida restages—while repeatedly claiming not to—the "stormy discussion"[33] that began in 1963 with Derrida's critique of Foucault's reading of madness in Descartes. Insisting on Foucault's ambivalence toward Freud, Derrida ultimately condemns *Madness* for "putting on trial" (244) an oedipal psychoanalysis that Foucault describes—*unjustly* in Derrida's view—as invested in the authority of Father and Judge. Reading Freud as the "doorman" [*huissier*][34] to the age of psychoanalysis, Derrida discovers *within* Foucault the disavowed psychoanalytic "borderline" (233), "hinge," or "lure" (*charnière*)[35] that ushers in "the very possibility of a history of madness" (229).

As I'm sure is by now quite clear, my sympathies here are more aligned with Eribon's admittedly polemical stance than with the pro- or middle ground positions represented by Davidson and Derrida. That said, I concede the obvious point—made visible by Derrida but not by Eribon—that in an age fully colonized by a psyche-logos we cannot simply choose the "either" against the "or" to stand outside a hermeneutic machinery that consumes us. And, if Derrida asserts that Foucault fails to conceptualize psychoanalysis as "that from out of which he speaks" (232), that assertion is made dubious by the numerous moments where Foucault insistently bemoans our modern imprisonment within psychoanalytic knowledge. But, like Foucault, I do not take that recognition of our embeddedness in a psychic order to mean, as Derrida implies, that we should give up on the effort to dismantle the machinery or, to use a Nietzschean metaphor, to hammer away at the foundations of the "fortress" (*M* xxxii) that imprisons us.

My sketch of the ongoing critical disagreements about psychoanalysis in Foucault establishes an interpretive context for my reading of the psyche in *Madness*. Unlike Derrida, I see Freud as the figure who, mirroring Descartes, functions not as *Madness*'s disavowed borderline but as one of the book's two central targets of critique. Indeed, the psychoanalytic concept of disavowal itself subtly privileges Foucault's interpreters as would-be analyst-doctors who claim to know more about Foucault than he knows about himself. The critical gesture of ferreting out, within Foucault, symptoms of his failure to know himself serves to authorize commonly held assumptions about his supposed ambivalence toward psychoanalysis. But, as *Madness* clearly shows, the "ambivalent" diagnosis is ill-founded. In fact, such a diagnosis—one that allows readers to make sense of Foucauldian symptoms they otherwise cannot understand—more likely reflects the interests and investments of his reader-doctors than they do Foucault's own position. Not wanting to entertain the possibility of a full-scale Foucauldian attack on psychoanalysis, readers choose to argue that he goes both ways.

This widespread phenomenon of psychoanalyzing Foucault in order to explain away his clearly unwelcome denunciations of Freud provides yet another explanation for queer theory's persistent Freudo-Foucauldianism. In the most general sense, the yes-of-course-psychoanalytic or kinda-psychoanalytic readings of Foucault exemplified by

Davidson and Derrida end up contributing to an interpretive ethos, reflected in much queer theory, that confidently and decisively sums up Foucault's views on psychoanalysis as "always uncertain, divided, mobile, some would say ambiguous, others ambivalent, confused, or contradictory."[36] Davidson's formulation epitomizes the truth-claiming position that characterizes such an interpretive ethos: "Despite the *genuine complexities* and *real ambiguities* that characterize Michel Foucault's attitude toward psychoanalysis, one can at least say *with confidence* that the Freudian discovery of the unconscious represented for him a *decisive* epistemological achievement."[37] That pervasive but seriously underanalyzed critical *certainty* about Foucault's *ambivalence* toward psychoanalysis serves indirectly to authorize the Freudo (Lacanian)-Foucauldianisms of queer theory that I, like Eribon, want to contest. If there is ambiguity in Foucault, it is due not to a wavering about psychoanalysis itself, but rather to a recognition that its contestation can only happen from within a *logos* that has captured our psyches already.

As a diagnosis of our historical present, *Madness*'s critique of our psychoanalytic capture constitutes its driving critical force, drawing together toward the vanishing point we now inhabit the spiraling repetitions of the seventeenth-, eighteenth-, and nineteenth-century stages of unreason that constitute the three-part structure of the book. Having described in part 1 of *Madness* the seventeenth-century coup that produced the division between reason and unreason, in parts 2 and 3 Foucault examines the historical consequences of that great division in the gradual establishment of scientific knowledge about madness over the course of the eighteenth and nineteenth centuries.

In congruence with his Nietzschean critique of morality, Foucault insists on this temporal emergence of the modern sciences of the psyche, where classical unreason as moral negativity gradually becomes modern madness as an objectified truth of science that excludes the perspective of the mad. Within the three-part schema outlined above, Foucault brings attention to the experience of unreason in the seventeenth century—the practice of confinement and the concomitant production of interiority as moral conscience—as the *moral* foundation for modern *scientific* understandings of mental illness: "classicisim shaped a moral experience of unreason, which still today forms the bedrock of our 'scientific' knowledge of mental illness" (*M* 106/*F* 121). Over a 150-year period, the negative moral valuation of those who are confined by the repressive forces of the seventeenth-century gives way, in the eighteenth century, to a positive revaluation of the mad as objects of scientific knowledge: "the *moral negativity* of the madman began to be nothing other than the *positivity* of what one can *know [connaître]* about him" (*M* 183/*F* 201; translation modified, emphasis added). Importantly, this productive transformation of moral negativity into scientific truth assumes, from the start, the *absence* of the point of view of the mad themselves; it is the mute negativity of madness that gives birth, "in the *silent* labor of the *positive*" (*M* 180/*F* 198; emphasis added), to a scientific view of madness. In this process, "the madman will become . . . the object of rational analysis, fullness offered to knowledge, and evident perception" (*M* 183/*F* 201; translation modified).

The most important institutional and conceptual structure that frames the emergence of the psyche over time is the vertical relation between the subject of knowing and the known object. *Madness* dramatizes the role played by the scientist-doctor-analyst as the agent who transforms moral negativity into the objectified positivity of a scientific content. The "doctor-patient couple" (*couple médecin-malade*) (*M* 205/*F* 222; translation modified) emerges as the modern figure of the hierarchical structure that pits knower against known. In the gradual transformation of unreason into madness as mental illness over the course of the eighteenth century, that couple comes to exemplify the unequal relations through which scientific expertise asserts itself. More important, that strange couple constitutes the hinge, to redeploy Derrida's term, on which Foucault's critique of Freud will turn. For if psychoanalysis prides itself on its dialogic practice, *Madness* exposes the historical foundations of that dialogue as a sham. In the eighteenth-century period when the doctor-patient couple first appears, the communication between the doctor—the one who knows madness—and the mad—the object to be known—is never direct: "there is no possibility of dialogue" (*M* 171/*F* 189; translation modified).

This absence of dialogue allows science to define madness as something in which there is nothing to hear or see. In the place of dialogue there is only the mad blank of the split that divides doctor from patient: "in the between-two [*l'entre-deux*], nothing, a void" (*M* 205/*F* 223; translation modified). As sheer, mute negativity, the blank of madness that both sutures and separates doctor and patient comes to constitute the hollow "bedrock"—the groundless ground—of an objectifying knowledge that separates itself from the madness it both excludes and captures. The mad patients themselves do not speak their own madness: "entirely excluded on one side, entirely objectified on the other, madness is never *made manifest* for itself, and in a language of its own that would be proper to it [*un langage qui lui serait propre*]" (*M* 171/*F* 189; translation modified). And, because institutional practices are such that doctors do not hear or see the mad directly, medical knowledge about madness proceeds to constitute itself not through empirical observation but through an imaginative labor that draws, ironically, on the realm of unreason.

In this way, the negativity of madness as "deformations of moral life" (*M* 196/*F* 214; translation modified) acquires a content or positivity through the mediated transmutation of images. And, if Foucault describes this as "the labor of imaginary realisations shared by doctor and patient" (*M* 205/*F* 223; translation modified), it is important to remember that the patient's part in that labor is a silent one. In that sense, the patient functions as a negative foil, the blank of a placeholder, for the productive imagination of a truth-wielding scientific project that will eventually fabricate, in the nineteenth century, our modern "pathological forms" (*M* 205/*F* 223) of madness. Thus, from the moment of the establishment of the doctor-patient couple in the eighteenth century and into the modern period, the "true work of knowledge [*savoir*]" (*M* 205/*F* 223; translation modified) occurs not through direct contact or empirical observation, but within a created world of imaginary forms.

This radical recasting of empirical psychology as the fabricated product of a solipsistic imagination places scientific reason squarely in the domain of unreason. Indeed, Foucault takes the argument one step further to describe the scientific labor of positivist psychology as the ritualistic work of exorcists and magicians. Looping back to Descartes in the seventeenth century, Foucault labels the imaginative process through which madness acquires a content an "exorcism" (*conjuration*) (*M* 244/*F* 262).[38] This consignment of the cogito to the realm of the ritualistic, the religious, and the irrational highlights Foucault's assertion that the doubt-driven Cartesian "work of negativity can never be simply the void of a negation" (*M* 206/*F* 224), just as an exorcism can never be simply an expulsion but is also a summons or conjuration. Alluding perhaps to Descartes's own conjuration and exorcism of an "evil genius," Foucault writes, "the Cartesian progression of doubt is certainly the great exorcism of madness" (*M* 244/*F* 262). This act of exorcism—a driving out of the mad demon summoned by Descartes in the repeated incantations that constitute systematic doubt—paradoxically fills in the blank produced by the exclusion of madness from the thinking cogito. In the place of the empty negativity that defines Cartesian error, images appear; the gap of the false becomes the fantastic production of *phantasma*.

Thus madness as an absence—as exorcized error, as reason's negation, as the nothingness that shatters thinking—becomes, paradoxically, a conjured "plenitude" (*M* 242):

> Madness fills the void of error with images, and binds fantasies [*fantasmes*] together through the affirmation of falsehood. In one sense, then, madness is plenitude, joining the figures of night to the powers [*puissances*] of day, and the forms of fantasy [*fantaisie*] to the activity of the waking mind. . . . Madness, at bottom, is *nothing*. . . . But as for this *nothing*, its paradox is that it *manifests* nothing, makes it burst into signs, words [*paroles*], and gestures. . . . For madness, if it is nothing, can only manifest itself by coming out of itself, and by acquiring appearance in the order of reason; it becomes in this way the opposite of itself (*M* 242/*F* 261; translation modified).

As nothing, madness can only be exorcized [*conjurée*] through an incantation or bringing out that allows it to manifest itself. Both summoned and driven out, madness becomes a plenitude that can appear in the order of reason, as "the opposite of itself," to give science "a rational grip" (*M* 243/*F* 261) on "the void of error." Beginning as a "knowledge [*connaissance*]" (*M* 243/*F* 261) that will soon become a science, a priestly reason both conjures and exorcizes the negativity of madness to authorize and give a content to its positivist project.

Foucault's description of madness as that which is conjured and exorcized through a religious ritual situates the interiority of madness not only within a singular mad body but also against the horizon of the collective social body. The conjuration of madness establishes its socially exceptional status; in its social internalization, the exception among others becomes an exorcized strangeness *within*. The same transformation that both conjures and exorcizes an imaginary content for madness—one that bursts into signs, words, and gestures when, eventually, madness begins to "speak"—also conjures and exorcizes madness as an interiority. In that conjuration, the singular alterity of madness is established as the exception to the general alterity of others; in this way, alterity is doubled—"a double system of alterity" (*M* 181/*F* 199)—through a madness that marks the exceptional against a backdrop of the universal: "The madman is the other in relation to the others: the other—in the sense of an exception—amongst others—in the sense of the universal. Every form of interiority is now exorcized [*conjurée*]" (*M* 181/*F* 199).[39] Through its repeated conjuration, "that singular Other that is the madman" (*M* 181/*F* 199) is both created and captured as the negativity of difference against which the universality of the social is constituted:

"the madman is more or less different within the group of others which is, in its turn, more or less universal" (*M* 181/*F* 199; translation modified).

In this way, repetitive incantation exorcizes any possibility of coextensive subjectivations that would be coincident with alterity, but not the objects of social exclusion—those desubjectivating forms of becoming that emerged in chapter 2 as wind, atmosphere, storm, or folds in the sea. Instead, those potential points of emergence of nonobjectifying forms of alterity are transformed into the absolute difference of abnormality, now captured and arrested within a system of relative norms. Thus the profile of the mad detaches itself—as the one inhabited by a singular strangeness—against the exterior space of generality and normality: society, the group, the universal other. The internalization which will locate that singular alterity *within* "abnormals" is the consequence of a conjuration that both invokes and drives out "*the difference of the Other in the exteriority of others*" (*M* 181/*F* 199).

That strange interiority—as a store of images—will eventually become the psychic object of psychiatry and psychology. As the internalized profile of a singular strangeness within a horizon of generality, the interior psyche is both the excluded blankness of normalizing forces and, at the same time, a positive content inhabited by images. "As a result of the work of images" (*M* 277/*F* 295; translation modified), the void of exclusion becomes a space of strangeness into which passions, dreams, and desires are deposited, then manifested or expressed as "a delirious discourse" (*M* 237/*F* 255). To put it back into the historical terms of Foucault's temporal narrative about the psyche's emergence, if madness was locked up and silenced in the seventeenth century, over the course of the eighteenth century it begins to speak the content it has been given. But, again, madness does not speak "in a language of its own that would be proper to it" (*M* 171/*F* 189; translation modified); its speech and appearance occur as an "inner" form—what will eventually be called the psyche—elaborated by medical knowledge. And, ultimately, that form will be linguistic: "language is the primary and ultimate structure of madness" (*M* 237/*F* 255). It is through "the discursive knowledge [*connaissance*] of madness" (*M* 251/*F* 269) that "the *negativity of madness*" (*M* 251/*F* 269) comes to manifest itself "in a positive manner" (*M* 251/*F* 269).

Having established this narrative about the transformation of moral negativity into the positivity of what science can know about the mad, Foucault draws out the paradoxes of conjuration to make a conceptual link between the internalizing work of scientific imagination and the

Nietzschean internalization of the moral soul. For, in *Madness,* the rationalist conjuration of madness as form is also an act of moral conjuration. Referring to those immoral perils regarded by a bourgeois order
with both desire and fear, Foucault writes: "morality dreams of exorcizing them [*conjurer*]" (*M* 360/*F* 380; translation modified).⁴⁰ Both science and morality give madness a content by drawing on an ancient
imaginary of good and evil. The specific moral form madness takes—as
the object of modern medical knowledge or the figure of impurity that
threatens bourgeois morality—comes about through "a strange return"
(*M* 358/*F* 378) to ancient images brought to the surface of cultural
memory. These images of madness—as corruption, impurity, conta-
gion, and monstrosity—give science a foothold in the negativity of unreason and, at the same time, determine the bourgeois management of
madness as a moral disorder in need of purification. Again, madness is
interiorized through an act of conjuration whose meanings are explicitly moral. That conjuration borrows from the buried language and visual representations of Western Christianity, from Augustine and Justinian to the late medieval paintings of Bosch.

For example, one description of an eighteenth-century madhouse
draws on a vocabulary that links specifically gender-deviant and homoerotic forms of obscenity with crime, repeating the Latin terms for debauchery from Christian patristic texts and early legal formulae: "It is
said that numerous prisoners, *simillimi feminis mores stuprati et constupratores* [like women of debauched morals and practioners of male-male
sex], returned *ex hoc obscaeno sacrario cooperti stupri suis alienisque* [from
this obscene secret place covered over with their own debaucheries and
those of others], lost to all chastity and ready to commit all manner of
crimes" (*M* 360/*F* 380; translation modified).⁴¹ Similarly, eighteenth-
century descriptions of the mad draw on the strange visual representations of desire and pain produced by artists of earlier centuries: "Nights
are peopled with inaccessible pleasures; these corrupt and ravaged figures suddenly become faces of voluptuousness; and within these dark
landscapes strange forms of pain and delight emerge that repeat Hieronymus Bosch and his delirious gardens" (*M* 360/*F* 380; translation
modified). If the seventeenth century suppressed and blotted out the
ancient voices and images of madness, eighteenth-century science and
bourgeois morality together reactivated them by tapping into "a prodi-
gious reserve of the fantastic, a sleeping world of monsters that was
believed to have been buried in the Bosch night that had once allowed
them to emerge" (*M* 361/*F* 380; translation modified).

Because science is ultimately a moral project, truth and morality work together. Positivism needs this store of fantastic images in order to have something over which it will maintain its objectifying hold: the "nature" that will become its object of knowledge. At the same time, that reserve of images as "the symbolism of the Impure" (M 358/F 378) authorizes the social exclusions of a bourgeois order whose categories of ostracism and judgment are not scientific, but moral. Again, in the eighteenth century, madness is established as an object of knowledge through the reactivation of a reserve of images rendered silent in the great confinement of the seventeenth century. As a form of "knowing," this positivist experience of mental illness redoubles the silencing, interiorizing fold of alienation into the "objective" perception of a science that speaks a "truth." In this way the Cartesian rejection of madness from the cogito culminates in the rationalist assertion: I "know" madness. But that "knowing" can only occur as the degradation of unreason—the wandering subjectivity of the ship of fools—into madness as an object of analytical perception: "This fall into objectivity," Foucault writes, "was a far deeper and more effective means of mastering madness than its previous enslavement to the forms of unreason" (M 443/F 463; translation modified).

Foucault interprets this tragic "fall" into an age where science masters madness by "knowing" it as the first figure of man's objectivization as truth (M 461–462/F 481). That truth will be secured through the modern technologies of psychological cures. With the creation of psychiatry comes the birth of the myth of a medical and objective recognition of madness, the production of knowledge, and the reorganization of internment into a world of healing (M 434–35/F 455). With science and its focus on healing mental illness, techniques are developed that combine internment with the possibility of a cure; by constraining madness in order to cure it, modern medical techniques thus "free" madness and, so doing, secure its truth. "For the first time," Foucault writes, "an idea is formulated that will weigh heavily on the history of psychiatry up until the psychoanalytic liberation" (M 436/F 456). In this ironic description of psychoanalytic freeing, Foucault demonstrates "that in these constraints, this closed-off vacuum, this 'milieu,' confined madness finds a privileged element in which the essential forms of its truth can surface" (M 436/F 456).

In this way, Foucault establishes a direct, historical line of scientific and moral truth-telling: from the "constraints" put into place in the seventeenth century emerge the "liberating" reforms of Philippe Pinel (figure 3.1) and William Tuke, in France and England, respectively, at the end of the eighteenth century; these reforms are consecrated by Charcot and the asylum of the nineteenth-century to produce, finally, Freudian "liberation" in the twentieth-century talking cure.

The transformation of the house of internment into the reformed asylum of the nineteenth century produces this idea of a medicalized "caged freedom" (*M* 436/*F* 456): the "caged freedom" that will eventually express itself as "liberated language" (*M* 436/*F* 457) is also the "liberated language" (*M* 436) of psychoanalysis. But it is only as a result of confinement—the conjuration of a psychic space of interiority, which also produces a moral conscience within the ethical constraints of a bourgeois order—that the "truth" of madness can be produced: "it is in the closed but empty space of confinement that madness formulates its truth and liberates its nature" (*M* 437/*F* 457; translation modified).

In this complex construction of madness the human psyche itself emerges as the result of a double, mutually constitutive process: the scientific transformation of human subjectivity into object and the social production of human truth against the moral horizon of an always scandalized bourgeois conscience that judges and confines. That construction is expressed, through the language of science, as the psyche

FIGURE 3.1 Robert Fleury, Philippe Pinel at the Salpêtrière, 1795

made manifest: as its "truth." In this way, "psychology in Western culture became man's truth" (*M* 453/*F* 473; translation modified). More than simply an otherness within to be feared and rejected, madness brings with it the paradoxical figure of the psyche as the inner motor that drives human behavior. Further, the human sciences that take up this figure as the basis of their truths—psychiatry, psychology, and psychoanalysis—are built on the nonscientific, contradictory foundations of a paradoxical conjuration. The universal truths about "man" they set out to establish are grounded in the singularity of the exceptional madman who is both summoned and exorcized within the social body. Put slightly differently, "man's truth" comes about through his objectification as mad, as other, as the difference that separates him from the universality of others. That paradoxical truth is produced through a process that is equally paradoxical: articulated as the "liberation" of man's "inner" nature, the freeing of the psyche comes about through constraint, imprisonment, and a denial of his freedom.

It is important to recall here what I asserted earlier about the impossibility of making madness "speak": as an object whose truth is constituted by the deceptive rituals of normalizing science and bourgeois morality, madness and the psyche have no real content and, therefore, have nothing to say. As madness and the psyche begin to "speak" in psychiatry and psychology and, so doing, to "free themselves" as truth, they do so in a language that is not their own. The voice of madness does not convey the experience of madness from the perspective of the mad; rather, it relays an understanding of madness—and, thus, of the psyche itself—through the alienating grid of positivist, moralizing "knowing." This consistently scientific conception of madness underlies the vagaries of its permutations from the seventeenth to the twentieth century: because madness is the product of reason, "the ultimate language of madness is that of reason" (*M* 233/*F* 252). When madness begins to "communicate," "it becomes communicable" (*M* 442/*F* 462; translation modified) within the forms it is given by the sciences of the psyche: communication occurs "in the neutralised form of offered objectivity" (*M* 442/*F* 462). Madness can only speak its truth "under the gaze that now envelopes it" (*M* 443/*F* 463; translation modified) as "a thing invested with language" (*M* 443/*F* 463). Of course, even in the age of positivist perception, madness as psyche is the exorcized demon of a nonscientific act of incantation: "a figure exorcized [*conjurée*] once it is seen" (*M* 443/*F* 463; translation modified). Like a ventriloquist with his doll, the psychiatric doctor conjures madness and makes her speak. Of course, because her words are not "her own," in making her speak, he silences her.

In this section of my engagement with *Madness*, I have brought out the paradoxical constitution of the psyche as inner truth to lay the groundwork for Foucault's critique of psychoanalysis as a talking cure. To be sure, in historical terms, Foucault's assertions about a madness that speaks appear to be contradictory. On the one hand, Foucault describes a historical trajectory from a "profound silence" (*M* 171/*F* 189) in the seventeenth century to "voices where madness speaks" (*M* 393/*F* 414) in the nineteenth and twentieth. At the same time, against the grain of this general progression from silence to speech, Foucault describes an opposite movement that devolves from a dialogue, however muted, in the classical age to absolute silence in the modern era: classical internment "had set up [*nouait*] a muted dialogue between reason and unreason" (*M* 497/*F* 517; translation modified), but "that dialogue itself is now undone [*dénoué*]; the silence is absolute" (*M* 497/*F* 517; translation modified).

This seeming inconsistency in Foucault's narrative constitutes, perhaps, a gap in his reasoning. However, if such is the case, the gap is appropriate, for it highlights the contradictory structure of reason itself, wherein madness as an experience is torn between the knowledge that describes it and the practice of internment that limits its freedom: "a 'medical analytics' and an 'asylum perception' that never managed to overlap" (*M* 393/*F* 414). This irreconcilable split within the experience of madness produces its "always fractured meaning" (*M* 163/*F* 181; translation modified). "A certain non-coherence" (*M* 163/*F* 181; translation modified) inhabits madness as an experience lived in that empty space that divides scientific theory from the concrete practice of an artificially imposed confinement and within which no contact between them occurs. Thus even when madness speaks for itself—"madness strangely conquered a language that was its own" (*M* 393/*F* 414; translation modified)—it can only do so from the space of alienation within which culture has captured it. Indeed, it is only within a structure of alienation—"the human milieu . . . as the negativity of man" (*M* 376/*F* 397)—that modern society comes "to finally pay attention to all that madness could say about itself" (*M* 394/*F* 414). But, even in that moment when society pretends to listen, madness cannot "speak."[42]

This incongruency between the unspeakable incoherence of the experience of madness and the coherence of the psyche as science defines it raises the important question of the reality of madness and, by extension, of the sexual deviance that is one of its avatars. Misunderstandings can easily occur, particularly in the wake of the antipsychiatric movement's uptake of Foucault's work in the late 1960s to bolster their thesis that madness is socially constructed and therefore not real. This is clearly not Foucault's position. When Foucault says madness cannot speak except in a scientific language that is the result of social alienation, he is not denying the experience or the reality of madness itself. For Foucault, whose 1950s training in psychology involved observing psychotic patients, madness is unquestionably "real." But at issue for Foucault are the terms and perspectives that are culturally available to those whose experience differs from the norm—that is, those who come to be labeled as mad, including those who are named as sexual deviants.

Foucault's purpose in *History of Madness* is therefore to interrupt a certain knowingness about madness—including sexual abnormality—that attempts to suture inchoate experience—the "fractured meaning" of "a certain noncoherence"—to specific diagnostic categories. As we have seen, Foucault describes that knowingness within a historical structure which corresponds to a Nietzschean perspective on the emergence of the modern subject. That structure reveals a division within time itself: the premodern "time" of unreason and the modern "time" of madness (M 363–63/F 383). But, as a temporal mapping that is already spatial, Foucault's linear division of time into premodern unreason and modern madness is doubled by a nonlinear description of time that coexists with the linear conception. Indeed, linear temporality is itself a product of the age of reason; the seventeenth-century division between reason and unreason that ushers in the modern era gives us, paradoxically, a conception of time in which unreason has no place. The modern era is the age of the linear, analytical time of madness whose "rupture with immediacy" (M 371–72/F 391) separates modern madness as mental illness from the undifferentiated, nonlinear time of return that characterizes the world of unreason. The knowingness about madness that constitutes modern medical diagnosis is a function then, not only of historically embedded spatial exclusions but also of an exclusionary temporality that cuts off madness from the tragic, lyrical, circling time of unreason. This temporal dimension of madness's history explains how the age of reason diminishes the range of languages of unreason through which the "mad" might articulate the reality of their experience: a reality that includes a "premodern" and therefore "now" unspeakable relation to oneself, to others, to time, and to the sensible

world (M 371/F 391). In the modern era—in the age of madness and rationalist, linear time—the amorphous experience of unreason as non-
subordinated difference can only be named in the objectifying, diagnostic language of pathologies to be isolated and specified.

The temporal and conceptual inaccessibility of madness—and also,
by extension, of sexual deviance—as the immediate experience of a subject in the world lays the foundation for a critique of psychoanalysis and
the concept that grounds it: namely, the psyche as an inner essence,
cause, or core truth of a human subject. But Foucault's argument in
Madness is tricky and easily misconstrued as only a partial critique of
psychoanalysis. If the scientific language of positivism silences madness by alienating it as an object, psychoanalysis would appear, unlike
psychiatry or psychology, to heal that temporal alienation by creating
the unconscious and thereby restoring the ancient dialogue between
reason and unreason. So doing, it would also appear to heal the historical rift that separates the mad subject from lyricism, the tragic, the time
of return, and the complex thickness of the sensible world. "It is for that
reason," Foucault writes in a passage made famous by Derrida, "that we
must do justice to Freud. . . . Freud took up madness at the level of its
language, reconstituting one of the essential elements of an experience
that positivism had reduced to silence. He . . . restored . . . the possibility
of a dialogue with reason to medical thought" (M 339/F 360). In these
assertions, Foucault clearly describes psychoanalysis as differentiating
itself from its positivist precursors by giving access to "an experience of
unreason that psychology, in the modern world, was meant to disguise"
(M 339/F 360).

By all appearances, here at Madness's center, or Derridean "hinge,"
Foucault seems to paint a positive picture of Freudian psychoanalysis, as
a force of demystification, reunification, and restoration that gives subjects access to their own experience. That picture would seem to support commonly held queer views about the Freudian psyche as a freeing
concept. But appearances are nothing if not deceptive. For even here, in
one of the first passages in Madness where Foucault explicitly mentions
psychoanalysis and, for all intents and purposes, gives it its due by
doing "justice to Freud," he already hints at a problem also noted by
Derrida: Freud's contribution to the management of madness is described not as a discovery but as "the sovereign violence of a return" (M
339/F 360). But where Derrida reads this as the beginning of Madness's
"deterioration," I read it, by contrast, as the place where the possibility of
a certain erotic ethics of freedom begins to appear. Deploying once

again the Nietzschean language of the internalizing fold, or return, as an act of sovereign violence that produces the illusion of an inner moral conscience, Foucault plants the seeds for his critique later in the book of the paradoxical logic that fashions freedom out of imprisonment. The same logic structures both positivism and psychoanalysis: "confined freedom heals on its own, just like the liberated language of psychoanalysis" (M 436/F 456–457; translation modified). Like the "caged freedom" (M 436/F 456) that characterizes a psyche captured and objectified by science, the "liberated language" of the psychoanalytic talking cure ultimately rests on an illusion of freedom.

How exactly is the "liberated language" of psychoanalysis merely an illusion of freedom? The answer to this question returns us, once again, to the doctor-patient couple and the sovereign structure that governs both the familial logic of psychoanalysis and the positivist logic of medical science. If the doctor-patient couple described earlier produces the positivist apotheosis of the doctor-scientist, that apotheosis is mirrored by the figure of the father who reigns over the oedipal structure of psychoanalysis. "The whole existence of madness," Foucault writes, "is enveloped in what we might describe by anticipation as a 'parental complex.' The privileges of patriarchy are revived once more around it in the bourgeois family. It is this historical sedimentation that psychoanalysis will later bring to light again, using a new myth to endow it with the meaning of a destiny" (M 490/F 510; translation modified).

Again, it is useful to read this passage through a Deleuzian lens, where the patriarchal parental complex that governs madness in the modern era appears as "an emergence of forces which doubles history."[43] That is, the Freudian coup that establishes paternal authority within the sovereign structure of the Oedipus complex repeats the Cartesian coup of reason that established the sovereignty of a thinking subject who could not be mad. Similarly, the appearance of the family within the psychoanalytic Oedipus myth doubles the juridical authority of the bourgeois family that judged and confined the abnormals of the Age of Reason. Just as the sovereignty of the cogito asserted itself within a bourgeois order of family morality, so too, with the advent of psychoanalysis, reason and morality work together within a structure of authority that arrests thinking in the formation of psychic interiority.

This understanding of the psychoanalytic return of the family complicates the meaning of Foucault's earlier description of psychoanalysis as "the sovereign violence of a *return*" (M 339/F 360); in this doubled, repeated historical sense, madness is literally "twice alienated inside the family" (*M* 490/*F* 510). In addition, this return repeats the *retour* we saw in the 1977 interview where Freud turned nineteenth-century dege-nerescence "inside-out, like a glove."[44] These repeated Nietzschean in-versions, founded in violence, highlight the redoubled loopings that characterize Foucault's conception of historical repetition and change. Further, the Deleuzian frame brings out psychoanalysis both as a con-crete institutional practice and as a figure for thinking; in both senses, psychoanalysis repeats and redoubles the effects of an exclusionary, normalizing history of family morality. This reading of psychoanalysis situates it, then, as an effect of historical and conceptual repetition. The "half-real, half-imaginary dialectic" (*M* 490/*F* 510) of the oedipal family in the twentieth century both repeats and cuts off the nonlinear, back-and-forth time of the "half-real, half-imaginary" (*M* 11/*F* 22; translation modified)[45] Renaissance ship of fools. And, like the seventeenth-century hospital that confined alterity by internalizing it as Nietzschean "bad conscience," the oedipal family constrains otherness through a turn in-ward—indeed, a *retour*—that is both a lived reality and a figure for thought thinking itself. Thus Freudian psychoanalysis repeats the Nietzschean inward turn through which an act of violence produces an inner conscience governed by the moral norms of the bourgeois fam-ily—producing, as Foucault puts it, "the castle of our own conscious-ness" (*M* 11/*F* 22) and conscience. These repetitions clarify the psycho-analytic fusion of morality and science in the amalgamation of Nietzschean "bad conscience" with the Freudian unconscious. As the result of a violent, sovereign act of constraint—"the sovereign violence of a *return*" (*M* 339/*F* 360)—the freedom of the talking cure that re-leases the unconscious is indeed only an illusion of freedom: a "caged freedom" (*M* 436/*F* 456).

Freudian psychoanalysis thus constitutes another instance of the rep-etition that Deleuze identifies as "Foucault's greatest historical princi-ple": that "everything is always said in every age."[46] But, in yet another twist, Foucault insists that historical repetition always happens with a difference in "*an emergence of forces which doubles history*, or rather envel-ops it, according to the Nietzschean conception."[47] Thus the internaliz-ing fold, or force, of the seventeenth century is repeated in the twentieth as psychoanalysis, both doubling and enveloping history. This does not mean that everything is always exactly the same, a repetition of events or forces that never change. Rather, as Deleuze puts it, "forces are in a perpetual state of evolution" (85). A moment in history—what Deleuze calls the "diagram" (there is a Greek diagram, a Roman diagram, a feudal diagram, a Napoleonic diagram, and so on)—is an exposure of "a set of relations between forces" and, as such "is the place only of mutation" (85). The mutation here—in the doubling of history from the inward turn of the great confinement to the psychic depth of psychoanalysis— is the transformation of a sovereign order—Nietzsche's "blond beast"— into a patriarchal structure that has internalized sovereign violence in the figure of the bourgeois father. Although paternal authority was always there—in the sovereign order as much as in postrevolutionary society—the emergence of "the privileges of patriarchy" (*M* 490/*F* 510) in the psychoanalytic Oedipus myth bring attention, importantly for queer theory, to patriarchy's specifically modern meanings.

Let me focus for a moment on this place of "patriarchy" in Foucault's book. As a feminist reader of a queer Foucault, my ears prick up at his uncharacteristic use of the term. Its deployment is even more surprising given its historical context—1961—before the rise of the second wave of feminist movements in Europe and the U.S. And, given the backdrop of numerous later feminist readings of Foucault that will decry his supposed antifeminism, his insistence on patriarchy in this key passage about psychoanalysis becomes all the more noteworthy. So what, in that context, is the precise relevance of this singular moment in Foucault?

From a feminist perspective, the term *patriarchy* might well apply to every diagrammatic moment in Foucault's history of madness, from the patriarchal sovereignty of Descartes to that of the positivist doctor. But Foucault never uses the term to describe Descartes or Pinel or Charcot. In fact, he applies it directly only to psychoanalysis in its connection to the bourgeois family. The singularity of Freud's naming as patriarchal suggests that patriarchy is not only revived in him, but augmented and fortified in the modern psychoanalytic management of madness within a new biopolitical structure that manages life. For we may recall that, in *Sexuality One*, the modern father's appearance as the "fallen" despot who has lost his authority in the public sphere disguises his continuing paternal sovereignty as the transfer point between private family alliances and public medicalized sexualities.[48] The oedipal father is a fallen king who continues to reign in a domestic role of supposedly private domination, thereby masking his function in the more totalizing "technology of power centered on life" that is biopower.[49] The mask turns out to look like nothing other than love; as with all structures founded in violence, that private bond is neither free nor reciprocal, saturated with the sediment of age-old structures of domination and exclusion. Indeed, in the modern sexual family the only recipient of that most precious of gifts we call love is the father, "elevated" by an oedipal patriarchy both old and new as "an object of *compulsory* love."[50]

In *Madness*, psychoanalysis thus brings to light *again* (*remettra à jour*, F 510) the sedimentation of a patriarchal past that will take on the inescapable meaning of a projected future—"the meaning of a destiny" (M 490/F 510)—in the form of a timeless Oedipus myth. And, although psychoanalysis presents itself as offering "a new myth" (M 490/F 510) as "the myth of a *disalienation*" (M 490/F 510; emphasis added), the Oedipus story emerges as a process of *realienation* that freezes time in the welding together of old and new, real and imaginary. Inheriting the familial institutional structures put into place by Tuke and his followers, psychoanalysis takes place within "a real [*réelle*] social structure" (M 489/F 509) and "a genuinely [*réellement*] alienating situation" (M 490/F 510) that emerged historically; at the same time, psychoanalysis reactivates an "ancient structure" (M 489/F 509) of domination within a mythic, timeless "imaginary landscape" (M 489/F 509).

The patriarchal power of Oedipus is thus derived from its welding of time-bound historical forces to timeless symbolic structures. In that light, Foucault's placement of the story of Tuke's eighteenth-century asylum reforms in the section of *Madness* that also critiques the psychoanalytic family structure takes on a similarly historical and symbolic meaning. Foucault's description constitutes both a recounting of actual practices located in history and an elaboration of a symbolic figuration of the familial production of subjectivity within psychology. Tuke opened the Retreat at York in England in 1796 with the goal of providing more humane treatment to the insane than that provided by traditional asylums. At the Retreat, treatment included occupational therapy, outdoor exercise in the form of walks and farmwork and, most important, a social environment modeled after the family. In all of those efforts, Tuke created what Foucault describes as "a simulacrum of the family, an institutional parody that was nonetheless a real psychological situation" (M 490/F 510).

Similarly, the patriarchal oedipal family of psychoanalysis is both "an institutional parody" and "a real psychological situation" (M 490/F 510). Like Tuke's asylum, Freudian psychoanalysis establishes itself as a freeing of constraints by putting in place another "simulacrum of the family" in the form of the oedipal unit. That family structure—both real and imaginary, old and new—is explicitly patriarchal, not only in its founding myth but also in the concrete institutional practices that, through the doctor-patient couple, repeat the unequal relations of Oedipus. With the new psyche of psychoanalysis emerges the figure of the child who, like the madman imprisoned in the asylum, is disempowered within a vertical family structure that empowers the father: "this ancient structure . . . turns him over, as a psychological subject, to the authority and privilege of the man of reason, who takes on for him the concrete form of an adult: that is, both a domination and a destination" (M 489/F 509; translation modified). Modeled on a logic of self-reproduction, the oedipal family repeatedly replays old structures of domination and regenerates itself as an illusion of the new. That illusion of the new as a destination for reproductive futurity masks the family's perpetuation of structures of domination. This masking produces what Foucault calls the image of a destiny of disalienation through "the purity of patriarchy" (M 490/F 510).

Although he is hardly engaging modern feminism here—it is, after all, 1961—Foucault's unmasking of a patriarchal Oedipus constitutes a withering feminist critique of Freudian psychoanalysis. In that critique, Foucault instigates a long line of French challenges to the oedipal model, from Deleuze and Guattari's *Anti-Oedipus* (1972) and Guy Hocquenghem's *Homosexual Desire* (1972) to Luce Irigaray's *Speculum of the Other Woman* (1974) to Jean-Joseph Goux's *Oedipus Philosopher* (1990) to Didier Eribon's *Echapper à la psychanalyse* (2005), to name just a few. In Foucault's view, patriarchy names a psychoanalytic logic that exploits, both conceptually and in actual practice, the dominating power of the doctor in the doctor-patient couple. Just as the "ancient structure" of the family puts the father in charge, so too the medical authority of the doctor is invested with patriarchal power. And, although dressed up as new and scientific, that power is ancient and ritualistic. Like the structure that enfolds him, the father-doctor derives his power from ancient, repetitive rituals of exorcism, incantation, and thaumaturgy. "Supported by the privileges that envelop the secrets of Family, Authority, Punishment, and Love" (M 507/F 526; translation modified), and "putting on the mask of the Father and Lord of Justice" (M 507/F 526; translation modified), the magician-priest-doctor "becomes the almost magical practitioner of the cure, taking on the appearance of a thaumaturge" (M 507/F 526; translation modified). As a consequence of these thaumaturgic practices, the patient will increasingly give herself over to the power of the doctor, passively abandoning herself into "the hands of a doctor . . . both divine and satanic" (M 509/F 528), accepting the magic of his prestige and the scientific knowledge which, like the power of divination, props him up. In this way the patient becomes the perfect, power-less complement to the doctor's power, a "pure object with no other re-sistance than her own inertia, ready to be the hysterical woman in whom Charcot exalted the marvelous powers of the doctor" (*M* 509/*F* 528; translation modified). And, rather than interrupting this long tradi-tion of priestly, patriarchal medical power, Freud draws his own power from it: "from Pinel *to Freud* . . . this objectivity is, from the start, a thin-gification [*chosification*] of a magical order" (*M* 509/*F* 528; translation modified, emphasis added).

Far more than simply a critique of psychoanalysis, Foucault's femi-nist diagnosis of the patriarchal structures of science, the family, and the production of the psyche highlights the *real and imaginary* gendered structures that transform human subjects into things.[51] As Foucault demonstrates repeatedly, that transformation is not only discursive and epistemological but also the concrete result of nondiscursive operations of power. Again, the patriarchal power Foucault describes here is both repressive and productive, and its description in *Madness* can be viewed as an early sketch of what Foucault will later call a dispositif. The divine and satanical doctor imposes his institutional authority onto the patient in a classic display of repressive domination; at the same time, the transformation of human subject into object occurs productively through "the complicity of the patient herself" (*M* 509/*F* 528; transla-tion modified), who, internalizing the powers she projects onto the doc-tor, polices herself as a psychic object.

It is precisely here, in his insistence on medical science as a structure invested with repressive and productive forms of power, that Foucault levels his most devastating blow against Freudian psychoanalysis. Again taking up the central "doctor-patient couple" (*M* 510/*F* 529), Foucault asserts that it is only through the power of the doctor that the void of positivist thought becomes a "concrete reality" (*M* 510/*F* 529): "Beyond the empty forms of positivist thought, all that remains is a single con-crete reality: the doctor-patient couple, in which all alienations are summed up, formed and resolved [*se nouent et se dénouent*]. It is in that respect that *all the psychiatry of the nineteenth century really does converge on Freud*, who was the first to accept the seriousness of the reality of the doctor-patient couple" (*M* 510/*F* 529; emphasis added). And if, with the talking cure, Freud completed a centuries-long process to release the mad from the structures of an asylum put into place in the seventeenth century, he did so only to reassert, in all seriousness, the theatrical and priestly, but nonetheless real patriarchal authority of the doctor.

First, we should note, as Derrida does, that "Freud demystified all the other asylum structures: abolished silence and the gaze" (*M* 510/*F* 529). We must recognize this shift "to do justice to Freud." However, in the same passage, Foucault then qualifies this assertion, which would appear to recognize a "psychoanalytic liberation" (*M* 436): "But, on the other hand, [Freud] exploited the structure that envelops the medical character [*personnage*]: he amplified his virtues as a thaumaturge, preparing an almost divine status for his omnipotence" (*M* 510/*F* 529; translation modified).

I can think of no critique of psychoanalysis—feminist or otherwise—more devastating than this one. In investing the psychoanalyst with the patriarchal powers of the doctor, Freud both creates new techniques of moral control and exploits the ancient power of priests and magicians. As a performer of miracles, he pretends to "free" the unconscious, but is only doing so in a gesture that reproduces the constraints through which the unconscious was produced in the first place. The "freeing" reforms of Pinel and Tuke produce a paradoxical situation where imprisonment itself is internalized; "more genuinely [*réellement*] confined than he would be in a dungeon or in chains" (*M* 496/*F* 516), the patient is imprisoned by none other than herself. And if that self-imprisonment restructures subjectivity as an alienated relation to oneself and to others, psychoanalysis mystifies that self-imprisonment and gives it a name: the unconscious. Having been freed from the walls and chains that confined her, the patient takes on the "outside" guilt and shame produced by bourgeois morality as the "inner" condition that separates her definitively from a society of others: "the patient is trapped in a relation to the self that is of the order of guilt [*faute*], and in a nonrelation to others that is of the order of shame [*honte*]" (*M* 496–97/*F* 516; translation modified). In this way "guilt is displaced toward the inside" (*M* 497/*F* 516; translation modified) in yet another rendering of the Nietzschean swamp of bad conscience that reproduces the psyche as an alienated interiority.

Having thus become her own alienation as guilt and shame, the patient only appears to be "freed" of her burden in the release of the psychoanalytic talking cure. For if the movement from the Renaissance to the modern era traces a progression from dialogue to silence, the corollary of that silence is the putting into place of the language of confession. Again, that language draws on an ancient reserve of Christian terms and *phantasma* which give a content to the pure negation of the self that had come about in the interiorization of error by sovereign reason. That which is "freed" in the talking cure is simply the confessional parroting of a language of guilt and shame that had already been deposited "inside" the psyche by historical and philosophical processes of exclusion and confinement. Thus the Freudian unconscious is like a psychic bank account where those shame-ridden deposits are held and from which withdrawals are made. The language of that withdrawal is not the mad other's "own" language, but simply the reproduction of a deposited language that was already there.

This exposure of psychoanalysis as a patriarchal, mimetic structure explains the devastating meaning of Foucault's ultimate, unambiguous condemnation of psychoanalysis: "psychoanalysis cannot and will never be able to hear the voices of unreason nor decipher on their own terms the signs of the insane" (M 511/F 530). In other words, Foucault asserts here that psychoanalysis cannot do that which it claims to do with its famous listening ear: to hear the voice—of alterity, of unreason—that rationalism cannot hear. Although it may succeed in unraveling "a few forms of madness" (M 511/F 530; translation modified), that unraveling remains separate from the deeper structures of unreason which, over the centuries, have been repressed and silenced by the work of reason. Two forms of sovereignty thus confront each other: the familiar, despotic sovereignty of reason and, less clearly, the "sovereign work of unreason" (M 511/F 530) pushed underground by sovereign reason. And in relation to that older, deeper, muted but sovereign work of unreason, psychoanalysis in fact has nothing to say: "it can neither liberate nor transcribe, nor a fortiori explain, what is essential in that labor" (M 511/F 530; translation modified).

Thus Foucault exposes the sovereign, patriarchal despotism of psychoanalysis as repeating the despotism of philosophical reason. In this, Freud is Descartes. Although seemingly a release from the constraints of rationalism, psychoanalysis endlessly performs and augments the Cartesian coup of the seventeenth century. In what Foucault calls in a 1965 interview a psychological *confiscation*[52] of the human sciences in the modern period, Freud repeats and fortifies the earlier rationalist "great *confiscation* of sexual ethics by family morality" (M 89/F 104) by exploiting the patriarchal distribution of power within the bourgeois family.[53] Rather than freeing the bodily unreason repressed and constrained in the great confinement, psychoanalysis reactivates the positivist, thaumaturgic language of madness as mental illness within a moral discourse of alienation. Psychoanalysis does not heal the mind-body split that excludes the erotic from the thinking cogito; instead, like

Descartes, Freud ensures the expulsion of eros. Psychoanalysis therefore constitutes the culmination of erotic assujettissement in the production of subjectivity as a dead psychic object—the submissive child, the ventriloquist's doll—who can only repeat what has already been programmed into her. In this way, the psychoanalytic talking cure takes its place within the larger frame of "these alienations that cure" (*M* 511/*F* 530) and which, as such, can never hear or speak the suffocated strangeness of the erotic other.

This condemnation of Freud can be specifically linked to the sexual questions that are queer theory's concern. The Foucauldian critique of psychoanalysis in *Madness* restages a scenario of erotic exclusion and repression that differs significantly from the repressive hypothesis Foucault demystifies in *Sexuality One*. Although it shares with *Sexuality One* a figuration of sexuality as a closeting, *Madness* elaborates on its moral dimensions in a way that *Sexuality One* does not. As I argued in chapter 1, *Madness* describes the modern, closeting suppression of the "mad love" of premodern "homosexual," lyrical expression as an "ethical reorganization" of the relationship between unreason and love. In that process of reorganization, modern sexuality is gradually installed as "a new moral unity . . . already close to modern forms of guilt" (*M* 88/*F* 102).

The new moral prison of that closeted unreason can now be linked to those modern forms of sexual guilt as they emerge in psychoanalysis. Specifically, the general logic that describes the psychoanalytic patient's alienated interiority as guilt and shame repeats the logic that governs sexual deviance. Thus, for example, the "homosexual" takes on the "outside" guilt and shame produced by bourgeois morality as the "inner" condition that separates him definitively from a society of others. In this way, the closet of sexual alterity is the result of a "gigantic moral imprisonment" (*M* 511/*F* 530) where psychoanalysis is but the latest, and in many ways most potent, of its many historical forms. The psychoanalytic "'reverse' discourse" (*discours "en retour"*)[54] of the talking cure repeats, in miniature, the great historical violent *retour* that is Freud's repetition of Descartes's despotic coup. In this famous "reverse discourse," too often seized upon by queer theorists as a blueprint for discursive political resistance, psychoanalysis creates the illusion of a release from that closet when finally, after centuries of silence, "homosexuality began to speak in its own behalf."[55] But, as *Madness* demonstrates with stunning clarity, as a form of madness, homosexuality can never be "*made manifest* for itself, and in a language of its own that would be proper to it [*un langage qui lui serait propre*]" (*M* 171/*F* 189;

translation modified) and therefore cannot speak on its own behalf. This logic of the closet revealed in *Madness* through the dynamism and detail of an emergence of forms over time serves to unravel what *Sexuality One* shows as the modern tail end of that historical process. Importantly, the explicit historicity of that picture in *Madness* makes it impossible to seize the psyche, as so many psychoanalytic theorists do, as a timeless and unchanging structure.

More important for a critical engagement with Foucault that takes seriously queer theory's feminist roots, in its critique of a patriarchal Oedipus, *Madness* offers a language for realigning a feminist critique of psychoanalysis with a queer perspective on sexuality. For, while *Sexuality One* explores the familial logic undergirding the production of modern sexuality, its relation to feminism is fraught, to say the least, because of a paradigmatically brief scene about the disciplinary consequences of a village idiot's indulgence in "inconsequential bucolic pleasures."[56] And, if feminists tend to read the Jouy passage as incontrovertible evidence of a rape that remains unacknowledged by Foucault, the brevity of the scene within *Sexuality One*'s montagelike structure makes it impossible to know whether or not the girl in the scene actually consented.[57] The angry feminist response to this "rape scene" in *Sexuality One*—along with Foucault's expression of controversial views regarding sexual punishment generally in the 1970s—has served to deauthorize gendered analyses of other feminist themes in Foucault, including, most crucially, a hystericization of women's bodies spectacularly dramatized in Charcot's puppetry at the Salpêtrière in the nineteenth century. Briefly evoked in *Sexuality One*, that crucial hysterical, feminized link in a chain that starts with amorphous unreason and ends with modern sexual specification is elaborated in great detail in *Madness*. Indeed, Foucault's treatment of the hysteric in *Madness* and, even earlier, his characterization of Dora in his 1954 Binswanger introduction as a figure of resistance to psychoanalytic despotism point to the need for a nuanced queer feminist reading of specifically female forms of sexuality in his work.[58] *Madness*'s description of oedipal models as relentlessly patriarchal opens the door to such readings.

Perhaps even more importantly for queer feminism, Foucault's privileging of the category of experience in *Madness* serves to align him with a feminist phenomenological critical lineage that begins with Beauvoir in the late 1940s. For, although Foucault was famously critical of Sartre, his more modulated views about other existentialist phenomenological thinkers—especially Merleau-Ponty, who was his teacher in the 1950s—

support possible connections between Foucault's and Beauvoir's approaches to sexual experience. The details of those connections are beyond the scope of this book. For the purposes of this chapter's focus on Foucault's challenge to Freud, I want to insist on the positivist tradition that, in Foucault's view, Freud inherits. As a dominance project of objectification, the "caged freedom" of psychoanalytic positivism is no freedom at all. Psychoanalysis cannot free us because its rationalist, moralizing structures preclude the possibility of speaking about sexual experience except as it is already captured by a patriarchal scientific gaze. And, as I've insisted throughout this book, an engagement with experience is crucial for an ethics of erotic freedom, as Foucault's later work on ethics attests. If we follow Foucault, through the byways of *Madness*, toward his devastating conclusion that psychoanalysis cannot hear the experience of unreason, any Freudian engagement with an ethics that would situate erotic alternatives to pathologization within the very psyche that secures those pathologies begins to look like a dead end.

Put somewhat differently, in the spinning game that is *Sexuality One*, Foucault has evacuated from the category of sexuality the experience of sexuality, except as one of discursive assimilation and control. And because it separates sexuality as discourse from any possibility of erotic experience, *Sexuality One* alone cannot yield an ethics or a politics that would hope to transform either individual or collective experiences of sexual exclusion. What is missing from *Sexuality One*—and what *Madness* gives us—is an argument that might lead from the negativity of critique to the constructive articulation of a different ethics; that argument, in turn, might produce a sustainable sexual politics. *Madness* gives us what *Sexuality One* alone cannot: the philosophical pieces for a reorganization of bourgeois sexual morality into what I am calling a political ethic of eros.

The Psychic Life of Identity

This chapter's return to *Madness* for its historicization of a psyche-logos we all inhabit is motivated by my sense of an ethical impasse specific to the present moment. That sense of impasse, or even exhaustion, is evidenced by an abandonment of politics in some quarters and a return to ethics in contemporary critical theory. My purpose in this section of the chapter is not to uncover all the paradigmatic instances in which queer theory reveals itself to be both Foucauldian and psychoanalytic. Indeed, the claim that queer theory has comfortably and almost invisibly settled into its Freudo-Foucauldian foundations is, I believe, indisputable. Even when Freud and Foucault are not explicitly cited, the implicitly Freudo-Foucauldian conceptual combinations that pepper queer discourse— "*jouissance*" with "historical consciousness,"[59] Žižekian "symptoms" with "normativity,"[60] the Lacanian "given-to-be-seen" with the material "archive,"[61] Freudian "erotogenicity" with Foucauldian "pleasure"[62]— attest to the phenomenon of the theoretical melding that characterizes queer "scavenger" theory. In that context, any project to obsessively ferret out the most egregious examples of such amalgamations would miss the Foucauldian point about the psychological "confiscation" of the human sciences, of which psychoanalysis is a part, that affects queer theory no less than other humanist projects. Indeed, as the manifestation of a confiscation, Freudo-Foucauldianism may be less a coupling than the most recent "episode," to use Foucault's word, of a hostile takeover that began when Descartes first exorcized madness from the cogito.

Despite the seeming no-win scenario of a modern knowledge project where we live in Freud like fish in water, I continue to argue that unreflective amalgamations of Freud with Foucault need to be questioned. For, if alterity itself has been confiscated by the sciences of the psyche, all the more reason to find alternative ways from within that confiscation to access the differences alterity names. That search for an alternative to the psychological models of Foucault's early training constitutes one of the vibrant threads that runs through his life's work. In that spirit, this book's restorative and revitalizing impulse has been driven, from its inception, by what I can only call a loyalty to Foucault and the archival specificity of his lifelong project. That loyalty is in part a response to the many readings of Foucault—some of them breezy, some of them serious—that collapse his uniquely generative work into, among other things, linguistic structuralism, Derridean deconstruction, and Freudo-Lacanianisms of various forms. Most important for the project of this book, loyalty names my inchoate but insistent sense that queer theory has eaten prodigiously of that juiciest of fruits we call Foucault, but has somehow not taken in, much less digested, the consistent critique of psychoanalysis to be found there.

Beyond loyalty, I want to uncouple the Freudian from the Foucauldian because I think their separation will be useful for the political and intellectual project of queer theory. Comparing his books to toolkits, farmers' shoes, or firecrackers, Foucault expressed his hope that they would "disappear" into the uses that might be made of them. And if

Sexuality One has been useful for queer theory, recontextualizing its ironic critique of psychoanalysis within the historicizing context *Madness* provides can make Foucault more useful now for the politico-ethical work I believe to be one of queer theory's most vital imperatives. *Madness*'s historical retraversal of the psychic moral territory that has been confiscated by a *psyche-logos* offers new conceptual and methodological tools for a queer political ethic. That retraversal not only exposes the inconsistencies of queer Freudo-Foucauldianism but, more important, establishes a new foundation for the difficult constructive task of rethinking subjectivation and erotic experience in new—other-than-psychic, other-than-moral—ethical terms.

In the previous chapter I drew on Butler's *Gender Trouble* to establish queer performative agency as a dialectical undoing of sexual identity through the reversal and sublation of subjective interiority conceived within a sociolinguistic matrix. I further distinguished the performative undoing of "sex" from a Foucauldian subjectivation in which the subject's historical emergence is conceived as coextensive with thinking, thereby differentiating the performative rupture of identity from the Foucauldian anonymity of an unfolding in which the subject disappears altogether. Queer theory's ongoing investment in the psyche as the site of identity's failure attests to the critical staying power of that performative logic.

I move now to build on my argument in chapter 2 by engaging Butler's more explicit reading of performativity and the psyche in *The Psychic Life of Power* (1997). In moving explicitly "toward a psychoanalytic criticism of Foucault,"[63] *Psychic Life* becomes, like *Gender Trouble*, a paradigmatic articulation of the problem of resistance to normative sexual identity that forms the backbone of queer theory. Because it builds on the dialectical reversals of performativity in *Gender Trouble*, *Psychic Life* serves to link my analysis of Nietzschean interiority in chapter 2 with this chapter's focus on the historical emergence of the sciences of the psyche. I would not, *pace* Sedgwick, describe *Gender Trouble* as "roughly psychoanalytic;"[64] indeed, the generative power of that volume in particular can in part be attributed to the wide-ranging "scavenger" qualities Butler and Sedgwick share. And although Butler's middle work displays an increasing investment in psychoanalytic frames for interrogating subjectivity, her thinking can certainly not be reduced to Freudian paradigms in any of its stages.[65] In fact, the often rival theories that come together in Butler's work form a theoretical tableau that looks more like a wrestling match than a harmonious coupling. In that sense, as in many others, Butler's work is useful for its exposure of the tensions that characterize much of queer theory, not least of which is a Freud-Foucault tension she readily acknowledges. From that perspective, *Psychic Life* can be seen as a foundational queer project to think "the theory of power together with a theory of the psyche."[66]

The Foucauldian foundation on which Butler erects her Freudian *Psychic Life* is established through a selective reading of Foucault's middle work that characterizes queer theory generally. Butler includes in her purview not only *Sexuality One* but also *Discipline and Punish*, which, published the year before *Sexuality One*, develops many of the concepts—particularly subjectivation as assujettissement—that will become central in queer theory's reception of Foucault. Responding to a historical present in which sexual assujettissement continues to normalize subjectivity and impose moralities that mire queer behaviors and forms of relation in the swamp of shame, Butler and Foucault share similar goals: to move "beyond normalization" (87) through the "breaking down" (95) of our subjectivation toward a "postmoral" (82) ethics of freedom. The question that worries Butler, as it does Foucault at the end of *Sexuality One*, is ultimately a political and ethical one: given our internalized subjectivation, how do we resist?

The problems that impel Butler's reflections on the psyche as the site where our internalized subjectivation resides are knots that emerge out of the condensations of *Sexuality One*. For if, unlike *Sexuality One*, *Discipline and Punish* is marked by an attention to the historicity of its subject, the sexual problems of *Psychic Life* derive from *Sexuality One*'s concentration on a Victorian portrait of the psyche. Butler's philosophical aims for thinking sexuality in *Psychic Life* include conceptualizing conscience as "the psychic operation of a regulatory norm" (5); giving "an account of subjection" that includes the subject's self-reproachful turning "against itself" (18–19); framing psychic life within a Nietzschean picture of "morality . . . predicated on a certain kind of violence" (64); and constructively imagining "the possibility of a postmoral gesture toward a less regular freedom" that, following Nietzsche, "calls into question the values of morality" (82).

Butler offers these reflections on the theme of psychic power as a supplement, a corrective, and a challenge to Foucault. In a comment that echoes Dean and Lane's declaration that Foucault rarely treated the topic of psychoanalysis in his work, Butler asserts, "Foucault is notoriously taciturn on the topic of the psyche" (18). Butler continues: "not only does the entire domain of the psyche remain largely unremarked in his theory, but power in this double valence of subordinating and producing remains unexplored" (2). Butler further interprets Foucault's silence on the psyche as the sign of an unacknowledged indebtedness to both Hegel and Freud. Uncovering the Freudo-Hegelian traces within Foucault that he "unwittingly" (34) fails to recognize, Butler sets the stage for a psychoanalytically driven, dialectical account of subjection and subversion in Foucault. Reinterpreting the unhappy consciousness of the Hegelian lord-bondsman dialectic as a psychic turning of the subject against himself, Butler's account of Foucault's psychic life produces Freudianism as the Foucauldian unconscious. Because the psyche remains unremarked in Foucault, its unspeakability becomes the Foucauldian symptom of a psychic foreclosure or "preemptive loss" (23) that "cannot be thought . . . owned or grieved" (24). Butler calls this loss that exceeds the thinking and expression of Foucault himself "a suppressed psychoanalysis in Foucault" (87).

Butler's psychoanalysis of Foucault is built on a dubious assertion—belied by the Binswanger introduction, *Mental Illness and Psychology*, *Madness*, *The Order of Things*, *Sexuality One*, and numerous interviews—that the psyche in Foucault remains unremarked. Further, each of the philosophical themes Butler raises as untreated in Foucault's account of subjection—the conscience as regulatory, the subject's turning against itself as negative affect, the violent underpinnings of moral conscience, and the gesture beyond morality toward an ethics of freedom—is treated in detail in *Madness*. I will not rehearse Foucault's account of those problems here, as they are already obvious as salient themes in the story I've been telling throughout this book. Moreover, my interest in *Psychic Life* centers not on its debatable claims about Foucault's foreclosure of the psyche but, more importantly, on the philosophical differences that emerge when we compare Foucault's extensive treatment of psychic life in the rise of science with Butler's account. For if *Madness* engages precisely the same questions that drive Butler's narrative about psychic life, it unravels them in different ways and from a different perspective. As I argued in chapter 2, whether Butler acknowledges *Madness* or not, in *Gender Trouble* the performative conception of subjectivity that frames her analysis differs significantly from Foucauldian subjectivation. And if that difference is already apparent in *Gender Trouble*'s dialectical resignifications, it becomes even more so in the Hegelo-Nietzschean, Freudo-Foucauldian combinations that *Psychic Life* stages. More than simply a difference of opinion about the heuristic value of psychoanalysis, the battle over the psyche that unfolds in *Psychic Life*

clarifies in ways that *Gender Trouble* does not two radically different philosophies of the subject and two distinct approaches to the ethical question of alterity.

Significantly, the philosophical distinctions between Foucault and
Butler that emerge through a reading of *Psychic Life* are, to a large extent,
a function of the temporally specific Franco-American contexts that
frame their vastly differing conceptions of subjectivity. As I already
noted in chapter 2, for Foucault madness is both a loss to be grieved and
the murmuring promise of a future freedom; that hope in an image of
the human face disappearing as sand at the edge of the sea frames the
philosophical antihumanism of Foucault's postwar generation. As
Moreno Pestaña's sociological reading of Foucault makes clear, his
thought reflects the thinking that constitutes his habitus and, at the
same time, distinguishes itself as distinctly Foucauldian within the
competitive intellectual environment of the French 1950s and sixties.[67]
Thus Foucault's disappearing subject cannot be reduced to an antihumanist position he shares with Lacan, Lévi-Strauss, or Derrida; at the
same time, it cannot be entirely extracted from that context either.

Butler, on the other hand, limits her antihumanism to a critique of
identity which, from a certain perspective, positions her within the humanist tradition Foucault spent his life challenging. Like Foucault, Butler both reflects the milieu that frames her thinking and strives to distinguish herself from other thinkers working within the same field.
Driven by the contradictions of a 1970s and eighties identity politics
specific to U.S. feminism and gay liberation, Butler's dialectical rework-
ings of "sex" constitute a philosophical response to the paradoxically
constraining liberation that characterizes political identity. And, within
the philosophical field itself, Butler's work creatively combines Hegelian dialectical idealism with the anti-Hegelian linguistic deconstruc-
tions that mark the imported French poststructuralism which began to
appear in the U.S.—and especially at Yale where Butler trained—in
the 1980s. In that context, Butler's anti-identitarian dialectizing moves
both troubled sex-gender and helped to create the "queer." And again,
as with Foucault, to situate Butler within this political and philosophical
frame is not to reduce her unique work to the effect of sociological
causes; rather, it is to provide an interpretive context for the distinctions
I'm making between the psychic investments of American Freudo-
Foucauldianism and Foucault's antipsychoanalytic French perspective.

In using Butler specifically to make assertions about queer theory
generally, I could, rightly enough, be accused of collapsing one into

the other. As I've repeatedly emphasized, queer theory's strands— including the psychoanalytic ones—are promiscuously multiple, over- lapping, and interwoven. As such, they present different knots to be untangled in a project to rethink psychic life in relation to Foucault. A detailed consideration of psychoanalytic Foucauldianism in Sedgwick, for example, would lead away from what she recognizes, unlike most queer theorists, as the "joke"[68] of the repressive hypothesis in *Sexuality One*. That consideration of Sedgwick would also involve the replace- ment of Freudianism and its developmental oedipal moorings with the "variety of reparative practices"[69] to be derived from the less paranoid, more hopeful, affect-oriented theories of Silvan Tomkins and Melanie Klein. The performative dimension of Sedgwick's queer theory would, correspondingly, present an overlapping but different set of problems to be considered in relation to Foucauldian subjectivation. Sedgwick's "perverse" close literary readings of fisting in James or masturbation in Austen would also open up different questions than those pursued within Butler's more specifically philosophical perspective. Other Fou- cauldian genealogies of psychoanalytic queer theory could also be un- dertaken with regard to Bersani, Edelman, Berlant, Halberstam, Eng, and so forth. But that is not my project. My more limited purpose is to focus on *Psychic Life* for its paradigmatic, even foundational, dramatiza- tion of the Freud-Foucault struggle. As we view that struggle through the lens of Butler's psychoanalytic perspective, the ethical differences between queer anti-identitarianism and Foucauldian antihumanism begin to emerge like holographic images we were unable to see before.

If *Gender Trouble*'s multiple analytical approaches, along with its clear critique of psychoanalytic heterosexism, make it something more than "roughly psychoanalytic," such is not the case in *Psychic Life*, where But- ler clearly speaks from a "first-person" (29) psychoanalytic perspective filtered through linguistic structuralism. Butler's grounding claims about "the incommensurability between psyche and subject" (87) are avowedly psychoanalytic: "*according to psychoanalysis*, the subject is not the same as the psyche from which it emerges" (94; emphasis added). Correspondingly, the conception of the subject that undergirds this claim is logico-linguistic. Butler insists: although "sometimes bandied about as if it were interchangeable with 'the person' or 'the individual,'" (10), the subject "ought to be designated as a linguistic category, a place- holder, a structure in formation" (10). In her psycholinguistic interpre- tation of subjection in Foucault, Butler thus adopts an analytical posi- tion that is doubly at odds with the Foucauldian project to rethink subjectivity not as the effect of a psycho-language, but as a discursive *and* nondiscursive experience whose historical structures can be traced through an immersion in the archive.

In the book's central chapter on Freud and Foucault, "Subjection, Resistance, Resignification," Butler admits to having "wandered into a psychoanalytic vocabulary" (92) of "sublimation" (58, 92), "interiority" (89), and "constitutive loss" (92) that is not Foucault's. But, through her psychoanalytic wanderings, Butler succeeds in transforming Foucault's antipsychoanalytic position into "a Foucaultian perspective *within* psychoanalysis" (87). Viewed through the lens of *Madness*, this transformation might be perceived not as a wandering but as a "confiscation," to use Foucault's oft-repeated term. For, in her psycholinguistic confiscation of Foucault, Butler respectfully but firmly plays Freud-the-analyst to a Foucauldian analysand in a paradigmatic doctor-patient pairing, skillfully deploying a psychoanalytic apparatus to uncover Foucault's psychic excess as "an excrescence" (17) of his own logic. And, if *Madness* demystifies as an object of science what Butler sees as "the psychoanalytically rich notion of the psyche" (87), it is not surprising that *Psychic Life* has no truck with such demystifying exposures of psychoanalysis as a despotic medical technology. For the performative political and philosophical goals that structure Butler's psychoanalysis of Foucault are very different from Foucault's nonperformative motivations.

But these differences are easily lost in the hologram—the dazzling transformations and dialectical reversals that produce, in *Psychic Life*, a sublated and "sublimated" Foucault who no longer looks like Foucault. Indeed, Foucault becomes, like the ventriloquist's doll we saw in *Madness*, the performative subject of an introjected psychic life who will speak, in a language foreign to him, the truth of identity's subversion. And although Butler repeatedly acknowledges Foucault's departures from theorists like Lacan, she subtly redeploys some of the trademark concepts made famous not only by Lacan but also by Althusser, Derrida, and Butler herself as if they were part of Foucault's conceptual arsenal. In the following passage, italics and brackets highlight the multiple poststructuralist utterances that appear to originate from the mouth of Foucault:

> Where Lacan restricts the notion of social power to the symbolic domain and delegates resistance to the imaginary, *Foucault* recasts the *symbolic* [*Foucault-as-Lacan*] as relations of power. . . . *In Foucault* . . . what is brought into being through the *performative effect* [*Foucault-as-Butler*] of the *interpellating demand*

[*Foucault-as-Althusser*] is much more than a "subject," for the "subject" created is not for that reason fixed in place: it becomes the occasion for a *further making* [*Foucault-as-Butler*]. Indeed, I would add, a subject only remains a subject through a *reiteration or rearticulation of itself as a subject* [*Foucault-as-Butler*]. . . . This repetition or, better, *iterability* [*Foucault-as-Derrida*] thus becomes the non-place of *subversion* [*Foucault-as-Butler*], the possibility of a *re-embodying* [*Foucault-as-Butler*] of the *subjectivating norm* [*Foucault-as-Foucault*] that can *redirect* [*Foucault-as-Butler*] its normativity. (98–99)

Notice that, of the multiple distinctive theoretical concepts that emerge in this passage about Foucault, only one can be characterized as recognizably Foucauldian. Indeed, by the end of the paragraph Foucault *is* Butler. In and of itself, this is not a problem; as a long-standing reader of Irigarayan mimesis, I appreciate the critical power of ventriloquisms of various kinds. And indeed, with regard to Foucault, it is worth remembering that he himself longed for his own disappearance into the multiple uses to be made of his books. But the ventriloquism we find here is neither Irigarayan (ironic) nor Foucauldian (desubjectivating). Ironically enough for a thinker of parody, Butler's ventriloquism in *Psychic Life* is nonparodic. Further, it is specifically psychoanalytic and identitarian. Put somewhat differently, the snag in the fabric of Foucault's "uses" here in *Psychic Life* is the manner of his transformation and reconstitution in a game called identity. So although Foucault disappears in a process that looks like Foucauldian desubjectivation, that disappearance is recuperated for the project of identity and its subversion. Thus, in the passage cited above, each of the terms Butler redeploys in her poststructuralist ventriloquism—*symbolic, performative, interpellating, reiteration, rearticulation,* and *iterability*—articulates an anti-identitarian unmaking and remaking which speaks to a contemporary American political reality framed within a psychoanalytic conception of identity and its undoing in the unconscious.

Let me be clear: my description of a ventriloquism in *Psychic Life* that makes Foucault speak about identity does not constitute a negative moral judgment about the value of identity work itself. Indeed, I am grateful to Butler for her toils in that field. My single point here is that it's not Foucauldian, and I believe that the time has arrived for queer theory to examine, as it has not yet done, the ethical and political implications of the differences that distinguish performative identity work from Foucauldian thinking about the subject. Correspondingly, I am not arguing, like François Cusset and others, that non-French meldings of multiple French poststructuralisms into new theoretical amalgams are necessarily suspect or risible. In fact, the poststructuralist performances to which we in the U.S. have been treated during the past three decades have served important, context-specific philosophical and political purposes.

Those purposes are multiple and temporally contingent. *Psychic Life*'s welding of Foucault with Freud could be viewed as a response to a theoretical impasse that emerges, within queer theory in the mid-1990s, precisely as a result of the Freudo-Foucauldianism of queer theory's beginnings. Such a contextualization of *Psychic Life* would include in its purview other queer theoretical maneuvers during the same period, revealing a more general sense of a growing unease with the contradictions embodied in queer theory's simultaneously Freudian and anti-Freudian Foucauldian investments. Thus, again in Sedgwick's work, the shifts away from oedipal psychoanalytic models in *Shame and Its Sisters* and *Touching Feeling* would serve as evidence of an increasing discomfort with Freudo-Foucauldianism. Sedgwick would exemplify, along the same lines, a pervasive attempt, within queer theory of the mid- to late-1990s, to access and theorize those dimensions of sexual experience—and, most especially, the experience of affect—that *Sexuality One* seems to have drained away. From that perspective, *Psychic Life*'s attention to self-berating, grief, guilt, love, melancholy, and rage could be read as a similar attempt to put some experiential flesh on a thin Foucauldian sexual dispositif that lacks sensibility or an inner life.

In that historically contextualizing spirit, I italicize *Psychic Life*'s queer ventriloquism not to denounce it, but rather to bring out the lessons it has to offer for queer theory today, over ten years after its original appearance and in the wake of the new English translation of *History of Madness*. Returning to my recurrent theme of a performative identity critique versus a desubjectivating challenge to subjectivity itself, attention to Butler's treatment of the psyche as identity's container exposes the philosophical rift that allows Butler to embrace psychoanalysis while Foucault rejects it. Unlike *Gender Trouble* or *Bodies that Matter*, *Psychic Life* subordinates identity's American political meanings to a conception of identity that is specifically psychoanalytic. Like a microscope, *Psychic Life* zeroes in on identity as it is defined *within* psychoanalysis, thereby bringing into greater theoretical focus the growing differences between performative identities and Foucauldian subjectivation.

In *Psychic Life*, and in accordance with its Freudian conception, identity names the normative dimension of the psyche. Correspondingly, in her reading of *Discipline and Punish*, Butler describes the disciplinary model of obedience that subjectivates the prisoner as a "normative ideal inculcated, as it were, into the prison [as] a kind of *psychic identity*, or what Foucault will call a 'soul'" (85; emphasis added). Further reinterpreting, through a psychoanalytic lens, Foucault's famous sentence in *Discipline and Punish* about the soul as a prison of the body, Butler redeploys a previously established analogy between the Nietzschean soul and psychic identity to counter Foucault's seeming totalization of the obedient subject in *Discipline and Punish*. In that redeployment of the soul as psyche, Butler strives to create a breach in the Foucauldian prison of subjective normalization. For, unlike the totalized subject of Foucault's disciplinary subjection, "the psyche," Butler asserts, "*includes the unconscious*" and "is very different from the subject" (86; emphasis added).

Butler's account of the psyche as the site of the subject's internal self-difference relies on a two-part logic: first, an equation that analogizes the psyche with identity and, second, a universalizing assertion about identity's failure. In that failure, psychic identity bleeds out an excess called the unconscious, which in turn produces the rupture of identity as nonidentity. Consequently, Foucauldian assujettissement spits out a subject who, having lost her coherence through identity's failure, achieves political agency *as a subject* by virtue of her failure to cohere *as an identity*. In this way, Butler produces an unconscious within Foucault as a force of psychic resistance that he himself is not able to perceive or acknowledge.

Importantly, the rupturing force of this distinctly queer Foucauldian unconscious leaves the subject disidentified, to use José Muñoz's term, but oddly intact as a political subject.[70] As Butler puts it in the ventriloquizing passage quoted above, "a subject . . . *remains*" (99; emphasis added). Significantly, it is precisely an *unconscious* psychic resistance—identity's excess within Foucault—that brings about, through a sublimation Foucault cannot recognize, the subject of reiterative, performative forms of agency that emerges in the ventriloquizing passage. Psychoanalysis—and, specifically, its Freudian form—thus allows Butler to transform the Nietzschean soul of *Discipline and Punish* into a concept of identity as a regulative ideal which contains within itself, as Foucault's unconscious, the subversion of that regulative ideal. This

Foucauldian unconscious allows her, in turn, to redeploy identity as a political term and to describe Foucault as an anti-identitarian performative subject who is "calling for an overthrow" of "identity politics" (100).

In the context I've laid out, this psychoanalytic narrative about Foucault begins to look like a disguise for a story that is not about him at all. As in *Gender Trouble*, Butler's conception of subjectivity in *Psychic Life* revolves around identity and its subversion. In *Psychic Life* specifically, Butler uses Freudian identity to enlist Foucault for a political agenda he doesn't share. As an antipsychoanalytic thinker whose work emerges out of the political tradition of French republicanism, Foucault displays few signs of thinking about the politics of subjectivity in either American or psychoanalytic identitarian terms. As I argued in chapter 1, *identity* is a word Foucault scarcely uses except in its mathematical meaning as equivalence; its most significant absence is marked by the passage in *Sexuality One* that most Anglophone readers have read as Foucault's "acts versus identities" theory of homosexuality.

This reading of *Psychic Life* serves to underscore precisely how psychoanalytic and identity-oriented readings of Foucault reinforce one another. For a ventriloquized Foucauldian "call to 'refuse' . . . identities" (102) and to overthrow the politics conducted in their name can only make sense from the Freudian perspective that produces identity and its excess as a Foucauldian unconscious. Further, despite attempts such as Dean and Lane's to separate psychoanalytic theory from its practice, Freudo-Foucauldianisms of various forms rely on Freud not only for the unconscious as a concept but also for the distinctively psychoanalytic hermeneutic critical practice it authorizes. For, as a concept attached to an analytic technology, the unconscious holds the key to the disavowed truths the analyst will uncover in the analysand. The queer psychoanalyst can thus discover in Foucault those hidden truths he himself was unable to discover without the help of the analyst. More important, the queer analyst can make Foucault speak: in a talking cure that corrects his errors and gives voice to his silent foreclosures, Foucault reproduces that which has been deposited in him as the unconscious of his work. The result of this psychoanalytic interpretive practice is a thaumaturgic transformation: Foucauldian antihumanist, nonstructuralist subjectivation becomes—through identity's psycholinguistic reversal and sublation as subversion—a form of political agency that resecures the subject of modern humanism.

This story about identity and a Foucauldian unconscious in psychoanalytic queer theory reveals the mutually reinforcing investments of a

psychoanalytic project to rupture identity and a humanist project to solidify the subject as identity's container. Investing the promise of identity's rupture within a sustainable humanist subject relies on a circular,
paradoxical logic that can describe identity, but not subjectivity itself.
For the psyche both secures the subject and destabilizes it with an unconscious that guarantees identity's failure. But, as the limited rupture
of a subject it also helps to secure, identity's failure within the subject
guarantees not the subject's failure but its recuperation against another,
unacknowledged alterity that is rendered invisible. In a well-known passage cited by Butler, Jacqueline Rose reveals the seductive dimension of
this psychoanalytic ruse about identity's failure as an alterity "at the very
heart of psychic life":

> The unconscious constantly reveals the "failure" of identity. Because there is
> no continuity of psychic life, so there is no stability of sexual identity, no posi-
> tion for women (or for men) which is ever simply achieved. Nor does psycho-
> analysis see such "failure" as a special-case inability or an individual devi-
> ancy from the norm. . . . "Failure" is something endlessly repeated and
> relived moment by moment throughout our individual histories. It appears
> not only in the symptoms, but also in dreams, in slips of the tongue and in
> forms of sexual pleasure which are pushed to the sidelines of the norm. . . .
> There is a resistance to identity at the very heart of psychic life.[71]

Rose's seductive assertions about a universally shared difference
within—assertions that amount to saying, as Dean and Lane do, that
psychoanalysis "effectively 'queers' all sexuality"[72]—are especially ap-
pealing when they're reworked, in *Psychic Life*, to produce new forms of
political agency. But if identity repeatedly fails in Rose's account, the
subject does not: she still has a history and an individuality that, "moment by moment," lives, dreams, speaks, and feels pleasure. There is
no other in Rose's account: identity's failure *within every* subject disguises the internalizing structure of violence that, in Foucault's Nietzschean account of subjectivity, erects some subjects on the backs of others, exorcizing those others from within the social body.

Such universalizing claims about identity's failure bring to the fore
Foucault's ethical concerns about psychoanalysis generally. For, if identity's failure is conceived as constitutive of all subjects in all times and
places, how can we account for the fact that some subjects are more deviant than others, more failed as subjects, so "pushed to the sidelines of
the norm" that they cease to be subjects? How can psychoanalytic iden-

tity's universal failure account for subjectivity's cost as an alterity that denies subjectivity to others? The subjective destabilizations Rose evokes are only partial failures in a ludic mode: the gentle ruptures of wild dreams, orgasms, verbal slips, kinky sex, and gender play that still leave the subject intact. These are the universalizing failures of a Freudian identity whose unconscious, in Dean and Lane's words, "makes all sexuality perverse."[73] But there is another kind of failure whose story would be written, if it could, in a tragic mode. That other failure, the unspeakable loss that haunts *Madness*, is more explicitly social and more deeply historical than the strange dreams or slips of the tongue that characterize identity's failures. Indeed, the failed subjectivities of that other failure are so illegible that they cannot be heard or measured.

Foucault's antipsychoanalytic, antihumanist view of alterity thus allows him to raise specifically ethical questions that he, a resisting analysand, can now ask of the psychoanalyst. For example, how can a conception of the psyche as a universal force of deviancy explain or heal the othering structures that produce those nonuniversal forms of alterity? How can psychoanalysis uncover or cure the centuries-old sedimentation of the abnormal and the pathological not as universal but as exceptionalizing categories of scientific and moral exclusion? How can it account for that queerest form of radical alterity called madness?

In a reprise of themes that will now be familiar, the answer to those questions can only emerge in a uniquely Foucauldian historical archiveology that distinguishes the ethical attention *Madness* brings to experiences of exclusion from understandings of alterity as the atemporal excrescences of a universal psyche. As *Madness* makes abundantly clear, Foucault locates the unconscious as a spatiotemporal emergence and connects it, specifically, to the technological transformations and institutional practices of a history of science. Queer Freudian thinking, by contrast, begins from within the static frame of a technology's capture as theory, thereby rendering invisible the practices and institutions from which the theory is derived.

This methodological and conceptual difference points to the widening chasm that separates Foucault from Butler and, by extension, from many of the queer uses to which he has been put. Although *Psychic Life* is concerned with the costs of identity—not only sexual normalization and the policing of gender but also negative affects that remain unresolved—as a theory whose telos is identity's subversion and resignification, *Psychic Life* does not attend to the historical costs of subjectivity itself. Indeed, I would argue that this is not its project. *Psychic Life*'s

UNRAVELING THE QUEER PSYCHE   177

concern is the "injury" of identity and identity politics, not the injuring that is subjectivity. And, although in its attachment to the self-wounding turn of a Nietzschean moral subject Butler's concept of injury might serve to link her to Foucault's self-injuring Nietzschean subject, the differences that separate them remain. For, if Foucault's antihumanist Nietzscheanism leads him into a historical wounding that swallows up subjectivity altogether, Butler's psychoanalytic Nietzscheanism leads her to recuperate injury as political agency.

Moreover, Butler's conception of psychic identity as injury reveals the paradoxical relation of subjects to themselves in their constitution through injury; this insight into what Wendy Brown calls identity's "wounded attachments"[74] also reveals what Butler calls the "self-colonizing trajectory of certain forms of identity politics" (104). In a final sublation that draws implicitly on psychoanalytic trauma theory, Butler reads this injury as "a necessarily alienated narcissism" (104) that can ultimately recuperate, through the unconscious, its own wounding as injury. It is the subject's attachment to her injury as identity that produces, for Butler, her political agency as a subject in the form of a "traumatic and productive iterability" (104).

Contrastingly, Foucault's focus in all of his work, but especially in *Madness*, is the historical injuring structure of subjectivity. Within that historical structure, Foucault might describe Butler's injury—the injury of *sexed* identity, the injury of what Foucault in *Sexuality One* calls simply "sex"—as the specifically nineteenth-century *sexological* injury of a psyche-logos that continues to produce "sex" not just as an identity, but as the explicitly modern form of subjectivity itself. Within Foucault's subjectivating logic, which is neither Butler's nor Freud's, the failure of "sex" would mean a failure of subjectivity, not the partial, orgasmic ruptures of the identitarian variety that universalize the queer as a sexual deviation which leaves the subject intact. Moreover, both the injury that is sex and the threat or promise of its failure would function, for Foucault, within the longer story this chapter traces about the rise of psychological science. Thus, where Butler's story about sex-as-identity's consolidation and failure ends with an infinitely productive self-wounding, Foucault's story about the consolidation or failure of sex-as-subjectivity would hinge on what he repeatedly calls in the 1961 preface the "tragic structure" that erects the subject and its history "against the backdrop" of a wounding that is the "absence of history" (*M* xxxi).

Ultimately, then, at stake for Foucault in his critique of psychoanalysis is a postmoral political ethic. As a product of rationalism and morality, the sexed psyche of a psychoanalytic, sexological thinking that is still with us shores up exclusion precisely when subjectivity emerges against the horizon of the other's disappearance. Psychoanalysis, for all its attention to sexed identity's failure as a psychic unconscious, cannot hear or see that *other* failure of "sex"-as-subjectivity because to acknowledge that failure would be the undoing of psyche-logos itself. Indeed, as *Madness* insists, psychoanalysis functions historically to ensure the other's burial. And if there will be resistance to that other's burial—which there will be—the resistance will not come from within the psyche or its identity. For Foucault there is no identity or anti-identity, not so much because it's American—Foucault liked the U.S., after all—but because as a psychoanalytic concept identity is ahistorical and fails, ethically, to account for the historical other whose traces Foucault finds in the archives.

Most important, despite what Freudo-Foucauldians often claim—that Foucault's condemnation of the psyche offers no way out—he in fact opens a path toward a resistance to moral rationalism's exclusions from a *within* that is not static but explicitly historical or genealogical. For, if we believe the "half-real, half-imaginary" story *Madness* tells, no one, including Foucault, can stand outside psyche-logos. Indeed, Foucault's recognition of that fact is something Derrida repeatedly refused to see in a philosophical battle that continued to drag on, ironically enough, well beyond Foucault's death. Foucault undoubtedly would have enjoyed that irony, especially given one of the Deleuzian images of Foucauldian subjectivation as a "becoming-battle."[75]

Foucault recognizes that because psychoanalysis has conquered and confiscated the human knowledge we hold about ourselves, resistance to psychoanalysis must come from within psychoanalysis. But resistance from within is always tricky, and it is easy to become the very thing we're resisting in ever-new confiscations. In reading *Madness* against *Psychic Life*—and, by extension, Foucault against Freudo-Foucauldian versions of him—it becomes clear that Foucault's "within psychoanalysis" is different than Butler's. If both stand inside that well-girded fortress of the psyche, Butler's anti-identitarian bricolage leaves the subject-producing foundations of humanism undisturbed. By contrast, Foucault's historicizing blows at the subject are aimed exactly at humanism's foundations. And, if he doesn't quite succeed at bringing down the fortress, his becoming-other conception of desubjectivation as a function of history and thinking itself is among the most radical of late-twentieth-century philosophical attempts to challenge the tarnished dream of rationalist humanism.

Many thinkers of the psyche will want to claim, with the concept of the unconscious, that psychoanalysis levels a similar, equally powerful blow to the philosophical structure that captures the human within rationalism. But *Madness* will tell them to historicize that claim in an *archival* retraversal of the emergence of the concept that grounds their assertion within temporally shifting technologies and practices. Those thinkers of the psyche might come to find hope in such a charge. For if, as Deleuze puts it, history is "an emergence of forces which doubles history," that redoubling movement can change history itself, opening toward different futures of freedom. Indeed, from that perspective, what we generally tend to think of as Foucault's final and limited "ethical" work—his return to Greco-Roman and early Christian practices of freedom in volumes 2 and 3 of *History of Sexuality*—might not be seen as the sum total of Foucault's attempts to conceptualize, along Nietzschean lines, a nonwounding postmoral ethics. Rather, they might be seen as the two "final" episodes in a series of historical or genealogical studies—including *History of Madness*, *Discipline and Punish*, and the three volumes of *History of Sexuality*—that constitute Foucault's ethical work. And if *Madness* has been generally perceived as belonging to the pregenealogical period of Foucault's oeuvre, I have argued throughout this book for situating *Madness* differently. That argument hinges on *Madness*'s historical treatment of the moral dimension of rationalism's injuring structures. In this sense, that truly *grand récit* that is *Madness* might be seen as the first of a series of genealogical investigations of ethics as a historical question. In the redoubling of history those investigations put in place, Foucault's ethical stories—his histoires—emerge as forces—as book-events—that both change history and promise a different future.

Queer Exhaustion

Let me end the chapter with a brief return to that other scene of ventriloquism with which I began: an analyst's advice to today's queer children as the failed prodigals of the oedipal family. Over the course of this chapter I have asked the question: if we, queer children, thought we were orphans of a parentally imprinted Freudian family, how is it that we now find ourselves not to be orphans, not to be such great forces of rupture after all—not children from Mars with fantastically prodigal, extravagant psyches, as Sedgwick had imagined herself in her own family[76]—but the normalized children of nineteenth-century heteropatriarchal structures of alliance? And if queer theory's promiscuous birth promised an escape not only from our own childhood, that "trap for adults,"[77] but also from childhood's moral family and its suffocating, dangerous values, why does queer theory still find itself so often mired in a Nietzschean swamp of shame?

In contrasting promiscuity with heteronormative families, I will not charge forward with a story about that specifically queer but amorphous beast we call sex itself: the more I think about "sex itself," the less I know what it means. Nor will I open a moral interrogation into those behavioral rules—including the odd proposition that there will be no rules—that would generalize for everyone—or at least for all queers—whether or not we should be monogamous, multipartnered, celibate, single, soldered to another in a holy place, a sex club, cyberspace, or a brothel, for life or ten minutes, with one or with many, or none of the above. As Sedgwick puts it in my favorite, oft-repeated axiom: "people are different from each other."[78] On the other hand, if I've learned anything from Foucault, it's that the "anything goes" forms of sexual freedom often put forward as a queer eschatology are simply the inverted reflections of Enlightenment autonomy. So I'm not arguing, as some have in response to old-fashioned normalizing moralisms—be they of the family values, feminist, or gay sex panic variety—that barebacking or orgies or public sex or erotic vomiting or sex-positive feminisms or late-night schedules in and of themselves will subvert those moralisms: "every assasination of painting is still a painting."[79] Nor am I arguing, as some sex panickers have, that we need to chastely albeit with bitter nostalgia reinvent ourselves in an attempt to undo the damage of our youthful orgiastic pleasures. If some of those pleasures produce horrible injury, in all the senses of the term, that is not a reason to give up on the many vibrant, capacious, generous forms of self-and-other coextensions promiscuity names. The promiscuous is a concept to be inhabited and explored. But it is not a free fall and requires the patient work of retraversal that Nietzsche practiced as a transvaluation of values. In that Nietzschean spirit, the promiscuous can be another name for the multiple, unexpected, and unforeseeable geometries of thinking, bodies, and forms of relation that delineate an erotic ethics.

Looking back at this chapter's beginning in a psychoanalytic prodigal theory that chafed, I see now it was the increasing predictability of queer theory's moralizing rehearsal of itself as the best-because-sexiest theory on offer that made its unacknowledged sexological investments and Freudian introjections of Foucault so chafing. But having traced here a retrospective interpretation of the Freudo-Foucauldian story, I now, oddly, feel more sympathetic toward prodigal queer theory than I did before. Chafing is a rubbing that happens over time. So the chafing feeling in those queer Freudo-Foucauldian encounters was in large part the result of the passage of time and the changes that came with that passage. Why have I spent the last few years reading more Foucault and less psychoanalysis, becoming more enamored with the former and less with the latter? I would not call it a conversion exactly. Raised on structuralism and its poststructuralist descendants, in the 1980s I too was enthralled with Lacan (although always Irigarayan, even to this day, with the lens I brought to my reading of him). But my shift away from such interpretive models to my current immersion in Foucault is not a supersession or the replacement of one model with another. Like Irigaray (whose *Speculum* I contemplated for years on end), I felt excluded from the Lacanian *Ecole freudienne* from the moment in graduate school when I first cracked open the rune-strewn pages of *Ecrits*. And, like Irigaray, I approached all the theory I read in those years (including, belatedly, Foucault) with the suspicious sense of distance that was (and is) my feminism. (Always hopeful, I will also forever be paranoid.)

So my immersion in Foucault, against Freud, as it were, is not a conversion but a deviation: a squiggling perversion in the line of thinking whose well-worn track I'd been following. I see this perverse deviation as enriching: not a renunciation but an accumulation. As with most acquisitions, adding Foucault to my store of precious treasures has required letting go of some of the stuff that I once adored but is no longer useful for engaging the queer ethical questions that our contemporary moment sets before us. The changes are, hopefully, evidence of thinking and not its refusal. For it was Foucault who taught us, following Nietzsche, that to think means to change our thinking.

Times have changed, and I've changed. In some ways that sums up Foucault's Nietzschean lessons about the historicity of the "I." This need to challenge is not simply the result of the arbitrary vagaries of my personal will, but emerges against the larger horizon of a collective thinking within our historical present. What worked for feminism or queer theory ten years ago doesn't necessarily work now, and the questions asked then are obviously no longer new. The queer psyche as a concept is one of those questions. And, if Nietzsche taught us that the psyche is another word for shame, that insight correlates with a distinctive queer "sense of identity" that Sedgwick describes as "tuned most durably to the note of shame."[80] Even when, in the early years of queer theory, we tried to turn back the virulent shaming that had been directed against us—when we pointed our fingers at those Bible-toting gay pride protesters and said "shame on *you!*"—that Nietzschean game of self-reflection spun shame around again to settle in the place in us it had never left, even as we yelled together and pointed our fingers. And there we were again, in our queer shame: we were the monster that had been there lurking all along in the filthy water. Recognizing this, queer theory didn't quite follow Nietzsche's advice to retraverse the historico-philosophical territories of rational morality that nurture shame. Rather, as Sedgwick points out, shame came out sideways in new forms of critical finger-pointing, written back into the "moralisms of the repressive hypothesis."[81]

This story about queer shame transfigured as critical moralism retells a De Manian lesson Sedgwick herself recalls: that the positive resignifications of "transformational shame"[82] have a life of their own, in their "necessarily 'aberrant'"[83] relation to their own reference. Remembering that lesson, Sedgwick chooses in her final work to move away from both Freudianism and what she called over twenty years ago, in *The Coherence of Gothic Conventions* (1986), "the Foucauldian paranoid."[84] In their place, Sedgwick proposes a "not particularly Oedipal"[85] Kleinian reparative "*seeking of pleasure*" that, for her, "inaugurates ethical possibility."[86] Grounded in what Sedgwick must see as the other-than-paranoid ethical Foucault of the 1980s, such possibility assumes a subject and a "care of the self"[87] that sets shame aside. But, as Foucault's historical lessons about sexual subjectivity, the psyche, and morality suggest, shame will continue to haunt us unless we wade through its culturally specific, temporally sedimented layers.

An especially visible public happening on the theme of queer shame illustrates my paranoid, genealogical Foucauldian point that we cannot really set shame aside, nor can we feel or think its edges before we've explored, historically, the lived experiences that take us there. In a 2005 special issue of *Social Text*, David Eng, Judith Halberstam, and José Muñoz bring together an array of mostly young queer voices on topics ranging from the racialization of sexuality to queer diasporas to critiques of what the editors call a regressive new "queer liberalism." In a collec-

tion that reflects, quite often, the kind of finger-pointing moralism Sedgwick decries, the editors, somewhat ironically, call for an "ethics of humility," which would recognize, from within an arrogant U.S. militarism,
"that we cannot be the center of the world."[88] And, while this call for humility is certainly welcome in the U.S. context the editors describe, in
their tone and self-certain epistemological positioning many of the essays reproduce an antihegemonic moralism that is anything but humble.
I point this out not to silence the important work of making visible a multiplicity of queer experiences and perspectives on race, sexuality, ethnic-
ity, and nation, but rather to suggest that the volume's ironically moralizing call for an ethics of humility is, in part, a response to shame. For
both at its edges—in the volume's introduction—and in its center—in
essays by Hiram Perez and Judith Halberstam—the reader tastes that
bitter residue of a specifically American historical erection of the human
on the backs of dehumanized others. Both Perez and Halberstam, in different ways and from different positions, respond to what they perceive
as the dehumanization of people of color at a now infamous 2003 University of Michigan conference on gay shame which, while spectacularly
excluding scholars of color, entertained and titillated its mostly white gay
male audience with performances and images of hypersexualized black
and brown male bodies. Without going into the details of that particular
scene, I evoke its repetition in the *Social Text* volume to argue for a queer
paranoid critical labor in the shaming, shame-ridden swamp called race
and to *not* do so through the *Freudo*-Foucauldian lens—reading psychic
"trauma" with disciplinary "normalization"[89]—that queer theory often
takes as a theoretical given.

For if the gay shame conference demonstrates that we cannot know
ahead of time the racialized edges of our sexual shame, those edges are
hardly determined by an ahistorical conception of the psyche. As an
instance of queer shame that is nothing less than allegorical in its capi-
talization of the problem, Gay Shame dramatizes the psyche's undeni-
ably historical dimensions. Staged against a backdrop of race made invisible by a focus on sexual shame, gay shame popped up in the corners
of a queer moral conscience where no one was looking and where it was
not expected to appear. The ricocheting movement of that particularly
virulent form of shame, spawned from the historical muck of racialized
sexualization in the U.S. context where the conference took place, demonstrates not only the need for Foucauldian archiveologies of nonwhite,
non-European, non-Western sexualities but also for ongoing critical archiveologies of the white, European, Western sexual formations that

continue to leak shame in the form of race and racism. These paradigmatically paranoid genealogical projects—"suspicious archeologies of the present, the detection of hidden patterns of violence and their exposure"—are not, as Sedgwick might claim, "infinitely doable and teachable protocols of unveiling."[90] On the contrary, these ethical excavations of the cultural spaces where shame settles as the very ground we walk on are infinitely fraught, complicated, and labor intensive: difficult to teach and even harder to do.

This chapter offers a modest contribution to that difficult work. In its call for further Foucauldian archiveologies of the conceptual tools we use to think about ourselves, this book does not represent an archiveology of queer sex in its own right, except, importantly, in its archiveology of "Foucault" himself: not an uncovering of his queer psyche, but another immersion into the layered accumulation of discourses that bear his name. In its current configuration within queer theory, the psyche has consistently been thought ahistorically, as a force of rupture that exists in a conceptual plane outside of space and outside of time. This does not mean that the psyche cannot be rehistoricized, perhaps in ways that Foucault never would have imagined.

As for the Freud-Foucault uncoupling that emerges out of this chapter's reading of the difficult relations between *Sexuality One*, queer theory, and *Madness*, I have repeatedly described *Sexuality One* as the Victorian culmination of the story of *Madness*: a tail end to the story that we still inhabit. And if most of us were, from the start, drawn deep into that tail end of a long sexual history, never quite getting to its beginnings in *Madness*, that queer inversion of a start-to-finish reading of Foucault might today serve to give us, retrospectively, a new picture of ourselves through the renewed beginnings *Madness* offers. This is not to diminish the value of the tail end that is *Sexuality One*: in the tail end we find those "pleasures of the anus"[91] that, like the infinitely expandable sac of a Jamesian sentence, have proven over and over to be truly "inexhaustible."[92] But, if some of us feel, at least for the moment, more than a little bit exhausted, the "begin again" message of *Madness* can revitalize the promiscuous project that is queer theory—even, especially, in its seeming exhaustion.

Postscript: Becoming-Laughter

In giving an account of Butler in *Psychic Life*, I also give an account of myself. I too speak in a confiscating, ventriloquizing voice from within that great confiscation of the human sciences that is psychoanalytic thinking. Like Butler, I engage in the messy and ethically fraught work of cutting and pasting someone else's words to advance my own position. In addition, as an American queer feminist theorist, I speak from a place of identity politics and its critique that Butler and I share. I live, after all, in that most identitarian of fields, "women's studies." And while I have pointed to some limits of performative thinking by examining *Gender Trouble* and *Psychic Life*, in Butler's later work she moves in directions that could also be construed as acknowledging the limits of performativity. Like the best of thinkers, Butler displays changes in her thinking over time that we might see, along with Foucault, not as evidence of philosophical inconsistencies, but as signs of thinking. Further, although I have raised *Madness*'s ethical themes—illegibility, alterity, invisibility, grief—differently than Butler, the work she undertakes after *Psychic Life*—in *Antigone's Claim* (2000), *Precarious Life* (2004), *Undoing Gender* (2004), and *Giving an Account of Oneself* (2005)—constitutes an array of variations on these topics. Precisely engaging in how Foucault's treatment of those themes differs from Butler's is not my purpose in this chapter. Rather, I want to acknowledge the necessary differences and complicities that bind my account of Butler to a self-accounting, but where alterity serves as a reminder that I cannot be reduced to her nor she to me. As Butler herself puts it, "when the 'I' seeks to give an account of itself, it can start with itself, but it will find that this self is already implicated in a social temporality that exceeds its own capacities of narration."[93] Hopefully, the gap such exceeding names can open sites not for stern-faced attacks and counterdefenses, but for generative contestation and even laughter.

Further, although I am fully sympathetic to the difficult philosophy Foucault attempts to practice, I do not claim to know how to do it. As I admitted in my "Wet Dreams" interlude, I do not know how to undo the subject and, frankly, I don't think Foucault does either. For all his criticisms of Descartes's rejection of madness, even Foucault is reduced to *dreaming* of a subject-free, future becoming-other. And, as Descartes points out, dreaming is different than actually thinking you're something other, like a shard of glass or a hollowed-out shell.

That said, I do not want to abandon what we might think of as Foucault's wet dream of a future that would refuse the eros-negating exclusions of a rationalist, humanist project bent on disguising its own violence. However paranoid the critical trench work of that project might be, the movement of that dream—and it's only a dream—must happen in a Nietzschean labor of retraversal: suspicious, serious, sometimes tedious, often dangerous in its slide toward thinking's dark-wooded edges, but heralding a *something better* which, as far as I'm concerned, is a promise we can't live without. Call me Pollyanna, but I want a future: not a heteronormatively reproductive future-as-prison, but an erotic, yes-saying, queer heterotopia: "a space of the outside."[94] For if, as Nietzsche might put it with regard to queer theory, we have tried to proceed "as if all these things—the problems of morality—were really not worth taking quite so seriously,"[95] I agree with Foucault that the necessarily sexual problems of morality continue to demand our serious attention. As Nietzsche affirms, "there seems to be nothing more worth taking seriously" than morality, a territory whose excavation will render the future rewards "of a long, brave, industrious, and subterranean seriousness."[96] Among those rewards will be what Nietzsche names as cheerfulness. Such hope in cheerfulness is something Foucault and Nietzsche shared, as Deleuze reminds us in his descriptions of Foucault's inimitable laughter. So perhaps the quintessentially Foucauldian cheerfulness of a self-shattering, life-affirming laughter will be the reward of a practice of thinking Nietzsche calls, in his own queer language, "a gay science."[97]

Third Interlude

OF METEORS AND MADNESS

Working on Foucault's critique of psychology and psychoanalysis has made me very nervous around my numerous friends who are enthusiastically committed to the project of the psyche as either therapists, analysts, or patients. The cause of my nervousness was confirmed one morning at breakfast with friends, one of whom is a therapist. Over eggs and coffee, I casually mentioned Foucault's *History of Madness* as the focus of my current scholarly investigations.

I should say here that, although I've never been psychoanalyzed, I myself have spent years in therapy and respect those practioners, like my friend, who work hard at listening and helping us feel better. But, over the course of more than a decade of relentlessly talking about myself, I grew not only bored by my own story but also increasingly disillusioned, experientially speaking, by the talking cure. Carefully working through Foucault's critique of Freud in *Madness* has helped me to see why, to find a conceptual and historical language for that inchoate sense of dissatisfaction I felt, which, ultimately, led me to quit therapy. It has also led me, in my intellectual work, to question my previously unreflective use of psychoanalysis as a master code for deciphering the mysteries of the world.

In any event, four of us were there—two lesbian couples—enjoying a sunny Sunday brunch on a restaurant patio in Atlanta. We were talking about *Madness* and my partner, Tamara, enthusiastically said, "Yeah,

Foucault basically argues that we don't really know what madness is, that it's socially constructed."

The therapist friend, call her Laura, immediately replied: "I strongly disagree." She paused for a moment, then continued: "Here's my coming out . . . much more important than my coming out as a lesbian. Compared to this other thing, that was nothing."

She went on to tell us that she was bipolar, and had been on medication for years. Working now as a psychotherapist, she says her experience with mental illness gives her special insight into her patients' suffering.

"When I was nineteen, I was homeless and crazy," she told us. "I was forcibly committed to Bellevue, twice. Do you know how crazy you have to be to be committed to Bellevue? To be picked up off the streets of New York and locked up? Madness is real."

I nodded in sympathy, but was feeling defensive. I had to explain about "madness as a social construction." A little voice in my head was whispering: she doesn't get what Tamara just said, that something socially constructed can still be real.

"In Foucault, it's a bit more complicated," I began. "He's really critiquing philosophical rationalism, going after Descartes. Plus the moral exclusions of bourgeois culture that result in the confinement not only of 'crazy people,' but of prostitutes, poor people, beggars, sodomites, homosexuals, nymphomaniacs, and libertines. He's tracing the historical movement or structure that defines an experience we have come to call madness."

I paused. I'd been writing and thinking about madness so much lately, it came out of me automatically, like a prerecorded message:

"He's asking us to question the category of 'unreason' that produced this great mass of excluded 'others' and locked them all up together, never to be seen or heard from again. It resulted from the Cartesian exile of the body from the mind, which allows the thinker to say: 'I'm not mad.'"

Laura and her partner looked at me quizzically, polite and attentive but also, I thought, wondering how anyone could talk in weird paragraphs like that. Another kind of crazy. I finished my thought:

"Foucault's work was taken up by the antipsychiatry movement, by David Cooper and others. They used it to contest the psychiatric establishment. To say that madness wasn't real. But Foucault himself was never part of that movement."

I had said my piece, but, still, it felt lame. My work felt like a big fat balloon, all puffed up, then suddenly pricked by the expert voice: the voice of psychosis and also the therapeutic voice that holds the key to the cure. It was the voice that "knew" better than I ever could.

But what am I to do with this true voice of madness that combines the perspective of the expert doctor and the suffering patient? I've had bouts of "madness" myself, never diagnosed except as clinical depression. Those years in the early nineties, when I was living in France, I was close to the edge of something deeper than depression. I don't know what to call it. Alcohol-induced psychosis? Suicidal despair? Was my "madness" like the madness Foucault experienced, also in France, as a young man in the 1950s? He too drank until he blacked out, was repeatedly suicidal, almost went over the edge:

> He would often be immobilized by emotional exhaustion for several days running after a nocturnal visit to a gay bar or cruising place. Following a suicide attempt in 1950, Foucault wrote to one of his friends, "Don't make me say anything. . . . Let me get used to lifting my head again; let me leave behind the night with which I have grown used to surrounding myself even at midday." There were several occasions on which Dr. Etienne [the doctor at the Ecole Normale Supérieure] had to intervene to prevent Foucault from taking his own life. . . . Foucault's father took him to a psychiatrist . . . the famous Professor Jean Delay. . . . It is easy to imagine how damaging, how dangerous even, it must have been for a young gay man to find himself in this man's office. The possibility of hospitalizing Foucault at Sainte-Anne was taken under serious consideration. It was probably Louis Althusser, who had gone through such a hospitalization a few years earlier, who talked Foucault out of it. . . . During the same period, Foucault became a serious alcoholic, to the point of needing to go through a detoxification treatment. (People recount that during his time in Sweden there were still moments when he would pass out, stone drunk).[1]

Madness is everywhere, I think, as I look back on the strange similarities between my experience and Foucault's. Like me during my teens, twenties, and part of my thirties, Foucault was "mad" with alcohol even during the time he was writing *Madness*. In fact, I muse, it was there from the start, even in the family in which I grew up. My mother had narcolepsy (I think of her when I see Glenda Jackson playing Charlotte Corday in the Peter Brook production of Peter Weiss's play, *Marat/Sade*).

As a "sleeping sickness," my mother's narcolepsy would have earned her the title of "mentally ill" and a berth in an asylum, like Charenton, along with Sade and the raving lunatics who theatrically replay, in a brilliantly inverted mise en abyme of the society that excludes them, the bloody glories of an "enlightened" Revolution carried out in the name of the "Rights of Man." But there's more. My mother is not only a narcoleptic but also a lesbian, just like me. We've both been lucky, historically speaking, to escape the great confinement, if not for her narcolepsy or my alcoholism, then certainly for the perversion we both embody. My sister, who ran away from home as a teenager, didn't escape, and was locked up for a while in a mental hospital in Denver. My brother, like me, is a recovering alcoholic. And my father, in the late 1960s, not long after *History of Madness* was published, was hospitalized for several months after suffering a nervous breakdown. So it is not an exaggeration to say, in a very real sense, that my entire (all-American) family is "crazy."

"I know madness too," I wanted to say to Laura.

I didn't say it. I just sat there and listened, feeling deflated. But that voice is familiar, the one that says: "I know madness." It sounds like Descartes. Was Laura speaking as someone with bipolar disorder or as the expert who can now talk about it and heal it in others? Turning madness into the object of scientific perception is part of what Foucault calls the effect of a suffocated strangeness: silenced and hidden away, unreason only reappears in the modern era as manageable, perceivable, measurable mental illness. To describe it as such is in itself an act of distancing: alcoholism, narcolepsy, bipolar disorder, lesbianism, perversion. To speak about madness as an object of knowing is tantamount to saying: I'm not mad.

So here's the truth—no, not the truth, but a truth-effect, as Foucault might put it. I don't really know how to juggle all these "mad" voices: Foucault's, my friend's, my mother's, my father's, my sister's, my brother's, the multitudinous ones that swirl around in my own head. This project, in places so heady and philosophical, is closer to the core than I'd like to admit. And, ultimately, it leaves me not knowing.

It leaves me not knowing, and I don't know what to call it. The experience is real, but I cannot name or diagnose it. Every experience is specific, singular: untranslatable. "It is strictly original," Foucault says in *Mental Illness and Psychology*.[2] "It's idiosyncratic," Kay Redfield Jamison tells us in her memoir about her own madness:

> People go mad in idiosyncratic ways. Perhaps it was not surprising that, as a
> meteorologist's daughter, I found myself, in that glorious illusion of high

FIGURE 3.2 Catherine wheel (breaking wheel)

FIGURE 3.3 Catherine wheel (firework)

summer days, gliding, flying, now and again lurching through cloud banks
and ethers, past stars, and across fields of ice crystals. Even now, I can see in
my mind's rather peculiar eye an extraordinary shattering and shifting of
light; inconstant but ravishing colors laid out across miles of circling rings;
and the almost imperceptible, somehow surprisingly pallid, moons of this
Catherine wheel of a planet.[3]

What an exquisite description of a singularly beautiful but painful experience. Perhaps this is what Foucault means in the 1961 preface when he describes *Madness* as tracing the "rudimentary movements of an experience" (*M* xxxii). Like the Catherine wheel, the experience of madness is both the wheel of torture (figure 3.2) on which human spirits are broken and a magnificent spiraling firework of colored sparks and flames (figure 3.3). There is, I think, rereading *Mental Illness and Psychology*, something in this movement of madness that is repeated, an eternal recurrence of the Catherine wheel of history. As a professor of psychiatry who suffers from bipolar disorder, Jamison is, like my friend, the crazy expert. And Foucault himself, in his magisterial command of the history and language of psychiatry, is another expert fractured by madness. So there's more of a connection—a swirling movement, perhaps—that links Foucault to Jamison—than either of them would be likely to admit. It's there in the doubling, the turns of language that, *without knowing*, repeat themselves as images of crystallization and flight. For when, in *Mental Illness and Psychology*, in a passage initially written in the 1950s, Foucault describes "schizophrenia" decades before Jamison published her memoir, he sounds like the meteorologist's daughter: "Thinking has disintegrated and proceeds in isolated fragments. . . . All that still emerges, as positive signs, are stereotypes, hallucinations, verbal schemata crystallized in incoherent syllables, and sudden affective interruptions crossing the demential inertia like meteors."[4]

As a mad literary critic, I can't help but see it. The serendipitous convergence is there: Jamison's "fields of ice crystals" are like Foucault's "verbal schemata crystallized;" the "meteorologist's daughter . . . flying past stars" strangely, chiastically, mirrors Foucault's "affective interruptions crossing . . . like meteors." The terms are set, between an emergence of crystallization as stasis and a movement of crossing as flight. And movement is the way out of the trap. "If Foucault was able to recover from his psychological problems," Eribon writes, "it is because he chose flight."[5] And flight, Foucault writes in a 1954 letter to Jean Barraqué, brings "frightful pleasures of which I had no inkling . . . of incomprehensible languages": "the pleasure of being unnecessary, in excess."[6]

The rotating Catherine wheel of history, of a planet, traces the movement of crystals and meteors, stasis and flight. The images keep converging, building on each other, serendipitously reconverging into new constellations among Jamison's "circling rings" and "pallid moons."

But I still don't know what madness is. However poetic or precise the language to describe it might be, on some level that language remains "incomprehensible." For me, in the singularity of my encounter with Foucault's queer madness, the crystals and the stars say it better than any diagnostic language of science.

Untranslatable, I reach toward myself as I'm left behind: the shattered light of a comet.

4 / A Queer Nephew

They bring tramps, poor wretches, or simply mediocre individuals
onto a strange stage where they strike poses, speechify, and declaim,
where they drape themselves in the bits of cloth they need if they
wish to draw attention in the theater of power. At times they remind one of a poor troupe of jugglers and clowns who deck themselves out in makeshift scraps of old finery to play before an audience of aristocrats who will make fun of them. Except that they are
staking their whole life on the performance.

—Michel Foucault, 1977

Theatrum Mundi

Foucault, Deleuze reminds us, is haunted by the double. All of Foucault's work, and *Madness* in particular, is peopled by ghosts, figures,
personages, and characters: the twins of those who "really did exist" (*M*
9) but whose lives have been lost to history. These figures function as
masks or overlays for the traces of unreason whose rendering by reason
betrays them: they are the doppelgängers who haunt Foucault's present.
Rendered as fictions to rewrite the past, they traverse and disturb Foucault's histoires. They are the "poor wretches" Foucault finds in the archives, performing in a "theater of power" whose stakes are life itself.[1]
That theater—the archival space as a stage of power—dramatizes the
effects of rationalism's exclusions.

Foucault's archival practice reworks and reconfigures that theater of
power. Confined in their death as they were in life, the traces of existence Foucault finds in the archives are transformed by an aesthetic
practice that shifts the sociohistorical roles they have been given in a
Cartesian script. In Foucault's rendering, these lives become open to
transformation through the fiction-making practice of histoire. Like
fools in a ship, they reshape history, circling back and forth between
past and present as characters in a floating *theatrum mundi*.

In *Madness*, Foucault dramatizes the late-eighteenth-century moment,
on the cusp of our modern age, when such possibilities of transforma-

tion are both revealed and foreclosed. Specifically, at the beginning of part 3, Foucault stages a literary figure caught in the breach between reason and unreason at the moment of the Enlightenment birth of the modern Western subject. That figure is Rameau's Nephew, the titular character of Denis Diderot's satire written on the eve of the French Revolution. In the Nephew, Foucault finds a figure of subjective instability who both incarnates unreason and, simultaneously, exposes its disappearance within a post-Enlightenment project that turns unreason into reason's object in the form of a madness as mental illness. The Nephew is, as Foucault puts it, "the last character in whom madness and unreason are united" (M 344), but also in whom the modern "moment of their separation is prefigured" (M 344).

The original text by Diderot in which the Nephew appears serves as a condensing lens through which to focus the historical and conceptual shifts of Foucault's larger text. As the inaugural character who introduces the final, "modern" (M 344) section of Madness, the Nephew captures, in a single emblem, the paradoxes and oppositions of a story of unreason that stretches from the Renaissance to the modern era. And if, in temporal terms, the Nephew functions as "a shortened paradigm of history" (M 344), in conceptual terms he exposes the general Hegelian "perversion"[2]—the moment of "ironic reversal" (M 345) of the dialectic— in which "each is the opposite of itself."[3] As a figure not only of the "necessary instability" (M 345) of the subject but also of its ironic reversal, the Nephew embodies reason's servitude to unreason in a Hegelian reversal of lord and bondsman: "unreason slowly creeps back to that which condemns it, imposing a form of retrograde servitude upon it" (M 345).

Standing at the threshold of modernity, the Nephew exposes both the cost and the promise of an Enlightenment event whose legacy is modern biopower. However entrenched the Western subject might seem, his modern genesis in the Age of Reason is unstable and open to reversal or change. Indeed, the Nephew's eighteenth century is, in the words of Jürgen Habermas, a moment that "marks the peripeteia in the drama of the history of reason."[4] The Nephew performs both the culmination of a Cartesian rationalism where "man moves from certainty to the truth through the work of the mind and of reason" (M 350) and an "anti-Cartesian" (M 350) contestation of reason. Like the cogito's ghost in the seventeenth century, the Nephew exposes a breach, a time of division that repeats the Cartesian moment of the great confinement, and after which unreason will disappear beneath the nineteenth-century specification of forms of madness as scientific objects. In this sense, the Nephew is a tear in history's fabric; after the cogito, he gives birth to a Western subject as the object of reason. At the same time, in a satirical discourse that mixes high with low, science with art, and tragic with comic, the Nephew destabilizes his own objectification through irony and parodic performance.

As a literary character, Rameau's Nephew holds an unusually prominent place in the history of philosophy not only for Foucault but also for an entire generation of French philosophers trained in the 1940s and fifties. Perhaps unknown to many of today's Anglophone readers, the Nephew would have been deeply familiar to Foucault's French readership at the time of the first publication of *History of Madness* in 1961. As a key actor in Hegel's *Phenomenology of Spirit* (1807), the Nephew figures prominently in the story of a mid-twentieth-century French Hegelianism Foucault was, by the late 1950s, trying to shake. With his brief appearance at the heart of Foucault's *Madness*, the Nephew raises a question I've been asking throughout this book: is it possible to undo the logic of Hegelian dialectical thinking?

As the figure who, in the *Phenomenology*, stands at the place of reversal in the dialectic, the Nephew opens, for Foucault, the possibility of desubjectivation at the moment of the birth of the Enlightenment subject. But Foucault receives the Nephew via Hegel, whose teleological motor shuts down the opening of desubjectivation. From the vantage point of our historical present, to remain in the back-and-forth perversion of realities by their opposites—what Foucault calls the "indivisible domain designated by the irony of *Rameau's Nephew*" (M 352)—is no more possible for us than the back-and-forth movement of a premodern ship of fools. The coexistence of opposites the Nephew performs will come to be sublated into the progress of rationalist history. We can only catch glimpses of that other domain exposed by the Nephew, from within the unreason that gives birth to the Age of Reason, in that familiar litany of artists: "Hölderlin, Nerval, Nietzsche, Van Gogh, Raymond Roussel and Artaud" (M 352). In this sense, *Rameau's Nephew* functions as a figure for the thought of the outside examined in chapter 2, the mark of a transgression that is the illumination of the limit: "in an instant [this character] illuminates like a bolt of lightning the great broken line that stretches from the Ship of Fools to the last words of Nietzsche and perhaps Artaud's cries of rage" (M 344).

Of course, paradoxically, these artists speak unreason only in their failure to speak: Nietzsche sinking down, silent. This failure of expression is the "tragic consequence" (*M* 352) of a venture into a region which, as it silences, "prepare[s] the way for the new idea."[5] In this sense the Nephew exposes the artist's fall into madness and the absence of an oeuvre as a potential opening toward something other. As Foucault puts it on the final page of *Madness*: "Nietzsche's madness, i.e. the collapse of his thought, is the way in which that thought opens onto the modern world. It is that which made it impossible that makes it present to us" (*M* 537). Thus the madman's *silence* "repeats with the insistence of time the same question" (*M* 352), the ethical question of difference: "Why is it not possible to remain in the difference that is unreason?" (*M* 352). With this ethical question Foucault names the cost of Western subjectivity as the silencing of unreason: the muting of the historical other. It is the question that opens toward a Foucauldian erotic ethics of alterity I will develop more fully in the final chapter.

Apprehending the place of *Rameau's Nephew* in *Madness* is thus crucial for understanding the ethical stakes of rationalist moralism as a modern question about the subject in time. Yet, despite the Nephew's importance for Foucault's ethical thinking and for an entire generation of French philosophers, there has been little sustained critical analysis of the Nephew in Foucault.[6] Indeed, it is fair to say that the significance of the Nephew in Foucault's thinking has, to this day, remained unacknowledged. No doubt Foucault's Nephew has been ignored by most non-French speakers because the nine pages devoted to him in *History of Madness* were excised from the original 1961 book for the abbreviated translations.[7] And, even for French readers, it would be easy to ignore him altogether, so brief is his blink-of-an-eye appearance.

I engage *Rameau's Nephew* as the place in *Madness* that stages the aesthetic transformation of rationalism as a "shortened paradigm" (*M* 344) of the subject in time. It functions, in that sense, as a kind of dress rehearsal for the transformative, archival *ars erotica* I describe in chapter 5 as Foucault's ethical practice. In his ironic instability, the Nephew is trapped in an objectifying capture, but also becomes unmoored, opening subjectivity, after Hegel, to the possibility of a desubjectivating practice of freedom. In that sense, the Nephew marks the peripeteia of *Madness*, to reinvoke Habermas's term, the place where both the disappointment and the promise of the Enlightenment resides.[8] *Rameau's Nephew* signals the beginning of a humanist project that will produce the violent objectifications of positivist science and its twentieth- and twenty-first-century descendants. At the same time, as a more promising aesthetic moment within *Madness*—and within the Enlightenment—that puts the philosophical subject of reason into question, the delirious Nephew announces a practice that will transform, as an art of living, those forms of unreason silenced and locked away in the great confinement.

If Foucault needs the Nephew in his story of madness, I too need him in my story about Foucault and queer theory. Specifically, I use him as the hinge between the critical project of the first three chapters—the critique of acts versus identities (chapter 1), the Nietzschean retraversal of queer theory and morality (chapter 2), and the challenge to queer theory's Freudo-Foucauldianism (chapter 3)—and the ethical question: how do we become free? The Nephew allows me to ask crucial questions to set up my argument about an erotic ethics in the final chapter. Specifically, unlike those who argue that Foucault's ethics leads him to reembrace an Enlightenment subject, I have argued throughout this book that his ethical project is inseparable from an undoing of the self and a philosophy of the limit.

But how can we have an ethics without a subject? The Nephew guides me in approaching this question not only conceptually but also historically, as a question about subjectivity and truth in history. To ask about the subject as a historical question engages, once again, the problem of the alterity of a past whose traces are found in the archives. But this raises a related, equally difficult question: how do we apprehend that historical alterity? If teleological history is itself a rationalist structure, how can we have a history without reason, without a telos? These related questions about an ethics without a subject and a history without a telos set the stage for my engagement with the Nephew as a Hegelian figure who emerges, in Foucault, at a historical moment when "madness takes on a new meaning for the modern world" (*M* 347). For, if the Cartesian rejection of madness parallels the institutional confinement of the mad, the end of the eighteenth century marks the age of Pinel and the freeing of the mad from their confinement.

Of course in Foucault this release from confinement is another form of a "caged freedom" we find a century later in the Freudian talking cure. But the Nephew is crucial for understanding a restructuring that takes place, at the end of the eighteenth century, in the architecture of Western reason. That restructuring takes the form of the rise of medical knowledge about insanity in the nineteenth century. The development of science means, for Foucault, positivism's inclusion of madness *within* reason. Hardly a freeing of the mad, this *inclusion* of madness is nonetheless "anti-Cartesian" (*M* 348), since Descartes *excluded* madness from reason. So if Descartes gives birth to the modern subject of reason, this does not explain how modern reason comes to include madness within itself. To explain that inclusion, Foucault uses Hegel, the dialectical philosopher of reason who includes madness within the subject as a necessary stage in the development of consciousness. As with all Foucault's births, the birth of the rational Western subject is repeated in *Madness*: first Descartes, then Hegel.

To be sure, Foucault doesn't give us Hegel directly, but refracts him through the lens of the Nephew. As a Hegelian figure born before Hegel, the Nephew in Foucault is a split subject: both Hegelian and pre-Hegelian, both dialectical and not. This means that Foucault doesn't simply give us Hegel; Foucault also undoes Hegel from within. Thus this chapter traverses a historical terrain that renarrates the birth of the Western subject in a Foucauldian remaking of Hegel.

In order to situate this Hegelian heritage of the Nephew in Foucault, I begin with a consideration of ironic reversal as a classic Hegelian mechanism for apprehending the subject of a telos in the dialectic of history. This consideration of irony allows me to trace a story of deviation and aporetic limits within a straight philosophical narrative that stretches from the time of Diderot's writing to Foucault's reading of a Hegelian Nephew in the 1940s and fifties to the Nephew's appearance in *Madness* in 1961. Retold as a Hegelian birth of the subject within *Madness*, the Nephew's emergence opens the possibility of dedialectizing Hegel and of queering reason's heteronormative filiations. I then consider the Nephew as a heterotopian mirror in which the modern "I" both constitutes himself in a humanist logic of self-reflection and, at the same time, makes the "I" strange and therefore open to an ethical relation to an other. Finally, I pursue the question of ethical self-undoing as a relation to an other through the figure of the Nephew as a modern Diogenes whose "militant" practices of dispossession might serve as a model for contemporary queer theory.

Irony's Edgework

Having ended part 2 of *History of Madness* with the Freudian return to an ancient violence, Foucault opens part 3 by returning to that French revolutionary time of a more recent bloodletting through the cynical irony of *Rameau's Nephew*. The ironic edge of Diderot's split subject cleaves *Madness* in two, revealing the dissonances in the book's narrative harmonies. In his torrential speech and parodic gestures, the self-mocking Nephew laughingly undermines the epistemological, ethical, and aesthetic rationalizations of an enlightened *Moi*. Like *Lui* with *Moi* in Diderot's text, the Nephew in *Madness* implicitly confronts Foucault-the-philosopher with his own self-mocking double. Indeed, *Rameau's Nephew* functions as a mise en abyme of *Madness* itself, mimetically ironizing the tragic, lyrical strains of Foucault's story about reason and unreason. This ironic tear at the heart of *Madness* raises the problem of the form—narrative or theatrical, tragic or comic, lyrical or ludic—for apprehending the subject in time.

Let me describe the original eighteenth-century work by Diderot that became so important for a nineteenth-century Hegel and the French Hegelians of the twentieth century. The plot of *Rameau's Nephew* is simple. Strolling one afternoon in the garden of the Palais Royal in Paris, Diderot (*Moi*) runs into Jean-François Rameau (*Lui*), a well-known eccentric and the nephew of the great composer Jean-Philippe Rameau. Over the course of the next eighty pages, the two engage in conversation. In this conversation, Diderot stages reason's (*Moi's*) encounter with unreason (*Lui*) as a mocking confrontation: "Aha, there you are, Mr. Philosopher,"[9] the Nephew says in the dialogue's opening. The Nephew is a dilettante who makes his living giving music lessons and entertaining his patrons, and his encounter with *Moi* occurs in the wake of the Nephew's dismissal from his post as jester-servant at the household of the wealthy state treasurer, Bertin, and his actress-mistress, Mademoiselle Hus. In his role as a bourgeois court jester, the Nephew is an object of amusement whose fortunes rise and fall at the whim of others. Having been fired from Bertinhus, the Nephew proceeds to entertain Mr. Philosopher as he would his wealthy patrons, commenting on various moral, political, social, musical, economic, and literary themes, sometimes reasonably, sometimes nonsensically. In his role as clown, the Nephew's mercurial behavior and comic perspective threaten to muddy the Enlightened clarity of Mr. Philosopher's thoughts and values.

Variously seduced and horrified by the Nephew's entertainment, *Moi* becomes almost completely unraveled by *Lui's* periodic shifts into sudden outbursts of pantomime. Specifically, in four separate moments, the torrential verbiage of *Lui's* conversation breaks off into the silent, gestural mimicry of various social, domestic, and aesthetic scenes, each one increasingly exaggerated as the Nephew's contorsions eventually propel him, toward the end of the dialogue, into a delirious frenzy. The dialogue ends with the parting of *Moi* from *Lui*, leaving the reader wondering what has happened and if anything has changed.

Throughout this book I have insisted on the importance of irony for an understanding of Foucault's thinking, especially in *Sexuality One*. But, if *Sexuality One* is ironic, *Madness* is written in a tragic mode: its lyricism tunes it to the notes of a grief—in what Derrida famously calls its pathos—that marks the loss "of those obscure gestures, necessarily forgotten as soon as they are accomplished, through which a culture rejects something which for it will be the Exterior" (*M* xxix). This seemingly classical tension in Foucault between tragic and ironic rhetorical modes is both dramatized and made strange by the Nephew's performance at the heart of *Madness*. In his presentation of Diderot, Foucault insists repeatedly on the Nephew's role as an ironist in a tragic world: "a tragic confrontation between need and illusion . . . the delirium of Rameau's Nephew is also an ironic repetition of the world" (*M* 349). But, if "it is tempting to classify Rameau's Nephew among the ancient lineage of fools and clowns" (*M* 346), his position at the cusp of modernity deprives him of the truth-telling wisdom of his premodern forebears.[10] No longer "an insouciant operator of truth" (*M* 346) with "strange powers" (*M* 346), the Nephew embodies a madness whose "power is made of nothing but error" (*M* 346). Thus the "powers of irony" (*M* 346) of ancient fools and clowns become, with the Nephew, simply the empty reversal of truth as error. Unlike the irony of the age of the ship of fools that "reveals who is good" and "unmasks rogues" (*M* 346), the Nephew's irony is aporetic and therefore deeply unsettling.

In the 1961 preface to *Madness*, Foucault writes: "to interrogate a culture about its limit-experiences is to question it at the confines of history about a tear that is something like the very birth of its history" (*M* xxix). As a modern fool whose aporetic "powers of irony" (*M* 346) are made of "nothing but error" (*M* 346), the Nephew is like a tear in the Enlightenment matrix that gives birth to the modern subject as a relation to truth. Unlike Aristotelian irony, whose emotionally cathartic reversals "knot[] the tragic to the dialectic of history" (*M* xxx), the Nephew's irony illuminates, in a flash, the violence of a "colonising reason" (*M* xxx) founded on illusory truths such as freedom and justice. This illuminating function is not a disclosure of a deeper truth, but rather an exposure of the void upon which the positivity of knowledge is erected. In this way, the Nephew embodies what Foucault calls one of "these limit-experiences of the Western world" (*M* xxx) whose unsettling irony explodes all form, including the tragic ones which, for Hegel, constitute history.

I am interested in Foucault's treatment of irony in the Nephew for two reasons. First, it gives this chapter's guiding question—how can we have an ethics without a subject and a history without a telos?—a specifically rhetorical frame. In its philosophical role as the trope of reversal, irony is important not only for Aristotelian tragedy but also, more significantly, for a Hegelian dialectical thinking from which Foucault wished to free himself. Based in a logic of cause and effect, the ironic reversal at the heart of dialectical philosophy is the teleological motor of rationalist history. But Foucault's deployment of the Nephew in *Madness* exposes a nondialectical, aporetic irony in Diderot's work that is papered over by Hegel's powerful dialectical machinery. In that sense the Nephew's irony leads us to that familiar Nietzschean impasse between being mad and pretending to be mad, between a silent aporia and an impossibly expressive madness. This makes the Nephew not a subject at all, but the space of a gap in which Nietzsche disappears as he falls into madness, leaving behind him a silhouette: a literary character, a shadow cast by something as it's leaving. To read the Nephew's aporetic irony is to read that shadow.

Second, in its aesthetic function, irony exposes affect or feeling as a crucial component of the limit-experience Foucault spent his life exploring. As I will argue more fully in chapter 5, if Foucault is a thinker of the limit, that limit is not defined by thought alone, but includes an affective dimension. Foucault is not only interested in desubjectivation as a function of thinking but also as a function of feeling. As Nietzsche puts it: "we have to learn . . . to feel differently."[11] And if art and literature give us modes for accessing the affective component of our thinking, the catharsis we might experience through familiar forms such as tragedy or comedy fail to transform us precisely because, like history itself, its forms are pregiven. Thus, with tragedy—when we imagine, for example, "the space, both empty and peopled" (*M* xxxi) of the mad who are lost to history—even our grief is already given to us in a preformed package. To put it in the terms Foucault will develop in the 1970s, affect itself is invested with power, "endowed with [psychiatric] rationality."[12]

The affective dimension of the Nephew's ironic disturbance has implications for the ethical transformation at the heart of Foucauldian desubjectivation. In *Rameau's Nephew*, *Moi*'s reaction to the Nephew's performance illustrates the cognitive and affective dissonance produced

by what Linda Hutcheon calls "irony's edge": "I was torn between opposite impulses and did not know whether to give in to laughter or furi-
ous indignation. I felt embarrassed. A score of times a burst of laughter
prevented a burst of rage, and a score of times the anger rising from the
depths of my heart ended in a burst of laughter."[13]

This unsettling duplicity—irony's edge—produces irony's "affective
'charge,'"[14] implicating aporetic irony in a set of problems that are not
only formal, epistemological, or rhetorical but also ethical and political.
As a rhetorical structure that engages and unsettles the emotions, such
irony differs from simple ambiguity: "irony is decidedly edgy."[15] Foucault's attraction to aporetic irony is not surprising, given that its edgi-
ness weights its social meanings, both cognitively and affectively, "in
favor of the silent and the unsaid."[16] Further, in the context of queer
theory, irony's status as a rhetorical structure that privileges the unsaid
has led to numerous claims, including performative ones, for its politically subversive capacities. But, as Sedgwick points out in her reading of
Diderot's The Nun, a discursive strategy that privileges the unsaid can
just as easily buttress a conservative as a progressive political position.[17]
As a rhetorical structure, irony itself is a political chameleon: as Hutcheon repeatedly insists, it is transideological.

Rather than making a political claim about irony in Foucault, I want
to follow Hutcheon in focusing for a moment on irony's "moral dimension"[18] and the edge work it might do to open a space, beyond Madness,
for an erotic ethics of freedom. The Nephew's ironic "play on the edge"[19]
that separates reason from unreason produces delight in his audience
through the comic deflation of tragic, serious life. But that delight is
troubled by an unsettling dissonance, as we just saw with Moi, that destabilizes the cognitive, emotional, and moral clarity of simple farce,
slapstick, or truth-telling comic forms. In its Foucauldian context, the
Nephew's ironic play on the historical and rhetorical edge of madness—
the edge of the void on which knowledge is erected—threatens to "force
people to the edge, and sometimes over it."[20] Further, because irony is
cognitively and emotionally unsettling, it is also, as Hutcheon puts it,
ethically "inscrutable,"[21] challenging the audience's need for harmonic
stability and closure—for the packaged feeling of catharsis—with a contaminating dissonance.

As the etymology of "satire" as "mixture" in Rameau's Nephew: Second
Satire suggests, this is a mixed, delirious discourse: a promiscuous
genre that pulls us to the edge of rationalist moral certainties.[22] Thus,
for example, in Diderot's dialogue, Lui's irony reveals Moi's self-

contained detachment as a hairsbreadth away from an uncontrolled delirium: on the edge of a mixing of reason and unreason that threatens to infect everyone who hears or sees it. As a contaminating structure, irony reveals, in rhetorical form, the Nietzschean historical point analyzed in chapter 2: the line separating genius and insanity is thinner than you think. As *Lui* puts it in a common expression: "great wits are oft to madness allied."[23] And later he says, "I had persuaded myself I was a genius," but I see "that I'm a fool, a fool, a fool [*un sot*]."[24] This hairsbreadth distance between reason and madness has ethical implications as well, as *Lui* puts it: "I did not say that genius was inseparable from wickedness or wickedness from genius."[25]

The Nephew, of course, is no common ironist, but one who illuminates the Foucauldian limit. Put somewhat differently, if ironists in general play on the edge of madness, the Nephew stands out as completely mad. Unlike those common ironists who stay in control, the Nephew not only plays but repeatedly and systematically goes over the edge as well, moving in and out of full-fledged delirium. "I am rare among my kind," he boasts, "yes, exceedingly rare. . . . I was for [my patrons] an entire Petites-Maisons."[26] This line, reinscribed by Foucault as the epigraph to part 3 of *Madness* (*M* 343), refers to the eighteenth-century French "home of the mad *par excellence*" (*M* 384) in the Rue de Sèvres where the severest cases from Bicêtre and the Salpétrière were taken. Rewritten as Foucault's epigraph to the section of *Madness* that opens toward modernity, the Nephew's declaration of his own madness announces what Foucault will call the "destiny of madness in the modern world" (*M* 346) where, through nineteenth-century positivism to its culmination in Freud, patients will be required to say, "I am mad." As ethical statements about the relation between subjectivity and truth, such utterances will of course be, like the Nephew's, ironic in the aporetic, modern sense: forms of truth telling whose "power is made of nothing but error" (*M* 346).

In the context of queer theory, it is also worth noting that, as an illumination of the limit of reason, the Nephew's ironic utterance—"I am mad," "I [am] an entire Petites-Maisons"—is also explicitly sexual. As Foucault informs us in part 1 of *Madness*, because Petites-Maisons was reserved "more or less exclusively for the insane and the venereal" (*M* 86), the Nephew's unique, systematic fall over irony's edge plays on the "kinship between the pains of madness and the punishment of debauchery" (*M* 86) that conflates madness with sexual deviance and impurity. As an "entire Petites-Maisons," the Nephew is not only mad but queer.

In his queer role as "Rameau the lunatic [*fou*],"[27] the Nephew doubles irony's play into discursive and nondiscursive—spoken and gestural— forms of aesthetic rupture on the edge of modernity and scientific reason. As discursive play, the Nephew's irony laughingly punctures *Madness*'s *grand récit* tragic movement. Diderot is an ironist who, like Foucault, revels in the conceptual power of rhetorical duplicity—the undecidable hovering between the said and the unsaid that characterizes nondialectical, aporetic irony. For both *philosophes*, such irony's value lies in its capacity to destabilize moral rationalism with a form of speech that cannot be philosophically controlled. Irony is a kind of rupturing unreason within reason, a break or interruption within discourse that would speak madness—if it could speak. In that sense, the Nephew really is a ghost of madness: "the shadow of a shadow" (*M* 348) we think we can hear.

What we do actually hear is the voice of the Nephew's silence ventriloquized by the loquacious language of positivist science. Specifically, in the Nephew's silent pantomimes, he gives a form to the mutism of madness. The paradox of this performance is that in giving madness a form—by making it "speak" as silence—the Nephew's pantomimes pin madness down by making it into an object that medical knowledge will name as aphasia. From the Greek *phánai*, to speak, *a-phasia* is madness as speechlessness. From an eighteenth-century perspective, the pantomimes can be "heard" as the artistic transformation of a madness made mute by the Cartesian exclusion of unreason from the cogito. But, from the postpositivist perspective of our historical present, the specification of mutism in scientific terms marks the biopolitical power of a colonizing reason.

However one receives their hovering meanings, the Nephew's pantomimes make visible again an internal fracture—a split within a split— already introduced at the end of part 1 of *Madness*, where the Cartesian separation of the mind from the body produced another split, within unreason, between animalistic and moral forms of deviation from reason. In part 3, Foucault redescribes that split, in eighteenth-century aesthetic terms, as a breach between animality and artificiality: between the "immediate necessity" of being (*M* 347)—the human subject's animal need for food, shelter, evacuation of the bowels—and the "nonbeing of illusion" (*M* 347)—the human subject's immersion in a world of mirrors, reflections, and aesthetic play. This classical split happens again, in an introduction to modernity, at the moment of the *Nephew*: the Enlightenment moment of classical unreason's transformation into positivist madness. That modern moment repeats and modifies the paradoxical experience of a classical unreason split between the "monstrous innocence" (*M* 158) of human animality—the bodily "incarnation" (*M* 158) of a bodiless reason as "the scandal of the human condition" (*M* 158)—and the culpability of a moral perversion—unreason as the condition of an ethical deviation from "the moral valorisation of reason" (*M* 158).

This split between incarnated animality and artificial illusion redescribes the Nietzschean impasse we saw in the first interlude, between "actual" madness and "pretending" to be mad, as the site of a rationalist moral control over those whose deviance makes way for the new idea. In using pantomime as a silent, bodily art—a corporeal ars erotica—to pull the mystifying rug of language out from under reason's feet, Foucault exposes the limits of the rationalist game where both bodily necessity and creative edge play will become equally pathologized, in the nineteenth century, as forms of madness at the limit of the human. And, although a classical unreason split between the bodily "fury of the animal world" (*M* 159) and an "ethical experience" (*M* 158/*F* 176; translation modified) of moral exclusion will be unified by that modern pathologizing gaze, "positivism never really escapes" (*M* 159/*F* 177; translation modified) a conception of madness still inhabited by that mind-body split, between the "ethics of unreason" (*M* 159/*F* 177; translation modified) and "the scandal of animality" (*M* 159/*F* 177; translation modified).

This summary of the ironic edge work performed by the Nephew "at the heart of madness" (*M* 349) brings into relief this chapter's relation to the previous chapter about the despotism of Freudian reason. If the discursive structure of psychoanalysis is the eternally caged freedom of a psychic thaumaturgy, the discursive and nondiscursive ironies of the *Nephew*'s mad theater both mimic the Freudian magic of the talking cure and replace it with a different dialogical vision that, unlike psychoanalysis, has access to the realm of unreason. Unlike the doctor-patient couple of psychoanalysis, the *Moi-Lui* couple of Diderot's dialogue opens, as a limit-experience, the possibility for a prepositivist, nonpsychoanalytic splitting of the subject: a different kind of desubjectivation that would include in its purview not only cognition but also eros: the affective and bodily dimensions of lived experience.

It is also worth mentioning, in terms of this book's structure, that my own shift from a focus on Freud in chapter 3 to this chapter's focus on a text by Diderot mimics a similar shift in Foucault, where the passage from Freud to Diderot occurs across the fold that separates parts 2 and 3 of *Madness*. That structural fold is also a temporal passage—from a Freudian twentieth century back to the Age of Reason—out of which, in a historical doubling of Enlightenment structures, the modern humanist subject will emerge. This double fold within *Madness* and within the spiraling temporality of history constitutes what Jacques Derrida has called the book's "hinge" or "lure" (*charnière*).[28] Pivoting around the *charnière*-as-hinge, Freud is the doorman who, in part 2, opens the passage to a humanist present refracted in part 3 through the lens of Diderot's vision. The mad art of that other doorman, Diderot, retells the story of humanism's birth, making way for a passage to a posthumanist future where madness itself would cease to exist. That other future ushered in by Diderot—through the back door, as it were—begins to trace Foucault's vision of a postmoral ethics of erotic experience that would contest the violent erasures of humanist history.

At the same time, the *charnière*-as-lure baits us into lingering inside the static, timeless fold of representation, a discursive gallery of mirrors where events are captured and endlessly redoubled as mimetic copies of never-quite-accessible models. That ghostly mimetic space is the space of aesthetic language. Internalized within *Madness* in the form of an ironic *Rameau's Nephew*, art becomes *Madness*'s internalized double. In this, Foucault mimics Hegel, who placed a literary Nephew at the heart of his philosophy of reason. But, unlike Hegel, Foucault deploys the Nephew to undo philosophy, dialectics, and the triumph of reason. His ironies lead elsewhere than to the Hegelian self-reflection Kristeva describes as "the sovereignty of the Self who doubles himself, becoming at the same time both his master and his slave."[29] Further, *Madness*'s aesthetic "inside," unlike the *Phenomenology*'s, reactivates within modernity a premodern conception of representation where, as we saw in chapter 1, reason and unreason remain in dialogue with each other, refusing the final movement of sublation that Freud will harness for the scientific talking cure.

Thus the mad artistic language of the modern period taps into a premodern language of noncoincident resemblances—distorting mirrors—that *Madness* represents as the back-and-forth movement of the ship of fools, a "sailing vessel" Foucault later describes as "the heterotopia par excellence."[30] Inside that ship—a theatrum mundi—the philosopher repeatedly confronts the "laugh of the madman" (*M* 15) in a manner that will be replicated in *Rameau's Nephew* and later by Diderot's mad nineteenth- and twentieth-century descendants. In that sense, as a late-eighteenth-century writer on the cusp of the modern period, Diderot both repeats a premodern dialogue between reason and unreason and, at the same time, prefigures the modern and postmodern struggle with madness, whose "frequency," Foucault says, "must be taken seriously" (*M* 536). This struggle of madness at the edge of form does not mean madness "slip[s] into the interstices of [an] oeuvre" (*M* 536): "Nietzsche's last cry . . . is . . . the destruction of the oeuvre itself, the point at which it becomes impossible, and where it must begin to silence itself" (*M* 536). But, in that impossibility, as "the hammer falls from the philosopher's hand" (*M* 536), the possibility of a different, noncolonizing relation between subjectivity and truth emerges in a "formless, mute, unsignifying region where language [*le langage*] can find its freedom."[31]

Let me note here the nonutopian, unsettling nature of any ethical or political vision that might come to light through these Foucauldian struggles at the edge of madness. Throughout his life, Foucault was suspicious of utopian thinking, from his diagnosis of the modern episteme in the 1960s to his critique of Habermasian communicative practice in the 1980s.[32] As he puts it in the preface to *The Order of Things*, "utopias afford consolation [*les utopies consolent*]."[33] By contrast, the bursts of laughter produced by the aporetic ironies of modern and postmodern forms of aesthetic language prefigured in *Rameau's Nephew* are always inhabited, as we saw with *Moi*, by "a certain uneasiness . . . hard to shake off."[34] No more consoling than the Borgesian text—a heterotopian "Other of order"[35] that cracks open *The Order of Things* with a disquieting laughter—the Diderotian space at *Madness*'s center is best described, as I have mentioned, as the heterotopian disorder "without law or geometry, of the heteroclite."[36] Heterotopias are "real places, actual places, places that are designed into the very institution of society, which are sorts of actually realized utopias in which the real emplacements, all the other real emplacements that can be found within a culture are, at the same time, represented, contested, and reversed, sorts of places that are outside all places, although they are actually localizable."[37] As a heterotopian space that is also, importantly, a temporal passage—"a piece of floating space, a placeless place"[38] like the ship of fools—*Rameau's Nephew* offers possibilities for tracing differences—thinking the outside—within the cracks that rupture the Same, but without any safety net of certainty or comfort. "Heterotopias are disturbing," Foucault writes in the preface to *The Order of Things*: "they secretly undermine language [*le langage*]" in the manner of aphasics who, unable to arrange "differently coloured skeins of wool on a table top," repeatedly create groups only to disperse them again, "destroying those that seem clearest, splitting up things that are identical, superimposing different criteria, frenziedly beginning all over again."[39] Heterotopias are, like satires, a kind of promiscuous genre.

As a heterotopia, the theatrical space the Nephew inhabits in *Madness* resounds with an aporetic laughter which, somewhat unsettlingly, calls forth a future: his speech and antics produce a rupture, before its time, of the modern specifications of madness, and of which aphasia—the "atopia"[40] where unreason resides—would be but one explicit example. The Nephew speaks and pantomimes a limit, before his time, of what will be pinned down and specified with the rise of science in the nineteenth century. And, if this aporetic irony is deeply unsettling—indeed, ruinous—we might follow Nietzsche, in his gay science, and greet it cheerfully, welcoming the artful possibilities it holds open. In this, we might also follow Foucault, who, in staging his own double as the modern fool of an Enlightenment *philosophe*, implicitly ironizes his own rationalist gesture as the writer of a history of madness. So doing, he makes a tear within his own project, giving birth to a passage to a different madness where, paradoxically, madness would disappear altogether. As Foucault puts it in the opening line of his 1964 essay, "Madness, the Absence of an Oeuvre": "One day, perhaps, we will no longer know what madness was" (*M* 541). What happens with the Nephew is not simply a movement of negativity in a Hegelian dialectic, but an aesthetic practice of "nonpositive affirmation"[41]—an illumination of the limit that, "one day, perhaps" will make madness "no longer . . . intelligible" (*M* 541).

A Hegelian Birth

This chapter's guiding question—how can we have a history without a telos and an ethics without a subject?—prepares the way for the final chapter by opening a space for a desubjectivated ethics as an ars erotica. In *Madness*, Foucault hints at this practice of desubjectivation by staging the subject of reason as episodic, multiply born, the "shadow of a shadow" (*M* 348), the "silhouette" (*M* 12) of a "fragmentary figure" (*M* 27) that is the effect of a disappearance over history's horizon. At the beginning of part 1, *Madness* famously opens with the birth of the subject in Descartes. Here, at the beginning of part 3, Foucault stages another nativity scene, the rebirth of the subject in Hegel. This staging of another of the subject's many births in Foucault—they are especially frequent in *Abnormal* and *Sexuality One*—binds Descartes to Hegel through a series of characters who "tell" a history of madness. This binding of the father of modern philosophy to the modern philosopher of reason—who, as Foucault once put it, "at the end . . . stands motionless, waiting for us"[42]—links Foucault's contestation of a rationalist ontology—"I think therefore I am"—to his ethical work on subjectivity and truth as a nonteleological practice of thinking the limits of freedom. Such a practice requires a contestation of a Hegelian character—*homo dialecticus* (M 543)—who makes "man" both "the sovereign subject and the dominated object of all the discourses on man" (M 543). Put simply, if Foucault's project is to dedialectize the subject of reason, he has to go through Hegel. In *Madness*, Foucault does this most visibly in his use of the Nephew.

But, if Hegel gives birth to Foucault's Nephew, it takes a while for that Foucauldian Nephew to be born. No birth is more deviant than that of the promiscuous Nephew. Conceived in 1761, exactly two hundred years before its appearance in *Madness*, *Rameau's Nephew* was initially drafted in 1762, then repeatedly revised for over a decade, probably up until 1779. Then the manuscript composed in Diderot's hand disappears into a dizzying proliferation of doubles. Never published or circulated during Diderot's lifetime, it fails to appear in Naigeon's 1798 posthumous edition of Diderot's *Oeuvres*. Nor is it mentioned eighteen years later in the 1816 list of Diderot manuscripts offered for sale by Naigeon's heirs to Diderot's daughter, Madame de Vandeul. In fact, *Rameau's Nephew* doesn't appear in an official critical inventory of Diderot manuscripts until Herbert Dieckmann's 1951 listing. During the intervening years—from the dawn of the nineteenth century to the 1950s when Foucault will mischievously place it, like a tiny explosive, in the middle of *Madness*—we discover a story of disappearance, translation, copying, and reappearance worthy of Borges. For, until 1891, when Georges Monval, the librairian of the Comédie-Française, unexpectedly discovered an autograph manuscript in a Parisian bookseller's box on the Quai Voltaire, few readers realized that the *Nephew*'s appearance over the course of the nineteenth century constituted a series of deceptive doubles.

That proliferation of doublings begins with the 1805 appearance in Leipzig of a *Rameaus Neffe*, a German translation by Goethe of a French *Nephew* that had been lent to him by an admiring Schiller but which, once returned to Schiller, seems to have vanished. This German double of a French manuscript whose source was most likely Catherine the

Great's collection of copies of Diderot's works—sent to her by Madame de Vandeul, per Diderot's agreement, after his death in 1784—was itself thus the translated copy of a copy of a copy of a copy. Rescripted clandestinely in French by Klinger, a German officer and dramatist posted in St. Petersburg, this copy of Catherine the Great's copy had been passed on to Schiller, who passed it on to Goethe, who translated it into the copy which became the Leipzig version: a copy of a copy of a copy of a copy. That series of copyings was redoubled again in the form of a retranslation from Goethe's German version back into French. This French retranslation—the copy of a copy of a copy of a copy of a copy—disguised itself as Diderot's original when it appeared in Paris in 1821 as *Le Neveu de Rameau: Dialogue*. Understandably upset at this blatant posing of a copy for an original, Madame de Vandeul published yet another version of the manuscript in her possession under the stewardship of Brière in 1823. And, although this copy of the *Nephew* became the official source of its subsequent editions for the next sixty years, its numerous deviations from what scholars now believe to be the manuscript's most "authentic" version confirm its errant status.

The manuscript that finally appears after a century of hiding had been tucked away in a closet and came to light only after lying dormant as part of a private three-hundred-volume collection of rare eighteenth-century erotica bound in leather and titled by its owner, the Marquis de la Rochefoucauld-Liancourt, as *Tragédies et oeuvres diverses*. Before that autograph "original" was secreted away by the Marquis, Diderot had most likely given it to his friend Baron von Friedrich Melchior Grimm, the German diplomat and editor of the privately circulated *Correspondance littéraire* where other scandalous works like *The Nun* were first published and distributed to a tiny clientele that included, among others, Catherine the Great. But, unlike *The Nun*, which was published and circulated after Diderot's death, *Rameau's Nephew* was never officially disseminated by the *philosophe*'s faithful editor and friend. Instead, it left France as a sheaf of private papers packed in a suitcase when Grimm returned to Germany during the Revolution, in 1792. Tucked away as a kind of silent residue of a failed Enlightenment and its bloody Revolution, the *Nephew* finally traveled back, sometime in the nineteenth century, to the land where it was first created. And there it sat, along the banks of the Seine, like the scandalous, erotic heart of a nested, self-replicating Russian doll, waiting for someone to make it beat again.

As the "original" *Nephew* sat there, waiting to be freed from the Marquis's closet, Hegel snatched up his German double—the 1805 Goethe translation of the copy brought to Jena in 1804—and deposited him in the middle of the immense central section of Spirit (488–595) in the third part of his *Phenomenology* (1807).[43] Fast-forwarding to the twentieth century, this Phenomenological *Nephew* became a central figure of the French Hegelianism Foucault's postwar generation would reject. And, just as the Nephew appears in *Madness* at the place of a hinge— where Freud is reversed and degraded as freedom's despotic sham—so too, in the *Phenomenology*, the Nephew appears as the pivot around which Spirit's content is dialectically reversed as "the perversion of every Notion and reality, the universal deception of itself and others."[44] Indeed, when in his later years Foucault criticized *Madness* for what he saw as its lingering Hegelianism, he could have been referring, at least in part, to the Nephew's mediating function there. And although, contesting Hegel, Foucault will refuse to sublate the Nephew's perverse "shamelessness" and self-conscious "deception" into "the greatest truth,"[45] the Nephew's mediating function at the point of *Madness*'s dialectical reversal and negation of Freud is undeniable. As we saw in chapter 3, Derrida interprets this anti-Freudian moment as the beginning of an unfortunate deterioration. But, from a different, less psychoanalytically invested perspective, one might read this moment of reversal as irony's uncontrolled reverberation in the return of a Hegelianism Foucault cannot fully escape. To requote the lines from Diderot cited in the *Phenomenology*, the *Nephew* not only exposes the "evenness of the notes" of Foucault's narrative about madness as "a rigamarole of wisdom and folly"[46] but also, in another turn of irony's screw, laughingly reveals a dialectical moment in Foucault's dedialectizing project.

Like his contemporaries, Foucault needs Hegel—that "old dragon"[47]— for his own ironizing, dialectical reversals, where reason becomes unreason, inside becomes outside, repression becomes production, and life becomes death. More specifically, he needs a Hegelian Nephew. Suzanne Gearhart explains that "the nephew incarnates the consciousness of the contamination"[48] of good by bad, of nobility by servility, and of opposites generally. His "consciousness of the contamination of these opposites by each other"[49] symbolizes the mediating moment in the journey of Spirit where opposites are reversed and thereby perverted. As Hegel puts it in the *Phenomenology*: "the disrupted consciousness . . . is consciousness of the perversion, and, moreover, of the absolute perversion."[50] In his absolute perversion—"the consciousness of the contamination of all opposites in and by each other"—the nephew is irony itself: the mediating term of the dialectic as a contaminating, perverting movement of reversal.

If Foucault needs Hegel's Nephew for his mediating role in a dialectical reversal, he also needs him, albeit differently than Hegel, as an aesthetic figure within philosophy. In the Hegelian journey toward a perfect knowledge [*das absolute Wissen*] only consummated in philosophy, the Nephew's literary role is crucial. Shoshana Felman points out that, in *Madness*, Diderot's Nephew announces, for the first time, a literary madness that will continue "to gain strength and ground in Romanticism."[51] And literature's perverting role in a history of reason is made philosophically explicit by a Romantic Hegel. Not only within the *Phenomenology* but also within the larger frame of a Hegelian oeuvre the *Phenomenology* introduces, knowledge requires a literary Nephew to make way for the philosophical overcoming of art by Spirit. As Gearhart puts it: "Hegel's reading of *Le Neveu* is a dress rehearsal for the sublation of morality by art and of art by philosophy in the *Aesthetics*."[52] In this sense, Hegel uses literature as a tool for philosophy, but only for the ultimate subordination of the aesthetic in the final apotheosis of philosophical knowledge.

To be sure, Hegel's reliance on literature for philosophical thinking is hardly unprecedented: the philosophical use of literature is as old as philosophy itself. But, as we can see in Hegel's use of *Rameau's Nephew*, philosophy typically uses literature in a mediating role for a thinking that culminates in philosophical knowledge. In that sense, traditional literary-philosophical genealogies are most accurately conceived as marital, patriarchal, and reproductive. As Gearhart points out, in this self-reproducing philosophical machinery, literature and art function as "the dutiful complements—one could almost say *the wives*—of philosophy."[53] The literary wife may prove to be helpful to her husband—"Mr. Philosophy," the *Moi*—but only in her mediating, reflective role as an illustrative unreason to be eventually excluded from Mr. Philosophy's final truth.

This story about the Nephew as a Hegelian legacy raises questions about literature and subjectivity in Foucault that I will explore further in chapter 5. To be sure, the queer Nephew who appears in *Madness* is not Mr. Philosophy's literary wife. Like other philosophers of his generation, Foucault implicitly questions Hegel's picture of absolute Truth in "the shape of self-certainty"[54] by staging the Nephew as the illuminated limit of thinking. And if, as Philippe Lacoue-Labarthe suggests, the question of "a possible literary *filiation* of philosophy" constitutes "a question that Hegel himself never asked as such,"[55] it is not clear that Foucault uses the Nephew to propose such a filiation. Indeed, Foucault's consistent treatment of genealogies as temporal discontinuities argues against a Foucauldian reversal of Hegelian philosophical filiations in favor of literary ones.

Such a refusal of literary filiation challenges Hegelo-Derridean readings of literature in Foucault. Felman, for example, suggests that "literature is, for Foucault, in a position of excess, since it includes that which philosophy excludes by definition: madness. Madness thus becomes an overflow, that which remains of literature after philosophy has been subtracted from it. The History of Madness is the story of this surplus, the story of a literary residue."[56] This deconstructive reading of literature as philosophy's excess and residue transforms Foucault into a champion of the literary, which becomes, for Felman, the madness that philosophy excludes. But such a reading not only continues the Hegelian logic of dialectical reversal, sublating literature over philosophy to support Derrida's claim that Foucault's *philosophy of madness* is "the inverted and irrefutable sign of the constitutive *madness of philosophy*."[57] It also simply ignores Foucault's repeated assertion that madness is the *absence* of an oeuvre, literary or otherwise. If literature "includes" madness, as Felman claims, it is no longer madness. Madness, by definition, cannot speak: "*where there is an oeuvre, there is no madness*" (M 537).[58]

Foucault is less interested in literature or art per se than he is in what he will later call an aesthetic practice of freedom. To be sure, the question of literature is tricky in Foucault, especially if we compare his writings of the sixties with his later work where literature becomes less prominent.[59] Unlike Derrida and Felman, who want to privilege Foucauldian literary texts as "mad in their 'undecidability,'"[60] I want to argue that literary discourse is one of the many discursive "fictions"—historical, scientific, pedagogical, philosophical—that participate in games of truth. In that sense, Foucault does not reverse Hegel, creating a literary filiation over a philosophical one. Rather, he dedialectizes the Hegelian vertical relation between literature and philosophy by placing both discourses beside him [*à côté de lui*],[61] in a horizontal or sideways relation, thereby releasing them—along with the traces of those delinquents, fools, and lunatics he finds in the archives—into the series of events to which they belong. This democratizing desublation of the philosophy-literature reversal we find in Hegel thus allows Foucault to bring an aesthetic practice to the space of the archive where he finds the lives of "infamous" men and women.

Foucault's implicit refusal of both literary and philosophical filiations in the context of the archive and reason's plotting of history frames the larger problem of filiation as a structure of power. As the story of the Nephew's deviant birth suggests, the Hegelian subject born with the Nephew exposes genealogy as a potentially deviating movement within a seemingly rationalist structure. The perversion of genealogy or filiation the Nephew performs—both within the text and in the story of its genesis—contests precisely the oedipal and Cartesian structures of a family morality Foucault left behind at the end of part 3 of *Madness*. As the Nephew's arboreal name—*rameau*, or branch—suggests, *Rameau's Nephew* not only names the lines of an aesthetic filiation between the Nephew and his composer uncle but also queers the genealogical lines of a family tree. In its exaggerated attention to the diagonal kinship relation of uncle and nephew rather than the oedipal, dialectical verticality of father and son, the *Nephew* perverts those family genealogies on which both Cartesian and Freudian patriarchal despotisms depend. Indeed, if the *Nephew* is "oblique"[62]—that is, *quer*, or queer—then the diagonal slant of his avuncular filiation links him to Sedgwick's antioedipal proclamation in *Tendencies*: "Forget the Name of the Father. Think about your uncles and aunts."[63]

The Nephew's birth is thus doubly deviant, born not from a father but "deviated through the avunculate" for a form of subjectivity James Creech describes as "broken thus plural, displaced thus displaceable."[64] Indeed, toward the end of the dialogue, *Lui* perverts father-son descent as a genealogy of fools: "And look at the name I bear—Rameau. Being called Rameau makes things awkward. . . . The old trunk branches out into an enormous bunch of fools [*sots*], but who cares?"[65] Once again, the theatrum mundi is a ship of fools.

This queer filiation in Diderot also queers the Hegelian subject of reason who is born, in *Madness*, in the theatrical space of *Rameau's Nephew*. This queered subject slants the story I told earlier about *Rameau's Nephew* as part of the French Hegelianism of the postwar period. For, as a post-Hegelian thinker, Foucault is himself part of a filial structure of philosophical descent. Specifically, the seemingly straight line of descent from a Hegelian father to his French sons is historically mediated by a French avuncular figure: Jean Hyppolite, the famous French Hegelian whom Foucault first met at the elite *lycée* Henri IV in Paris in

1945. Although Hyppolite remains faithful to Hegel while Foucault does not, Foucault and Hyppolite remain queerly faithful to each other, even and especially beyond Hyppolite's death in 1968. Indeed, it was in his absence that Hyppolite most powerfully helped to propel Foucault to the pinnacle of French intellectual power, when his death created the vacancy at the Collège de France that Foucault would fill in 1970.

As Foucault's tribute at a memorial gathering in Hyppolite's honor suggests, Foucault's Hegelian teacher and predecessor allowed Foucault, paradoxically, to contest the Hegelianism that dominated French philosophy in the postwar period. In Foucault's eulogy, he presents Hyppolite as a Hegelian thinker whose direct contact with the immediacy of lived experience produces an encounter between "philosophical thought"—as "this twisting and redoubling"[66]—and its perversion as the nonphilosophical. This philosophical contact with the nonphilosophical in Foucault's tribute twists and redoubles Hegel into something we might not recognize as Hegel: an endless, risk-taking thinking—"in excess of any philosophy"—where the nonphilosophical appears as "a light which kept watch [veillait] even before there was any discourse, a blade [lame] which still shines even as it enters into sleep."[67] This interpretation of an Hyppolite whom Foucault describes at Henri IV as the ventriloquized "voice of Hegel" might, in the eyes of some, distort Hegel beyond recognition.[68] But Foucault will push his anti-Hegelian twistings of Hegel even further three years later. In "Nietzsche, Genealogy, History," published in 1971 in a collection of essays honoring Hyppolite, Foucault surprisingly bypasses Hegel to celebrate Nietzsche.[69] Importantly, Foucault's invisible transformation of Hegel into Nietzsche, in what will become one of his most widely cited essays, sheds light on the Nephew—whom we might now call the Nietzschean figure of a Hegelianism gone mad—as Madness's central image of philosophy's limits. Indeed, just as Foucault biographer David Macey ultimately finds it "strangely fitting that [Foucault's] final homage to Hyppolite should take the form of a eulogy of Nietzsche,"[70] so too we might find it strangely appropriate that Foucault stages a Hegelian Nephew at the center of his Nietzschean Madness.

In light of Foucault's somewhat odd description of Hegel in Hyppolite, we might further reread Hyppolite as an "older man," avuncular figure who allows Foucault to rethink the seemingly straight Hegelianism represented by the Nephew in Madness. For, however faithful Hyppolite's filial relation to father Hegel might be—including, importantly, his admiring reading of Hegel's *Nephew* in *Genesis and Structure of the Phenomenology of Spirit* (1946)—Foucault will reinterpret those faithful readings as a kind of perverted Hegelianism, where the philosopher of absolute knowledge becomes a Nietzschean thinker of the immediacy of experience, of eros, of the nonphilosophical. Never reading anything straight, Foucault thus becomes the queer nephew of an Hyppolite who, paradoxically, becomes a queer Hegelian uncle to Foucault while simultaneously maintaining his position as a straight Hegelian son. From that perspective, we might correspondingly read Hyppolite's straight interpretation of the *Nephew* in Hegel through an avuncular lens that queers the Nephew in *Madness*: "He openly shows himself as he is, but in fact he never finds himself in a definitive way. He is never what he is, always outside himself, and returning to himself when he is outside himself."⁷¹ Like the Nephew Hyppolite describes, Foucault is "always outside himself." In that sense, Foucault's widely acknowledged Nietzscheanism is also oddly Hegelian: literally taking the place, at the Collège de France, of postwar France's most famous Hegelian, Foucault queers that place as Hegel's Nietzschean thought-at-the-limit.

So too, in *Madness*, the Hegelian Nephew becomes something other than Hegel: "always outside himself," he embodies the heterotopian experience of the limit. In that sense, Foucault restores a radical strangeness to Diderot that had been taken away by Hegel. For, if Hegel's Nephew, as absolute perversion, is implicitly queer, he comes to Foucault all straightened out—"a stranger to himself who becomes familiar once more" (*M* 543)—in the *Phenomenology*'s final sublation of perversion as absolute knowledge. In the pre-Hegelian Nephew, by contrast, thinking begins and ends in deviance; as the *Moi* puts it on the very first page: "my thoughts, they are my whores [*catins*]."⁷² Thinking itself becomes promiscuous, straying not only beyond the father but, in its whoring, beyond the moralism of family values. The theatrum mundi becomes a brothel; like the ship of fools, it is a heterotopia: "the greatest reservoir of imagination."⁷³

As a *philosophe*'s thoughts-as-whores, the Nephew is a reservoir of imaginative deviations that expose the limits of reason. However, if we recall Emma Goldman's insights into a heterosexual "traffic in women" that binds prostitution to "legitimate" marriage, the deviant brothel starts to look more heteronormative than heterotopian. This was certainly the case for Diderot, whose married status also included the pleasures of a mistress, Sophie Volland. Of course, there exists in the dialogue between *Moi* and *Lui*—and especially in the figure of the Nephew—the ever-present possibility of the queering of hetero-marriage and its typical infidelities. But that queer possibility can only occur in the Nephew's deviant future as Foucault's *Madness*. Rerouted through the grid of the homoerotic and sexually deviant proclivities *Madness* describes, the whoring thinking becomes, like one of Fou-cault's bathhouse "tricks," "another trick that madness play[s]" (*M* xxvii) to contest rationalism's *heteronormative* moral investments. Restaged within *Madness*, the Nephew's discursive and nondiscursive appear-ances—his mocking descriptions of marital couplings as forms of eco-nomic exchange, his celebratory focus on defecation and other shame-tainted bodily activities, his gender-rupturing pantomimes of musical instruments and Parisian social posturing—all reappear as queer alter-natives to *Moi's* heteronormative economy.

Finally, all this exposes the place of the "nonphilosophical" in Fou-cault's own life: the place of his queer experience as an intellectual competitor-in-training in the French 1940s and fifties. Trying to stake a claim as a not-yet-established thinker in a cutthroat environment, Fou-cault writes *Madness* in the wake of an explicitly homosocial philosophi-cal training: a boy's club if ever there was one. Especially at the Ecole Normale Supérieure, where Foucault prepared in the late 1940s as a future member of the intellectual elite, the club is also a chain that links generations of thinkers before and after Foucault, including Sartre, Du-mézil, Canguilhem, Hyppolite, Althusser, Bourdieu , Genette, Badiou, Derrida, Balibar, Macherey, and Rancière, to name just a few. The boys play a game—a "traffic in thoughts"—that will render, as the profits of a fixed economy, the intellectual capital of individual careers and reputa-tions.[74] In this French intellectual environment, a philosopher's thoughts are indeed his whores: the game commodifies thoughts as objects of exchange that serve to enrich the thinker who pimps them.

But if Foucault is as much a trafficker in thoughts as anyone else, in the 1940s and fifties his net worth in that homosocial economy is poten-tially diminished by his homoerotic proclivities. Like many of his anti-humanist peers, Foucault will use philosophy to challenge philoso-phy from within, from his adolescence at Henri IV to his last years at the Collège de France. But, with the exception of Jacques Martin—Foucault's brilliant, latently schizophrenic gay friend at the Ecole Nor-male who, having written nothing, eventually committed suicide in 1963—Foucault is virtually alone in an erotic attraction to boys and men that he painfully hid from his peers. Haunted by a queer "ghost of failure"[75] in the image of Martin, Foucault's standing in a field whose homophobia is often explicit is threatened by his singular homoeroticism. As Macey asserts, in postwar France "rumours of homosexuality could and did break academic careers,"[76] and homophobic prejudices were backed up by a 1946 statute that limited the possibility of employment by the state—including, most importantly, university teaching—to persons of "good morality."[77] The homophobic environment in which Foucault received his philosophical training helps to explain the appearance, at the close of the 1950s, of a history of madness that is also, indirectly, both a genealogy of sexual deviance and an affirmation of eros. Diderot's mad *Nephew*—filtered, in *Madness*, through a queered Hegelianism—exposes both the dangers and pleasures of a homoeroticism that differentiates Foucault from his antihumanist peers. It remains to be seen if *Madness*'s queering of French antihumanism also functions as a proto-feminist challenge to a homo-philosophical traffic that is not only heteronormative but also exclusively gendered. That is a final question *Madness* might pose for the contemporary project of a queer feminism.

A Heterotopian Mirror

As a Hegelian subject who is both there and not there, mad and not mad, the Nephew returns us to the problem of the "I" that first emerged with the Cartesian cogito. But, unlike Descartes, who excludes madness from the "I," Hegel includes madness within the dialectic as the other face of a self-reflective subject. "The capacity for self-reflection is given to man alone," Hegel writes. "That is why he has, so to speak, the privilege of madness."[78] As Daniel Berthold-Bond points out in *Hegel's Theory of Madness*, "madness and the 'normal' mind are not sheer opposites for Hegel. Not only does Hegel refer to madness as a 'necessary' and 'essential' stage in the phenomenology of human consciousness, but there are certain basic structures of madness which are equally structures of the developed, rational mind."[79] Hegel's ontology of madness is an "ontology of origins" (3): "Like Freud some eighty years later, Hegel saw madness as a reversion to and recovery of psychic origins: in madness, the mind 'sinks back' into the earliest phases of the development of the soul, the domain of the unconscious play of instincts, or what he calls 'the life of feeling'" (3). In the dialectic, this life of feeling is "retained and integrated within the rational self" (3). According to Hegel, "insanity is not a . . . loss of reason" but more of a regression, a "derange-ment," "a contradiction in still subsisting reason" (3).

I have already shown how reason's perversion as madness, embodied by the Nephew, is sublated in Hegel while it is not in Foucault. Berthold-Bold's explication of Hegel's ontology of madness in the *Encyclopedia* helps to clarify how the Hegelian Nephew functions, in Foucault, as reason's mirror: its own madness. "That man is *my* madman," Foucault says. And as Berthold-Bond puts it, in Hegel "madness is the *mirror* of the developed consciousness" (3; emphasis added); its ontology reveals an "inward 'doubleness' or self-division" (7) that, in Foucault's hands, exposes the reasoning subject to a radical instability. This is not the same as saying, as Derrida does, that philosophy becomes mad through the textual play of *différance*. Rather, the Nephew in his coextension with the sensible world becomes a mirror that flattens out all that Hegel will have sublated: the life of feeling, instinct, and the functions of the body to which the Hegelian self regresses when he "sinks" into madness. This is why Foucault insists on the continuity between the "drunkenness of the sensible" (*M* 351) in Rameau's Nephew and the "consecration of the sen-sible in Nerval" (*M* 351) or the "return to immediacy" (*M* 351) in Hölder-lin's late poetry. Hegelian self-reflection and the rise of pathologies in the nineteenth century help to explain why reason's mirror turns the "ver-tigo of the sensible" (*M* 351) into the "confinement of madness" (*M* 351). Here again we find Nietzsche "going mad": "The moment of the *Ja-sagen*, of the embrace of the lure of the sensible, was also the moment [he] re-treated into the shadows of insanity" (*M* 351).

In this section I focus on this self-reflective Hegelian logic as a doubling structure that provides a frame for approaching desubjectiva-tion as an ethical question. If self-reflection in Hegel, in the service of reason, ultimately turns the self-doubling subject into the self-same, self-reflection in Foucault happens in a distorting mirror that opens the sub-ject to the other. And, because reason's own madness entails the "lure of the sensible" (*M* 351), that opening toward the other includes a sensible dimension: the call of eros as instinct, the body, and the life of feeling.

In a positivist, post-Hegelian world, that realm of immediacy is cap-tured by science and specified as pathologies because, as Foucault puts it, "in all post-Hegelian thought, man moves from certainty to the truth through the work of the mind and of reason" (*M* 350). That work of the mind turns erotic subjects into objects. So my inquiry into the Nephew as a self-reflective "I" begins with a question that emerges out of chapter

3: if human subjectivities and sexualities are fully captured as objects of a modern psyche-logos, what nonobjectifying alternatives remain available to us? This question reopens *Madness*'s structural center or *charnière* (hinge and lure), where the "I" sees himself reflected in what Foucault calls the subject's modern objectification as truth. As a hinge, the Nephew marks a revolutionary turn of the subject from the Age of Reason to its nineteenth-century apotheosis in the rise of medical science. As a lure, the Nephew draws attention to the Hegelian moment in Foucault's argument where Descartes and Freud converge. The power of the lure is attested to by Derrida's repetitive return to these pages both in 1963 and again in 1991, in his essays on Descartes and Freud, respectively. Indeed the lure is the place where Derrida finds a confirmation of the madness of philosophy he already posited in his reading of Descartes. Here, with Diderot, Derrida defends Freud as a Nietzschean madman, one of "those worthy heirs of Rameau's Nephew."[80] But, for Foucault, the Nephew functions as a different kind of mirror to reflect *Madness*'s Cartesian beginning back, as an ending, into a psychoanalytic present where Descartes joins Freud in a twinned sovereign rule over modern knowledge as psyche-logos. The Nephew is therefore a condensation, a pleating of time "just below the temporality of historians" (*M* 344), a narrative contraction whose reflective stain replicates the father of modern philosophy as the father of psychoanalysis.

Indeed, one of the Nephew's most important qualities as a character is his mirroring function: his mimetic talents, his ability to ape the world. Quoting from Diderot, Foucault presents the Nephew as "an ironic repetition of the world" (*M* 349):

> shouting, singing, twirling like a man possessed, acting at the same time all the roles of all the male and female dancers and singers, a whole orchestra, an entire opera, dividing himself into twenty different roles, running around in circles, before suddenly stopping like a man possessed, his eyes wild, foaming at the mouth. . . . He cried, shouted and sighed, he looked moved, tranquil and furious; he was a woman fainting in agony, a miserable creature filled with despair, a temple that rose up, the birds that fall silent with the setting sun . . . he was night with its darkness, he was shadows, he was silence (*M* 349).

Diderot's mimetic Nephew performs the modern "I" in its coextension with the world, in what Foucault calls "the indefinite reflection of a mirror" (*M* 347). But, as a mad "I" who also illuminates the limit-as-void, the Nephew does not produce the image of a self as a substance at the center of a world that swirls around him. To use Irigarayan terminology, he does not produce the "I" as a reflection of the same. If the Nephew is a mirror, he is a "troubled" one: "a distorting mirror" (*trouble miroir*) (M 354–355/F 374) that, rather than reflecting a Cartesian "I" back to himself in yet another exclusion of madness, distorts the cogito with an unthinkable utterance: "I am mad." As Foucault puts it: "Descartes became aware that he could not be mad. . . . But Rameau's Nephew knows very well—and it is the most permanent feature among his fleeting certitudes—that he is mad" (M 343). This moment in *Madness* where a rational subject (*Moi*) recognizes and names his own madness (*Lui*) is crucial. We might, at first glance, conclude that Foucault is using the Nephew to turn Descartes with his cogito into a madman, as Derrida does in his famous critique of *Madness*. "The act of the Cogito is valid *even if I am mad*, even if my thoughts are thoroughly mad,"[81] Derrida asserts. But, despite the apparent similarities between Derrida's Hegelian universalization of madness as developed consciousness's sublated mirror and reason's contamination by madness in the Nephew, the implications of the statement "I am mad" become dramatically distinct in their Derridean and Foucauldian contexts.

To be sure, raised on Hegel, both Derrida and Foucault begin with a familiar Hegelian move by using ironic reversal to expose reason's dialectical negation of itself as madness: the perversion in the mirror of the "I"'s self-reflection. But, unlike Foucault, in his "Cogito" essay Derrida deconstructs, in a Hegelian logic, the reason-madness opposition, thereby negating a rationalist cogito and transforming it into philosophy's supreme figure of madness: "I philosophize only in *terror*, but in the *confessed* terror of going mad [*d'être fou*]."[82] Foucault, by contrast, refuses to sublate irony's dualities, moving instead toward its unsettling edge. So if, in reversing Hegelian absolute knowledge as a Cartesian absolute madness, Derrida uses the dialectic to recuperate madness for philosophy, Foucault does no such thing. Rather, he allows madness to sit there "beside him" as the sharp edge of a tear, a disquieting aporia.

This contrast between Derrida and Foucault at the place of the "I" in his self-reflection can be linked to Foucault's critique of Freud as another kind of mirroring structure. As I demonstrated in the previous chapter, Freudian dialogue recaptures madness in the self-objectifying utterances of the talking cure. In that context, when a psychoanalytic patient utters the self-reflective utterance "I am mad," his confession of madness is, unlike the Nephew's, forced by rationalism's despotic power. Inscribed within a psychoanalytic objectifying practice, "I am mad" is not the sign of the subject's truth, but the effect of a technology that is the historical result of Hegel's rationalist telos. As Foucault demonstrates in *Psychiatric Power* (1973–74), and again in the opening of "Sexuality and Solitude" (1981), Leuret's patient, Dupré, finally gives in to the doctor's treatments—which include cold showers, the recitation of names, and forced diarrhea—by saying, "I am mad."[83] Within the dialectical dispositif of a rationalist economy whose sublation, or profit, is "the statement of truth,"[84] Dupré's admission of madness paradoxically signals a return to sanity and the conclusion of his medical treatment. This mindless parroting of the doctor's words in an impossible self-recognition makes Dupré's truth, like that of the talking cure, as empty as the Nephew's. The self-reflective speaking of unreason—"I am mad"—is exposed as a therapeutic weapon to legitimate the analyst-doctor's power-knowledge.

By contrast, the Nephew's utterance—"I am mad"—occurs in a non-medical dialogical context where the "I"'s perversion as madness remains unresolved. In this sense, the *Nephew*'s madness remains as an emergence, both inside and outside of time, that cannot be appropriated, deciphered, or fully theorized. Thus, where the Freudian talking cure recaptures the subject in a "caged freedom," Foucault's subject is potentially freed into a heterotopian "space opened by the words [*la parole*] of the Nephew" (*M* 344/*F* 364).

Remembering, again, "that everything is always said in every age,"[85] we can thus read the Nephew, in his ironic hovering inside and outside of the psychological time of madness, as himself doubled in a temporal mirroring that works both backward and forward in the linear time of history. For, in a modern conception of historical time, the Nephew becomes, as Foucault puts it, "the last character in whom madness and unreason are united" (*M* 344/*F* 364). Thus, as a figure of modern madness, the Nephew simultaneously repeats ancient and premodern figurations of unreason. That prior unification of madness and unreason points, further, to a seventeenth-century moment when Descartes and the general hospitals captured unreason in the great confinement. And, in yet another doubling, this "last character" of the unification of unreason and madness also "prefigures" a later moment when positivist science will definitively separate them: "Rameau's Nephew is also the one in whom the moment of separation is prefigured" (*M* 344/*F* 364; translation modified). Finally, the Nephew opens a future aesthetic space of contestation in "the last texts of Nietzsche or . . . Artaud" (*M* 344/*F* 364) in which the "philosophical and tragic dimensions" (*M* 344/*F* 364) of that unification-separation will reemerge from within unreason's capture by modern rationalism.

Thus the Nephew both provides the mirror and "troubles" the reflection of the humanist subject as truth. This lens on the Nephew as a mirroring subject offers another figure for the heterotopian theme I've been developing in this chapter. To the theatrum mundi, the ship of fools, and the brothel we can now add the mirror. The mirror is a certain kind of heterotopia: it offers the "kind of mixed, intermediate experience"[86] that forms "between utopias" and the "utterly different emplacements"[87] that are heterotopias:

> The mirror is a utopia after all, since it is a placeless place. In the mirror I see myself where I am not, in an unreal space that opens up virtually behind the surface; I am over there where I am not, a kind of shadow that gives me my own visibility, that enables me to look at myself there where I am absent—a mirror utopia. But it is also a heterotopia in that the mirror really exists, in that it has a sort of return effect on the place that I occupy. Due to the mirror, I discover myself absent at the place where I am, since I see myself over there. From that gaze which settles on me, as it were, I come back to myself and I begin once more to direct my eyes toward myself and to reconstitute myself there where I am. The mirror functions as a heterotopia in the sense that it makes this place I occupy at the moment I look at myself in the glass *both utterly real,* connected with the entire space surrounding it, *and utterly unreal*—since, to be perceived, it is obliged to go by way of that virtual point which is over there.[88]

Like the "half-real, half-imaginary" ship of fools that opens Foucault's story of *Madness,* the subject's instrument of self-reflection is "both utterly real . . . and utterly unreal." As an "intermediate experience," the heterotopian mirror is unstable: it both performs the Hegelian magic of allowing me to "come back to myself"—to "begin once more to direct my eyes toward myself and to reconstitute myself there where I am"— and, at the same time, it dedialectizes Hegel in a continual process of self-estrangement: "I discover myself absent at the place where I am, since I see myself over there."

In its nonutopian, heterotopian dimension, the mirror describes the structure of an ethical encounter, where the self-reflective symmetry of the "I" is disrupted by an actual alterity that puts the reasoning subject

into question. In the context of the Nephew, within the mirrored structure that binds *Moi* to *Lui* and reason to madness, this ethical encounter is reframed within the real political space of the social. Foucault asserts that *Rameau's Nephew* marks the "first time since the Great
Confinement that the madman becomes once again a character on the
social stage" (*M* 353/*F* 373; translation modified), a figure who enters
into conversation with others. The Nephew becomes one of the mad
"'planners of crackpot [*tête fêlée*] projects'" (*M* 354/*F* 374) observed by
Mercier in *Tableau de Paris* (1781), mimicking the *philosophe* who would
build a new society on reason's back. Ironically performing the serious
work of the rationalist Enlightenment's planners and constitution writers—work that will lead to the mad, passion-driven bloodbath of the
French Revolution—the Nephew reveals the madness that is "not external to thought but lies at its very heart":[89] the absolute emptiness where
the "I" encounters—in himself and in society—"the ironic perversion
of his own truth" (*M* 350/*F* 370). That appearance of madness on a social stage also corresponds to the moment when, in the late eighteenth
century, the mad begin to be released from the asylums. This dialogue
of madness on a social stage thus makes visible the asylum—a "heterotopia[] of deviation"[90]—at the moment of its diminishing importance as
a technology of confinement, just as the experience of a premodern
homosexual eros became visible in its disappearance *into* the asylum
150 years earlier.

In the chiastic crossings of those oppositional movements—where
things appear in their disappearance—the "I"'s experience of madness
emerges in the "intermediate experience"[91] of the heterotopian mirror:
a gap in time and in form—between past and present, between tragic
and comic—that troubles the ethical certainties of the modern subject.
In the larger context of Foucault's archival ethical project, the Nephew's
ludic condensation of the archive's traces of madness exposes the illegible alterities of history and, through mimicry, makes them speak. In
the silence of the queer pantomimes—another heterotopian form of
mirroring—emerge the traces of a nondiscursive, gestural *theatrum
mundi*. Restaged as *Madness*'s mise en abyme, those pantomimes give
voice to an archive of madness that could only speak discursively, like
Leuret's patient, in the distorting and therefore impossible mimetic language of reason. By contrast, the mimetic performances of Diderot's
lunatic virtuoso function in *Madness* as scenes of retrieval where silence,
impossibly, speaks. In that sense, the Nephew's appearance in *Madness*
constitutes a moment of what Foucault calls eventialization: "the bring-

ing to light of 'ruptures of evidence.'"[92] As heterotopian mirrors, the Nephew's queer pantomimes are figures of visibility that bring to light those real forms of alterity history has rendered illegible. As the nondiscursive residue of both a discursive reason and a rationalist Revolution that failed to deliver on its high-minded promises, the Nephew's pantomimes can be "heard," then, as corporeal instantiations of unreason's silent "voice." This unsettling "speaking" has ethical implications: the experience of unreason in the Nephew's pantomime changes the one who "hears" it, engaging the listener's experience through the affective dimension of irony's heterotopian, slightly disturbing edge. "Did I admire?" *Moi* asks. "Yes, I did. Was I touched with pity? Yes, I was. But a tinge of ridicule ran through these sentiments and denaturalized them."[93]

Post-Hegel, this contestation of reason's self-reflection is a late-eighteenth-century event to which we in the present have no access. In a present-day, rationalist temporality that will have captured and sublated unreason, in the nineteenth century, into madness as a pathological object of science, that discourse is no longer available to us. "The nineteenth century, in all its inflexible seriousness, rends the indivisible domain designated by the irony of *Rameau's Nephew*, tracing an abstract line through what was formerly inseparable, demarcating the realm of the pathological" (*M* 352/*F* 372). It is precisely the abstraction of scientific positivism and its increasingly minute specification of forms of abnormality that reduces the experience of unreason performed by the Nephew to a list of specific pathologies to be diagnosed. In the nineteenth century, the possibility of heterotopian reversals like the Nephew's are shut down, their ironies sublated as absolute knowledge and thus "impossible . . . for us" (*M* 352).

However, if we allow the Nephew to help us remember that the linear, sublated time of a scientific madness is split by the dedialectizing time of unreason, the positivist muting of unreason becomes opened to an ethical contestation: a light-bringing encounter which, "like a bolt of lightning" (*M* 344), fractures the Age of Reason. In the midst of historical impossibilities, different possibilities reopen. And those openings, or flashes, are the "trouble" in the mirror whose instability might free the "I" from the stasis of its own self-identical reflection. Ironic reversal once again troubles subjectivity, but in a nonlinear time, creating an opening for a nonself-reflective "I": "I discover myself absent at the place where I am, since I see myself over there."[94] Moving back and forth in time like the ship of fools, that heterotopian opening moves in and out of the paralyzing time of pathological madness and the spiraling time of ironic unreason. As a fold in time, it shuttles back toward old forms of unreason like the "buffoonery" of the "Middle Ages" (*M* 344) and forward toward "the most modern forms of unreason, those that are the contemporaries of Nerval, Nietzsche, and Antonin Artaud" (*M* 344). In ethical terms, it is not a silencing of reason so that unreason might speak, as so many of Foucault's interpreters have claimed. It is, rather, the opening of a passage, within reason, less for speaking than for an archival listening: the creation of a pathway for a different hearing.

In the next and final section of this chapter, I will show how this opening might lead to new possibilities for a dialogue between madness and queer theory. Here I want simply to note that the opening of a heterotopian mirror can help frame the thinking of an erotic ethics that would not sublate the life of feeling and instinct that Hegel associates with madness. In its capture of everything—including a contaminating madness rejected by Descartes and then recuperated by Hegel and Freud—reason's mirror is distorted: it becomes heterotopian. Both in his torrential speech and his gestural silences the Nephew destabilizes any meaning we might attach to the lives he mimics: any "straight" commentary we might extrude from the Nephew on the important themes, characters, and public figures that surround him is continually thwarted by an ironic perspective that mocks them. In a "systematic will to delirium" (*M* 347) that repeats and rivals Cartesian systematic doubt, the Nephew embraces and becomes all that which Descartes would have excluded from the cogito as error: "that noise, that music, that spectacle, that comedy" (*M* 348). For Foucault, this satirical "fascination with what is the most exterior" (*M* 348/*F* 368; translation modified) marks an ironic challenge to the sovereign, internalized moral order of a coherent, self-reflective subjectivity whose self-realization excludes the other, either through outright exile or, in a dialectical reversal, through Hegelian universalization. Irony turns that overly serious subject inside out, producing a radically different ethical experience—"a total experience of the world" (*M* 347)—in which the subject is thrust away from himself—and his own philosophical structures of knowledge—toward the alterity of the outside. "I would like to be somebody else,"[95] the Nephew says. That porous figure of an ethical becoming-other "open to the winds" (*M* 343) will reappear, twenty years later, in

Foucault's anonymous dream of an ethical "curiosity" as "care"[96] that would "listen to the wind," summoning or inventing "signs of existence" not heard before.[97]

Madness's critical contestation of bourgeois reason's universalizing structure of self-reflection in the central figure of *Rameau's Nephew* is thus crucial to its movement toward an ethics. In ethical terms, the Nephew might be described as a paradigmatically Foucauldian effect of desubjectivation whose radical coextensivity with the external world constitutes an opening toward the other. To be sure, the same irony that opened the subject to the world can easily destroy the subject's contact with immediacy as the mad virtuality of a Deleuzian becoming-other.[98] In other words, the laughing subject's mad generosity toward the lived, corporeal particularities of the world can easily be recuperated as a mimetic representation that leaves the fleshy world behind: "the ironic repetition of the world, its destructive reconstitution in a theatre of illusion" (*M* 349). But, as I've insisted throughout this book, Foucault seems willing to take that risk—the Nietzschean risk of an ironic, simulated becoming-other—for its challenge to the mystified violence of rationalist humanism. That challenge is an opening, a light-bringing event whose flash illuminates the possibility for a nonviolent ethics of erotic experience in the form of a practice of freedom. Mounting a challenge to the illusory, even murderous "freedoms" of a Cartesian rationalism or a Freudian talking cure, this ethical freedom affirms a different conception of subjectivity or, rather, a freeing of the subject from subjectivity altogether.

This ethical affirmation of an erotic becoming-other whose condition of possibility is freedom links the complex reflective structure I've described in this chapter to the "troubled mirror" that is sexuality. Foucault will take up the project of erotic subjectivity as a self-undoing in the last two volumes of *History of Sexuality*. Here in *Madness*, through the Hegelian Nephew, Foucault exposes the erotic costs of a self-reflective logic that weds unreason's sexual possibilities to a confining moral order. So if we were to ask the Nephew the question we have asked so many times before—why have we made sexuality into a moral experience?—how might he respond? Of course we cannot know what "his" answer would be, because "he" is no other than our own troubled reflection. Indeed, Rameau's Nephew, as the "distorting mirror" (*M* 354–355) in which we become "a sort of harmless caricature" (*M* 355) of ourselves, ultimately decimates both the question itself and all our prior answers to it by mocking the seriousness of the quasi-philosophical "we" that would produce such a question in the first place. He would, no doubt, laughingly remind us of the place "we" occupy, without acknowledging it, the moment "we" ask the question: the Cartesian place of a shared reason, the Freudian place of a shared morality always bent, in Hegelo-Derridean seriousness, on "doing justice."[99] Only when the question of sexuality can be released from the already captured place of the subject who asks it can a different ethical experience of eros emerge.

So, in a Cynic's gesture of self-deflation, I will allow the Nephew to do his work here by letting go of the question that has, up to now, structured my interrogation of sexuality and madness. I imagine the question becoming, as in the Nephew's pantomimes, one of those "absurd masks"[100] his performances create for "the faces of the most pompous individuals":[101] prelates, judges, monks, ministers, first secretaries,[102] and—why not?—university professors. The "why" was touched on in previous chapters: we have made sexuality into a moral experience because we have repudiated erotic love in a Cartesian splitting of the mind from the body (chapter 1), reducing eros to the internalized violence of a shame-infested bad conscience (chapter 2), and securing our sexual objectification in the talk-producing project of a despotic psyche-logos that continues to define modern subjectivity (chapter 3). Now it is time to release the "why," along with its theory-saturated "we," into the possibilities of a different erotic experience no longer bound by the structures of reason and morality, subjectivity and truth, that allowed the question to be articulated at all. The Nephew sets the stage for a different ethics. Neither the violent moralism of a bourgeois order that locks up the fleshy other nor the equally violent reactive rupture of moralism's negation, this ethics will take the shape of a poetic and corporeal opening toward the real alterity of the world. Its mimetic language will shift from the philosophical drone of an endlessly repeated, abstract question to the ludic, aleatory, gestural articulation of a sensibility that allows unreason, in all its erotic generosity, to be heard. Like Diogenes, who responded to Alexander the Great's offer of favors with a simple request—"Stop blocking my sun!"[103]—it is a fame-mocking erotic ethics.

A Modern Diogenes

How does all this relate to queer theory? Diderot is certainly not irrelevant to the queer. His *Bijoux indiscrets* (1748), about talking vaginas, serves as an emblem of a modern sex-that-speaks in *Sexuality One*, the bible of queer theory. And Sedgwick famously develops an argument about the "privileges of unknowing" through a reading of Diderot's *La Religieuse*. Less obviously queer than the scandalous tale of a lesbian desire whose contamination of an illusory moral innocence exposes the hypocrisy of the Age of Reason, the Nephew's centrality in Foucault nonetheless makes him important for queer theory. And, as I will show more clearly in the following chapter, the ethics he makes possible are vastly more generative than either recent queer moralisms of various kinds or a "no future" negative ethics. Foucault's Diderot—the mad Diderot of *Rameau's Nephew*—can guide us in constructing an ethical vision which, like the self-undoing practices of the self we find in volumes 2 and 3 of *History of Sexuality*, acknowledges subjectivity as dialogic and therefore relational. Further, the Nephew's nondiscursive practices of self-making and unmaking suggest technologies of the self invested in a body unsplit from a thinking subject. Through the exaggerated gesture of pantomime, the Nephew engages subjectivity's corporeal dimension in a post-Cartesian exercise of freedom that sutures the wound separating the mind from the body, mimetic illusion from animal necessity, reason from unreason.

In that sense, *Madness*'s Nephew is a queer shadow, silhouette, or ghost who moves in and out of our historical present in a time-altering ship of fools. And, unlike the elite Greco-Roman practices Foucault examined as experiments in ethical freedom, the Nephew's practices emerge from the heart of an Enlightenment ethos we still inhabit. Not only does the Nephew stage a language of silence that can be heard as a different "voice" for unreason that speaks from within our psychic capture, but his pantomimes bear the traces of an erotic deviance we have come to call queer: "metaphorical ass kissing" can just as easily be the "simple," literal, pleasurable kind.[104]

As the Nephew's Nietzschean transvaluation of a bondsman's slavish "ass kissing" into a perverse eroticism suggests, the corporeal self, however objectified, is promiscuously open to transformation. This transvaluation of ass kissing is not a performative resignification *à la* Butler but rather a heterotopian retraversal of a land of morality which reveals the (anal) void as the pleasurable site of a desubjectivation that happens in a relation to an other. That image of self-undoing in an erotic relation—a common enough experience that most of us "get," however abstract the philosophical language that names it—offers a way of approaching a more difficult practice, after sex,[105] in a relation to history's others I call Foucault's ethical ars erotica. The Nephew's multiple performances are thus not performative, in the queer Butlerian sense, because the breakdown of self they embody undoes not just identities—as "woman," "man," "dancer," "singer" (in M 349)—but subjectivity itself: he becomes "a temple that rose up," "birds that fall silent," "night with its darkness," "shadows," "silence" (in M 349). Not a ludic game, but a "hystericized discourse with psychotic borders,"[106] the Nephew's pantomime forces an ethical engagement with a moral structure invested in reason where contact with the other serves to replicate the self.

If rational moralism colonizes the contact between self and other within the powerful self-reflective machinery of humanist philosophical abstraction, the Nephew's experience of the immediate and the sensible within a philosophical theater of illusions registers once again the questions Foucault raised in his tribute to Hyppolite about philosophy's own relation to the nonphilosophical. Foucault highlights Hyppolite's position as an historian, within the space of philosophy, who "wanted to describe the way in which all philosophies take up within themselves an immediacy [un immédiat] that they have already ceased to be."[107] And Hyppolite finds in Hegel, Foucault continues, the drama of thinking's relation to experience, "the play of philosophy and non-philosophy" (812). Foucault's Hyppolite recognized, as other Hegelians did not, "the moment when [philosophy] traverses its own limits to become the philosophy of non-philosophy, or perhaps the non-philosophy of philosophy itself" (812). To do philosophy, then, meant not "to describe an object" or pin it down but rather "to open it, to trace its ruptures, its lags, its blanks, to establish it in its irruption and its suspense, to unfold it in the lack or the unsaid through which philosophy speaks for itself" (809). If philosophy is reason, to trace its ruptures is to write the madness that describes philosophy's relation to that which it is not. No description better captures Foucault's own project: a "philosophical thinking" as an "incessant practice" (813), "a certain way of putting non-philosophy to work" (813).

This avuncular relation that links Foucault to Hegel through a certain madness in Hyppolite's thinking[108]—the madness of the nonphilosophical realm of instinct, bodily experience, and the life of feeling that philosophy sublates as reason—turns the dialectic into something other: an unsettling hovering at the limits of thinking. This is perhaps why Foucault hints, in his brief nine pages on Rameau's Nephew, that the Nephew is a modern Diogenes. Like Diogenes, Foucault's Nephew lives a life of immediacy in direct contact with the nonphilosophical: "Rameau's Nephew is hungry and says so" (*M* 347). We don't know, of course, if when he wrote these lines Foucault was thinking of the well-known anecdote about Diogenes who said, when rebuked for masturbating in the public square, "if only I could soothe my hunger by rubbing my belly." Foucault does mention the anecdote years later, in 1984, in his last course at the Collège de France, the second half of which is devoted to the lives of the Cynics.[109] But, in *Madness*, Foucault explicitly links the Cynics to Diderot's character, insisting that "cynicism . . . is occasionally reborn in [the Nephew]" (*M* 347). As the Nephew himself puts it at the end of the dialogue, "so Diogenes danced the pantomime too."[110] Thus Foucault's famous thinking of the limit might be imagined here as indebted to the Cynic whose challenge to Socrates in "a dialogue of flesh and blood" led Plato to call him a "'Socrates gone mad.'"[111] Another erotic contestation, in "flesh and blood," of the power of the dialectic. Another anti-Cartesian character in the ship of fools (figure 4.1).

Let me conclude this chapter with a confession. In somewhat surreptitiously reading the swishy mad Nephew who inhabits the salons of

FIGURE 4.1 Diogenes, Democritus, and two fools standing around the globe. From *Das Narrenschiff*, 1497

eighteenth-century France as a filthy, flea-bitten Cynic,[112] I admit to being a bit like Doctor Leuret, who deviously slipped calomel into his patient's food. If Leuret's treatment gave Dupré diarrhea in the form of an utterance—"I am mad"—these dashes of Diogenes have the power to unleash a philosophical case of the runs from which neither I nor my readers might ever recover. But, then again, as the Nephew puts it, "The important thing is to evacuate the bowels easily, freely, pleasantly, and copiously every evening. *O stercus pretiosum!*"[113] As strange as it may seem, I am tempted by the promise of a defecating, masturbating, urinating Diogenes—as Foucault was tempted in his last course—as a radical figure of a self-undoing subject: a philosopher ethically transformed by the nonphilosophical. As Foucault suggests in "The Courage of Truth," Diogenes might be a useful model not only for a difficult, courageous *parrhesia* but also, more powerfully, for a difficult practice of ethical living. Unlike a "beneficent" Socrates, Diogenes might be the "militant" we need to become something other than what we have been.[114] As Louisa Shea puts it, Foucault "recognizes Cynicism in mendicant orders of the Middle Ages, in revolutionary movements of the nineteenth century, and above all in modernist art of the turn of the twentieth century. Speaking out against scholars who relegate Cynicism to the past, Foucault insists on the enduring vitality of Cynicism as an engaged, militant attitude, which, in its uncompromising critique of social institutions, cannot but remind one of Foucault's own life-long philosophical project."[115] Like the Nephew in the Enlightenment, cynicism plays the role of a "broken mirror where the philosopher comes to see himself and, at the same time, doesn't recognize himself."[116] This heterotopian broken mirror comes about through the Cynic's belief in an embodied life, a "'homophonic' relation between word and deed,"[117] and an ethical parrhesia as a *"pratique à deux"*[118] that requires not only the courage to speak but also, more importantly, the courage to listen "to this other who has retained and arrested me."[119] And finally, in his commitment to animality—not a natural "given" but a "duty," an "exercise," and an ethical "practice"[120]—Foucault's Cynic lives an ethic of dispossession: an ethic of undoing through a scandalous animality as a model of getting free of oneself.

As an ethical achievement, that practice of self-undoing is not merely the serendipitous result of an explosive art of performative reversals. In his own thinking practice—his philosophy of nonphilosophy as Cynic—Foucault undoes himself through the long process of a disciplined, de subjectivating archival labor. But, in our love affair with the performative rupture of a linguistic poststructuralism, queer theorists have missed this Foucauldian practice and taken a dialectical path. That path leads directly to Hegel, who still lurks around every corner. And if Socratic and Hegelian ironies can continue to command our admiring attention, as any brilliant dialogue of talking heads always does, we might follow Foucault who, as we have seen, turned from Socrates, as he had from Hegel, to follow Diogenes toward the "scandalous banality" of living.[121]

As a modern Diogenes, the Nephew might offer us, as does Sloterdijk's "kynic," an ethical attitude for our cynical present. But, unlike Sloterdijk's masculinist, self-freeing Diogenes—like a little boy with his penis who has gleefully learned that anti-Hegelian "art of pissing against the idealist wind"[122]—Foucault's Nephew is an effeminate militant whose bodily practices must inform a thinking and feeling that acknowledges the sexual unfreedom of the swishy, the transgendered, the abnormal, and the limp-wristed. If ethics, as Foucault puts it, is the "conscious [réfléchie] practice of freedom,"[123] as pantomiming beggar, the Nephew knows this freedom of the "ontological condition of ethics" is available to few.[124] An ethical cynicism for our historical present must attend to the fraught social and political relations that subordinate less-than-human others to human subjects.

Even in our *highest* forms of queer feminist knowledge making, we can learn to practice the "pantomimic materialism"[125] of a Cynic's "*low theory*"[126] by remaining curious about the bodily traces of the "infamous" lives we find in the archives. In his strange, silhouetted, fractured beauty, the Nephew is a ghost who "speaks" those archives of madness. As an anti-Enlightenment "*éclaireur*"[127] the Nephew, like Diogenes, illuminates those lives through an erotic practice—an *alethes bios*—in the public square, in a place where "the sun lights up the swift joys of the *depraved animal.*"[128] That nonphilosophical light, in excess of philosophy, keeps watch as a different *surveillance*-as-care.[129] In a bodily parrhesia that engages the other, *bios* is transformed by eros. Hardly a nostalgic longing for a presocial state of nature—as Sloterdijk reminds us, Diogenes is an urban figure—this erotic ethics is "not a given."[130] Nor is it a utopia, a dream, or a projection. It is a heterotopian ars erotica—both "utterly real" and "utterly unreal"[131]—we can learn to practice on ourselves.

Fourth Interlude

A SHAMEFUL LYRICISM

After my encounter with the Nephew's blistering irony, I can't help but recall Foucault's ironic voice in the 1972 preface to *History of Madness*. Does the Nephew's emergence in the middle of *Madness* signal, like the rewritten preface, an ironic repudiation of an earlier lyricism? There is surely a resonance—it's unmistakable—between the homosexual lyricism that was left behind in the Renaissance and the lyrical pathos of the 1961 preface that Foucault suppressed. Reading it again, through the lens of *Rameau's Nephew*, I wonder if Foucault's irony really does succeed in effacing the lyricism of an earlier, tragic voice. And, if it does succeed, does that mean an erasure of his own homosexual lyricism as well?

For now I hear in that first preface the heartbreak of an ending, its voice speaking with "a lump in its throat, collapsing before it ever reaches any formulation and returning without a fuss to the silence it shook off" (*M* xxxii). After two attempted suicides, in 1948 and 1950, in the midst of a postwar French society that did not hesitate to diagnose as pathological abnormality what could have been a "happy world of desire" (*M* xxx), Foucault met his first lover, Jean Barraqué, in 1952. His biographers tell us that the relationship with the composer changed him: "There is no doubt," Eribon writes, "that this meeting provoked a 'transformation' in Foucault."[1] In a 1954 letter to Jacqueline Verdeaux,

Foucault writes: "I have decided to make the effort to live. But I have only taken the first few breaths. I am keeping an eye on the mirror to make sure I don't turn blue."[2]

Foucault's critique of psyche-logos tells me not to read the 1961 preface through the psychologizing lens provided by biography where Foucault's passion for Barraqué would shed new personal light on the preface's philosophical meanings. And yet something in me resists such directives. Perhaps, in this resistance, I remain perversely faithful to Foucault, who himself admits that any escape from psychology is a "doubly impossible task" (M xxxii). Perhaps to indulge in the language of psychological struggle is simply to give in to that fact. Of course, if there is a perverse faithfulness in my submission to psychology, that faithfulness is ironic. Psychology will not give me access to what I seek. For indeed, in my self-indulgent surrender to the kind of psychological reading Foucault would have resisted and did resist all his life (knowing, all the while, that his resistance was "doubly impossible"), I know I will miss the experience of love altogether. As Foucault now reminds me, to recreate, in writing, "the rudimentary movements of an experience" (M xxxii) of love means the experience itself has been distorted by "a world that has captured [it] already" (M xxxii). To perfectly reproduce an experience in writing is clearly impossible; to write that experience in a non-captured language is doubly so.

If the 1961 preface speaks in an anguished voice ripe for a psychologizing reading, the 1972 preface speaks in an ironic mode that adamantly refuses any sentimental interpretation of a tragic self. The relationship between the two, I now understand, hinges on an aporetic irony exposed in the revolutionary moment of *Rameau's Nephew*. In 1972, Foucault fully grasps, with some embarrassment, how mistaken he was in 1961 to indulge in the lyrical language of a personal drama. Thus he stages a voice to double and destroy the tragic one that emerged in 1961. In this he mimics Nietzsche, who replaced the first preface to the *Birth of Tragedy* (1872) fourteen years later with a prefatory "Attempt at a Self-Criticism," complaining that art is "impossible." Like Nietzsche, throughout his life Foucault had trouble with births and beginnings. He wrote numerous prefaces and introductions, like birth announcements, to a progeny that never came: "A Preface to Transgression," *History of Sexuality One: An Introduction*, the "Preface" to *History of Sexuality Two*. And *History of Madness*, his "first" major work, was the most problematic birth of all. For Foucault, as for Nietzsche, there can be no beginning, except as failure, a thinking that collapses in on itself as

unreason. "All things that live long are gradually so saturated with reason that their origin in unreason thereby becomes improbable," Nietzsche says at the opening of that matutinal book, *Daybreak*, which starts
him on a journey against morality. To begin in unreason is so improbable that it becomes "impossible," like the speaking of madness in Foucault or art in Nietzsche. Like the leper's ghost, the beginning appears,
again and again, as a figure of failure. And yet, as Foucault puts it in *The
Use of Pleasure*, the only way to work is to begin again, always in error:
"to begin again and again, to attempt and be mistaken, to go back and
rework everything from top to bottom, and still find reason to hesitate
from one step to the next."[3]

And so Foucault's 1972 scorching of the lovelorn figure who lingers in
his youthful preface is as swift as it is relentless. Here, in 1972, the "I" of
the 1961 preface is depicted not as a grieving lover but as a ruthless despot: "the monarch of the things that I have said" whose "eminent sovereignty" (*M* xxxviii) held sway over the meanings he intended to convey.
The lyrical language of the tragic voice with a lump in his throat is revealed, from the distance of 1972, as merely a seductive disguise. Beneath the disguise is a despotic subject whose lyricism masks a "declaration of tyranny" (*M* xxxviii) that must be resisted.

As I reread this passage from 1972, I can almost feel Foucault blush-
ing at his former folly, so blatantly exhibited for all the world to see. I
want to remark on the pain of this noncoincidence of self with self, to
note it as a kind of shame to be violently expunged in an act of self-
annihilation. I want to look it in the face and ask it questions: Shame,
where did you come from? What deeper, shame-ridden self are you hiding? I know these are despotic, self-identical, psychological questions.
And yet, I think, as I reread the passage: the shame is real. But I also
know that to ferret it out and ask it questions is to stubbornly, arrogantly
play at being Freud again. To play the father. So I remain here, trapped,
between the rock of Foucault's critique of Freud and the hard place of a
seemingly impossible resistance to a psychoanalytic perspective we inhabit like the air we breathe. No wonder Foucault checked the mirror
for signs of asphyxiation.

The failed preface is, not surprisingly, a figure that haunts the 1975
Droit interview as well. Early in the conversation, Droit turns to the
issue of the suppressed 1961 preface. After some vaguely negative remarks about the preface by Foucault, Droit counters that it wasn't all
that ugly. And Foucault responds: "Yes . . . that is, she [the preface] had
the faded beauties, not the faded beauties, she had the slightly ridicu-

lous beauties of a still green little girl who, to play the grand lady, puts a wad of make-up on her cheeks. . . . I was wearing a wig."[4]

The lyrical voice of the 1961 preface is a little girl playing dress-up. If the preface was beautiful, Foucault seems to say, it was a false, make-believe kind of beauty that didn't really know what it was saying, its embellishing words mere ornaments on a structure to which, ultimately, there was not much substance. That structure, I see now, is the structure of the limit, a "hollowed-out void" (M xxix) or "white space" (M xxix) Foucault will embellish with images: "a sterile beach of words" (M xxxi), "sand that has run its course" (M xxxi), "the charred root of meaning" (M xxxii), or "the murmur of dark insects" (M xxxiii). Such "dressing up" language reeks of aestheticism and a belles lettres sacralization of beauty. And yet, behind this image of Foucault as a little girl playing dress-up there's something shocking—is it shame again?—a certain gender trouble beneath the surface. For in his description of this elle, this she-preface, Foucault is speaking of himself.

And, indeed, as Eribon tells us, "right up to the end of his life," "Foucault would often speak in the feminine (about himself or others) when he was in the company of his gay friends. He made notable use of certain traits characteristic of gay conversation, feminizing first names by preceding them with a 'la' or using the 'la' in front of the surname—and, when possible, giving that surname a feminine form."[5] La Michelle Foucault? Michel la Foucault?

This is not performative resignification. There's something else going on here, a different kind of gender trouble. "She," the little-girl-as-preface, uses fancy, old-fashioned, grown-up words to make herself appear as something she is not: the lyrical preface-as-grand-lady. This grand lady preface is none other than Foucault, the "I" who mirrors himself-as-book back to himself-as-preface in what is ultimately, we may remember from the 1972 preface, the despotic act of a tyrannical monarch. Is the grand lady, perhaps, a queen?

She just might be, as another sort of preface or opening to a book: the "imperial prude" who stands as an emblem, in the very first paragraph of Sexuality One, as the illusory sexuality-as-repression that the book will throw into question. At the time of the interview in which the little-girl-as-lady image appears, Foucault was in the midst of writing that volume over which Queen Victoria presides. She's the symbol—a blason, like Diderot's talking vaginas[6]—for a psychologized sexuality of dispositifs from which erotic experience has been drained. That might explain why Foucault dislikes himself as grand lady so much. By dressing himself up in the lyrical language of tragedy, Foucault plays the queen whose fading sovereignty masks the rise of disciplinarity and biopower.

Thus Foucault as monarch—the sovereign "I"—describes his own lyricism as "disgusting" and morally reprehensible: "It's pretty disgusting to conduct an analysis and then tip your hat to it in a great solemn gesture and pay reverence to this experience and speak about it with enough emphasis and lyricism to appropriate it a bit, but too much distance in fact to let it pass, so I find that those passages in my book are morally not good."[7]

Indeed, it is precisely lyricism's moral dimension that troubles Foucault the most: "It's rather the moral failing that bothers me in those passages, where one makes something shudder, one makes the words shudder, it's not so difficult after all, this habit of the scribbler! . . . One makes the words shudder and then it's not the experience itself."[8]

There we are again: the ethical question of how to render "experience itself." Lyricism becomes associated with the moral failings of a belles lettres tradition of dressed-up writing, one that makes the words shimmer, shudder, and tremble but cannot capture the experience it describes. So is literary lyricism's moral failing the same as that of a scientific language equally inadequate to the task of transmitting the experience itself? Better, it seems, to play the humble artisan whose attitude toward his work is strictly utilitarian: "I think one needs to have an artisanal sense of this, just as one should do a good job making a shoe, so one should do a good job making a book."[9]

Ashamed of his former dress-up behavior, playing the queen in his silly wig, or solemnly tipping his hat with an aristocratic flourish, Foucault in the 1975 interview becomes a simple worker, perhaps even a peasant, never an artist, but simply an artisan. Foucault, the bookmaker, is like a shoemaker, and the shoe itself is not an object of fashion, but rather the functional shoe of a laborer. Unlike écriture, which serves no useful purpose, his livre must be, however beautiful, transformative like a bomb: "My dream is the explosive, that is, something that is useful like an instrument, efficacious like a bomb, and pretty like fireworks."[10]

Like the farmer's shoe, the book disappears into the job it performs and, so doing, changes the landscape; like the shoe, it is a useful instrument. Writing is not something to be lingered over; rather, it has a job to do: "To open doors, create openings, put in place kinds of pathways, breaches, through which it will be possible to hear those who speak."[11]

Writing is a strategy, an assault on the adorned structures that mask the limit-as-void, a method for finding their point of weakness "so that one can make the walls fall down."[12] It is an opening of a passage, through the unraveling of the self, so that another "speaking" might be heard.

To linger over the preface (as both I and Foucault, ironically, have been doing) is to construct an image of oneself in a shameful act of self-reflection. It is to fall, like Narcissus, into the trap of self-identity. The figure of the author, of the "I" itself, is nothing but a great magnifying mirror in which the book-as-bomb or useful tool dresses itself up as a false, socially coded, puffed-up exaggeration of what is neither more nor less than a humble disappearance into the series of events to which the book belongs.

And so Foucault sums up his shameful lyricism in the 1961 preface:

> I retranscribed it in a kind of emphatic lyricism that I'm not proud of. So it was the first thing that struck me in this preface and the second thing that horrified me because I absolutely do not remember it, was the use of the word structure which reappears every ten lines or almost, when there's nothing in the book that brings to mind in any way an analysis of the structural kind, but it was ultimately, between these two things, the lyricism and the recourse to this notion of structure, the relationship was clear, to the extent that I wanted absolutely to escape this malaise inherent in the recourse to experience.[13]

Hinting, perhaps, that his own experience has something to do with what he says in the preface, the word *lyricism* opens a door to something—is it love? heartbreak? longing?—that the word *structure* closes down. The analysis in the book itself, Foucault assures us, is hardly structural. So the word *structure,* obsessively repeated in the 1961 preface, serves a function other than that of introducing the method to follow. I'm no Lévi-Strauss, Foucault tells his interviewer, but, nonetheless, "I was clinging to something that was this notion of structure."[14] Why the clinging? Because "I wanted to escape this malaise inherent in the recourse to experience," Foucault explains, referring to his training in phenomenology.

And yet, as Foucault rereads the first preface in the early 1970s—one that he had completely forgotten, it seems—something like an experience appears. This is not the experience of phenomenology. Foucault does not name it, and neither can I. But it is nonetheless there, in the space between a "lyricism" that would conceal it and a "structure" that would deny it. And appearing, as it does, in a preface to "madness," I can't help but think that the experience is erotic: another form of living.

5 / A Political Ethic of Eros

A long time ago I made use of documents like these for a book. If I did so back then, it was doubtless because of the resonance I still experience today when I happen to encounter these lowly lives reduced to ashes in the few sentences that struck them down.
—Michel Foucault, 1977

I have never written anything other than fictions.
—Michel Foucault, 1977

We want to be the poets of our life—first of all in the smallest, most everyday matters.
—Friedrich Nietzsche, 1882

The Mad Subject of Ethics

Foucault's ethical project in *History of Madness* is built on a paradox. The paradox is familiar: to explain unreason or make it speak is to betray unreason with reason's language about madness. The stakes of that paradox are epistemological—what can we know?—and ethical—to whom are we accountable? They are also thoroughly historical: to explain unreason is to return, impossibly, to the time before a great division, an epistemic break that cannot be breached. Unreason exposes the alterity of history, the untranslatability of the historical other. The historical other, unreason's ghost, remains on the far side of modernity, in an irrecuperable time. The modern subject who wants to know unreason is thus caught in this ethico-historical paradox: to recuperate, in language, the truths of the past is to betray unreason and the alterity of history.

This paradoxical articulation of ethics in Foucault as a problem of history would appear to leave us in an aporia. But aporia is tricky and, as I've argued, not necessarily a dead end; in its refusal to settle on one side or the other, aporia can generate new possibilities. Such possibilities can be found in the ethical questions raised by Foucault in *History of Madness*, questions he takes up again and again in his life's work. A phrase from one of Foucault's last courses, *Hermeneutics of the Subject*

(1981–82), captures the generative possibilities of this ethico-historical paradox. In his reflections on the self in the Greco-Roman world, Foucault enjoins us "to become again what we never were."[1]

Like Foucault's earlier return to unreason, this call to return to a subjectivity that never was is seemingly impossible, an imperative to reinhabit the ghosts of selves that never existed: "to become again what we never were." Those past selves are, like the figures of unreason that haunt reason, untranslatable into modern language. But the "we" of becoming—brought into the present as a plurality of first-person subjects connected, by the "again," to the persistence of the past—articulates the possibility of our own transformation, the possibility of our own becoming-other: "to become again what we never were." In the terms of *Madness*, that self-transformation is the possibility of becoming mad. But, articulated as a "we," the mad other is no longer the singular other set apart from the generality of others; rather, as a "we," the alterity of madness is transformed, in a time we cannot know, to become something other than the object pinned down, the straitjacketed psychotic or the convulsing hysteric on the scientific stage. As Foucault puts it in "Madness, the Absence of an Oeuvre," the "we" enters a time where madness ceases to have any meaning: "One day, perhaps, we will no longer know what madness was" (*M* 542). Becoming-other is thus a process of stripping away the structures of thought that produce reason and madness: an unlearning or releasing of the rationalist subject.

But how can this unlearning, releasing, or stripping away be, at the same time, Foucault's famous "return" to the self and a "return" to ethics? And how can we distinguish that return to ethics from a recuperation of bourgeois morality, the liberal humanist land of shame and internalized violence that Nietzsche diagnoses in his *Genealogy*? In this final chapter, we might begin again with the principle of transformation we find in the phrase "to become again what we never were." We might go so far as to call transformation the basic ethical principle in Foucault. Except, of course, that the notion of a principle would suggest that Foucault's thinking about ethics is propositional. I prefer to call Foucauldian transformation a "poetic attitude" and practice, recalling the etymology of *poiesis* as making: a making or fashioning attitude. As Foucault himself puts it: "The key to the personal poetic attitude of a philosopher is not to be sought in his ideas, as if it could be deduced from them, but rather in his philosophy-as-life, in his philosophical life, his ethos."[2] As a lived poetic attitude, Foucauldian transformation is always, necessarily, a movement of return. As Johanna Oksala puts it in *Foucault on Freedom* (2005): "philosophy as a critical practice is a movement of always having to turn back."[3] "Advancing toward the self," Foucault says in *Hermeneutics*, "is at the same time a return to the self, like a return to port."[4] To think the history of the present is to turn back, again and again, to the history of the subject: a history that repeats itself, but always with a difference. The history of the subject can be, for Foucault, a history of ethical transformation.

Thus the ethical stakes of this book engage the question: what is it stake in self-transformation? How, to echo Nietzsche in *The Gay Science* (1882), do we become "the poets of our life?"[5] And how, as the ethical poets of our life, can we become again what we never were? To ask about ethics in this way is to pose ethics as a question about subjectivity. And to ask about ethics from a queer feminist perspective is to ask about a desubjectivating ethics of eros. Such an erotic ethics practices the art of living as a specifically historical, archival task whose political stakes are the transformation of the present.

This practice, this task, and this art are what I'm calling a political ethic of eros in Foucault. An ethics of eros is hardly a new concept, especially from the perspective of feminist theory. Simone de Beauvoir, Luce Irigaray, and Audre Lorde are just three feminist thinkers associated with an ethics of eros.[6] My purpose here is not to draw any systematic links between these thinkers and Foucault's ethics of eros, although I will point to places of convergence. I hope rather to draw out the specificity of a Foucauldian ethics traced from the perspective of *History of Madness*.

If an ethics of eros hinges on transformation, the idea of transformation—openness to change, mutability, the capacity to shape-shift—suggests that Foucault's ethics can only be understood as the opening of a question, something to be articulated on the way to something else. As Charles Scott argues, to ask the question of ethics in Foucault *must* mean to insist on the noun—*the question*—over and above its prepositional object—*ethics*. Such an insistence on the question leaves ethics open, indefinite, mutable. Not a body of values by which a culture comes to understand itself as good or bad, this postmoral ethics is an interrogation of the assumptions underlying the constitution of those values. To ask the question of ethics from this perspective is to ask "how questioning can occur in a manner that puts into question the body of values that led to the questioning."[7]

This conception of ethics differs significantly from common understandings of the term. In its traditional and everyday usage, ethics is not sharply distinguished from morality; both morality and ethics generally refer to normative principles by which a culture judges conduct and values. Many progressive thinkers have eschewed ethics understood in this sense, and for good reason; in its traditional conception, ethics undergirds the normalizing violence of biopower. In its most insidious forms, ethics is the mask donned by biopower to justify and distort its subjectivating violence: from business ethics to bioethics to neuroethics to ethics centers, ethics is central to governmentality. Thus, to take a specifically queer example, there is little structural distinction between this common understanding of the "ethics" of "ethics centers" and the moralism of "family values." To be sure, disagreements occur between ethical agents about what counts as good or bad; a gay couple's dream to enjoy the full privileges of marriage is a Christian fundamentalist's nightmare. But the structural relation between thought and values is the same for the gay couple and the Christian fundamentalist. Both assume an ethical agent—a subject—whose capacity to think and produce certainty—a truth—remains unquestioned.

This common conception of ethics is obviously not Foucault's ethics, although some of his interpreters have argued otherwise.[8] Following Nietzsche, Foucault distinguishes between ethics and morality; he famously calls morality "catastrophic."[9] Further, the catastrophe of morality springs, for Foucault, from the Western subject as morality's ground. Specifically, Foucault puts into question the subject of truth: the ethical agent whose moral judgments presume epistemic certainty about the world. From this perspective, ethics in Foucault can be explicitly linked to the question of the rational moral subject whose undoing is the work of *History of Madness*. Just as *Madness* begins, in Foucault's reading of Descartes, with what we might describe as unreason's interrogation of the subject of truth, so too Foucault's later work on ethics begins with the *question* of the rational moral subject.

As a book that raises this ethical question of the subject, *History of Madness* thus functions as an ironic nativity scene, the first of many births that will give us Foucault. This polycephalous Foucault of multiple births—the birth of the clinic, the birth of the prison, the birth of the homosexual, the birth of the hermeneutics of the subject—is a mad, delirious, repeated labor of telling and retelling the story of the birth of the Western subject in relation to truth. More specifically, *Madness's* insistently repeated, inaugural exposure of the divisive gesture that separates reason from unreason puts into question, as ethics, the rational, moral, normative subject built on the back of the other.

This conception of ethics is consistent with Foucault's own retrospective view of his life's work as an extended interrogation of the problem of the relation between subjectivity and truth. "I have always been interested in this problem," Foucault tells his interlocutors in a 1984 interview. And, further, this problem begins with "madness":

> As I said when we started, I have always been interested in the problem of the relationship between subject and truth. I mean, how does the subject fit into a certain game of truth? The first problem I examined was why madness was problematized, starting at a certain time and following certain practices, as an illness falling under a certain model of medicine. How was the mad subject placed in this game of truth defined by a medical model or a knowledge?"[10]

Foucault clarifies this link between madness and the relation between subjectivity and truth by insisting on his attempts to undo the self-identical Western subject in all his work:

> What I rejected was the idea of starting out with a theory of the subject—as is done, for example, in phenomenology or existentialism—and, on the basis of this theory, asking how a given form of knowledge was possible. What I wanted to try to show was how the subject constituted itself, in one specific form or another, as a mad or a healthy subject, as a delinquent or nondelinquent subject, through certain practices that were also games of truth. . . . [The subject] is not a substance. It is a form, and this form is not primarily or always identical to itself."[11]

These comments made by Foucault not long before his death frame my approach to an ethics of eros that begins and ends with the question of the subject. If Foucault is known for his 1970s work on subjectivation, his ethical project from the 1980s is generally viewed as an attempt to get out from under the subjectivation that characterizes modern disciplinary and biopower. This standard view of Foucault is not inaccurate. But the view is flawed by its lack of attention to the ethical thinking that emerges from the beginning of Foucault's work. Specifically, if we reread Foucault retrospectively, through the lens of *History of Madness*, and thus also prospectively, from *Madness* forward to the as yet unwritten "becoming again," we find already in his first major book an ethics of freedom that asks about the relation between subjectivity and truth. Thus the ethics of eros we find in *Madness* constitutes the beginnings of a desubjectivating thinking that links the "madness" project to the "delinquency" project to the "sexuality" project to the "final" ethical project that was, we now see, always there in Foucault from the very start.

In contrast to many of Foucault's interpreters, I argue here that Foucault was always asking about ethics because, from "madness" to "ethics," he was always asking about the subject and the other; he was always, from the start, trying to find a way out from under those modes of subjectivation that keep us, and others, unfree. Never a substance, never pregiven, Foucault's subject cannot be assumed as the ready-made agent of high-minded moral projects; for Foucault, there is no presumed subject of an ethics that will then be applied, through the agency of the subject, to a given field: bioethics or business ethics or any of a multitude of moralizing assertions of contemporary biopower. Indeed, even as a form—a character or a figure, such as those that appear over the course of Foucault's writings, as madmen, hysterics, abnormals, homosexuals, delinquents, or Greek *erastes* and *eromenos*—the subject is "not a substance." Rather, the subject is a geographically and temporally specific configuration of meanings; it is a spatiotemporal process of emergence and disappearance, persistence and erasure. And, as a "form . . . not primarily or always identical to itself," it cannot be assumed or taken for granted.

This chapter points to that process of nonself-identical subjective emergence and disappearance as a way to name ethics in Foucault. As a question about the subject, this ethics is not unrelated to a certain thinking about alterity epitomized in the work of Levinas. For Foucault, as for Levinas, subjectivity must be thought as the interruption of the self by an other; alterity precedes the subject and puts it into question through an always prior sociality. But, unlike Levinas, Foucault rejects any divine principle of exteriority or God; as he puts it in "A Preface to Transgression," we exist "without God."[12] In his refusal of God, Foucault offers an alternative to a Levinasian conception of alterity as a transcendental movement away from history and the realm of the social. This nontranscendental approach to the other undergirds Foucault's archival philosophical practice; his conception of ethical alterity demands an attention to the lived specificities of the concrete world. Foucault's others are the ghosts of history, those leprous figures who populate the pages of *History of Madness* as the half-real, half-imaginary traces of a past that

can only be made visible through the fiction-making operations of histoire. Foucault's political ethic is motivated, in this sense, by a stubborn
persistence, a kind of fidelity to the ghosts of history, to the never-absent
nonpresence of the subject's other, the repudiated alterity of Western
humanism whose afterimage hovers over us but cannot be captured.

In naming that faithful attention an ethics of eros, I also hint at the
political dimensions of the emergence and disappearance of history's
ghosts. As forms of nonpresence, those ghosts are dead, killed by the
obliterating violence of official History: "these lowly lives reduced to
ashes in the few sentences that struck them down,"[13] as Foucault puts it
in "Lives of Infamous Men." But, as stubborn persistences that are
never quite absent, the ghosts live on; they are traversed by an eros—
another mode of life we might call artistic or spiritual—that touches but
evades the grids of intelligibility which manage life as bios.

But what does it mean to say these persistences are traversed by eros?
If lives become ashes, how are they illuminated again, for us? In his
book on Foucault and Lacan, *Truth and Eros*, John Rajchman asks,
"What is the eros of thinking?"[14] Focusing on Foucault's ethical work of
the 1980s, Rajchman argues that, in his return to the Greco-Roman self,
Foucault "re-eroticized the activity of philosophical or critical thought
for our times" by linking truth and eros.[15] "Foucault's problem about
truth," Rajchman writes, "was . . . the problem, in short, of a 'new
erotic.'"[16] Rajchman specifically links eros to the "*parrhesiac* situation"[17]
of "frank speech" or truth telling in the ancient world: "we might again
become uncertain and curious as to how to tell the truth about our eros,
and the eros of doing so. And so we might give a more precise sense of
the 'wonderment' or 'bewilderment' through which philosophy had
sought to describe the passion to know, or the 'will to knowledge.' We
might define a kind of critical 'curiosity.'"[18]

This erotic will to knowledge—a "curious, experimental, critical passion,"[19] as Rajchman puts it—can be linked to the courageous, ethical
listening I evoked in the last chapter: a "*pratique à deux*" that requires
"courage on the part of the interlocutor who agrees to receive, as true, the
wounding truth he hears."[20] Such a listening undoubtedly conjures up
images of the famous psychoanalytic listening ear. But, in returning to a
prepsychological subjectivity, Foucault seeks a practice of desubjectivation that might reframe the caged freedom of listening within psyche-
logos. Foucault's erotic attention to subjectivity as a historical formation
contests a modern psychoanalytic practice built on an ahistorical, biological will to knowledge. Foucault's ethics of eros contests bio-logos.

Drawing on Rajchman's argument about an erotic ethics in Foucault's return to the ancients, I want to argue that this erotic will to knowledge characterizes an ethics that informs all of Foucault's thinking. Viewed through the lens of ethical parrhesia, *Madness* is a drama about the impossibility of erotic knowledge—a different truth telling— from within the confinement of modern rationalism. The confinement of the mad is the confinement of eros. And, from our position in the present—within a psychological bio-logos—we cannot access eros directly, except as the shadow cast by something as it is leaving. Those shadows gather in the dusty corners of the archives where Foucault spent his days tracing the emergence of lives lost to history.

The archive thus becomes, in this ethical parrhesia, the site of an erotic, courageous listening. It is useful to imagine the archive as another heterotopia. As the space that preserves the traces of rationalism's power to wound, the archive is "utterly real."[21] But, as the site of a different listening by one "who agrees to receive, as true, the wounding truth he hears," the archive is also "utterly unreal."[22] Like the heterotopian mirror, the modern archive becomes the site of an ethical encounter where the self-reflective symmetry of the knowing "I" is confronted by a real alterity that puts the reasoning subject into question.

In his 1961 preface, Foucault imagines such an ethical listening by "anyone who lends an ear" (*M* xxxi) to the "great space of murmurings" (*M* xxxi) he finds in the archives. "Perhaps, to my mind," Foucault writes in the preface, "the most important part of this work is the space I have left to the texts of the archives themselves" (*M* xxxv). Then in 1977, in "Lives of Infamous Men," Foucault returns to the murmuring of that very same archive whose traces generated a *History of Madness*. "A long time ago I made use of documents like these for a book," Foucault tells us, elliptically referring to *Madness*. In the "Lives" essay, which, like so many of Foucault's "beginnings," serves as an introduction to something that never comes, Foucault articulates the stakes of his own self-transformative relation to the archive, to a truth that changes him. Foucault tells us, specifically, that the documents he first encountered while writing *Madness*—the police orders, *lettres de cachet*, and other traces of the lives of those locked up in the great confinement—still produce a "resonance" in him fifteen years later. Thus his return to the archive is not only a return to *Madness* but a return to himself: his attempt to become what he never was by listening, once again, to what he finds there.

But how is this return an example of what Rajchman calls "the eros of thinking"?[23] Foucault specifically describes the "intensity that sparks through" these archival traces and the "jostling violence of the facts they tell."[24] He uses the word *intensity* again and again to evoke these "flash existences" (159), these "poem-lives" (159), from "the first intensities that motivated [him]" (158) in the 1950s when he was writing *Madness* to "the intensity they [still] seem to have" (159) when he returns to them in the late 1970s. And the archives themselves are traversed by intensities, for they hold in their shadows "particles endowed with an energy all the greater for their being small and difficult to discern" (161). Each archival trace is a particle of life: "the most intense point of a life, the point where its energy is concentrated" (162) when it "comes up against power" (162).

These particles of life are not "life itself": not the biological molecules to be found through the microscopic technologies of modern bio-power.[25] They are not a substance, and the erotic intensities they hold are not an essence or property of the lives themselves, but rather the result of their encounter with power: "the most intense point of a life . . . when it comes up against power."[26] That intensity is erotic because it engages the real: "Real lives were 'enacted' ['*jouées*'] in these few sentences."[27] Or, put somewhat differently, their intensity bears witness to the fact that, like the ship of fools, "they really did exist" (*M* 9) and had "a genuine existence" (*M* 9). It is the stuff of life that makes these "fragments of discourse" (160) erotic: "traps, weapons, cries, gestures, attitudes, ruses, intrigues" (160), bodies that lived and died. And it is this erotic intensity that distinguishes them from literary figures: "none of the dark heroes that [literature has] invented appeared as intense to me as these cobblers, these army deserters, these garment-sellers, these scriveners, these vagabond monks, all of them rabid, scandalous, or pitiful" (160), Foucault writes. Unlike literature, the erotic intensity of these "poem-lives" comes, quite simply, from "the mere fact that they are known to have lived" (160).

So it is in the "play" of these "poem-lives" in their "encounter with power" (161)—"illuminated," like Girodet's Endymion (figure 5.1), by a "beam of light" (161)—that they become, in Foucault's hands, erotic. It is important to note that the clash with power alone is not enough to illuminate these lives for us: not enough for an ethical parrhesia. Rather, it is in *Foucault's* own archival encounter with these texts "trailing the fragments of a reality they are a part of" (160)—in his own historico-philosophical game of power—that these lives become "poem-lives" with an erotic intensity: a luminous persistence that "snatche[s] them from the darkness" (161). When Foucault enters the archive, the archival "body" is transformed: new parts of the archive are eroticized in a new

FIGURE 5.1   Anne-Louis Girodet, *The Sleep of Endymion*, 1791

clash between the poem-lives and power. This sex play in the archives creates new configurations of the shadows and profiles of the archival body. In that sense, Foucault's encounter with the archives is a strategic one, like the amorous game he describes in "The Ethics of the Concern for Self as a Practice of Freedom": in his approach to the archives, he "wield[s] power over the other,"[28] the historical other he finds in the darkness. But in that encounter between knower and known—between Foucault and the historical other—the relation of power becomes "a sort of open-ended strategic game"[29] where the archives—the known—act on the knower. Thus, "the situation [of power] may be reversed"[30] by an erotic, ethical listening that undoes the subject in his will to knowledge, producing vibrations, physical sensations, and feelings in the knower that, paradoxically, cannot be known or named. The power play that is recorded in the dusty archive—the site that preserves the claw marks of rationalism's wounding—is thereby transformed in a new game of power that, in Foucault's poetic refashioning of those lives, becomes "a part of love, of passion, and sexual pleasure."[31]

This strategic reversal in an archival game of power gives a specific shape to that faithful attention I'm calling Foucault's ethics of eros. To be sure, the archive is not the only place such strategic reversals can happen. But I do want to argue that for Foucault and his "archiveology,"[32] that particular power game is crucial. It allows us to reconceive the archive of modernity as a heterotopia.[33] And like all heterotopias, the archive becomes unstable: both there and not there, both real and not, the site of an "absolute break" from "traditional time."[34] More important than the site itself is the "poetic attitude" and practice the archival encounter brings to light. And, from that perspective, Foucauldian eros can be conceived more generally as an alternative thinking and practice of life within the subjectivated living called biopower.

Rajchman argues that the "question of truth and eros"[35] involved Foucault "in a long and involuted reflection on ethics"[36] Rajchman links, specifically, with "the passion of thought."[37] This sense of Foucault's ethics defines both its power and what Rajchman calls its "difficulty for *us*," which comes from a passion that creates an "experience of thought."[38] This experience of thought is an ethical experience, both for Foucault in his encounter with the other and for us when we encounter Foucault. And, as an erotic experience—an experience of passion—this encounter with thinking has ethical consequences: it reshapes the way we might think about ethics *tout court*. More specifically, Foucauldian eros helps us to delineate a postmoral ethics—a rethinking of the relation between subjectivity and truth in the face of the other—that implicitly engages the political question of governmentality and freedom. As Foucault insists, governmentality is linked to the (self)-government of the subject, and what we might think of as the "stuff" of politics and political theory—namely, freedom—is also the "stuff" of an ethics of eros: "freedom," Foucault says, "is the ontological condition of ethics;"[39] and again, he says, "the freedom of the subject in relation to others . . . constitutes the very stuff [*la matière même*] of ethics."[40] Significantly, this does not mean that freedom is an ontological condition or characteristic of the subject; as Oksala points out, "there is no inherent freedom."[41] Nor does it mean, as Nancy Hirschmann suggests, that the purpose of freedom is to "create the self."[42] Rather, Foucault "refers to the ontological contingency of the present: freedom is the opening up of possibilities of an age."[43] Foucault practices this freedom in the space of the archive, a site of rationalist violence where the present appears as the "accumulation of time in a place that will not move."[44] Ethical freedom is the erotic transformation of this biopolitical present.

I will develop the vast question of an ethics of eros here in this chapter by stepping back a bit from the detailed texture of *History of Madness* to allow the nonself-identical shape of another ethics—the historical ghost of the question of ethics—to emerge. Specifically, I will draw out that shape by pairing *Madness* and *Sexuality One* with Foucault's work on ethics from the early 1980s: the second and third volumes of *History of Sexuality*; his 1981–82 course at the Collège de France, *Hermeneutics of the Subject*; and the essays, lectures, and interviews gathered together in *Ethics: Subjectivity and Truth*. I will then return to Foucault's 1977 essay, "Lives of Infamous Men," to reengage the question of "the experience of thought" as passion. Taken together, these ethical writings across Foucault's oeuvre bear witness to the production and exclusion of history's ghosts. From *Madness* to the final works on the ancient world, Foucault's ethics are generated out of a faithful attention to the cast-off remains of an official past. This ethical attention to the alterity of the past is, moreover, an attention to the exclusions of our historical present. Indeed, what I'm calling the persistence of ethics in Foucault is inseparable from the historical question I asked in the first chapter: what persists? The historical question of persistence and erasure, of that which remains and that which disappears, gives a singular shape to Foucault's poetic attitude and practice of ethics. In his fidelity to the great murmur of history, Foucault traces the outline of a lingering nonpresence that is not an absence but strange forms of survival. This ethical commitment to the past's strange survivals depends, paradoxically, on our own capacity to change our relation to ourselves in the present: to make ourselves pleasurably, erotically strange in our strategic games of power. I call the possibility of these strange, self-transformative survivals of the present Foucault's political ethic of eros.

The Ethics of Sex

In chapter 1, I pointed to an oft-noted divergence between feminist ethics and a queer repudiation of moral norms. From the perspective of the larger critique of the Enlightenment which situates Foucault's thinking, that feminist-queer squabble may appear as a distraction which keeps us from attending to larger issues like war, economic exploitation, and the suicidal degradation of the earth's environment. But, before we dismiss this squabble as a distraction, we might do well to remember what Foucault teaches us: that the modern subject is the sexual subject. Or, more precisely, the modern, post-Enlightenment, Western subject of violence is also a sexual subject.

Like both feminist and queer theorists, Foucault understands "sex as a political issue."[45] But sex is political for Foucault in ways that are different from the sexual politics most commonly associated with queers and feminists. For what is ultimately at stake in Foucault's linking of sexuality with modern subjectivity are not restricted forms of sexual expression or state-imposed limits on the ability to engage in certain bodily acts or gender-specific forms of violence. What is at stake for Foucault in sexuality is biopower. It is biopower that most clearly demonstrates why the modern subject—always a sexual subject—is also a subject of life-administering violence.

For Foucault, modernity is defined through biopower, when the stakes of power are life itself: "what might be called a society's 'threshold of biological modernity' is reached when the life of the species is staked [*entre comme enjeu*] on its own political strategies."[46] This "life of the species" is biological existence—life as bios—and its temporal form is biohistorical. Modernity marks a "new mode of relation between history and life" (143); bios is "no longer an inaccessible substrate that only emerges from time to time, amid the randomness of death and its fatality" (142), but rather "passes into knowledge's field of control and power's sphere of intervention" (142). This passing of life into power-knowledge—"into the realm of explicit calculations" (143)—is, in many ways, the most dangerous aspect of the Enlightenment legacy. For the same Enlightenment that, through sexuality, made the subject intelligible to himself—"made man the offspring of an imperious and intelligible sex" (78)—also manages and orders biological life. In its most virulent form, biopower paves the way for "Nazism," a "racism of expansion" (125), and the "eugenic ordering of society" (149). In its more common, current form, biopower unfolds at the molecular level where, as Nikolas Rose puts it, "there is nothing mystical or incomprehensible about our vitality—anything and everything appears, in principle, to be intelligible."[47]

If queer theory owes its emergence as a field at least in part to an almost obsessive reading of *Sexuality One*, that queer reading has, for the most part, skirted biopower.[48] Foucault himself commented on the general nonreading of the biopower argument he made in the last chapter of his book. In a 1977 interview, he says, "No one wants to talk about that last part. Even though the book is a short one, but I suspect people never got as far as this last chapter. All the same, it's a fundamental part of the book."⁴⁹ And indeed, like Foucault's readers generally, most queer theorists seem not to have noticed the importance of biopower for an understanding of sexuality in Foucault. Again, and very briefly, Judith Butler's work is paradigmatic of this tendency in queer theory to evade a direct discussion of biopower. In *Gender Trouble*, Butler refers to the final chapter of *Sexuality One*—"Right of Death and Power Over Life"— where Foucault introduces biopower, but only to retrieve Foucault's definition of "sex" as a "fictive unity" for her own performative reading of the "regulatory production of identity-effects" in Foucault.⁵⁰ Similarly, in "Sexual Inversions," a 1993 article that criticizes Foucault, in the context of the AIDS crisis, for his failure to account for death in modernity, Butler again focuses on the chapter in *Sexuality One* where biopower emerges without ever using the term *biopower* directly. Butler argues, somewhat idiosyncratically, that Foucault's theory of life as the site for the elaboration of power expels death from Western modernity. What she calls Foucault's "vitalism" leads,⁵¹ she says, to a Foucauldian theory of modernity where power is described as "ward[ing] off death" by exchanging it for sex (86). Foucault is "mistaken" (94), Butler continues, in his presumption that modern "technology will ward off death" and "preserve life" (94). "What promise," she asks, "did Foucault see in sex, and in sexuality, to overcome death, such that sex is precisely what marks the overcoming of death, the end to the struggling against it?" (96) This promise of modernity Butler reads into Foucault—where sex-as-life has overcome death—amounts, in her view, to a "phantasmatic projection and a vainly utopian faith" as a hallmark of Foucault's thinking about modern sexuality (94).

The implications of this reading of *Sexuality One* for queer interpretations of Foucault are important, especially in the link that can be drawn between the American obsession with identity in Foucault and a concomitant nonreading of biopower required by an identitarian reading that focuses on individuals rather than populations. I have already argued, in chapter 1, why the identity reading of Foucault is open to challenge. I also showed, in chapter 4, why the "vain" utopianism with which Butler charges Foucault misreads his insistence on the heterotopias of the present. Here I want to question, in somewhat different terms, the queer misreading of biopower for which Butler's work serves as a foundation. Foucault does not, in fact, describe modern biopower as an expulsion of death, as Butler claims. Rather, he contrasts modern power with sovereign power and the latter's "power of life and death";⁵²

this "right to death" of the older, sovereign model is the power "to take life or let live."[53] "Right to death" and this power to take or not take life is linked to what Foucault calls, more broadly, the power of deduction (*prélèvement*): the power to take away or subtract. With modernity, the power of deduction—the general form of the power of life and death—"has tended to be no longer the major form of power but *merely one element among others.*"[54] With this modern power, "bent on generating forces, making them grow, and ordering them,"[55] the "right to death" does not disappear. Rather, "the ancient right to take life or let live is replaced by a power to foster life *or disallow it to the point of death.*"[56] This is a far cry from Butler's claim that in Foucault "death is effectively expelled from Western modernity."[57]

The above might amount to nothing more than a quibble about a minor matter, were it not that biopower constitutes a key element for thinking about the ethics of sex in Foucault. And as I will show in the final section of this chapter, the life administered by biopower is the modern form of a bios Foucault describes in his ethical work on the Greco-Roman and early Christian worlds. Bios persists, then, over the course of Foucault's work on the history of sexuality, as a term that is crucial for thinking the ethical relation between subjectivity and truth. Queer theory, on the other hand, has tended to focus only on disciplinary power—those forms of modern power Foucault describes as "centered on the body as a machine"[58] and as "an anatomo-politics of the human body."[59] This individual body-centered form of power is connected to and part of biopower, but only constitutes one dimension of its function. The "second" and chronologically "somewhat later" form of modern power is what Foucault calls biopower. Its focus is the "species body, the body imbued with the mechanics of life and serving as the basis of the biological processes"[60] that will be supervised by "a biopolitics of the population" (139).[61]

If bios persists, from *Sexuality One* through the later ethical writings, it is worth asking why that is so. How is bios part of the puzzle of the question of an ethics of sex in Foucault? If Foucault called *Sexuality One Madness*'s "twin,"[62] is bios the bad twin of the ghost of *Madness*? And, if bios is crucial for the deployment of the grid of modern sexuality, might there be another concept of life that promises transformation? This is where eros becomes important, for in its etymology eros refers not only to a notion of passionate love but also to a life force, what Audre Lorde calls, like Nietzsche, "the *yes* within ourselves."[63] Might an ethics of eros be articulated as a possibility of life to transform the violence of biopower?

Another Cartesian Moment

Transforming biopower through an erotic practice is a specifically modern historical task. So let me return for a moment to Foucault's first modern history and the place of the Nephew as its hinge. As I argued in chapter 4, despite its brevity, the nine-page passage devoted to *Rameau's Nephew* forms the crux of Foucault's exploration of the ethical stakes of subjectivity as a function of the limits of reason. As a queer figure, the Nephew opens the door to a modernity that both objectifies madness in positivist science and, at the same time, dedialectizes Hegelian reason to undermine his own objectification. Here in this chapter, the heterotopian space of the Nephew who stands in the breach we call the Enlightenment can be linked more explicitly to the ethical language that emerges in Foucault's later work on the ancient world. If ethics is ultimately about the question of the subject and, specifically, the cost of subjectivity as the ghost of the other, the Nephew makes the stakes of that subjectivity clear. For it is the Nephew who first raises the ethical question of the relation between subjectivity and truth Foucault will return to at the end of his life.

With the Nephew, Foucault links a mad subject, an "I," to unreason as truth; in *Rameau's Nephew*, Foucault writes, we find "a language where madness was permitted to speak in the first person, uttering in the midst of the empty verbiage and the insane grammar of its paradoxes something that bore an essential relation to the truth" (*M* 517). Contra Descartes, Foucault's Nephew instantiates life as paradox: the possibility of impossibles, of mad cogitos and their insane truths. In exposing this antiphilosophical possibility of a relation between a mad subject and truth, Foucault brings together what Descartes insisted on keeping apart. For, if Cartesian certainty allows the cogito to dream but not to be mad, such is not the case for Foucauldian games of truth:

> What madness says of itself was, for the thought and the poetry of the early nineteenth century, what dreams say in the disorder of their images; a truth of man, very archaic and very near, very silent and very threatening, a truth that underlies all truth, *the truth closest to the birth of subjectivity*, and the most widely spread at the very level of things; a truth that is the deep retreat of man's individuality, and the inchoate form of the cosmos. (*M* 517; emphasis added)

As I argued earlier, throughout his work Foucault stages the birth of subjectivity, in different times and from different perspectives, but always with a concern for this ethical question of the relation between the subject and truth. Madness lies at the heart of that question, since the stakes of madness are the stakes of rational subjectivity. The Nephew, born after Descartes in the Age of Reason and its exclusion of madness from subjectivity, can be seen to inaugurate his own objectification, as mad, as a truth of nineteenth-century positivist science. At the same time, and paradoxically, the Nephew inaugurates another temporality and another truth for an other-than-Cartesian subject. As the passage from *Madness* suggests, in the "thought and poetry of the early nineteenth century" (*M* 517), the mad "I" that spoke in the Nephew's eighteenth-century paradoxes emerges in the disordered imagery of nineteenth-century Romantic dreams. Referring, no doubt, to the lineage of mad poets and artists—Nerval, Van Gogh, Nietzsche—he invokes over the course of *History of Madness*, here Foucault heralds the birth of another relation between subjectivity and truth—another subject of "disorder"—at the moment when truth is being objectified, measured, calculated, and codified as what will become the ordering of life called biopower.

Surprisingly, this possibility of rupture at the moment of birth of the modern biopolitical sexual subject is not just the work of poets, artists, and mad philosophers. Foucault repeats, in *The Hermeneutics of the Subject*, his identification of the nineteenth century as an era of subjective transformation. In the second course lecture, he describes the nineteenth century as a time "that poses, at least implicitly, the very old question of spirituality and which, without saying so, rediscovers the care of the self."[64] In "almost all" of nineteenth-century philosophy, Foucault continues, "a certain structure of spirituality tries to link knowledge, the activity of knowing, and the conditions and effects of this activity, to a transformation in the subject's being" (28).

But what is this spirituality to which Foucault refers? And what promise does it hold for philosophical reflection as a transformative, artistic practice of thinking? In the first course of *Hermeneutics*, Foucault unfolds an argument that will distinguish between philosophy and spirituality as two modes of relation between subjectivity and truth. In the first course lecture, Foucault asks, "In what historical form do the relations between the 'subject' and 'truth,' elements that do not usually fall into the historian's practice or analysis, take shape in the West" (20)? Responding to his own question, Foucault begins by offering a distinction between *epimeleia heautou*, "care of the self," and *gnothi seauton*, "know yourself" (3). In Socrates, Foucault points out, these precepts are "twinned" (4), but always with a privileging of self-care over self-knowledge. Indeed, according to Foucault, throughout Antiquity—from the fifth century BCE to the fourth and fifth centuries CE—*gnothi seauton* is subordinated to *epimeleia heautou*: "You must attend to yourself, you must not forget yourself, you must take care of yourself. The rule 'know yourself' appears and is formulated within and at the forefront of this care" (5).

Modern biopower, by contrast, is marked by the privileging of self-knowing to the exclusion of care of the self. Correspondingly, the ethico-historical, archival questions Foucault poses in *Hermeneutics* for "us, now, today" (12) become: "Why did Western thought and philosophy neglect the notion of *epimeleia heautou* (care of the self) in the reconstruction of its own history? How did it come about that we . . . left in the shadow this notion of care of the self?" (12). These questions expose the historical dimensions of Foucault's ethical reflections by demonstrating, again, how knowledge makes us forget: knowing too much, we pass something over. Like the ghosts of *Madness* that haunt the archive, care of the self—the practice of self-transformation—has been neglected, "left in the shadow of" official history and philosophy. But, like a ghost, care of the self as transformation continues to haunt our historical present.

In *Hermeneutics*, as in *Madness*, Foucault identifies the "Cartesian moment" (14) as the moment when self-transformation is no longer possible: the moment when philosophy makes "know yourself"—and not care of the self—"into a fundamental means of access to truth" (14). This "Cartesian moment" defines the ethos of the modern biopolitical age: "I think the modern age of the history of truth begins when knowledge itself and knowledge alone gives access to truth. That is to say, it is when the philosopher (or the scientist or simply someone who seeks the truth) can recognize the truth and have access to it in himself and solely through his activity of knowing, without anything being demanded of him and without him having to change or alter his being as subject" (17). This modern relation between subjectivity and truth, where access to truth does not require self-transformation, is what Foucault calls, in *Hermeneutics*, philosophy.

In contrast to philosophy, Foucault names the other mode of access to truth spirituality, that mode of relation between subjectivity and truth we have already seen, both in *Madness* and *Hermeneutics*, in the mad dreamers of the nineteenth century. This spirituality that characterizes the subject of truth in Antiquity and Romanticism alike is "the search, practice, and experience through which the subject carries out the necessary transformations on himself in order to have access to the truth" (15). This transformative truth "brings the subject's being into play" (15): with spirituality, "there can be no truth without a conversion or a transformation of the subject" (15). In the ethical relation of the subject to truth, spirituality is the possibility of becoming-other: the subject "must be changed, transformed, shifted, and become, to some extent and up to a certain point, other than himself" (15). Significantly, one of the two major modes through which that self-othering can occur is erotic. Conversion or transformation "may take place in the form of a movement that removes the subject from his current status or condition. . . . Let us call this movement . . . the movement of *eros* (love)" (15–16).

The Cartesian moment, by contrast, denies the possibility of self-transformation: it denies the possibility of eros. This denial of eros forms the foundation of the modern sexual subject. For if, as I have argued, the Cartesian moment in *Madness* is the moment of the sexual deviant's simultaneous production and exclusion—the moment of the great confinement—that moment corresponds to the birth of the subject of modern philosophy from whom the possibility of madness has been excluded. That exclusion of madness in the Cartesian moment parallels philosophy's rejection of an erotic spirituality through which the thinking subject would be transformed. To refuse to be transformed is to refuse the madness of eros: "In order to know the truth one must not be mad" (18), Foucault reminds us in his comments on Descartes in *Hermeneutics*, implicitly recalling *History of Madness*. The subject of reason is thus the product not only of the cogito's exclusion of madness but also of a more general refusal to be transformed by erotic love. With the Cartesian moment, that other "enlightenment" (18) which would spiritually transform the violent rationalist moralism of Western Enlightenment cannot occur. Thus biopower is born, along with the Western subject, as a repudiation of eros: in modernity, "the subject's transfiguration by the 'rebound effect' on himself of the truth he knows, and which passes through, permeates, and transfigures his being, can no longer exist" (18).

Recalling, again, the passage I cited from *History of Madness* about the birth of subjectivity in *Rameau's Nephew*, we can now hear its resonances with what Foucault calls the "beginnings of the hermeneutics of the subject" in the Greco-Roman and early Christian worlds. Further, Foucault's early language about madness and the birth of subjectivity resonates with his later, explicitly ethical language in volume 2 of *His-*

tory of Sexuality about desubjectivation or what he calls, in *Hermeneutics of the Subject*, the "testing of the self." In the chronological unfolding of Foucault's work, the birth of the *Nephew* at the heart of *Madness* is the first of many births of the Western subject: not as the taken-for-granted, self-identical substance we generally encounter in ethics, but as the nonself-identical subject of a test. That self-testing, forged in the ethos of *epimeleia heautou* as the practice of self-transformation, reconfigures subjectivity in its relation to truth not only in Antiquity, but as the possibility of alteration in our historical present. As the erotic practice that characterizes what I've called the poetic attitude of transformation, self-testing puts the coherence and solidity of the subject into question not as a self-enclosed, solipsistic exercise, but as a relational practice of freedom. That relation extends to others not only in their incarnation as other subjects but also to alterity as a more pervasive form of existence: as modes of life in a movement of becoming-other. This is what Foucault calls, in the *Madness* passage about the Nephew I have quoted, a form of relation "at the very level of things" (*M* 517), the subject's coextension with the "inchoate form of the cosmos" (*M* 517). This radicalization of becoming-other that cosmically extends the subject into the world of things is precisely what Descartes calls madness: to believe oneself to have an earthenware head, to be a hollowed-out shell, or to be made of glass. And, as we have seen, that Cartesian madness is implicitly erotic.

To return to this chapter's opening reflections on the paradox of becoming again "what we never were," ethico-historical transformation requires an erotic testing of the self. That testing is, paradoxically, both a return to the self and a release of the self: the process of stripping away or unlearning that Foucault calls in the second volume of *History of Sexuality* self-undoing. The term he uses—*se déprendre de soi-même*,[65] to release oneself from oneself—means we are no longer ourselves, no longer caught in the grip of teleological history. As *History of Madness* suggests, to release the self from the shackles of biopower requires a return to the birth of that self and the tracing of a genealogy of the formation of those shackles. The ethical project of transformation is thus, like philosophy, a project of return.

But what are we to make of Foucault's return to the ancient world to seek that which the West has forgotten about itself? It does not mean, importantly, that the Greeks will be part of a task of recovery, becoming a model for us to emulate. In the last interview before his death, Foucault asserts that they were neither exemplary nor admirable;[66] in another interview he calls them "disgusting."[67] *Pace* Foucault's numerous feminist critics, Foucault repeatedly acknowledges the elitism of the masculine world he describes.[68] Eros is "an ethics of men made for men,"[69] he says in *The Use of Pleasure*. In "On the Genealogy of Ethics," Foucault emphasizes that the "Greek ethics of pleasure is linked to a virile society, to dissymmetry, exclusion of the other."[70] "Moderation was a man's virtue,"[71] he continues in *The Use of Pleasure*, and the "femininity" of self-indulgent, passive Greek men marked their difference from virile men. But gender was not organized as it is in modern biopower: "The traditional signs of effeminacy—idleness, indolence, refusal to engage in the somewhat rough activities of sports, a fondness for perfumes and adornments, softness (*malakia*)—were not necessarily associated with the individual who in the nineteenth century would be called an 'invert,' but with the one who yielded to the pleasures that enticed him."[72] Although the sex-gender system we know today was not in place—the great dividing line was not men and women but active versus passive with regard to pleasures—this does not mean that Foucault's return to the Greeks will give us a model for nonsexist living beyond gender. Nor does the institutionalization of man-boy sex in the relation of *erastes* to *eromenos* mean that ancient Greece is some lost paradise of homosexual freedom. As Foucault makes clear:

> For [the Greeks], reflection on sexual behavior as a moral domain was not a means of internalizing, justifying, or formalizing general interdictions imposed on everyone; rather, it was a means of developing—for the smallest minority of the population, made up of free, adult males—an aesthetics of existence, the purposeful art of a freedom perceived as a power game. Their sexual ethics, from which our own derives in part, rested on a very harsh system of inequalities and constraints (particularly in conjunction with women and slaves).[73]

If the Greeks are not an alternative model for us, how are we to read Foucault's return to them as a mode of access into the erotic transformation of biopower? In a comment he made at Berkeley in 1980, Foucault calls his ethical project an exploration of the "beginning of the hermeneutics of the self."[74] Specifically, with the rise of Christianity and the monastic precept to confess, Foucault identifies a transformation that "starts what we would call the hermeneutics of the self."[75] Foucault finds in the transition from the ancient to the Christian world the birth of a subjectivity we might compare with the Hegelian birth of subjectivity in the Enlightenment *Nephew*.

Foucault's Berkeley comment refers, specifically, to a set of two lectures he gave at Dartmouth in 1980, a year before his course on *Hermeneutics*. The first lecture, "Subjectivity and Truth,"[76] makes explicit the link I've been developing between ethics and madness. It begins with the dialogue I examined in chapter 4, between Leuret and a patient who is compelled by the doctor to say "I am mad." In a modified version of the lecture in the *Ethics* volume, "Sexuality and Solitude," Foucault reflects on Leuret's technique with the following comment: "About twenty years ago," he says, "I kept in mind the project of analyzing the form and the history of such a bizarre practice."[77] So even here, in the 1980s, with his turn to the ancient world, Foucault insists on the persistence of a modern *Madness* as fundamental to his analytical project. Specifically, he recalls here, as he does elsewhere, that from start to finish the madness problem is the problem of the "philosophy of the subject."[78] And just as *Madness* describes the ethical costs of that subjectivity, so too Foucault's Dartmouth lecture and the *Hermeneutics* course can be seen as an interrogation and critique of those costs. The subject is something Foucault wants to change, and Foucault articulates that change in political terms: "I have tried to get out from the philosophy of the subject through a genealogy of the subject, by studying the constitution of the subject across history which has led us up to the modern concept of the self."[79] Foucault continues: "This has not always been an easy task, since most historians prefer a history of social processes, and most philosophers prefer a subject without history."[80] Distinguishing himself from both philosophers and historians, Foucault historicizes a subject "that can eventually change."[81] "That," he adds, "is politically important."[82]

The idea that the subject can eventually change is, of course, politically important, and Foucault's lifelong project is nothing if not a thinking about thinking as a practice of change. But transformation is never simple: it is not a springing free into that which we are not. Foucault's heterotopias—the ship, the brothel, the library, the mirror—are here and now, not in some "elsewhere" we can only imagine. And, if transformation is in fact a movement as freedom—or rather, if, as we have seen, the ontological condition of change is freedom—that freedom is itself conditioned. In *History of Madness* modern freedom is conditioned by the hospital, the asylum, the straitjacket, and the psychoanalytic talking cure: freedom in modernity is always a caged freedom. But that doesn't mean there's no way out of those conditioned spaces, as some of Foucault's interpreters have argued. Although freedom is conditioned by historically specific institutions, it is also conditioned by structures of thinking in their relation to those institutions. Freedom is therefore determined not only by our sociohistorical condition but also by our capacity to critically reflect on ourselves, not for self-knowing, but for self-transformation. In that sense, transformation is always historical, always involves critical reflection, and always involves a movement of return. The ethics of the self as a practice of freedom is, above all, the practice of a critical reflection that will allow us to practice a different living through the art of ethical self-transformation: "to become again what we never were."

In his ethics of the self, Foucault is specific about the sexual meanings of a hermeneutics of the subject; in "Sexuality and Solitude" he calls it the "seismograph of our subjectivity" in the West.[83] The centrality of the subject throughout Foucault's work thus allows us to specify the ethical links between the "madness" project and the "sexuality" project. Specifically, how does Foucault's ethical thinking about sexuality relate to the ethical costs of subjectivity Foucault first articulated in *History of Madness*? To put it simply, Foucault cares about sexuality because he cares about the subject, and that care is ultimately ethical. It is also insistently historical. In "Sexuality and Solitude," Foucault describes the transformation that marks the beginning of the hermeneutics of the subject by contrasting the "wet dreams" of Artemidorus to those of Augustine, where the former poses the problem of penetration as a problem of the relation to an other and the latter poses it as an erection and therefore a rebellion of the self in its relation to the self. This shift from the pagan dream to the Christian dream "bears witness," Foucault says, "to a new type of relationship with Christianity established between sex and subjectivity."[84]

Thus the hermeneutics of the modern self involves a double movement in the self's relation to the self exemplified by Augustine's troubling erection. First, the Christian self's erection requires a diagnosis of truth and illusion, what Foucault calls a permanent hermeneutics of oneself, a persistent form of self-scrutiny that is as unremitting as it is long-lasting. Second, and this brings us back to Leuret and his mad patient, the self's sexual erection in the post-Christian era produces what we might call compelled speech: the discursive production of the sexual self made so famous by Foucault in *Sexuality One*. As Mark Blasius explains in his introduction to the Dartmouth lectures: "Christianity inaugurated a new attitude of people not so much toward sexual acts and the code of sexual ethics, but toward themselves."[85] This attitude is what we might call "nowadays," as Foucault puts it at the end of his second Dartmouth lecture, "the politics of ourselves."[86] The politics of today are the politics of ourselves, for better or worse. And the seismograph of our political selves must necessarily be the seismograph of our sexuality. Thus the erection of the modern self involves both a continuous process of self-scrutiny—the hermeneutic principle—and the speaking of that hermeneutic project—what Blasius describes as the "self's iteration and social reinforcement through an ongoing verbalization of this self-decipherment to others."[87]

To release the subject—to get out from under this philosophy of the subject dramatized in the scene with Leuret's patient—involves, for Foucault, a retraversal of historical moments—the epistemic breaks or shifts from one system of subjectivity to another. To locate these moments is difficult: "the stake, the challenge," Foucault says in *Hermeneutics*, "is precisely that of grasping when a cultural phenomenon of a determinate scale actually constitutes within the history of thought a decisive moment that is still significant for our modern mode of being subjects."[88] *History of Madness* is Foucault's first attempt to locate such a moment in the history of thought: an event he will call, twenty years later, the Cartesian moment. It is one beginning of subjectivity to place alongside another beginning, the birth of the subject in the early Christian era.

In the Dartmouth lecture, Foucault repeats the critique of the Cartesian moment we have already seen in both *Hermeneutics* and *Madness*. Foucault refers to the philosophy of the subject that dominated Europe in the period preceding and following the Second World War; this philosophy, he says, "began with Descartes"[89] and "set as its task *par excellence* the foundation of all knowledge and the principle of all signification as stemming from the meaningful subject."[90] Foucault's histories, of course, are never linear: elsewhere, in *Hermeneutics*, he associates Aristotle with the Cartesian moment, describing him as "the founder of philosophy in the modern sense of the term."[91] But, whether it happens in the ancient world or with the rise of reason in the seventeenth century, the Cartesian moment is the moment "philosophy" denies the possibility of "spirituality." In the "wet dreams" distinction I have outlined, the philosophical moment is the moment of the erection as a problem of the subject, and the fading away of the problem of penetration as a relation to others. The problem of penetration is the problem of transformation in relation to others: the subject's transfiguration of truth's "rebound effect" on him, when he is himself passed through or permeated by that effect.

However, we cannot undo the subject—release him, unlearn him, unravel him, or strip him away along with the violence of his other-obliterating erection—by simply returning to an idyllic moment of penetration that would leave us blissfully free in our desubjectivation. The erotic penetration of the flesh might appear to do this, if only for a moment, and many of Foucault's most enthusiastic queer commentators have made much of flesh-driven forms of self-shattering.[92] But the specific practices of bodies are not in themselves either freeing or constraining, and even the Greek "obsession with penetration" was,[93] for Foucault, linked to forms of exclusion he abhorred. Thus even Foucault's paradigmatic historical example of self-undoing through penetration—the Greek moment of Artemidorus—includes, as Foucault readily admits, its share of exclusions, subjugations, and violence. He is not enjoining us to be like Artemidorus. Our own transformation will not come about through the simple adoption of the practices of others, be they ancient or non-Western forms of ars erotica. Rather, we can only "become again what we never were" by performing a critical ontology of ourselves, a spiritual self-traversal: "The critical ontology of ourselves has to be considered . . . [as] an attitude, an ethos, a philosophical life in which the critique of what we are is at one and the same time the historical analysis of the limits that are imposed on us and an experiment in the possibility of going beyond them."[94] This analysis of the limits of ourselves brings us back to *Madness* and that decisive gesture—the establishment of the limits by which reason and unreason are constituted, by which a society produces and excludes that which it deems as other. The possibility of going beyond the limits is, in this perspective, not only something we are ethically called to do, but part of the modern "politics of ourselves" we are called to practice.

A Political Ethic of Eros

The birth of *Rameau's Nephew* at the heart of Western reason is one of many births in Foucault's oeuvre: a "birth of subjectivity" that we also see in his course, *The Hermeneutics of the Subject*, twenty years later. *Rameau's Nephew*, like the Epicureans or the Stoics, inhabits a moment of transition where the self is tested and where the division that separates reason from unreason also sets the limits of the self. From the perspective of *Hermeneutics*, the Hegelian Nephew opens the possibility of another "spiritual" event after the catastrophe of the Cartesian moment. Indeed, as we have seen, the Nephew inaugurates what Foucault identifies as the spirituality of the nineteenth century. In his repetition of earlier "births" of other subjects in their relation to truth, the Nephew's "first speaking" of madness can only happen in the mode of irony and paradox, that point of turning in the Hegelian dialectic where positives are perverted into their own negation. Thus the Enlightenment truth he marks is the coupling of madness with the birth of subjectivity: "madness is permitted to speak in the first person" and, so doing, speaks "the truth closest to the birth of the subject" (517).

In the terms I've been elaborating over the course of this chapter, the moment of the Nephew might thus be seen as the moment of a new division between the eros of spirituality and the bios of positivism. But this historical division, inaugurated by the ironic "birth" of the modern subject in the Nephew's first-person utterance "I am mad," should not be construed, in the nineteenth century that paves the way for our own age, as a simple opposition between the erotic spirituality of literature versus the biopolitical philosophy of positivist science. As the Hegelian dialectic so powerfully shows, literature can easily be another cog in the philosophical machine of absolute knowledge. Further, in the age of modern, antispiritual philosophy that is Foucault's ultimate political concern, life is increasingly organized in the mode of biopower: what in an earlier age might have been called erotic emerges, in the age of biopower, as sexuality. Thus, for example, "same-sex" eroticism in the ancient Greek world is recoded in biopower as one of sexuality's many perversions.

The recoding of eros as sexuality is the result of the great division between reason and unreason Foucault identifies with the Cartesian moment. This recoding links Descartes to Freud, as I demonstrated in chapter 3. And as Shadi Bartsch and Thomas Bartscherer explain, Freud's psychoanalysis "became the dominant analytical paradigm for approaching eros throughout much of the twentieth century. His theory placed biological sexual instincts firmly at the root of erotic phenomena."[95] From Descartes to Freud, eros is eventually swallowed up by bio-logos, reemerging in Freud as a mystification of actual life through the tragic theme of the origin of civilization expressed, as Rajchman puts it, "through a fictive anthropology or prehistory of the 'primal.'"[96]

Writing "against such erotic archaism"[97] as the mystified sublimation of bio-logos, Foucault aligns eros with unreason to explain its disappearance beneath history's horizon. Specifically, in *Madness*, in the post-Cartesian world which follows the great confinement, Foucault grieves the loss of a premodern "homosexual lyricism" he links to an erotic "Platonic culture" (*M* 88/*F* 103) that associates love with unreason, either as "a blind madness of the body" (*M* 88) or as "the great intoxication of the soul where Unreason is in a position of knowledge" (*M* 88). As a form of knowledge that includes madness, eros will be banished by the "I" of the cogito. We could continue to narrate this story about the exclusion of eros from modern subjectivity along the lines of the tale Foucault tells more explicitly about modernity's exclusion of unreason. And, like unreason, eros doesn't disappear altogether; rather, it becomes a ghost, the trace of an absence whose silhouette we still discern in the modern reorganization of love and unreason within the grid of modern sexuality. After Descartes, in Foucault's story, eros is divided into two forms of love: "either reasoned or governed by unreason" (*M* 88). If before the great division, the intermingling of love and madness included everyone in the back-and-forth movement of the ship of fools, with the Cartesian moment, homosexuality and the other perversions will be consigned to the realms of love "governed by unreason": they will be excluded, measured, calculated, and pinned down by the mode of knowledge that is biopower.

To invoke eros, then, as I'm doing here, is to face again the paradox of unreason. To explain eros is to return, impossibly, to the time before an epistemic break that cannot be breached. As a form of unreason, eros exposes the alterity of the past. Like unreason, eros is untranslatable. Those past lives eros might name—the Renaissance homosexual lyricism to which Foucault alludes, for example—can only be stuttering, suffocated voices, trapped in a time before biopower we cannot know. The modern subject who wants to know eros is thus caught in this ethico-historical paradox: to recuperate, in language, the forms of an erotic past is to reduce that past to ashes.

If we perceive eros across an epistemic breach that keeps it distant from us, to identify it in modernity is to betray it. To seek out, today, those bodily practices or forms of relation that resemble what we think eros might have once been is to distort its otherness and, more generally, to betray the alterity of history. It is tempting, of course, to look for it anyway, so seductive are eros's promises. But we must be careful, as Foucault warns us, not to indulge in utopian consolations, those nostalgic recuperations of nonexistent pasts we harness as projections of our own future freedom. We must be especially wary of those modern sites where eros appears to emerge, magically escaping biopower, in all its ancient, Greek-inflected glory.

One of those sites is the space of literature which, as we've seen, Foucault explicitly distinguishes from the "poem-lives" of his "infamous" men and women. To be sure, in *History of Madness*, Foucault gestures toward the literary language of certain writers—Nerval, Nietzsche, Hölderlin, Roussel, and Artaud—as discourses that use the erotic to challenge the limits of reason. But, as Foucault insists, to the extent a writer's oeuvre can be heard at all, it is heard in the nonerotic, "sexual" language of reason. To speak madness is to cease to exist, and even literature cannot bring into the present the voice of an erotic unreason. Like psychoanalysis, literature's freedom to speak unreason is, in biopower, a caged freedom. "Literature," Foucault says in "Lives of Infamous Men," belongs to the same "great system of constraint" (173) that governs the discursive apparatus of biopower. The compelled speech of psychiatric knowledge is in fact intensified in literary language. "A kind of injunction to ferret out the most nocturnal and most quotidian elements of existence," Foucault writes, "would mark out the course that literature would follow from the seventeenth century onward, from the time it began to be literature in the modern sense of the word" (173). Literary language, Foucault continues, "more than any other form of language . . . has the duty of saying what is most resistant to being said—the worst, the most secret, the most insufferable, the shameless" (174). If psychiatric power produces the perverse implantation Foucault decries in *Sexuality One*, literature is embedded in that grid of power.

Eros is not a timeless form of expression delimited by genre or discursive form. Nor is it a libidinal, Marcusian energy waiting to be liberated—either through the talking cure or literary language—with a promise to transform the conditions of work, the economy, and social institutions. Rather, eros is the name we can give to an ethical practice of embodied subjectivity in relation to truth. As an attitude that characterizes a present disposition, eros is both ancient and always changing. For the modern sexual subject, eros names a practice of retraversal: a genealogy of the land of sexual morality where the cogito lives. This erotic retraversal is a postmoral, ethical, self-transformative labor that exposes the Cartesian subject to her own undoing. In that undoing, the subject becomes erotic: her relation to herself and the past changes. This means, specifically, a change in the relation between subjectivity and truth. Becoming erotic through her own undoing, the subject is "marked with a touch of impossibility" (173); she becomes, like a fable, "traversed and transfigured" (173) by the unreal realities of unknown worlds. Like the fools in the Renaissance ship, the fabular subject of this modern theatrum mundi engages in practices of self-transformation that negotiate the limits of the imaginary and the real: she plays the "game of the 'exemplary fabulous'" (173). This game of the fabulous is an erotic game of truth whose rules are not those of biopolitical knowledge—what Foucault calls philosophy—but rather the self-transformative conditions of spirituality. But, unlike decorporealizing forms of spiritual practice, this game of truth restages the body as the claw-marked flesh trapped in the archive: "men who lived and died, with sufferings, meannesses, jealousies, vociferations" (160). This is why Foucault returns, again and again, to the archive. It is both the site of a rationalist wounding that "mark[s] [lives] with its claw" (161) and, as the space for a *poiesis* of lives, the site of an erotic transformation.

Foucault's ethics of eros is thus a transformative rethinking of life: if bios is a life form captured by modern power, eros is biopolitical life's transfiguration: spiritual, affective, intellectual, corporeal. In *Hermeneutics*, Foucault defines bios as existence as the object of techniques—bios as "the correlate of a *tekhne* (486); in the ancient world, this means bios, or existence, is also "a material for an aesthetic piece of art" (485). Foucault pursues this idea in "On the Genealogy of Ethics," where he says: "the general Greek problem was not *tekhne* of the self, it was the *tekhne* of life, the *tekhne tou biou*, how to live. . . . The idea of the *bios* as a material for an aesthetic piece of art is something that fascinates me" (260). Foucault is struck by the fact that, "in our society, art has become something that is related only to objects and not to individuals or to life," and only practiced "by experts who are artists" (261). "But," Foucault asks, "couldn't everyone's life become a work of art?" (261).

Much has been made of Foucault's arts of existence: critical commentary ranges from accusations of apolitical dandyism[98] to arguments for the political potential of aesthetic life as exemplified by modern forms of gay culture. But if life is an art in the specific context of modern biopower, the stakes of that life extend beyond the fashioning of individual style or the cultural particularities of contemporary forms of social belonging. Again, the focus of biopower is not simply the disciplining of individual bodies, but the ordering of life itself. Indeed, if bios has become, in the modern era, that which is managed, measured, and calculated within the subjectivating grids of science, Foucault's call to transform bios is a call to transform the modes of rationality through which that ordering is carried out.

Both in *Madness* and in *Sexuality One*, Foucault makes clear the role psyche-logos plays in the capture of life by science. As we have seen, even in the language of psychoanalysis, bios remains caught in the caged freedom of the modern subject-object pinned down by positivist knowledge. Still, Foucault says in *Sexuality One*, the capture of bios is never total: "it is not that life has been totally integrated into techniques that govern and administer it; it constantly escapes them."[99] In *Madness*, we find such escapes in the mad pantomimes of the Nephew or the "poetic conversions" (*M* 351) of the nineteenth-century hysteric. But, given what we know about Foucault's refusal of utopian thinking, this language of escape should give us pause. What sort of escape does he have in mind here? Are these escapes mere flashes of freedom, like the "painful irony" (*M* 351) of a hurt "without exchange" (*M* 351) at the hysterical theater of the Salpêtrière? How does life persist in escaping the grids of biopower?

If we read, retrospectively, this possibility of escape through the lens of *tekhne tou biou*, we might answer by suggesting that we escape biopower through the aesthetic transformation of bio-logos, by living our life as a work of art. This has led some to suggest that S/M practices and other forms of erotic gaming are examples of Foucault's ethics in practice. Most famously, David Halperin asserts the importance of S/M practices of "degenitalization" in which Foucault is reported to have participated and suggests that fisting in particular might be a modern version of the arts of the self described in Foucault's work on the ancient world.[100] According to Halperin, the new erotic practices of which fisting serves as an emblem are all practices that work to pulverize the self into the "sensorial continuum of the body."[101] Halperin continues: "The transformative potential of the queer sexual practices that gay men have invented" creates "a queer praxis that ultimately dispenses with 'sexuality' and destabilizes the very constitution of identity itself."[102] The implication of this argument is that the biopolitical subject can be undone by gay fisting.

Like many others, I find this argument to be unpersuasive. As Peter Hallward puts it, "nothing is more consistent with [Foucault's] critique [of specification] than his adamant refusal to specify an alternative model of sexual practice or understanding. Nothing is more foreign to Foucault's conception of critical *thought* than what he derides as 'the Californian cult of the self.'"[103] Neither the pages of literature nor the back rooms of sex clubs *necessarily* constitute the site of our erotic de-subjectivation. Indeed, nothing can be inferred one way or the other from these half-imaginary, half-real heterotopias. As nonutopias, they are unstable, open only to the continually shifting transformations brought about by specific practices. As heterotopias, they appear and disappear like Deleuze's ships: "an inside which is merely the fold of the outside, as if the ship were a folding of the sea."[104] The eros they promise is not a substance any more than Foucault's Nietzschean subject. It is not pregiven, like some inherently disruptive force of nature that shatters Greeks, Romantics, and Freudians alike. Indeed, as we have already seen, the queer self-shattering argument is both politically American and conceptually psychoanalytic: it depends on a mutually reinforcing investment in identity politics and a psyche to be disrupted. And, given Foucault's warnings about emulating the Greeks, to simply transpose the erotic arts of the self from the fourth century BCE to the twentieth century—from between the thighs to "anal yoga"—seems dubious at best.[105]

The erotic practices of new arts of living will not be found in any specific discursive form, nor will they be found in particular body parts or configurations of bodies, although the body is still there, as the fleshy stuff to be erotically illuminated in the archive. Indeed, these practices will not be found in a conception of the present that papers over the otherness of history. To read eros as solely about discourses or bodies in the present is, indeed, to buy into the great, ahistorical Cartesian mind-body split that Foucault spent his life dismantling. Rather, eros is the practice of the subject in relation to herself and others, through which the relation between subjectivity and truth will be transformed. That transformation must engage not only the contemporary practices of subjects in society but also the relation of those subjects to their own history. Foucault's historical approach to philosophy is a lifelong labor that works with the traces of forms of bios. And if bios is life as the object of techniques, Foucault's genealogies of the present are conceptual modes of working with bios. But, where rationalist modes of working with bios capture lives by pinning them down as objects of knowledge, Foucault's approach to bios is an art of living that, as we have seen, he describes as a "poetic attitude": his philosophy-as-life, his philosophical life, his ethos as a nonphilosophical philosopher.

Although much has been made of Foucault's "stoic" attitude toward the end of his life, reinforced by comments such as "sex is boring,"[106] this poetic attitude reveals, in my view, a passionate "experience of thought" not confined to the thinking organ.[107] Indeed, such confinement of passion would make Foucault Cartesian all over again. Foucault's lifelong trajectory traces a passionate thinking toward thinking's limit as something other than thinking. That "something other than thinking" creates an opening, like the ship-as-fold, for the subject's undoing in her coextension with the alterity of the world: "a void, a time of silence, a question without an answer, it provokes a tearing without repair by which the world is forced to question itself " (M 537/F 556). In putting out this call, as a strange preacher or prophet, for this ethical "space of our work" (M 537; emphasis added), Foucault enjoins us to confront our own limits, and the limits of our truths, through a constant engagement with the borders of a world that we can never fully know, but to which, nonetheless, we are fully accountable. This, Foucault writes on the last page of Madness, is our promiscuous practice: "our mixed vocation as apostle and interpreter" (M 537/F 557; translation modified).

Such a prophetic, promiscuous "spiritual" thinking at the edges of thought is not only a call to think differently, although it is certainly that. "Philosophical discourse," Foucault says, "is entitled to explore what might be changed, in its own thought, through the practice of a knowledge that is foreign to it,"[108] by ethical practice—an ars erotica—as an activity of freedom: "to free thought from what it silently thinks, and so enable it to think differently."[109] But this prophetic call, as an ethics of eros, is not only about thinking but also about affect, sensation, sentiment, and feeling. Arlette Farge insists on the erotic dimension of Foucault's return to the archive in "Lives of Infamous Men," which he approaches, she writes, with "stupefaction" and "dread."[110] Indeed, Foucault writes, at the opening of the essay: the approach to these lives "was guided by . . . my taste, my pleasure, an emotion, laughter, surprise, a certain dread, or some other feeling whose intensity I might have trouble justifying."[111] Farge reads these feelings that guide Foucault's encounter with the poem-lives as a solicitation of the senses. "It is [the senses] that give meaning and interrogate, [the senses] that are the agents of thought [acteurs de la pensée]."[112] Reflecting on Foucault's "stupefaction" and "dread," Farge calls "these feelings" unleashed by the archive the "primary instruments of [Foucault's] thinking" (75; translation mine). So with the illuminated lives of "infamous" men—"in this burst of life (or in these burst lives)"—we touch "the emotion of the one who encounters [them]" (77; translation mine). Unlike Descartes, who cuts off the res cogitans from the orgasmic eruptions of the body, Foucault's thinking is driven by the "'physical vibration' experienced in consulting the archive" (78; translation mine).

Farge interprets Foucault's return to the *Madness* archives—his return to himself—in "Lives of Infamous Men" as a response to those who had criticized him: "a form of radical intervention about the mode of his encounter with his sources" (78; translation mine) as something other than the truth-telling of rationalist historians. In this intimate encounter in a space of feeling, sensation, stupefaction, and dread that "stirred more fibers" in Foucault "than what is ordinarily called 'literature,'"[113] Foucault is, once again, thoroughly Nietzschean. His encounter with the *infamous*—a word, Farge reminds us, that meant "homosexual" in the police reports and prison registers of the eighteenth century[114]— is an ethical encounter that transforms the rationalist moralism of Western thinking. As Nietzsche writes in *Daybreak*:

> It goes without saying that I do not deny—unless I am a fool—that many actions called immoral ought to be avoided and resisted, or that many called moral ought to be done and encouraged—but I think the one should be encouraged and the other avoided *for other reasons than hitherto*. We have to *learn to think differently*—in order at last, perhaps very late on, to attain even more: *to feel differently*.[115]

Foucault's archival *practice*—in all the meanings of the term, including action, thinking, feeling, listening—is his response to this Nietzschean call to "think differently" in order to "very late on, attain even more": the erotic practice of a different feeling. Eros informs Foucault's relation to his own histories of the present, to which he gains access through the alterity of the archives. Foucault's erotic attention to the archival other is at once fiercely concerned with the subjugations of the present and with the othering violences of the past. The great space of murmurings we encounter in *Madness* is the space of that othering in our historical present. It tells the story of existences—traces of bios—as the captured objects of biopolitical techniques. So doing, it gives us a series of characters and figures that dramatize forms of bios that have been captured by science in a garden of species of madness. But Foucault's tale of *Madness* is not only a capture narrative about "lowly lives reduced to ashes in the few sentences that struck them down."[116] In the poem-lives Foucault finds in the archives—lives illuminated and destroyed by their clash with power—something persists as the strange survivals borne out of Foucault's aesthetic practice. This fashioning of survivals extricated from the cage of power-knowledge is Foucault's work: his ars erotica.

That ars erotica is not only a labor on the traces of lives we call history. As an aesthetic practice and an art of living, Foucault's erotic transformation of bios is also a testing of the self. His ars erotica not only remakes history by fashioning a story that illuminates the lives of history's cast-off remains. Foucault's strange illumination of history's survivals also produces a rebound effect that transfigures him as a thinking, feeling body. In this sense, the archive becomes an ethical invitation to philosophical investigation as an aesthetic practice: an invitation to curiosity-as-care: "the care brought to the process of putting historico-critical reflection to the test of concrete practices."[117] It is curiosity, after all, that leads to self-release: "not the curiosity that seeks to assimilate what it is proper for one to know, but that which enables one to get free of oneself."[118] Foucault is a fiction maker—a maker of poem-lives—who refashions historical bios and allows himself to be refashioned. Opening his own life to spiritual transformation, he becomes a fabular subject. Thus his aesthetic is a practical art whose doing transforms the doer in the manner of what he calls, in *Hermeneutics*, *ethopoiein*: "making ethos, producing ethos, changing, transforming ethos."[119] This kind of thinking-feeling I'm calling erotic constitutes, for Foucault, a "useful"[120] knowledge that can help us in our "effort to think [our] own history."[121] It can help us to realize the ethico-historical paradox of transformation: to become again what we never were by "free[ing] thought from what it silently thinks, and so enable it to think"—and feel—"differently."[122]

This understanding of a thinking-feeling ars erotica as a practice of philosophy and history insists on the importance of the other in Foucault's ethical thinking. Unlike Butler, who faults Foucault for his "failure to think the other,"[123] I view Foucault's ethical ars erotica as explicitly concerned with alterity.[124] Especially with regard to the erotic arts, Foucault's primary ethical concern is, as he puts it, "the pleasure of the other."[125] More generally, with regard to Foucault's historico-philosophical ars erotica, the other shapes all of Foucault's work. From the beginning, *Madness* tells us that if history comes to us through the evidence of the archive, the evidence will not give us a singular truth of history. *Madness* dramatizes the problem of the relation between subjectivity and truth as a specifically ethical, archival question that confronts the investigator who will craft history. But, for the history-making subject's relation to truth to be free, the investigator must allow herself to be undone, even, perhaps especially, by emotions like stupefaction, dread, "or some other feeling"[126] whose intensity Foucault experiences but cannot name. To do otherwise—to proceed with the traditional investigative assumption that we already know what madness is and, therefore, know a pervert when we find one in the archive—is to deny the alterity of historical eros. It is to engage in a historico-philosophical form of biopower by pinning lives down as already-known objects, as sets of unities or causalities we project onto the evidence. This nonpoetic attitude toward the poem-lives of history gives us forms of bios already shaped before we write them and makes us complicit with biopower.

I have called this eros a political ethic by insisting on Foucault's engagement with governmentality in the context of practices of freedom. In *Foucault and the Art of Ethics*, Timothy O'Leary similarly calls Foucault's "art of freedom" the most significant component of his ethical thinking. But it is worth asking more specifically, from a feminist perspective, how Foucault's ethics of eros is specifically political. In her reading of eros in Audre Lorde, Cynthia Willett insists on the relation between the erotic as power and new forms of the self that contest liberal models of the individual against the state. Willett explains that this liberal model "poses freedom in opposition to constraints on autonomy,"[127] whereas Lorde and other thinkers of eros find freedom in our capacity to sustain relationality. As Willett puts it: "Freedom's most sublime meaning is eros" (180). Willett's reading of Lorde builds on her critique of eros and freedom in Marcuse, whose "new man" excludes women. Following Tina Chanter, she finds in Irigaray the ingredients of an ethics of eros that places the "amorous exchange" (134) at its heart. "Irigaray teaches us to see through Marcuse's dream" (141). Willett argues, by insisting on the "social eroticism that binds children to their mothers" (141). Finding much of value in Irigaray's ethics, Willett ultimately critiques her for binding eros to the heterosexual couple, thereby refusing to engage the "material subject" (152)—the servant or laborer "who must work so that her lovers can play" (151). This critique is important, and can be linked to the political ethic of eros I'm arguing for in Foucault. Willett wonders "how lovers can live without a source of labor" and questions an Irigaray who "imagines that lovers might cleanse their skin of the sedimentations of power and create a paradise out of nothing" (151). She wonders, like Foucault, how we can "ever escape wounds from conflicts past and present" (152). Like Foucault, Willett asks, "where are the ghosts of those who were lost?" (152).

Foucault's eros, like Lorde's and Irigaray's, is driven by an attention to a relationality that goes far beyond the relationship between the individual and the state. It redefines freedom and governmentality as a nexus of relations that animates and configures every fiber of our lives. But Foucault differs from Lorde and Irigaray in his explicit attention to the archival relation on which I've insisted, to the role power plays in the subject's relation to the alterity of history: to "the ghosts of those who were lost."

Foucault's erotic attention to historical traces of bios contrasts with what Nietzsche calls the "hallowed custom with philosophers" to engage in "unhistorical thinking."[128] Foucault, like Nietzsche, is an antiphilosophical historical philosopher (but antihistorical in his histories) who allows the philosophical to touch the nonphilosophical—what Foucault calls experience in his tribute to Hyppolite—and thereby transform him. This "spiritual" approach to traces of bios is Foucault's ars erotica: his artistic practice as a feeling thinker and his conception of art as a way of living. Unlike the pregiven packages of traditional scientific, historical, or belles lettres literary forms, art opens the spiritual possibility of transformation. Art is fiction making, an ethical *poiesis*: the awakening of new forms of life.

From the time of the publication of *Madness*, Foucault has been accused of romanticizing the irrational. But Foucault is neither romantic nor irrational: as a feeling thinker, his practice is erotic. In his repeated, spiraling, obsessive, perhaps delirious returns to the silhouettes of a faded unreason, Foucault brings to the fore a concrete practice of aesthetic work on bios—those ghosts of history who appear in modern bio-logos as the object of techniques. Illuminated by history in their clash with power, the infamous lives Foucault invokes are illuminated again by a different attention than the recording, calculating, ordering gaze of biopolitical surveillance. That different attention is Foucault's poetic attitude: an erotic attention, a curiosity-as-care, a transformative lingering that is love.

In that lingering love, Foucault follows Nietzsche into the space left open by the collapse of his thought. Nietzsche's transvaluation of values produced the warrior ethics of a will to power that could make no space for tenderness except as insanity: Nietzsche's moment of tenderness, when in 1889 he flings his arms around the neck of a horse being beaten, is historically registered as his fall into the abyss of madness. In Nietzsche's wake—after sex—Foucault's erotic care for the lives in the archives forces the world to confront its own capacity to wound, to account for the scraps of flesh made bloody by the claws of power. In the transfiguration of *erastes* and *eromenos* for a modern ethical parrhesia, this ethics of eros names the intense thinking-feeling—an erotic curiosity-

278 A POLITICAL ETHIC OF EROS

as-care—toward the wounded vulnerability of the beloved other. Thus Foucault's *Madness* makes way not only for the new idea, as Nietzsche would put it, but also for a tenderness that comes after Nietzsche: the same tender generosity I felt, in my own passionate encounter with the "fragments of a reality" of a philosopher's life, in the monastic space of the Normandy archives. There I found a *petit fou* named Foucault I will never cease to love.

A FOOL'S LAUGHTER

In August 2008 I returned to the Normandy archives to listen to Foucault's last course on the ancient Cynics, "Le Courage de la vérité." He died not long after his final, March 28 lecture, on 25 June 1984.

The wind howls through the library, hour after hour, as I listen to the ghost voice, sometimes lively, sometimes fading. I feel the loneliness of the twelfth-century monk and the twentieth-century farmer crouched in the debris of a Nazi bombardment. Foucault's voice grows weaker, faster, higher, the flash of a kite disappearing. It is the voice of the hysteric—*la folle*—the tail of a firecracker, screeching. His fleshy matter—the body of the brain—will be eaten away by the invading cells. This relentless devouring of the mind-as-body will be Foucault's ultimate proof of Descartes's error.

The wind howls louder as the day progresses, occasionally broken by peals of laughter—Foucault's students' and my own. Foucault is talking about Diogenes. Treated like a dog, he arrives at a banquet and is thrown a bone, then turns around and "pisses on the guests like a dog."[1] I can't help but laugh, drawing glances. At the Collège de France, the students laugh too. Another story: Diogenes eats raw flesh, purportedly dying after consuming a live octopus.[2] Another burst of laughter. But, beneath the hilarity, I feel the same uneasiness that Foucault felt when he was reading Borges. As with Borges, the laughter points me—this time through the "scandalous redoubling of the correct life" (*la vie droite*) in the Cynic's practice of a "barking life" (*la vie aboyante*)³—toward a disquieting shamelessness, the "thought without space"⁴ of the "other life" (*la vie autre*).⁵

Foucault would have appreciated my fool's laughter in the midst of this solemn monastic space, refurbished after the war's destruction to preserve the traces of History. His hysteric's voice is one of those traces, the shadow cast by something as it's leaving. Even as I'm listening, the voice grows weaker. I reach the end—March 28. "I had some things to tell you," Foucault says at last. "But it's too late, *voilà, merci.*"⁶ These are the last words I hear him utter. The kite disappears, carried off by a howl. Reluctantly I let go of the fragile string that held it there, hovering, just a little bit longer, for us.

Notes

Preface

1. Technically, Foucault's first book was *Maladie mentale et personnalité*, published in 1954 at the request of Louis Althusser for a series destined for students. But it does not appear in its final form until after the publication of *Folie et déraison* in 1961. At the request of his editor, Foucault significantly altered the original 1954 version to reflect his thinking in *Folie et déraison*. Against Foucault's wishes, the book was republished as *Maladie mentale et psychologie* (*Mental Illness and Psychology*) in 1962.

2. Throughout this book, I will use the following abbreviations to refer to Foucault's *History of Madness*: *M* for the 2006 English translation of *History of Madness*, *F* for the 1972 French edition of *Histoire de la folie à l'âge classique*. Full details for these sources can be found in the works cited list.

3. The French title of the first volume of *Histoire de la sexualité* is *La Volonté de savoir* (*The Will to Knowledge*). As many have noted, the title of the English translation, *The History of Sexuality: An Introduction* (1978), constitutes a significant elision, distorting the original French presentation of the book. In order to avoid confusion, I have chosen to refer to the published English translation as *Sexuality One*. I will refer to the second and third volumes of *The History of Sexuality* as *Sexuality Two* and *Sexuality Three*, respectively.

4. Droit, *Michel Foucault, entretiens* , p. 105 (translation mine).

5. Canguilhem, "On 'Histoire de la folie,'" p. 284.

6. Deleuze, *Negotiations*, p. 84.

7. Foucault, "Chronologie," p. 33 (translation mine).

8. The British version of the truncated English translation did not appear until 1967, with a preface by David Cooper, in the series Studies in Existentialism

and Phenomenology directed by Ronald D. Laing. From that time on, *Madness* was read by many English readers through the lens of *antipsychiatry*, a term coined by Cooper in 1962. And, although Foucault did not explicitly distance himself from the British antipsychiatric reception of his book, he was never a part of the movement.

9. For a recent overview of the book's history in light of the new translation, see Beaulieu and Fillion's "Review Essay."
10. Feher, "Les interrègnes de Michel Foucault," p. 262 (translation mine).
11. Foucault, "Final Interview," p. 10. Foucault poses a similar question in the introduction to volume 2 of *The History of Sexuality, The Use of Pleasure* (1984): "the question that ought to guide my inquiry was the following: how, why, and in what forms was sexuality constituted as a moral domain? Why this ethical concern that was so persistent despite its varying forms and intensity" (10). See Foucault, *The History of Sexuality*, vol. 2: *The Use of Pleasure*.
12. Foucault, "Se débarrasser de la philosophie," pp. 87–88 (translation mine).
13. Foucault, "Entretien avec Roger-Pol Droit," p. 58.

Introduction

1. Howe, *My Emily Dickinson*, p. 13.
2. Plaza, "Our Damages." For a similar critique see Soper, "Productive Contradictions." For a more balanced assessment of Foucault and the problem of sexual violence, see Fassin, "Somnolence de Foucault."
3. Cooper and Foucault, "Dialogue sur l'enfermement," p. 99 (translation mine).
4. Davis, "Racialized Punishment and Prison Abolition."
5. For these and other archival materials from the GIP movement, see Artières, Quéro, and Zancarini-Fournel, *Le Groupe d'information*. For a critical view of GIP's construction of prisoners' subjectivity see Brich, "The Groupe d'information."
6. See Foucault, *Discipline and Punish*; for the French original, see Foucault, *Surveiller et punir*.
7. Davis, "Racialized Punishment and Prison Abolition," p. 96.
8. Ibid., p. 97.
9. Feher, "Les interrègnes de Michel Foucault," p. 267 (translation mine).
10. Ibid., p. 267.
11. Ibid.
12. See Butler, *Trouble dans le genre*. For a brief overview of Butler's reception in France, see Fassin, "Résistance et réception."
13. See Sedgwick, *Epistémologie du placard*.
14. See Rubin and Butler, *Marché au sexe*.
15. Eribon, *Insult*, p. 250.
16. I am grateful to Didier Eribon for putting me in contact with the association, allowing me to gain access to the letters.
17. Although none of Barraqué's letters to Foucault seem to have been preserved, in the binder that holds the Foucault correspondence there is a draft, in Bar-

raqué's hand, of a letter written to Foucault sometime after 11 March 1956. (Foucault's last letter to Barraqué is dated 6 May 1956.) It is impossible to know if the actual letter from Barraqué was ever sent; in the draft Barraqué insists on the importance of his work and, more specifically, implores Foucault to listen to his new composition "Séquence." This music, he says, "is the only reality that can give a structure" to their exchanges. Barraqué also expresses "shame" at what Foucault has made of him: "I almost slipped and fell," he writes, but managed to escape the "vertigo of madness" (undated draft of letter, Jean Barraqué to Michel Foucault, 1956; translation mine). For a brief description of the relationship between Barraqué and Foucault, see Griffiths, *The Sea on Fire*, especially chapter 7.

18. According to Veyne, Barraqué taught Foucault about the "intransitivity" of art: "that forms were non-transitive toward society or toward a totality (the spirit of an age, for example)." See Veyne, *Foucault*, p. 39 (translation mine).
19. Foucault, "Qui êtes-vous, professeur Foucault?" 1:641 (translation mine).
20. Ibid. (translation mine).
21. Foucault, "Prisons et asiles," 1:1391 (translation mine).
22. Cited by Eribon, *Insult*, p. 256.
23. Howe, *My Emily Dickinson*, p. 13.
24. Barkley Brown, "'What Has Happened Here,'" p. 297.
25. Beauvoir, *The Ethics of Ambiguity*, p. 8.
26. Foucault, "Entretien avec Roger-Pol Droit," p. 118.
27. This resistance to History is what Foucault will come to call genealogy in the 1970s. For Foucault's clearest articulation of the difference between genealogy and history, see Foucault, "Nietzsche, Genealogy, History."
28. Droit, *Michel Foucault, entretiens*. The first article appeared in the 6 September 1986, edition of *Le Monde* as "Michel Foucault, passe-frontières de la philosophie" and is reprinted as "Se débarrasser de la philosophie" in the Droit collection. The second article appeared in the 1 July 2004 edition of *Le Point* as "Les Confessions de Michel Foucault" and is reprinted as "Je suis un artificier" in Droit. The Droit collection also includes an excerpt from a different, previously published 1975 interview (*Le Monde*, 21 February 1975) entitled "Gérer les illégalismes," also reprinted in *Dits et écrits* (1975) and Droit's *La Compagnie des contemporains* (2002).
29. Foucault, "What Is an Author?" 2:207. For the French original, see "Qu'est-ce qu'un auteur?" 1:822.
30. Foucault, "Entretien avec Roger-Pol Droit," p. 319 (translation mine).
31. Ibid., pp. 25–26 (translation mine).
32. Ibid., p. 29.
33. Butler, *Gender Trouble*, p. 101.
34. Deleuze, *Foucault*, p. 90.
35. For a helpful overview of such responses, see Beaulieu and Fillion, "Review Essay."
36. Scull, "Michel Foucault's *History of Madness*," p. 57.
37. Andrew Scull's more recent review of the 2006 translation is almost entirely negative and seems to have renewed old debates about the book's accuracy, as

indicated by an exchange of letters with Colin Gordon following the review in March 2007. In his 2007 review, Scull claims to prefer the truncated 1965 English translation both to its "plodding" original and the new English translation, which he calls "dreary," "dispirited," "unreliable," and "prone to inaccurate paraphrase" (4). He concludes his review by admonishing Paul Rabinow, R. D. Laing, and Nikolas Rose for their praise of Foucault, whom Scull describes as "cynical and shameless" (7). See Scull, "The Fictions of Foucault's Scholarship." For the response by Gordon, see "Extreme Prejudice."

38. For overviews of the historians' critiques see especially Midelfort, "Madness and Civilisation"; Megill, "The Reception of Foucault"; Gordon, "Histoire de la folie"; and Gutting, "Foucault and the History of Madness."

39. Megill, "The Reception of Foucault," pp. 133–134.

40. See, for example, Mandrou, "Trois clés"; Goldstein, Console and Classify; and Gutting, "Foucault and the History of Madness." For Colin Gordon's appraisal of the new translation, see his "Review of History of Madness."

41. Cited by Megill, "The Reception of Foucault," p. 117; also cited by Gutting, "Foucault and the History of Madness," p. 47.

42. Droit, Michel Foucault, entretiens, p. 132 (translation mine).

43. Ibid., p. 118 (translation mine).

44. See Habermas, "The Critique of Reason"; and Stone, "Madness."

45. For example see Quétel, "Faut-il critiquer Foucault?"; and Swain, Dialogue avec l'insensé.

46. See Derrida, "Cogito and History of Madness"; for the original see Derrida, "Cogito et histoire de la folie."

47. Winnubst, Queering Freedom, p. 138.

48. Ibid., p. 138.

49. Dreyfus and Rabinow, Michel Foucault, p. 12.

50. Dreyfus, "Foreword to the California Edition," p. xxviii.

51. Ibid.

52. For a reading of Foucault's "hermeneutics" see Caputo, "On Not Knowing Who We Are." Although I disagree with Caputo's characterization of Foucault's project in Madness as primarily a hermeneutical uncovering, his larger point about Foucault's project as a whole as a movement toward difference is consistent with my approach.

53. McNay, Foucault, p. 39.

54. Kaufman, The Delirium of Praise, p. 68.

55. Deleuze, Negotiations, p. 102.

56. Deleuze, Foucault, p. 97.

57. Ibid., p. 97.

58. Ibid., p. 43. I am persuaded by Peter Hallward's argument regarding the important difference between a Deleuzian philosophy without limits grounded in the singular and a Foucauldian philosophy of the limit grounded in the specific. As Hallward explains, "singularity tends toward a radical plenitude" and is always self-generating, while the specific "always eventually confronts the empty horizon of its extension" (Hallward, "The Limits," p. 99) as void. The Foucauldian "articulation of the specific recognises that the only pertinent cri-

teria for action are always external (i.e. specific) to the particular action itself—and thus a matter of conflict, deliberation, and *decision*" (99), while Deleuzian singularities are immanent, immediate, self-differing, and virtual. From the perspective of this difference, Deleuze's vitalistic terminology to describe the inside-outside unfolding of the subject as "an unformed element of forces" (*Foucault*, p. 43) is slightly inaccurate. Invoking coextension on the model of what Hallward calls an "ontological univocity" (94) that is categorical for Deleuze, the phrase distorts the play of relational, external, void-encountering forces that characterize coextension in Foucault. I have nonetheless retained the general frame of Deleuze's coextensivity argument in *Foucault* since, whether singular or specific, the subject's coextension involves the undoing of the subject through a confrontation with limits. See Hallward, "The Limits."

59. Deleuze, *Foucault*, p. 43.

60. Foucault, "The Thought of the Outside," 2:166. For the French original, see "La Pensée du dehors," 1:565–566.

61. Hallward, "The Limits," p. 103.

62. Droit, *Michel Foucault, entretiens*, p. 12 (translation mine).

63. For a similar argument along these lines, see Jeffrey Nealon's case for "ethical resistance" (77) to a "biopolitical 'ethical realm' . . . we all have in common" (89). Nealon concludes that Foucauldian "resistance is not a rare attribute of certain heroic subjects, but an essential fact of everyone's everyday struggles with power" (111). See Nealon, *Foucault Beyond Foucault*.

64. David Halperin also makes one brief mention of *Madness* in *Saint Foucault*: he compares "sexuality" to "madness" (40) and critiques James Miller's distorting use of *Madness and Civilization* (166). See Halperin, *Saint Foucault*.

65. Eribon, *Echapper à la psychanalyse*, p. 85 (translation mine).

66. Ibid., p. 81 (translation mine).

67. Foucault, "Entretien avec Roger-Pol Droit," p. 29; in Droit, *Michel Foucault, entretiens*, p. 94 (translation mine).

68. In Eribon, *Insult*, p. 259.

69. Miller, *The Passion of Michel Foucault*.

70. Foucault, "Prisons et asiles," 1:1392 (translation mine).

71. Fassin, "Genre et sexualité," p. 230 (translation mine).

72. For example, regarding *Sexuality One*, Gayle Rubin tells Judith Butler in an interview: "I was totally hot for that book." See Rubin with Butler, "Sexual Traffic," p. 78. Equally enthusiastic, although in a more devotional mode, David Halperin says in *Saint Foucault*: "I do worship him. . . . As far as I'm concerned, the guy was a fucking saint" (6).

73. Fassin, "Genre et sexualité," p. 230 (translation mine).

74. Nancy, *Being-Singular-Plural*, p. xiii.

1. How We Became Queer

1. See Halley, *Split Decisions*, p. 31.

2. Ibid., p. 31. In one of the early, article-length versions of the "Taking a Break"

project, first delivered as the Brainerd Currie Lecture at Duke Law School in November 2002, Halley takes on a masculine subject position as "Ian Halley." See Halley, "Queer Theory by Men." Also see Wiegman's remarks in "Dear Ian" on Halley's increasing identification "with and as a gay man" (93) and her implicit rejection of lesbian feminism.

3. William Turner argues that "the originators of queer theory are all feminist scholars," (34) and gives Teresa de Lauretis pride of place as the theorist to first use the term *queer* in 1991 (5). See Turner, *A Genealogy of Queer Theory*; and de Lauretis, "Queer Theory, Lesbian and Gay Studies." For an interesting argument on the specifically poetic lesbian-feminist roots of queer theory see Garber, *Identity Poetics*.

4. MacKinnon, *Feminism Unmodified*, p. 7.

5. Halley, *Split Decisions*, p. 20.

6. Ibid., p. 21.

7. Rubin, "Thinking Sex," pp. 34, 32.

8. In a 2006 article, Wiegman notes the reversal of this opposition. The association between queer studies and sexuality specifically has been complicated by the proliferation of queer work on transgender issues and what Wiegman calls the "transitivity of gender": "feminist, queer, and trans-ed studies, along with heterosexuality itself, share a desire for gender." See Wiegman, "Heteronormativity," p. 97.

9. See Butler, "Against Proper Objects"; and Weed, "The More Things Change."

10. Since *Sexuality One*, and as a direct result of Anglo-American gender studies, the paired terms *genre* and *sexualité* have begun to find their way into the vocabulary of a growing minority of French writers who work in this field. See especially Fassin, "Le genre aux Etats-Unis." Also see Fassin's preface to the 2005 French translation of Butler's *Gender Trouble*, "Trouble-genre."

11. Foucault, *History of Sexuality*, 1:154.

12. Foucault, *Sexuality One*, 1:103.

13. In this sense, Foucault's "sexuality" is conceptually indistinguishable from MacKinnon's collapsing of sex, sexuality, and gender. Along the same lines, when I use the term *sexuality* in my discussion of Foucault, the multiple meanings of what English speakers call sex and gender should be understood to be included within it.

14. Halley, *Split Decisions*, p. 123.

15. Foucault, *Sexuality One*, 1:130.

16. Eribon, *Insult*, p. 264 (emphasis added).

17. For examples of such readings see Dreyfus and Rabinow, *Michel Foucault*; Caputo, "On Not Knowing Who We Are"; and McNay, *Foucault*.

18. Foucault, *Discipline and Punish*; for the French original, see Foucault, *Surveiller et punir*.

19. As Roy Boyne points out, "the three pages on Descartes do not, at first glance, appear to be so important" (43), and were excised from the abridged version of *Madness* on which most of the translations were based. But as the Foucault-Derrida debate makes clear, Descartes's role in *Madness* is crucial. Descartes's excision from *Madness* for the abridged French version in 1964 and the 1965

English translation, *after* Derrida's 1963 lecture focusing on Descartes, raises questions about Foucault's strategic editorial maneuvers in his philosophical battle with Derrida. See Boyne, *Foucault and Derrida*.

20. Blanchot, *The Infinite Conversation*, p. 198; for the French original, see Blanchot, *L'Entretien infini*, p. 295.

21. See Irigaray, *Speculum of the Other Woman*; for the French original, see Irigaray, *Speculum de l'autre femme*.

22. Foucault, "Entretien avec Roger-Pol Droit," p. 25.

23. Scull, "Michel Foucault's *History of Madness*," p. 57.

24. Megill, "Foucault, Ambiguity," p. 358.

25. Gutting, "Introduction, Michel Foucault," p. 20.

26. Flynn, "Foucault's Mapping of History," p. 43.

27. Deleuze, *Foucault*, p. 43.

28. Ibid., p. 44.

29. The French term *le négatif* connotes both negativity as a philosophical abstraction and the more concrete meaning of a photographic negative as rendered in the new English translation: "something like a photographic negative of the city of morals" (*M* 74).

30. It is important to distinguish here between the political meaning of the French term *répression*, whose first definition signifies punishment, and the psychoanalytic meaning of *refoulement*, an unconscious defensive phenomenon of the "I" who rejects or refuses the sexual drives. And, while the French distinction between the terms is lost in the English translation ("repression"), in *Madness* Foucault uses the political term *répression* exclusively. For a more detailed definition of *refoulement* see Laplanche and Pontalis, *Le Vocabulaire de la psychanalyse*.

31. Deleuze, *Foucault*, p. 43.

32. The word for *savoir* (knowledge) is deleted in the English rendering of the French original.

33. This line is missing entirely from the new English translation. It should appear on page 80.

34. For example, John Caputo cites Foucault in a 1977 interview: "I think that I was positing [in *Madness and Civilization*] the existence of a sort of living, voluble and anxious madness which the mechanisms of power and psychiatry were supposed to have come to repress and reduce to silence. . . . In defining the effects of power as repression, one adopts a purely juridical conception of such power, one identifies power with a law which says no, power is taken above all as carrying the force of prohibition." See Caputo, "On Not Knowing Who We Are," p. 244. Not only is it possible that Foucault might not see all that is going on in his own work, but it is not clear from the comments quoted by Caputo that he only sees repression at work in his analysis of madness. The comment itself does not support the weight of the claim Caputo makes.

35. Ibid., p. 245.

36. One reason for this pervasive reading of Foucault is a critical insistence on reading productive power as purely and exclusively linguistic or discursive. As Caputo puts it: "this other form of [productive] power reflects not so much a

change in Foucault's thinking as a discovery about a change that takes place in the later history of power and madness. . . . At a certain point, instead of being repressed, unreason is forced to talk . . . to talk, talk, talk, for in the talking is the cure" (ibid.). But given Foucault's explicit understanding of power as both discursive and nondiscursive, this restriction of an understanding of productive power to "talk, talk, talk" seems skewed. Madness repeatedly demonstrates that even within a repressive confinement, the silencing of the mad is never total, and their "creation" as figures of alienation happens along a number of different vectors including corporeal, juridical, familial, institutional, and discursive. As *Discipline and Punish* so beautifully demonstrates, disciplinary subjects are produced in a multitude of ways. Discursivity is just one of many modes of subjectivation.

37. Ibid., p. 246.
38. Ibid.
39. For a useful overview of "experience" in Foucault, see O'Leary, "Foucault, Literature, Experience."
40. Caputo, "On Not Knowing Who We Are," p. 243.
41. Scott, "The Evidence of Experience," p. 408.
42. Deleuze, *Negotiations*, p. 100.
43. Ibid., p. 101.
44. Ibid., p. 100.
45. Nietzsche, *On the Genealogy of Morals*, p. 84.
46. Foucault, *Sexuality One*, 1:43.
47. Ibid., p. 105.
48. Spargo, *Foucault and Queer Theory*, p. 17.
49. Jagose, *Queer Theory*, pp. 11, 10.
50. Corber and Valocchi, "Introduction," p. 10 (emphasis added).
51. Foucault, *Histoire de la sexualité*, 1:59.
52. We find examples of this use of *identity* in Foucault in *The Order of Things* (to describe the Classical episteme of "identities [identités] and differences") and at the end of *Sexuality One* (to describe that aspect of an individual which "joins the force of a drive to the singularity of history"). See Foucault, *The Order of Things*, p. 50; for the French original, see Foucault, *Les Mots et les choses*, p. 64. Also see Foucault, *Sexuality One*, 1:156; for the French original, see Foucault, *Histoire de la sexualité*, 1:205–206.
53. Fassin, "Genre et sexualité," p. 226 (translation mine).
54. Ibid., p. 227.
55. Foucault, *Abnormal*. Many thanks to Mark Jordan for helping me to see this parallel between *Sexuality One* and *Abnormal*, especially in his presentation, "Are There Still Sodomites?" at the Remember Foucault symposium, Emory University, November 2007.
56. Rictor Norton describes Foucault's declaration of the birth of "the queer moment" as "slovenly": "Foucault got it wrong!" Norton gleefully asserts, in a typical irony-deaf reading. See Rictor Norton, "A Critique."
57. Jagose, *Queer Theory*, p. 11.
58. Foucault, *Sexuality One*, 1:35.

59. Ibid., 1:43.
60. Deleuze, *Foucault*, p. 43. This critique in Foucault of the "confinement of the outside" corresponds to what Peter Hallward calls his contestation of "the limits of our specification" (101), in contrast to the Deleuzian singularities that "create their own medium of extension or existence" (93). See Hallward, "The Limits."
61. Deleuze, *Foucault*, p. 54.
62. Foucault, *Sexuality One*, 1:43.
63. Eribon, *Insult*, p. 9.
64. Cvetkovich, *An Archive of Feelings*.
65. Deleuze, *Foucault*, p. 43.
66. Ibid., p. 89.
67. Caputo, "On Not Knowing Who We Are," p. 257.
68. Deleuze, *Negotiations*, pp. 100–101.
69. Halley, *Split Decisions*, p. 59.
70. "Prodigal Son," from the Stones' 1968 album *Beggar's Banquet*, is a remake of the 1929 song by Reverend Robert Wilkins, "That's No Way to Get Along."

First Interlude

1. Nietzsche, *Daybreak*, p. 13.
2. Foucault, "What Is an Author?" 2:207.
3. Hayman, *Nietzsche*, p. 340.
4. Nietzsche, *Daybreak*, p. 14.
5. Ibid., p. 14.
6. Ibid.
7. Hayman, *Nietzsche*, p. 341.
8. Ibid., p. 340.
9. Ibid., p. 11.

2. Queer Moralities

1. Foucault, "Nietzsche, Genealogy, History," 2:369–392.
2. Nietzsche, *Daybreak*, p. 13.
3. Hayman, *Nietzsche*, p. 340.
4. Nietzsche, *Daybreak*, p. 14.
5. "On the other hand, the existence on earth of an animal soul turned against itself, taking sides against itself, was something so new, so profound, unheard of, enigmatic, contradictory, *and pregnant with a future* that the aspect of the earth was essentially altered." Nietzsche, *On the Genealogy of Morals*, p. 85.
6. Hayman, *Nietzsche*, p. 349.
7. Foucault, "Nietzsche, Freud, Marx," 2:275 (translation modified); for the French original, see Foucault, "Nietzsche, Freud, Marx," 1:599.
8. Foucault, "Qui êtes-vous, professeur Foucault?" 1:640–641 (translation mine).

9. Nietzsche, *On the Genealogy of Morals*, p. 19.
10. Foucault, in Droit, *Michel Foucault, entretiens*, p. 113 (translation mine).
11. Ibid., pp. 113–14 (translation mine).
12. Ibid., p. 103 (translation mine).
13. For arguments supporting these various influences see Dreyfus and Rabinow, *Michel Foucault*; Scott, *The Question of Ethics*; Dumm, *Michel Foucault and the Politics of Freedom*; Elden, *Mapping the Present*; Moreno Pestaña, *En devenant Foucault*; and Nealon, *Foucault Beyond Foucault*.
14. Flynn, "Foucault's Mapping of History," p. 43.
15. Dumm, *Michel Foucault and the Politics of Freedom*.
16. Elden, *Mapping the Present*.
17. Philo, *A Geographical History*, pp. 17–50.
18. Foucault, "A Preface to Transgression," 2:70 (translation modified); for the French original, see "Préface à la transgression," 1:261.
19. See especially Allen, "The Anti-Subjective Hypothesis," for an astute analysis of "antisubjectivation" in Foucault. Also see Hallward, "The Limits," for a distinction between Deleuzian and Foucauldian forms of desubjectivation.
20. Deleuze, *Negotiations*, p. 115.
21. Deleuze, *Foucault*, p. 70.
22. In this passage, the crucial term *notre savoir* in the French phrase "le visage que leur reconnaît notre savoir" (*F* 291) disappears in its English translation as "the face that we still recognise today" (*M* 273).
23. Foucault, "A Preface to Transgression," p. 69 (emphasis added, translation modified); "Préface à la transgression," p. 261.
24. Foucault, *History of Sexuality*, 1:156; for the French original, see Foucault, *Histoire de la sexualité*, 1:206.
25. Foucault, *Sexuality One*, 1:157 and 159.
26. Nietzsche, *Daybreak*, p. 14.
27. Sedgwick and Frank, *Shame and Its Sisters*, p. 5.
28. Ibid., p. 5.
29. Ibid., p. 23.
30. Ibid., p. 23.
31. Nietzsche, *On the Genealogy of Morals*, p. 19.
32. Foucault, *Sexuality One*, 1:156 (translation modified); Foucault, *Histoire de la sexualité*, 1:206. The important conceptual correspondence between a Nietzschean *traversal* of violent morality and a psychoanalytic consolidation of that morality as sex *traversed* by a death instinct is lost in the English translation of *Sexuality One*, where the phrase in question reads: "sex is indeed *imbued* with the death instinct" (1:156).
33. Nietzsche, *On the Genealogy of Morals*, p. 21.
34. Dreyfus and Rabinow, *Michel Foucault*, p. 229.
35. Nietzsche, *On the Genealogy of Morals*, p. 23.
36. Deleuze, *Foucault*, p. 97.
37. Hallward, "The Limits of Individuation," p. 102.
38. Foucault, "The Thought of the Outside," p. 152; for the French original, see Foucault, "La Pensée du dehors," 1:551.
39. Foucault, "The Thought of the Outside," p. 152.

2. QUEER MORALITIES 291

40. Nietzsche, *Daybreak*, p. 14.
41. The translation of this phrase into English has been the source of misunderstandings and vehement disputes among historians. Originally translated as
"an easy wandering existence" (18) in the abridged 1965 American edition of
Madness and Civilization, numerous critics of Foucault have seized on this
phrase to align Foucault with the antipsychiatry movement and to label him
as "a thoroughgoing romantic" (Wing, *Reasoning About Madness*, p. 196) with
an unscholarly nostalgia for an age when the insane were happy and free. Roy
Porter similar accuses Foucault of a "romantic primitivism" that celebrates
"those good old days [when] madness really did utter its own truths and engage
in a full dialogue with reason" (Porter, *A Social History of Madness*, p. 14). Erik
Midelfort's (1980) famous critique of this passage is especially puzzling, since
it cites the original French but then grounds its criticisms in the inaccurate
English translation. See Midelfort, "Madness and Civilization." Peter Sedgwick
(1982) and, notoriously, Lawrence Stone (1982) draw extensively on Midelfort's
work to elaborate their critiques of Foucault. See Sedgwick, *Psycho Politics;*
and Stone, "Madness." For an informative overview of this debate, see Gordon, "*Histoire de la folie.*" Also see responses to Gordon by various writers and
Gordon's reply, "History, Madness, and Other Errors." Gordon retranslates the
original French sentence—"Les fous alors avaient une existence facilement
errante" (*F* 19)—as "the existence of the mad at that time could easily be a
wandering one." The solution offered in the new full English translation—
"itinerant existence" (*M* 9)—avoids the problems of the first translation. But it
avoids those problems by simply removing the adverb (*facilement*) that was the
primary cause of consternation and dispute, thereby distorting what Foucault
actually wrote. Moreover, none of the published translations offered thus far
capture the double meaning of *errante* as errancy *and* error, a connotation that
seems particularly important for Foucault's philosophical critique of Cartesian
certainty as the rationalist exclusion of error. Translations are never perfect;
they are destined, by definition, to be metaphorical approximations. Nonetheless, it is not clear to me why an obvious, more literal translation has not been
adopted. I propose, as a simple solution: "easily errant existence." This translation better conveys, it seems to me, what I take to be Foucault's meaning: in
the Renaissance, the mad wandering of the ship of fools symbolizes an ethos
where the divisions between certainty and error were less categorical and less
absolute than during the Age of Reason.
42. Caputo, "On Not Knowing Who We Are," p. 237.
43. Deleuze, *Foucault*, p. 60.
44. This phrase raises another set of translation problems that are not easily
solved. *Le négatif* includes, as the new translation suggests, the connotation of
"something like a photographic negative" as a concrete image of inversion and
reversal. But it also includes the more abstract philosophical connotations of
"the negative" as the oppositional negation that characterizes dialectical thinking. As for *la cité morale*, both possible translations—"the city of morals" or
"the moral city"—are valid, with each carrying slightly different connotations
that are captured together in the ambiguity of the original French phrase. "The
city of morals" suggests an actual environment governed by moral norms;

"the moral city," on the other hand, connotes a more flatly allegorical figure in a symbolic landscape. Since Foucault's geography is "half-real, half-imaginary" (*M* 11/*F* 22; translation modified), to choose one over the other seems inappropriate: an impossible translation.

45. Foucault, "Different Spaces," 2:185.

46. Foucault, "The Thought of the Outside," p. 150.

47. Nietzsche, *On the Genealogy of Morals*, p. 84.

48. It is worth noting that the temporal and spatial terms of this historical chronology follow precisely Foucault's description of normalization in *Discipline and Punish*, from sovereign torture and punishment to the increasingly diffused generalization of a disciplinary society. In Nietzschean terms, *History of Madness* and *Discipline and Punish* are thus historically and conceptually closely aligned. Both books offer powerful counterintuitive readings of the general phenomenon noted by historians of the last two hundred years—"less cruelty, less pain, more kindness, more respect, more 'humanity'" (16), as Foucault puts it in *Discipline and Punish*—by describing the modern internalization of cruelty and pain: first as morality in *Madness*'s "city of morals" (*M* 74), then as panoptical surveillance in *Discipline and Punish*'s "carceral city" (308). In that sense, both books describe the staggering costs of humanist reason. See Foucault, *Discipline and Punish*; for the French original, see Foucault, *Surveiller et punir*.

49. Deleuze, *Foucault*, p. 54.

50. Nietzsche, *Daybreak*, p. 9.

51. In its double connotation as both (moral) conscience and (general) consciousness, the French term *conscience* Foucault uses here presents yet another irresolvable problem of translation. Although the published translation of *Madness* (2006) renders the term as "consciousness," I have modified the translation as "conscience" in accordance with my Nietzschean reading of morality as "bad conscience" in *Madness*. This modification does not deny the validity of its translation as "consciousness," but rather suggests an equally valid possible translation that would support a Nietzschean interpretation of *Madness*. Along related lines, see Walter Kaufmann's comments on Danto's mistranslation of Nietzsche's *Schlechtes Gewissen* as "bad consciousness" in Nietzsche, *On the Genealogy of Morals*, p. 57n1.

52. Deleuze, *Foucault*, p. 60.

53. Ibid.

54. Ibid.

55. Foucault puts this succinctly in his 1982 essay on Pierre Boulez: "What he expected from thought was precisely that it always enable him to do something different from what he was doing. He demanded that it open up, in the highly regulated, very deliberate game that he played, a new space of freedom [*un nouvel espace libre*]." See Foucault, "Pierre Boulez, Passing Through the Screen," 2:244; for the French original, see "Pierre Boulez, l'écran traversé," 2:1041.

56. Nietzsche, *On the Genealogy of Morals*, p. 45.

57. Bell, *Culture and Performance*, p. 11.

58. Ibid.

59. Ibid.

60. This helps to explain Foucault's statement, in *The Order of Things* (1966), that "the end of man . . . is nothing more, and nothing less, than the unfolding of a space in which it is once more possible to think." See Foucault, *The Order of Things*, p. 342; for the French original, see *Les Mots et les choses*.

61. Bell, *Culture and Performance*, p. 11.

62. Ibid., p. 11.

63. Foucault, "The Thought of the Outside," p. 166.

64. Foucault, "A Preface to Transgression," p. 69.

65. Ibid.

66. Ibid., p. 70.

67. This phrase—*limite de notre conscience* (Foucault, "Préface à la transgression," p. 261)—from "A Preface to Transgression" raises the same translation problems as *château de notre conscience* (M 11/F 22; translation modified) in *Madness*. I have retained "consciousness" in the published translation of this essay on Bataille in order to highlight the simultaneity of the limit of our (general) consciousness and the limit of our (moral) conscience. No English translation perfectly captures the nuances of this double meaning.

68. Foucault, "A Preface to Transgression," pp. 69–70; Foucault, "Préface à la transgression," p. 261.

69. Foucault, "A Preface to Transgression," p. 70.

70. Ibid., p. 152.

71. Foucault, "The Thought of the Outside," p. 151.

72. Ibid., p. 152.

73. Ibid.

74. Ibid.

75. Deleuze, *Negotiations*, p. 115.

76. Foucault, "The Thought of the Outside," p. 152.

77. Foucault, "A Preface to Transgression," p. 74 (translation modified); Foucault, "Préface à la transgression," p. 265.

78. Ibid., pp. 78–79 (emphasis added, translation modified); ibid., p. 270.

79. Foucault, "The Thought of the Outside," p. 152. In his reading of *Madness*, Maurice Blanchot similarly asks: "if madness has a language, and if it is even nothing but language, would this language not send us back (as does literature, although at another level) to one of the problems with which our time is dramatically concerned when it seeks to keep together the demands of dialectical discourse and the existence of a non-dialectical language or, more precisely, a non-dialectical experience of language?" See Blanchot, *The Infinite Conversation*, p. 201.

80. Beauvoir, *The Ethics of Ambiguity*, p. 13; for the French original, see *Pour une morale de l'ambiguité*, pp. 17–18.

81. Foucault, "The Thought of the Outside," p. 150 (emphasis added).

82. Butler, *Gender Trouble*, p. x.

83. Ibid., p. xi.

84. Ibid.

85. Ibid., p. 7.
86. Cited in Winnubst, *Queering Freedom*, p. 211.
87. Ibid., p. xi.
88. Nietzsche, *On the Genealogy of Morals*, p. 45.
89. As Sedgwick puts it in her articulation of queer performativity: "there are important senses in which 'queer' can signify only when attached to the first person." Sedgwick, *Tendencies*, p. 9.
90. Butler, *Undoing Gender*, p. 219.
91. Ibid.
92. Ibid.
93. Ibid. (emphasis added).
94. Nietzsche, *On the Genealogy of Morals*, p. 85.
95. Ibid., p. 85.
96. Foucault, "The Thought of the Outside," p. 150.
97. Nietzsche, *On the Genealogy of Morals*, p. 38.
98. Butler, "Imitation and Gender Insubordination," p. 317.
99. See Bersani, "Is the Rectum a Grave?"; Bersani, *Homos*; and Edelman, *No Future*.
100. Nietzsche, *On the Genealogy of Morals*, p. 85.
101. Beauvoir, *The Ethics of Ambiguity*, p. 55.
102. Foucault, "On the Ways of Writing History," 2:289; Foucault, "Sur les façons d'écrire l'histoire," 1:623.
103. Deleuze, *Negotiations*, p. 115.
104. Foucault, "On the Ways of Writing History," p. 291 (translation modified); Foucault, "Sur les façons d'écrire l'histoire," p. 624.
105. Foucault, "The Masked Philosopher," 1:323; for the French original, see Foucault, "Le Philosophe masqué," 2:925.
106. Foucault, "On the Ways of Writing History," p. 289.
107. Ibid. (translation modified); Foucault, "Sur les façons d'écrire l'histoire," p. 623.
108. Foucault, "The Masked Philosopher," 1:325.
109. Foucault, "On the Ways of Writing History," p. 280.
110. Nietzsche, *Daybreak*, p. 14.
111. Foucault, "A Preface to Transgression," p. 75 (translation modified); Foucault, "Préface à la transgression," p. 266.
112. Ibid., p. 74; ibid., p. 266.
113. Foucault, "Structuralism and Post-structuralism," 2:450; for the French original, see "Structuralisme et poststructuralisme," 2:1268.
114. Deleuze, *Foucault*, p. 97.
115. Deleuze, *Negotiations*, p. 115.
116. Foucault, "The Masked Philosopher," 1:323.

Second Interlude

1. Howe, "Pythagorean Silence," *The Europe of Trusts*, p. 17.
2. Ray, *Ecology of a Cracker Childhood*, p. 97.

3. Jamison, *An Unquiet Mind.*
4. Ray, *Ecology of a Cracker Childhood,* p. 79.
5. Descartes, *Meditations,* p. 19.
6. See Foucault, "Different Spaces," 2:175–186.
7. Halperin, *Saint Foucault.*
8. Descartes, *Meditations,* p. 62.

3. Unraveling the Queer Psyche

1. Foucault, *Sexuality One,* 1:113. For French original see Foucault, *Histoire de la sexualité,* 1:149.
2. Foucault, *Sexuality One,* 1:113.
3. For a helpful analysis of Foucault's ventriloquism in *Sexuality One* and its implications for queer theory see Parker, "Foucault's Tongues."
4. Halley, *Split Decisions,* p. 31.
5. Foucault, *Sexuality One,* 1:111.
6. Ibid.
7. Dean and Lane, "Homosexuality and Psychoanalysis," p. 28.
8. Foucault, "The Confession of the Flesh," p. 211 (translation modified); for the French original, see Foucault, "Le Jeu de Michel Foucault," 2:314.
9. Ibid., p. 212 (emphasis added, translation modified); ibid.
10. Ibid.; ibid.
11. Not insignificantly, for the interpretation of this passage, the English translation adds the words *but the fact remains that,* a phrase that does not appear in the original French, where the independent clauses are linked simply with a semicolon, a grammatical hinging marked here in italics: "on peut bien aussi dénoncer le rôle joué depuis des années par l'institution *psychanalytique; dans* cette grande famille des technologies du sexe . . . elle fut, jusqu'aux années 1940, celle qui s'est opposée, rigoureusement, aux effets politiques et institutionnels du système perversion-hérédité-dégénérescence" (157–158). Although minor, the substitution of the rhetorically weighted "but the fact remains that" for a more neutral semicolon tips the back-and-forth of Foucault's negative and positive assertions about Freud in the passage toward a slightly more pro-Freud position.
12. Foucault, *Sexuality One,* 1:119; *Histoire de la sexualité,* 1:157–158; in Dean and Lane, "Homosexuality and Psychoanalysis," p. 10.
13. Foucault, *Sexuality One,* 1:119.
14. Ibid., p. 119.
15. Foucault, "The Confession of the Flesh," p. 212 (translation modified); "Le Jeu de Michel Foucault," p. 314.
16. The original French phrase reads: "Freud a retourné comme un gant la théorie de la dégénérescence" ("Le Jeu de Michel Foucault," p. 314). I have replaced the English translation of *dégénérescence* as "degeneracy" with "degenerescence" in order to reflect its exact repetition in *Sexuality One* as the term Foucault uses to describe the system of perversion-heredity-degenerescence in the passage cited by Dean and Lane.

17. Foucault, "The Confession of the Flesh," p. 209.
18. Elden, *Mapping the Present*, p. 95.
19. Foucault, *Sexuality One*, 1:122.
20. Bersani, "Is the Rectum a Grave?"
21. Rubin, "Thinking Sex."
22. Sedgwick, *Between Men*; Sedgwick, *Epistemology of the Closet*.
23. Butler, *Gender Trouble*.
24. Halberstam, *Female Masculinity*, p. 13. This "queer methodology," Halberstam writes, "uses different methods to collect and produce information on subjects who have been deliberately or accidentally excluded from traditional studies of human behavior. . . . [It] attempts to combine methods that are often cast as being at odds with each other, and it refuses the academic compulsion toward disciplinary coherence" (13).
25. Sedgwick, *Tendencies*, p. 74.
26. Davidson, "Foucault, Psychoanalysis, and Pleasure," p. 45. For the more detailed account of Davidson's argument regarding the historical relationship between Freud and Foucault, see his *The Emergence of Sexuality*, especially chapters 1, 2, 3, and 8. Davidson's essay in the Dean and Lane volume appears as an appendix in *The Emergence of Sexuality*.
27. Davidson, "Foucault, Psychoanalysis, and Pleasure," p. 45.
28. Ibid., pp. 43–44.
29. Eribon, *Insult*, p. 272.
30. Ibid., p. 273.
31. Eribon, *Echapper à la psychanalyse*, p. 86 (translation mine).
32. Derrida, "'To Do Justice to Freud,'" p. 234. For the French original, see Derrida, "'Etre juste avec Freud,'" p. 150.
33. Ibid., p. 228.
34. Ibid., p. 234; Derrida, "Etre juste avec Freud," p. 150.
35. Ibid.; ibid.
36. Derrida, "To Do Justice to Freud," p. 234. It is worth pointing out the obvious here, which is that neither Derrida nor Davidson is a queer theorist. Derrida's position vis-à-vis Foucault is well known; as for Davidson, his work on Foucault (especially *The Emergence of Sexuality*) and his role as editor of the English translations of the Collège de France lectures make his relationship to Foucault significant as well.
37. Davidson, "Foucault, Psychoanalysis, and Pleasure," p. 43 (emphasis added).
38. Both the 2006 and 1965 translations render the French word *conjuration* as "exorcism," thus avoiding the confusions that might result from a literal rendering of the word as the English *conjuration*. However, it is worth asking why Foucault repeatedly uses the French word *conjuration* and never the French term *exorcisme* with which it is almost, but not quite, synonymous. *Conjuration* presents us with something of a puzzle, especially when we set about to translate it into English. For, in English, *conjuration* means a *summoning* or invocation of supernatural forces. This meaning would appear to reverse, as one of those nasty *faux amis*, the French meaning of *conjuration* as exorcism—a *driving out* of evil forces. However, this knotty problem of translating *conjura-*

3. UNRAVELING THE QUEER PSYCHE 297

tion—for which there is no obvious solution—might serve, happily if inadvertently, to highlight Foucault's clear insistence that the Cartesian method is *both* an exorcism and an invocation: a driving out (*ex*-orcism) that assumes a prior summoning (*con*-juration) through the imaginative, ritualistic, repeated incantations that constitute systematic doubt.

39. Insisting, as I have in the preceding note 38, on the paradoxical meanings of *conjuration* and *exorcism*, I have substituted the verb *exorcized* for *banished* in the published English translation to more accurately render the double meaning of Foucault's original term, *conjurée*. In addition, as this chapter demonstrates, the repetition of the French terms *conjuration* and *conjurer* over the course of *Madness* semantically and conceptually binds Descartes to Freud. That insistent terminological repetition is lost in the English translation.

40. Again, the stream of "conjurations" I'm tracing here is lost in the English translation of *conjurer* as "taming."

41. The words *stuprati* (debauched), *constupratores* (mutual debauchers), and *stupri* (debauchery) repeat the language of Augustine and Justinian. In the 2006 English translation of the Latin phrases, the homoerotic meanings of the terms are lost. Many thanks to Mark Jordan for help with the translation and its patristic contexts.

42. Peter Hallward articulates a similar point in his analysis of Foucauldian despecification: "Madness itself has nothing to say, it does not itself *speak*. It simply interrupts, contests, and despecifies." See Hallward, "The Limits," p. 103.

43. Deleuze, *Foucault*, p. 85.

44. Foucault, "The Confession of the Flesh," p. 212.

45. The nuances of Foucault's repeated use of the phrase *half-real, half-imaginary* ("mi-réel, mi-imaginaire") to describe both the Renaissance navigation of the ship of fools (*M* 11/*F* 22) and the Freudian oedipal family (*M* 490/*F* 510) are lost in the English translation's rendering of the former as simply "real and imaginary" (*M* 11).

46. Deleuze, *Foucault*, p. 54.

47. Ibid., p. 85.

48. Foucault, *Sexuality One*, 1:130.

49. Ibid., 1:144.

50. Ibid., 1:130 (emphasis added).

51. In this specific way, Foucault's identification of psychoanalytic objectification as "patriarchal" anticipates important feminist arguments like those of Catherine MacKinnon about the relationship between scientific "objectivity" and the patriarchal "objectification" of women. See especially MacKinnon's *Toward a Feminist Theory of the State* for a full elaboration of this argument.

52. Foucault, "Philosophie et psychologie," 1:469.

53. In the 1965 interview Foucault says specifically: "This problem of the unconscious is very difficult. . . . That which, up to the present, had been excluded from a properly psychological problematic [physiology and the body, sociology and the individual with his milieu and his group] was brought together into the interior. . . . The simple discovery of the unconscious is not an addition of

domains, not an extension of psychology, but rather the *confiscation*, by psychology, of the majority of the domains covered by the human sciences. . . . . *After Freud* all of the human sciences became, in one way or another, sciences of the psyche. . . . Our body is part of our psyche. . . . At bottom, *now there is no longer anything but psychology*" ("Philosophie et psychologie," p. 469; emphasis added, translation mine). This passage highlights not only the obvious parallels between the two "confiscations" of the human by psychoanalysis and family morality but also Foucault's unambiguous description of Freudian psychoanalysis as part of the project of psychology.

54. Foucault, *Sexuality One*, 1:101; Foucault, *Histoire de la sexualité*, 1:104.

55. Foucault, *Sexuality One*, 1:101.

56. Ibid., p. 31.

57. In his 1974–75 course, "Les Anormaux," Foucault describes at greater length some of the details of the case of Charles Jouy and the little girl, whose name we learn is Sophie Adam. In *Abnormal* we also learn that there were two separate incidents involving Charles and Sophie that are merged in *Sexuality One*: the first, the game of "curdled milk," involved a second, unnamed little girl who watched as Charles got Sophie to masturbate him. In a subsequent incident a few days later, Charles dragged Sophie "(unless it was Sophie Adam who dragged Charles Jouy)" (292) into a ditch where "something happened: almost rape, perhaps" (292). As we can see, even in this more detailed narrative about the Jouy story, the problem of the gender asymmetries that frame questions of consent and sexual violence remain disturbingly undertheorized and unresolved. Foucault's own uncertainty regarding these feminist questions is reflected in his description of an "almost" happening whose almost victim was "more or less raped" (303). See Foucault, *Abnormal*.

58. In his 1954 introduction to Ludwig Binswanger's *Dream and Existence*, Foucault writes: "Dora got better, not despite the interruption of the psychoanalysis, but because, by deciding to break it off, she went the whole distance to that solitude toward which until then her existence had been only an indecisive movement" (56). See Foucault and Binswanger, *Dream and Existence*.

59. Freeman, "Time Binds," pp. 67 and 59.

60. Villarejo, "Tarrying with the Normative," 71 and 69.

61. Eng, *Racial Castration*, p. 50.

62. Bersani, *Homos*, p. 98. To be fair, I should point out that Bersani recognizes Foucault's conception of pleasure as being "decidedly nonpsychoanalytic" (99), although he goes on, regardless, in a classic Freudo-Foucauldian vein, to link Freudian masochism with the Foucauldian undoing of the subject through pleasure. Bersani's Freudo-Foucauldianism is also apparent in his early article "Is the Rectum a Grave?" (1987).

63. Butler, *The Psychic Life of Power*, p. 87.

64. Sedgwick, *Touching Feeling*, p. 129.

65. For a helpful overview of *The Psychic Life of Power* within the context of Butler's oeuvre as a whole, see Kirby, *Judith Butler*.

66. Butler, *The Psychic Life of Power*, p. 3.

67. Moreno Pestaña, *En devenant Foucault*.

68. Sedgwick, *Touching Feeling*, p. 9.

69. Ibid., p. 150.
70. Muñoz, *Disidentifications*.
71. Cited in Butler, *The Psychic Life of Power*, p. 97. For original context, see Rose, "Femininity and Its Discontents," pp. 90–91.
72. Dean and Lane, "Homosexuality and Psychoanalysis," p. 5.
73. Ibid., p. 4.
74. Brown, *States of Injury*.
75. Deleuze, *Negotiations*, p. 115.
76. Sedgwick, *A Dialogue on Love*.
77. Foucault, *Abnormal*, p. 304.
78. Sedgwick, *Epistemology of the Closet*, p. 22.
79. Beauvoir, *The Ethics of Ambiguity*, p. 55.
80. Sedgwick, *Touching Feeling*, p. 63.
81. Ibid., p. 64
82. Ibid., p. 38.
83. Ibid., p. 7.
84. Sedgwick, *The Coherence of Gothic Conventions*, p. xi.
85. Sedgwick, *Touching Feeling*, p. 146.
86. Ibid., p. 137.
87. Ibid.
88. Eng, Halberstam, and Muñoz, "Introduction," 15.
89. Perez, "You Can Have My Brown Body!" 183 and 174.
90. Sedgwick, *Touching Feeling*, p. 143.
91. Ibid., p. 96.
92. Ibid., p. 103.
93. Butler, *Giving an Account of Oneself*, pp. 7–8.
94. Foucault, "Different Spaces," p. 177.
95. Nietzsche, *On the Genealogy of Morals*, p. 21.
96. Ibid.
97. Ibid.

Third Interlude

1. Eribon, *Insult*, pp. 251–252.
2. Foucault, *Mental Illness and Psychology*, p. 26.
3. Jamison, *An Unquiet Mind*, p. 90.
4. Foucault, *Mental Illness and Psychology*, p. 27.
5. Eribon, *Insult*, p. 254.
6. Foucault, cited ibid.

4. A Queer Nephew

1. Foucault, "Lives of Infamous Men," 3:171. For French original see Foucault, "La vie des hommes infâmes," 2:250.
2. Hegel, *Phenomenology of Spirit*, p. 317.

3. Ibid., p. 316.
4. Habermas, "The Critique of Reason," p. 243.
5. Nietzsche, *Daybreak*, pp. 13–14.
6. Jacques Derrida invokes him briefly in his 1991 defense of Freud, "'To Do Justice to Freud,'" pp. 227–266; and Karlis Racevskis devotes a twelve-page article to him in "Michel Foucault, Rameau's Nephew." Diderot's place in *Madness* is briefly mentioned in Simon During's *Foucault and Literature*, p. 37, although the work in question is incorrectly identified as *Jacques le Fataliste*.
7. In the 1965 English translation of *Madness* as *Madness and Civilization*, both the epigraph from Diderot—"I was, for them, an entire Petites-Maisons"—and all but the first two paragraphs of Foucault's analysis of *Rameau's Nephew* have been removed.
8. As critics have pointed out, in the late 1970s Foucault began to modify his anti-Enlightenment rhetoric. Especially in the last of his three essays devoted to Kant's "What Is Enlightenment?" Foucault revisits Enlightenment thinking as "a mode of relating to contemporary reality" (309) that includes "thinking and feeling," "acting and behaving," "a relation of belonging," and "a task": "a bit like what the Greeks called an *ethos*" (309). Less a historical period than an attitude, for Foucault Enlightenment thinking becomes "a type of philosophical interrogation" or "philosophical ethos that could be described as a permanent critique of our historical era" (312). Although some would see this relatively generous view of the Enlightenment as diametrically opposed to Foucault's more hostile position of the 1960s and early-to-mid 1970s, Foucault's focus on the Nephew alludes precisely to the possibility of an ethos of critique within the Enlightenment that the later essay makes more explicit. Throughout his career, from *Madness* to the Kant essays, Foucault consistently defines the task of philosophy as the critical thinking of our historical present. See Foucault, "What Is Enlightenment?" For a similar view on the continuity between the 1984 Kant essay and Foucault's lifelong critique of the subject, see Nealon, *Foucault Beyond Foucault*, especially pp. 13–17.
9. Diderot, *Rameau's Nephew*, p. 36.
10. Here my argument differs from that of Racevskis, who finds in the Nephew's lack of hypocrisy a power of disclosure: "Rameau's rantings have the effect of *disclosing* the pretentiousness of Reason and its claims to Truth" (Racevskis, "Michel Foucault, Rameau's Nephew," p. 25; emphasis added). Foucault's clear distinction between the traditional fool's and the Nephew's relation to truth suggests a more complex relationship.
11. Nietzsche, *Daybreak*, p. 60.
12. Foucault, *Abnormal*, p. 250.
13. Diderot, *Rameau's Nephew*, p. 51.
14. Hutcheon, *Irony's Edge*, p. 15.
15. Ibid., p. 37.
16. Ibid.
17. Sedgwick, "Privilege of Unknowing," pp. 23–51.
18. Hutcheon, *Irony's Edge*, p. 120.
19. Ibid., p. 43.

20. Ibid.
21. Ibid., p. 10.
22. Many thanks to Mark Jordan for pointing out the significance of this etymology for understanding Foucault's relation to *Rameau's Nephew* and Horace's *Satires*; Diderot uses the latter—which stages a pre-Hegelian lord-bondsman dialectic in a dialogue between Horace and his slave—as a model for his own satire.
23. Diderot, *Rameau's Nephew*, p. 39.
24. Ibid., p. 115; Diderot, *Le Neveu de Rameau*, p. 98.
25. Diderot, *Rameau's Nephew*, p. 40.
26. Ibid., p. 87 (translation modified); Diderot, *Le Neveu de Rameau*, p. 65. Diderot's French is rendered differently in the various translations of the *Nephew* and its redoubling in *Madness*. Excised completely from the 1965 English translation of *Folie et déraison* as *Madness and Civilization*, in the 2006 full translation of *History of Madness* the Petites-Maisons epigraph is restored in English as "for them, I was the incarnation of the Petites-Maisons" (*M* 343). Leonard Tancock's 1964 translation of Diderot renders the sentence as "I supplied them with a complete madhouse" (Diderot, *Rameau's Nephew*, p. 87), while Margaret Mauldon's 2006 version translates it as "they saw me as a complete lunatic asylum of their very own" (Diderot, *Rameau's Nephew and First Satire*, p. 53). But, as my modification of the English translation of Diderot suggests, the queer specificity of "Petites-Maisons" in both Diderot and Foucault is crucial.
27. Diderot, *Rameau's Nephew*, p. 46; Diderot, *Le Neveu de Rameau*, p. 18.
28. Derrida, "'To Do Justice to Freud,'" p. 234; Derrida, "'Etre juste avec Freud,'" p. 150.
29. Kristeva, "La Musique parlée," p. 154 (translation mine).
30. Foucault, "Different Spaces," 2:185. In this 1967 essay, Foucault describes his concept of "heterotopias" as "sorts of places that are outside all places, although they are actually localizable" (178). They are "real places, actual places . . . sorts of actually realized utopias in which . . . all the other real emplacements that can be found within the culture are, at the same time, represented, contested, and reversed" (ibid.). Foucault's description of heterotopias repeats the "half-real, half-imaginary" characterization of the ship of fools in *Madness* as a contestation of the limit that echoes "Preface to Transgression" and "The Thought of the Outside": "These different spaces, these other places [are] a kind of *contestation, both mythical and real*, of the space in which we live" (179; emphasis added). And finally, Foucault asserts that "the sailing vessel is the heterotopia par excellence" (185): "a piece of floating space, a placeless place, that lives by its own devices, that is self-enclosed and, at the same time, delivered over to the boundless expanse of the ocean" (184–185).
31. Foucault, *The Order of Things*, p. 383; Foucault, *Les Mots et les choses*, p. 395.
32. In a 1984 interview, Foucault admits to his partial agreement with Habermas's work, confining his criticims of Habermas to what he sees as its utopianism: "I have always had a problem [with Habermas] insofar as he gives communicative relations this place which is so important and, above all, a function that I

would call 'utopian.' The idea that there could exist a state of communication that would allow games of truth to circulate freely, without any constraints or coercive effects, seems utopian to me. . . . The problem . . . is not to try to dissolve [power relations] in the utopia of completely transparent communication but to acquire the rules of law, the management techniques, and also the morality, the ethos, the practice of the self, that will allow us to play these games of power with as little domination as possible." See Foucault, "The Ethics of the Concern for Self," 1:298.

33. Foucault, *The Order of Things*, p. xviii; Foucault, *Les Mots et les choses*, p. 9.
34. Foucault, *The Order of Things*, p. xvii.
35. Gros, "De Borges à Magritte," p. 17 (translation mine).
36. Foucault, *The Order of Things*, p. xvii.
37. Foucault, "Different Spaces," p. 178.
38. Ibid., pp. 184–185.
39. Foucault, *The Order of Things*, p. xviii; Foucault, *Les Mots et les choses*, p. 9.
40. Foucault, *The Order of Things*, p. xix.
41. Foucault, "A Preface to Transgression," 2:74. See Nigro, "Foucault lecteur critique," for a useful explanation of how Bataille's notion of transgression in Foucault contests the positive-negative duality of the Hegelian dialectic.
42. Foucault, "The Discourse on Language," p. 235. The full quote reads: "We have to determine the extent to which our anti-Hegelianism is possibly one of his tricks directed against us, at the end of which he stands motionless, waiting for us."
43. See Schmidt, "The Fool's Truth," for an interesting consideration of the *Phenomenology* in light of the fact that "the words Hegel appropriated were not, strictly speaking, Diderot's" (626). Other commentators on Hegel's use of *Rameau's Nephew* include Jauss, "The Dialogical and the Dialectical"; Hulbert, "Diderot in the Text of Hegel"; Price, "Hegel's Intertextual Dialectic"; Gearhart, "The Dialectic and Its Aesthetic Other"; and Gearhart, *The Interrupted Dialectic*.
44. Hegel, *Phenomenology of Spirit*, p. 317.
45. Ibid.
46. Ibid., p. 318.
47. Foucault, "The Death of Lacan," p. 57.
48. Gearhart, "The Dialectic and Its Aesthetic Other," p. 1049.
49. Ibid., p. 1051.
50. Hegel, *Phenomenology of Spirit*, p. 317.
51. Felman, "Foucault/Derrida," p. 66.
52. Gearhart, "The Dialectic and Its Aesthetic Other," p. 1051.
53. Ibid., p. 1045.
54. Hegel, *Phenomenology of Spirit*, p. 485.
55. Lacoue-Labarthe, "L'Imprésentable," p. 54 (translation mine).
56. Felman, "Foucault/Derrida," p. 65.
57. Ibid., p. 60.
58. It is worth pointing out that to say madness cannot speak is different than saying, as Felman does, that madness "has no proper meaning" (68). Felman's rhetorical point about the "radical metaphoricity" of madness grounds itself

in a deconstructive, textual understanding of absence and presence that aligns her with Derrida rather than Foucault.

59. The best overview of literature in the work of Foucault is Simon During's *Foucault and Literature* (1992). During argues that if the "long story of madness is deeply embedded in the history of literature" (41), in Foucault "one finds and examines a different literariness than that proposed by traditional literary studies. It helps form no sensibility, no set of appreciative and evaluative responses to culture, no indviduals who may serve as exemplars to the young and who may be reproduced by them" (237). If During distinguishes Foucault from traditionalists, he also differentiates his take on literature from "a certain deconstruction" (42). Unlike writers like Derrida and Felman, Foucault "does not permit us to think of texts as mad in their 'undecidability'" (ibid.). Also see O'Leary, "Foucault, Experience, Literature," who argues that Foucault helps us to understand how literature can "force us to think otherwise" (5).

60. During, *Foucault and Literature*, p. 42.

61. Foucault, "A Preface to Transgression," pp. 78–79 (translation modified); Michel Foucault, "Préface à la transgression," p. 270.

62. Creech, "*Le Neveu de Rameau*," p. 996.

63. Sedgwick, *Tendencies*, p. 59.

64. Creech, "*Le Neveu de Rameau*," p. 996.

65. Diderot, *Rameau's Nephew*, p. 116; Diderot, *Le Neveu de Rameau*, p. 99.

66. Foucault, "Jean Hyppolite," 1:808 (translation mine).

67. Ibid. (translation mine).

68. Ibid., p. 807 (translation mine).

69. See Foucault, "Nietzsche, Genealogy, History."

70. Macey, *The Lives of Michel Foucault*, p. 233.

71. Hyppolite, *Génèse et structure*, 1:399 (translation mine).

72. Diderot, *Rameau's Nephew*, p. 3 (translation modified); Diderot, *Le Neveu de Rameau*, p. 3. Both Leonard Tancock's 1964 English rendering and Margaret Mauldon's 2006 revised English translation of *Rameau's Nephew* prudishly alter the meaning of the French *catins*, an eighteenth-century term for "whores," into something less shocking to an Anglophone audience: "wenches" (33) in Tancock and "little flirts" (3) in Mauldron. But even as conservative a scholar as Georges Poulet recognizes the less prudish meaning of *catin*, translating the original sentence, "Mes pensées, ce sont mes catins," as "My thoughts are my whores." Poulet, "Phenomenology of Reading," p. 56.

73. Foucault, "Different Spaces," p. 185.

74. See Moreno Pestaña, *En devenant Foucault* for a detailed Bourdieuian analysis of Foucault's early formation and, especially, the crucial years at the ENS in this high-stakes academic game.

75. Macey, *The Lives of Michel Foucault*, p. 26.

76. Ibid., p. 30.

77. Ibid., p. 30.

78. In Felman, "Foucault/Derrida," pp. 51–52.

79. Berthold-Bond, *Hegel's Theory of Madness*, p. 143. Berthold-Bond's book on madness in Hegel is based on the two-page section devoted to the topic in the

Encyclopedia of Philosophical Sciences (1817) and on lecture manuscripts and course notes gathered together by one of Hegel's students in 1845. Although Berthold-Bond devotes a chapter to the difference between Hegel's "pure ontology of madness" (179) and the social constructionist theories of Foucault and Szasz, he does not mention Foucault's treatment of the Nephew in *History of Madness*, asserting, incorrectly, that Foucault "never spoke of Hegel's theory of madness" (179). This omission may be explained by the excision of the Nephew from the abbreviated translation of *Madness* cited by Berthold-Bond.

80. Derrida, "'To Do Justice to Freud,'" p. 244.
81. Derrida, "Cogito and History of Madness," p. 55 (translation modified); Derrida, "Cogito et histoire de la folie," p. 85.
82. Ibid., p. 62; ibid., p. 96.
83. Foucault, *Psychiatric Power*; Foucault, "Sexuality and Solitude." Foucault omits both the repetition of names and the crucial detail about diarrhea from the published essay, "Sexuality and Solitude," focusing solely on the cold shower that causes "Mr. A" to cry at last, "Yes, yes! I am mad!" (175).
84. Foucault, *Psychiatric Power*, p. 157.
85. Deleuze, *Foucault*, p. 54.
86. Foucault, "Different Spaces," p. 179.
87. Ibid., p. 178.
88. Ibid., p. 179 (emphasis added).
89. Deleuze, *Foucault*, p. 97.
90. Foucault, "Different Spaces," p. 180.
91. Ibid., p. 179.
92. Foucault, cited in Canguilhem, "On 'Histoire de la folie' as an Event," p. 284.
93. Diderot, *Rameau's Nephew*, p. 103 (translation modified); Diderot, *Le Neveu de Rameau*, p. 84.
94. Foucault, "Different Spaces," p. 179.
95. Diderot, *Rameau's Nephew*, p. 43.
96. Foucault, "The Masked Philosopher," 1:324.
97. Ibid., 1:323.
98. See Hallward, "The Limits," on the distinction between a Deleuzian philosophy of singularities that include the virtual—a philosophy without limits—and a Foucauldian philosophy of the specific—a philosophy of the limit.
99. Derrida repeatedly invokes "justice" to distinguish himself from Foucault, not only in the 1991 essay "'To Do Justice to Freud'" but also in his famous 1963 response to *Madness*. Just as Derrida, in 1991, accuses Foucault of unjustly putting Freud on trial, so too in "Cogito and History of Madness" he denounces *Madness* for inappropriately putting reason on trial: "an impossible trial [*un procès impossible*], for by the fact of their articulation the proceedings and the verdict unceasingly reiterate the crime" (35/58; translation modified).
100. Diderot, *Rameau's Nephew*, p. 121.
101. Ibid.
102. Ibid.
103. Sloterdijk, *Critique of Cynical Reason*, p. 160.
104. Diderot, *Rameau's Nephew*, p. 49 (translation modified); Diderot, *Le Neveu de Rameau*, p. 21. The original French reads: "Entendons nous; c'est qu'il y a baiser le cul au simple, et baiser le cul au figuré."

105. For an example of queer theory's current movement toward a postsexual thinking, see the special "after sex" issue of *South Atlantic Quarterly* 106, no. 3 (Summer 2007), ed. Janet Halley and Andrew Parker.

106. Kristeva, "La Musique parlée," p. 174 (translation mine).

107. Foucault, "Jean Hyppolite," p. 809 (translation mine).

108. As Berthold-Bond points out, it was Hyppolite who argued, quite controversially, that "madness is a key underlying theme of the *Phenomenology*." Berthold-Bond, *Hegel's Theory of Madness*, p. 195.

109. In his 14 March 1984 lecture Foucault offers as a primary illustration of the nondissimulated life (*la vie non-dissimulée*), or *alethes bios* of the Cynics, the example of Diogenes masturbating in public. With this nondissimulated life, "the philosophical life [of the Cynics] appears as radically other to all other forms of life." Foucault, "Le Courage de la vérité," 14 March 1984, CD 69 (08).

110. Diderot, *Rameau's Nephew*, p. 123.

111. Sloterdijk, *Critique of Cynical Reason*, p. 104. Foucault, like Sloterdijk, points to the common characterization of cynicism as "a form of unreason." Foucault, "Le Courage de la vérité," 7 March 1984, CD 69 (06). In the same lecture, Foucault in fact mentions Sloterdijk's book, which appeared in German in 1983, but confesses to not having read it.

112. For a book-length examination of the Cynic's role in eighteenth-century France, see Shea's *The Cynic Enlightenment*, and especially chapter 8: "Cynicism as Critical Vanguard: Foucault's Last Lecture Course."

113. Diderot, *Rameau's Nephew*, p. 52. Jean Fabre, the editor of the 1950 French edition of *Le Neveu de Rameau*, points out that with this phrase, "precious fertilizer," the Nephew puts an unexpected twist on an ancient agricultural adage. See Jean Fabre, n. 84, in Diderot, *Le Neveu de Rameau*, p. 159.

114. Foucault, "Le Courage de la vérité," 21 March 1984, CD 69 (08).

115. Shea, *The Cynic Enlightenment*, p. 116.

116. Foucault, "Le Courage de la vérité," 21 March 1984, CD 69 (08) (translation mine).

117. Shea, *The Cynic Enlightenment*, p. 122.

118. Foucault, "Le Courage de la vérité," 1 February 1984, CD 69 (01).

119. Ibid. (translation mine). Foucault continues in the same lecture: "*Parrhesia* is thus in two words the courage of truth, the courage of truth in the one who speaks and who takes the risk to say, despite everything, all the truth he is thinking, but it's also the courage on the part of the interlocutor who agrees to receive, as true, the wounding truth he hears."

120. Foucault, "Le Courage de la vérité," 14 March 1984, CD 69 (08) (translation mine).

121. Ibid. (translation mine).

122. Sloterdijk, *Critique of Cynical Reason*, p. 105.

123. Foucault, "The Ethics of the Concern for Self," p. 284.

124. Ibid., p. 284.

125. Sloterdijk, *Critique of Cynical Reason*, p. 103.

126. Ibid, p. 102.

127. Foucault, "Le Courage de la vérité," 21 March 1984, CD 69 (08).

128. Foucault, "What Is Enlightenment?" p. 311. Foucault cites Baudelaire, who cites the artist Constantin Guys, in the section of "What Is Enlightenment"

where Foucault describes a Baudelairean "attitude of modernity" that, lingering at the Romantic place of passion's "*pose*" (311), opens the way to an ironic heroization of the present. This alternative description of an ironic romanticism might correspond to what Foucault describes as one of the forms of a "transhistorical cynicism" in the "revolutionary militantism" of the nineteenth century. See Foucault, "Le Courage de la vérité," 7 March 1984,, CD 69 (06) (translation mine).

129. In his 21 March 1984 lecture, Foucault describes the Cynic as the *veilleur universel*, a universal watchman whose *surveillance* of humanity takes care of the care of the other: "Prendre en souci le souci des hommes." Foucault's transformative play with the verb to watch over (*veiller*)—a verb we might recognize in the modern disciplinary *surveillance* of *Discipline and Punish* (*Surveiller et punir*)—brings attention to Foucault's use of the same verb in his 1969 tribute to Hyppolite. There, we may recall, *veiller* described a contact of the philosophical with the nonphilosophical as "a light which kept watch [*veillait*] even before there was any discourse, a blade [*lame*] which still shines even as it enters into sleep." See Foucault, "Jean Hyppolite," p. 808 (translation mine).

130. Foucault, "Le Courage de la vérité," 14 March 1984, CD 69 (08) (translation mine).

131. Foucault, "Different Spaces," p. 179.

Fourth Interlude

1. Eribon, *Insult*, p. 251.
2. Ibid., p. 392n7.
3. Foucault, *History of Sexuality*, 2:7.
4. Foucault, "Entretien avec Roger-Pol Droit," p. 44 (translation mine).
5. Eribon, *Insult*, p. 251.
6. See Foucault, *History of Sexuality*, 1:77, for his discussion of Denis Diderot's *Bijoux indiscrets* and one of society's "emblems," the "talking sex" (77).
7. Foucault, "Entretien avec Roger-Pol Droit," p. 48 (translation mine).
8. Ibid. (translation mine).
9. Foucault, "Je suis un artificier," in Droit, *Michel Foucault, entretiens*, p. 103; Foucault, "Entretien avec Roger-Pol Droit," p. 50 (translation mine).
10. Ibid., p. 105; ibid., p. 51 (translation mine).
11. Ibid., p. 102; ibid., p. 58 (translation mine).
12. Foucault, "Entretien avec Roger-Pol Droit," p. 90 (translation mine).
13. Ibid., pp. 42–43 (translation mine).
14. Ibid., p. 43 (translation mine).

5. A Political Ethic of Eros

1. Foucault, *The Hermeneutics of the Subject*, p. 95.
2. Foucault, "Politics and Ethics," p. 374.
3. Oksala, *Foucault on Freedom*, p. 173.

4. Foucault, *The Hermeneutics of the Subject*, p. 213.
5. Nietzsche, *The Gay Science*, p. 240.
6. On an erotic ethics in Beauvoir see Bergoffen, *The Philosophy of Simone de Beauvoir*, especially chapters 1, 5, and 6; on Irigaray see Chanter, *Ethics of Eros;* and Willett, "This Poem That Is My Body," pp. 123–156; also see Lorde, "Uses of the Erotic," pp. 53–59.
7. Scott, *The Question of Ethics*, p. 1.
8. For a helpful overview of Foucault's ethics, see O'Leary, *Foucault and the Art of Ethics*. Although I generally agree with O'Leary's characterization of Foucault's ethics as a process of self-making and unmaking, I disagree with his pro-Enlightenment conclusion that Foucault's ethical "affirmation of freedom places him firmly in the tradition of *les lumières*" (17.) For feminist perspectives on Foucault's ethics, see Taylor and Vintges, *Feminism and the Final Foucault*. Many of the contributions to this volume interpret Foucault's reading of the ancient world as an ethical model for contemporary contexts (consciousness-raising groups, Alcoholics Anonymous, queer sexual freedom, women's health counseling, feminist identity politics, the Mothers of the Plaza de Mayo). In doing so, some of the arguments reinstall an autonomous, individual Enlightenment subject at the heart of Foucault's ethics. See, for example, Helen O'Grady's argument ("An Ethics of the Self," pp. 91–117) that Foucault "believes the contemporary climate is ripe for a return to *a more individual-based ethics*" (101; emphasis added) or Jana Sawicki's claim ("Foucault's Pleasures," pp. 163–182) that Foucault's thinking about sexual pleasure involved "an expanded understanding of *erotic autonomy*" (180; emphasis added) that gives us a "positive account of sexual freedom" (165).
9. Foucault, "Le Retour à la morale," 2:1525 (translation mine).
10. Foucault, "The Ethics of the Concern for Self," 1:289–290.
11. Ibid., p. 290.
12. Foucault, "A Preface to Transgression," 2:70.
13. Foucault, "Lives of Infamous Men," 3:158.
14. Rajchman, *Truth and Eros*, p. 1.
15. Ibid., p. 1.
16. Ibid., p. 88.
17. Ibid., p. 140.
18. Ibid., p. 141.
19. Ibid.
20. Foucault, "Le Courage de la vérité," 1 February 1984, CD 69 (01) (translation mine).
21. Foucault, "Different Spaces," 2:179.
22. Ibid., p. 179.
23. Rajchman, *Truth and Eros*, p. 1.
24. Foucault, "Lives of Infamous Men," 3:157.
25. For an overview of contemporary molecular biopolitics see Rose, *The Politics of Life Itself*. Drawing on Foucault, Rose argues that "biopower is more a perspective than a concept: it brings into view a whole range of more or less rationalized attempts by different authorities to intervene upon the vital characteristic of human existence" (54).

26. Foucault, "Lives of Infamous Men," 3:162.
27. Ibid., 3:160; for the French original, see Foucault, "La Vie des hommes infâmes," 2:240.
28. Foucault, "The Ethics of the Concern for Self," 1:298.
29. Ibid.
30. Ibid.
31. Ibid.
32. Elden, *Mapping the Present*, p. 95.
33. In "Different Spaces," Foucault contrasts archives with museums and libraries. "Museums and libraries are heterotopias in which time never ceases to pile up and perch on its own summit" (182) and, so doing, become "heterochronias" (182). "By contrast, the idea of accumulating everything, the idea of constituting a sort of *general archive*, the desire to contain all times, all ages, all forms, all tastes in one place, the idea of constituting a place of all times that is itself outside time and protected from its erosion" (182) is, by implication, not heterotopian. From this perspective, Foucault's approach to the archive is an attempt to introduce the movement of "temporal discontinuities" (ibid.) into the modern archival "accumulation of time in a place that will not move" (ibid.). See Foucault, "Different Spaces," p. 182.
34. Ibid.
35. Rajchman, *Truth and Eros*, p. 2.
36. Ibid.
37. Ibid.
38. Ibid., p. 27.
39. Foucault, "The Ethics of the Concern for Self," p. 284.
40. Ibid., p. 300; for French the original, see "L'éthique du souci de soi," 2:1548.
41. Oksala, *Foucault on Freedom*, p. 188.
42. Like Oksala, Hirschmann implies that freedom is not an ontological condition of the subject. Foucault's vision, she argues, is "not the attainment of a 'free state,' as if freedom were a quality one could possess or a condition that one could attain." But she nonetheless insists on linking freedom to a subjectivating project at odds with Foucault's insistence on self-undoing. As Hirschmann puts it: "freedom is a model of activity and thought in which people participate by engaging in practices *that create the self.*" See Hirschmann, *The Subject of Liberty*, p. 211 (emphasis added).
43. Ibid., p. 188.
44. Foucault, "Different Spaces," p. 192.
45. Foucault, *Sexuality One*, 1:145.
46. Foucault, *Sexuality One*, 1:143 (translation modified); for the French original, see Foucault, *Histoire de la sexualité*, 1:188.
47. Rose, *The Politics of Life Itself*, p. 4.
48. A notable exception to this is Jasbir Puar's work on "homonationalism" within the frame of biopower. However, following Judith Butler and Achille Mbembe, Puar misreads Foucauldian biopower as a "constant march forward, *away from death*" (27; emphasis added). This description of biopower's denial of death contradicts Foucault's own description of biopower not only in *Sexuality One*

but also in his 17 March 1976 course, where he links racism to "the *death-function* in the economy of biopower" (258; emphasis added). See Puar, *Terrorist Assemblages*; Butler, "Sexual Inversions"; Mbembe, "Necropolitics" ; and Foucault, *Society Must Be Defended*.

49. Foucault, "The Confession of the Flesh," p. 222.
50. Butler, *Gender Trouble*, p. 106.
51. Butler, "Sexual Inversions," p. 88.
52. Foucault, *Sexuality One*, 1:136.
53. Ibid.
54. Ibid. (emphasis added).
55. Ibid.
56. Ibid., p. 138.
57. Butler, "Sexual Inversions," p. 85.
58. Foucault, *Sexuality One*, 1:139.
59. Ibid. Nikolas Rose argues that this bipolar distinction in Foucault begins to break down in the current period. "Now," he writes, "new kinds of political struggle could emerge, in which 'life as a political object' was turned back against the controls exercised over it, in the name of claims to a 'right' to life, to one's body, to health, to the satisfaction of one's needs. . . . The distinction between discipline and regulation—between strategies seeking the management of individual bodies and those focused on the collective body of the population—blurs" (Rose, *The Politics of Life Itself*, p. 53). For a similar point about disciplinary power's supersession by biopower, see Nealon, *Foucault Beyond Foucault*.
60. Foucault, *Sexuality One*, 1:139.
61. Ibid. In *Race and the Education of Desire*, Ann Stoler makes a similar point about the importance of biopower in *Sexuality One*. My analysis differs considerably from hers, however, on a number of points. Specifically, I disagree with Stoler's focus on biopower as a form of power invested primarily in the colonial state; rather, as Foucault argues, biopower functions beyond the state to include the myriad domains of existence he calls governmentality. Stoler's insistence on biopower as "state racism" leads her, inevitably, to dissociate the ethics of the sexual subject from biopolitics: "The transformation [Foucault] had explored in 1976 [in *Sexuality One*] from a 'discourse on the war of races' to 'state racism' never appears again, and the genealogy of racism was not pursued further. By 1978, 'governmentality' took its place entirely, leading Foucault back to sex in the governing and care of the self" (25). Unlike Stoler, I read "governmentality" and the ethics of sex as inextricably connected to Foucault's earlier work on biopower. See Stoler, *Race and the Education of Desire*.
62. In Macey, *The Lives of Michel Foucault*, p. 354.
63. Lorde, "Uses of the Erotic," p. 57.
64. Foucault, *The Hermeneutics of the Subject*, p. 28.
65. Foucault, *Histoire de la sexualité*, 2:15.
66. Foucault, "Final Interview," p. 2.
67. Foucault, "On the Genealogy of Ethics," 1:258.
68. Jean Grimshaw describes Foucault's ethics as "disappointing. . . . It seems

trapped in a highly masculinist view of ethics as the concern of a male elite to stylize their own lives" (70). Along similar lines, Kate Soper remarks: "Foucault, in short, by abstracting as much as he can both from the social context of the ethical codes he is charting, and from the dialectic of personal relations, defines the ethical so as to make it appear a very private—and masculine—affair" (41). Amy Richlin has this to say: "Not that women are the only glaring absence in Foucault's history; Foucault has reproduced for his readers an antiquity without Jews . . . without Africans, Egyptians, Semites, northern Europeans; without children, babies, poor people, slaves. All the 'Greeks' are Athenians and most of the 'Romans' are Greeks; in many ways these books are not salvageable" (139). And Biddy Martin argues that Foucault's ethics denies interiority, and refuses to acknowledge the ways in which people are constrained in their freedom. See Grimshaw, "Practices of Freedom"; Soper, "Productive Contradictions"; Richlin, "Foucault's History of Sexuality"; and Martin, "Feminism, Criticism, and Foucault."

69. Foucault, *The Use of Pleasure*, p. 83.
70. Foucault, "On the Genealogy of Ethics," 1:258.
71. Foucault, *The Use of Pleasure*, p. 83.
72. Ibid., p. 85.
73. Foucault, "On the Genealogy of Ethics," 1:253.
74. Foucault, "About the Beginning of the Hermeneutics of the Self," pp. 198–227. As Mark Blasius explains in his "Introductory Note" to two 1980 Dartmouth lectures given by Foucault, in the fall of 1980 Foucault lectured at a number of U.S. universities, including Dartmouth, Berkeley, Princeton, and NYU. The two Dartmouth lectures, delivered in November 1980, had been delivered at Berkeley in October. In the Berkeley lectures, Foucault commented that "the title of these two lectures could have been, and should have been, in fact, 'About the Beginning of the Hermeneutics of the Self'" (198), a remark Blasius honors in the title he gives to the two lectures, published together in 1993 in *Political Theory*. As Blasius points out, the first lecture, "Subjectivity and Truth," has been published in different form in various places, most notably as "Sexuality and Solitude," in *Essential Works of Foucault* 1:175–184.
75. Foucault, "About the Beginning of the Hermeneutics of the Self," p. 204.
76. This lecture is not to be confused with "Subjectivity and Truth" in the *Ethics* volume of the *Essential Works of Foucault* (volume 1), which is an overview of his 1980–81 course at the Collège de France. The *Ethics* volume piece that most closely follows the arguments of the Dartmouth lecture is "Sexuality and Solitude," although there are significant differences between the two.
77. Foucault, "Sexuality and Solitude," p. 175. Also see Foucault's more extensive comments on Leuret in his 1973–74 course, *Psychiatric Power*. In the course, Foucault emphasizes that in the course of his treatment, the patient, Dupré, moves from "a sort of *uncertainty between madness and reason*" (158) to the assertion of truth: "what [Leuret] wants above all is that his patient pin himself to his own history," but as "a truth imposed on him in a canonical form" (159). See Foucault, *Psychiatric Power*.
78. Foucault, "About the Beginning of the Hermeneutics of the Self," p. 202; Foucault, "Sexuality and Solitude," p. 176.

79. "About the Beginning of the Hermeneutics of the Self," p. 202.
80. Ibid.
81. Foucault, "Sexuality and Solitude," p. 177.
82. Ibid.
83. Ibid., p. 179.
84. Ibid., p. 182.
85. Blasius, "Introductory Note."
86. Foucault, "About the Beginning of the Hermeneutics of the Self," p. 223.
87. Blasius, "Introductory Note," p. 200.
88. Foucault, *The Hermeneutics of the Subject*, p. 9.
89. Foucault, "About the Beginning of the Hermeneutics of the Self," p. 201; "Sexuality and Solitude," p. 176.
90. Foucault, "About the Beginning of the Hermeneutics of the Self," p. 201.
91. Foucault, *The Hermeneutics of the Subject*, p. 17.
92. See, most famously, David Halperin's discussion of Foucault and fisting in *Saint Foucault*, especially pp. 85–106. For a founding queer Freudo-Foucauldian argument about self-shattering pleasure, see Bersani, "Is the Rectum a Grave?"
93. Foucault, "On the Genealogy of Ethics," 1:258.
94. Foucault, "What Is Enlightenment?" 1:319.
95. Bartsch and Bartsherer, "What Silent Love Hath Writ," p. 2.
96. Rajchman, *Truth and Eros*, p. 108.
97. Ibid.
98. For an overview of these critiques, especially those by Foucault's colleague at the Collège de France, Pierre Hadot, see O'Leary, *Foucault and the Art of Ethics*, pp. 70–73.
99. Foucault, *Sexuality One*, 1:143.
100. Gayle Rubin defines fisting as "a sexual technique in which the hand and arm, rather than a penis or dildo, are used to penetrate a bodily orifice. Fisting usually refers to anal penetration, although the terms are also used for the insertion of a hand into a vagina." Rubin, "Catacombs," p. 121.
101. Halperin, *Saint Foucault*, p. 95.
102. Ibid., pp. 96–97.
103. Hallward, "The Limits," p. 100.
104. Deleuze, *Foucault*, p. 97. Gayle Rubin's somewhat nostalgic picture of the San Francisco sex clubs of a bygone era speaks to this heterotopian movement that evades our attempts to pin it down. The Catacombs appear, in Rubin's loving rendering, as Foucault's Renaissance homosexuals do in *History of Madness*: as the shadows cast by something as it is leaving. See Rubin, "Catacombs."
105. Halperin, *Saint Foucault*, p. 91.
106. Foucault, "On the Genealogy of Ethics," 1:253.
107. Rajchman, *Truth and Eros*, p. 27.
108. Foucault, *The Use of Pleasure*, p. 9.
109. Ibid., p. 9.
110. Farge, "Michel Foucault et les archives de l'exclusion," p. 65 (translation mine).
111. Foucault, "Lives of Infamous Men," 3:157.
112. Farge, "Michel Foucault et les archives de l'exclusion," p. 73 (translation mine).

113. Foucault, "Lives of Infamous Men," 3:158.
114. Farge, "Michel Foucault et les archives de l'exclusion," p. 77.
115. Nietzsche, *Daybreak*, p. 103.
116. Foucault, "Lives of Infamous Men," 3:158.
117. Foucault, *The Hermeneutics of the Subject*, p. 319.
118. Foucault, *The Use of Pleasure*, p. 8.
119. Foucault, *The Hermeneutics of the Subject*, p. 237.
120. Ibid.
121. Foucault, *The Use of Pleasure*, p. 9.
122. Ibid., p. 9.
123. Butler, *Giving an Account of Oneself*, p. 23.
124. Timothy O'Leary's illuminating overview of Foucault's ethics similarly concludes that Foucault "fails to address one of the central questions of ethics, 'how should I relate to the other?'" O'Leary, *Foucault and the Art of Ethics*, p. 173.
125. Foucault, "On the Genealogy of Ethics," 1:258.
126. Foucault, "Lives of Infamous Men," p. 157.
127. Willett, *The Soul of Justice*, p. 180.
128. Nietzsche, *On the Genealogy of Morals*, p. 25.

Postlude

1. Foucault, "Le Courage de la vérité," 14 March 1984, CD 69 (08).
2. Ibid.
3. Ibid.
4. Foucault, *The Order of Things*, pp. xviii–xix.
5. Ibid.
6. Foucault, "Le Courage de la vérité," 28 March 1984, CD 69 (09).

Works Cited

Allen, Amy. "The Anti-Subjective Hypothesis: Michel Foucault and the Death of the Subject." *Philosophical Forum* 31, no. 2 (Summer 2000): 113–130.

Artières, Philippe, Laurent Quéro, and Michelle Zancarini-Fournel, eds. *Le Groupe d'information sur les prisons: Archives d'une lutte, 1970–1972*. Paris: IMEC, 2003.

Barkley Brown, Elsa. "'What Has Happened Here': The Politics of Difference in Women's History and Feminist Politics." *Feminist Studies* 18, no. 2 (1992): 295–312.

Bartsch, Shadi, and Thomas Bartscherer. "What Silent Love Hath Writ: An Introduction to *Erotikon*." In Shadi Barsch and Thomas Bartscherer, eds., *Erotikon: Essays on Eros, Ancient and Modern*, pp. 1–15. Chicago: University of Chicago Press, 2005.

Beaulieu, Alan, and Réal Fillion. "Review Essay: Michel Foucault, *History of Madness*." *Foucault Studies* 5 (January 2008): 74–89.

Beauvoir, Simone de. *Pour une morale de l'ambiguité*. Paris: Gallimard, 1947.

—— *The Ethics of Ambiguity*. Trans. Bernard Frechtman. New York: Citadel, 1976.

Bell, Vikki. *Culture and Performance: The Challenge of Ethics, Politics, and Feminist Theory*. Oxford: Berg, 2007.

Bergoffen, Debra. *The Philosophy of Simone de Beauvoir: Gendered Phenomenologies, Erotic Generosities*. Albany: State University of New York Press, 1997.

Bersani, Leo. *Homos*. Cambridge: Harvard University Press, 1995.

—— "Is the Rectum a Grave?" *October* 43 (Winter 1987): 197–222.

Berthold-Bond, Daniel. *Hegel's Theory of Madness*. Albany: SUNY Press, 1995.

Blanchot, Maurice. *L'Entretien infini*. Paris: Gallimard, 1969.

—— *The Infinite Conversation*. Trans. Susan Hanson. Minneapolis: University of Minnesota Press, 1993.

Blasius, Mark. "Introductory Note: About the Beginning of the Hermeneutics of the Self." Michel Foucault, "About the Beginning of the Hermeneutics of the Self: Two Lectures at Dartmouth." *Political Theory* 21, no. 2 (May 1993): 198–200.

Boyne, Roy. *Foucault and Derrida: The Other Side of Reason.* London: Unwin Hyman, 1990.

Brich, Cecile. "The Groupe d'information sur les prisons: The voice of prisoners? Or Foucault's?" *Foucault Studies* 5 (January 2008): 26–47.

Brook, Peter. *Marat/Sade.* Metro Goldwyn Meyer, 1967.

Brown, Wendy. *States of Injury: Power and Freedom in Late Modernity.* Princeton: Princeton University Press, 1995.

Butler, Judith. "Against Proper Objects." In Elizabeth Weed and Naomi Schor, eds., *Feminism Meets Queer Theory,* pp. 1–30. Bloomington: Indiana University Press, 1997.

—— *Antigone's Claim: Kinship Between Life and Death.* New York: Columbia University Press, 2000.

—— *Bodies That Matter: On the Discursive Limits of "Sex."* New York: Routledge, 1993.

—— *Gender Trouble: Feminism and the Subversion of Identity.* New York: Routledge, 1990.

—— *Giving an Account of Oneself.* New York: Fordham University Press, 2005.

—— "Imitation and Gender Insubordination." In Henry Abelove, Michèle Aina Barale, and David M. Halperin, eds., *The Lesbian and Gay Studies Reader,* pp. 307–320. New York: Routledge, 1993.

—— *Precarious Life: The Powers of Mourning and Violence.* London: Verso, 2004.

—— *The Psychic Life of Power: Theories in Subjection.* Stanford: Stanford University Press, 1997.

—— "Sexual Inversions." In John D. Caputo and Mark Yount, eds., *Foucault and the Critique of Institutions,* pp. 81–98. University Park: Pennsylvania State University Press, 1993.

—— *Trouble dans le genre: Pour un féminisme de la subversion.* Trans. Cynthia Kraus. Paris: La Découverte, 2005.

—— *Undoing Gender.* New York: Routledge, 2004.

Canguilhem, Georges. "On 'Histoire de la folie' as an Event." *Critical Inquiry* 21, no. 2 (Winter 1995): 282–286.

Caputo, John. "On Not Knowing Who We Are: Madness, Hermeneutics, and the Night of Truth in Foucault." In John Caputo and Mark Yount, eds., *Foucault and the Critique of Institutions,* pp. 233–262. University Park: Pennsylvania State University Press, 1993.

Chanter, Tina. *Ethics of Eros: Irigaray's Rewriting of the Philosophers.* New York: Routledge, 1995.

Cooper, David, and Michel Foucault. "Dialogue sur l'enfermement et la répression psychiatrique." In Collectif Change, ed., *La Folie encerclée,* pp. 76–110. Paris: Seghers/Laffont, 1977.

Corber, Robert J., and Stephen Valocchi. "Introduction." In Robert J. Corber and Stephen Valocchi, eds., *Queer Studies: An Interdisciplinary Reader,* pp. 1–20. Oxford: Blackwell, 2003.

Creech, James. "*Le Neveu de Rameau*: The 'Diary' of a Reading." *Modern Language Notes* 95, no. 4 (May 1980): 995–1004.

Cusset, François. *French Theory: Foucault, Derrida, Deleuze & Cie et les mutations de la vie intellectuelle aux Etats-Unis*. Paris: La Découverte, 2003.

—— *Queer Theory: La littérature française déshabillée par ses homo-lecteurs*. Paris: PUF, 2002.

Cvetkovich, Ann. *An Archive of Feelings: Trauma, Sexuality, and Lesbian Public Cultures*. Durham: Duke University Press, 2003.

Davidson, Arnold. "Foucault, Psychoanalysis, and Pleasure." In Tim Dean and Christopher Lane, eds., *Homosexuality and Psychoanalysis*, pp. 43–50. Chicago: University of Chicago Press, 2001.

—— *The Emergence of Sexuality: Historical Epistemology and the Formation of Concepts*. Cambridge: Harvard University Press, 2001.

Davis, Angela. "Racialized Punishment and Prison Abolition." In Joy James, ed., *The Angela Davis Reader*, pp. 96–107. Malden, MA: Blackwell, 1998.

Dean, Tim, and Christopher Lane. "Homosexuality and Psychoanalysis: An Introduction." In Tim Dean and Christopher Lane, ed., *Homosexuality and Psychoanalysis*, pp. 3–42. Chicago: University of Chicago Press, 2001.

De Lauretis, Teresa. "Queer Theory, Lesbian and Gay Studies: An Introduction." *Differences: A Journal of Feminist Cultural Studies* 3, no. 2 (1991): iii–xviii.

Deleuze, Gilles. *Foucault*. Trans. Séan Hand. Minneapolis: University of Minnesota Press, 1988.

—— *Negotiations: 1972–1990*. Trans. Martin Joughlin. New York: Columbia University Press, 1995.

Derrida, Jacques. "Cogito and History of Madness." In *Writing and Difference*, pp. 31–63. Trans. Alan Bass. Chicago: University of Chicago Press, 1978.

—— "Cogito et histoire de la folie." *L'Ecriture et la différence*. Paris: Seuil, 1967, pp. 51–98.

—— "'Etre juste avec Freud': L'histoire de la folie à l'âge de la psychanalyse." In Elisabeth Roudinesco, ed., *Penser la folie: Essais sur Michel Foucault*, pp. 139–195. Paris: Gallilée, 1992.

—— "'To Do Justice to Freud': The History of Madness in the Age of Psychoanalysis." Trans. Pascale-Anne Brault and Michael Naas. *Critical Inquiry* 20 (Winter 1994): 227–266.

Descartes, René. *Meditations and Other Metaphysical Writings*. Trans. Desmond M. Clarke. New York: Penguin, 1998.

Diderot, Denis. *La Religieuse*. Paris: Flammarion, 1993.

—— *Le Neveu de Rameau*. Genève: Droz, 1950.

—— *Les Bijoux indiscrets*. Paris: Flammarion, 1993.

—— *Rameau's Nephew and D'Alembert's Dream*. Trans. Leonard Tancock. New York: Penguin, 1966.

—— *Rameau's Nephew and First Satire*. Trans. Margaret Mauldon. Oxford: Oxford University Press, 2006.

—— *The Indiscreet Jewels*. Trans. Sophie Hawkes. New York: Marsilio, 1993.

—— *The Nun*. Trans. Leonard Tanock. New York: Penguin, 1974.

Dreyfus, Hubert L. "Foreword to the California Edition." Michel Foucault, *Mental Illness and Psychology*, pp. vii–xliii. Trans. Alan Sheridan. Berkeley: University of California Press, 1987.

Dreyfus, Hubert L., and Paul Rabinow. *Michel Foucault: Beyond Structuralism and Hermeneutics*. Chicago: University of Chicago Press, 1983.

Droit, Roger-Pol. *La Compagnie des contemporains*. Paris: Odile Jacob, 2002.

—— *Michel Foucault, entretiens*. Paris: Odile Jacob, 2004.

Dumm, Thomas L. *Michel Foucault and the Politics of Freedom*. Thousand Oaks, CA: Sage, 1996.

During, Simon. *Foucault and Literature: Toward a Genealogy of Writing*. London: Routledge, 1992.

Edelman, Lee. *No Future: Queer Theory and the Death Drive*. Durham: Duke University Press, 2004.

Elden, Stuart. *Mapping the Present: Heidegger, Foucault and the Project of a Spatial History*. London: Continuum, 2001.

Eng, David L. *Racial Castration: Managing Masculinity in Asian America*. Durham: Duke University Press, 2001.

Eng, David L., Judith Halberstam, and José Muñoz. "Introduction: What's Queer About Queer Studies Now?" *Social Text* 84–85 (Fall/Winter 2005): 1–18.

Eribon, Didier. *Echapper à la psychanalyse*. Paris: Leo Scheer, 2005.

—— *Insult and the Making of the Gay Self*. Trans. Michael Lucey. Durham: Duke University Press, 2004.

Farge, Arlette. "Michel Foucault et les archives de l'exclusion." In Elisabeth Roudinesco, ed., *Penser la folie: Essais sur Michel Foucault*, pp. 63–78. Paris: Galilée, 1992.

Fassin, Eric. "Genre et sexualité: Politique de la critique historique." In Marie-Christine Granjon, ed., *Penser avec Michel Foucault: Théorie critique et pratiques politiques*, pp. 225–250. Paris: Karthala, 2005.

—— "Le genre aux Etats-Unis." In Christine Bard, Christian Baudelot, and Janine Mossuz-Lavau, eds., *Quand les femmes s'en mêlent: Genre et pouvoir*, pp. 23–43. Paris: La Martinière, 2004.

—— "Résistance et réception: Judith Butler en France." In *L'Inversion de la question homosexuelle*, pp. 215–224. Paris: Amsterdam, 2008.

—— "Somnolence de Foucault: Violence sexuelle, consentement, et pouvoir." *Prochoix* 21 (Spring 2002): 106–119.

—— "Trouble-genre." Preface to Judith Butler's *Trouble dans le genre: Pour un féminisme de la subversion*, pp. 5–19. Trans. Cynthia Kraus. Paris: Découverte, 2005.

Feher, Michel. "Les interrègnes de Michel Foucault." In Marie-Christine Granjon, ed., *Penser avec Michel Foucault: Théorie critique et pratiques politiques*, pp. 251–300. Paris: Karthala, 2005.

Felman, Shoshana. "Foucault/Derrida: The Madness of the Thinking/Speaking Subject." In Emily Sun, Eyal Peretz, and Ulrich Baer, eds., *The Claims of Literature: A Shoshana Felman Reader*, pp. 51–69. New York: Fordham University Press, 2007.

Flynn, Thomas. "Foucault's Mapping of History." In *The Cambridge Companion to Foucault*, pp. 28–46. Cambridge: Cambridge University Press, 1994.

Foucault, Michel. *Abnormal: Lectures at the Collège de France, 1974–1975.* Trans. Graham Burchell. New York: Picador, 2003.

—— "About the Beginning of the Hermeneutics of the Self: Two Lectures at Dartmouth." *Political Theory* 21, no. 2 (May 1993): 198–227.

—— "A Preface to Transgression." In Paul Rabinow, ed., *Essential Works of Foucault, 1954–1984,* 2:69–88. 3 vols. New York: New Press, 1998.

—— "Chronologie." *Dits et écrits,* 1:13–90. 2 vols. Paris: Quarto Gallimard, 2001.

—— "Different Spaces." In Paul Rabinow, ed., *Essential Works of Foucault, 1954–1984,* 2:175–186. 3 vols. New York: New Press, 1998.

—— *Discipline and Punish: The Birth of the Prison.* Trans. Alan Sheridan. New York: Random House, 1977.

—— "Entretien avec Roger-Pol Droit." 9 cassettes. Paris: IMEC, June 1975.

—— "Final Interview." *Raritan* 5, no. 1 (1985): 1–13.

—— *Histoire de la folie à l'âge classique.* Paris: Gallimard, 1972.

—— *Histoire de la sexualité,* vol. 1: *La Volonté de savoir.* Paris: Gallimard, 1976.

—— *Histoire de la sexualité,* vol. 2: *L' Usage des plaisirs.* Paris: Gallimard, 1984.

—— *Histoire de la sexualité,* vol. 3: *Le Souci de soi.* Paris: Gallimard, 1984.

—— *History of Madness.* Trans. Jonathan Murphy and Jean Khalfa. London: Routledge, 2006.

—— "Jean Hyppolite, 1907–1968" (1969). In *Dits et écrits,* 1:807–814. 2 vols. Paris: Quarto Gallimard, 2001.

—— "'Je suis un artificier': A propos de la méthode et de la trajectoire de Michel Foucault." In Roger-Pol Droit, *Michel Foucault, entretiens,* pp. 89–136. Paris: Odile Jacob, 2004.

—— "La Pensée du dehors" (1966). In *Dits et écrits,* 1:546–567. 2 vols. Paris: Quarto Gallimard, 2001.

—— "La vie des hommes infâmes" (1977). In *Dits et écrits,* 2: 237–253. 2 vols. Paris: Quarto Gallimard, 2001.

—— "Le Courage de la vérité." 9 cassettes. Paris: IMEC, February-March 1984.

—— "Le Jeu de Michel Foucault" (1977). In *Dits et écrits.* 2 vols. Paris: Quarto Gallimard, 2001, 2: 298–329.

—— "Le Philosophe masqué" (1980). In *Dits et écrits,* 2:923–929. 2 vols. Paris: Quarto Gallimard, 2001.

—— "Le Retour à la morale" (1984). In *Dits et écrits,* 2:1515–1526. 2 vols. Paris: Quarto Gallimard, 2001.

—— *Les Mots et les choses.* Paris: Gallimard, 1966.

—— "L'éthique du souci de soi comme pratique de la liberté" (1984). In *Dits et écrits,* 2:1527–1548. 2 vols. Paris: Quarto Gallimard, 2001.

—— "Lives of Infamous Men." In Paul Rabinow, ed., *Essential Works of Foucault, 1954–1984,* 3:157–175. 3 vols. New York: New Press, 2000.

—— *Madness and Civilization: A History of Insanity in the Age of Reason.* Trans. Richard Howard. New York: Random House, 1965.

—— *Mental Illness and Psychology.* Trans. Alan Sheridan. Berkeley: University of California Press, 1987.

—— "Nietzsche, Freud, Marx" (1967). In *Dits et écrits,* 1:592–607. 2 vols. Paris: Quarto Gallimard, 2001.

—— "Nietzsche, Freud, Marx." In Paul Rabinow, ed., *Essential Works of Foucault, 1954–1984*, 2:269–278. 3 vols. New York: New Press, 1998.

—— "Nietzsche, Genealogy, History." In Paul Rabinow, ed., *Essential Works of Foucault, 1954–1984*, 2:369–392. 3 vols. New York: New Press, 1998.

—— "On the Genealogy of Ethics." In Paul Rabinow, ed., *Essential Works of Foucault, 1954–1984*, 1:253–280. 3 vols. New York: New Press, 1997.

—— "On the Ways of Writing History." In Paul Rabinow, ed., *Essential Works of Foucault, 1954–1984*, 2:279–296. 3 vols. New York: New Press, 1998.

—— "Philosophie et psychologie" (1965). In *Dits et écrits*, 1:466–476. 2 vols. Paris: Quarto Gallimard, 2001.

—— "Pierre Boulez, l'écran traversé" (1982). In *Dits et écrits*, 2:1038–1041. 2 vols. Paris: Quarto Gallimard, 2001.

—— "Pierre Boulez, Passing Through the Screen." In Paul Rabinow, ed., *Essential Works of Foucault, 1854–1984*, 2:241–244. 3 vols. New York: New Press, 1998.

—— "Politics and Ethics." In Paul Rabinow, ed., *The Foucault Reader*, pp. 373–380. New York: Pantheon, 1984.

—— "Préface, in Foucault (M.), *Folie et déraison: Histoire de la folie à l'âge classique*" (1961). In *Dits et écrits*, 1:187–195. 2 vols. Paris: Quatro Gallimard, 2001.

—— "Préface à la transgression" (1963). In *Dits et écrits*, 1:261–278. 2 vols. Paris: Quarto Gallimard, 2001.

—— "Prisons et asiles dans le mécanisme du pouvoir" (1974). In *Dits et écrits*, 1:1389–1393. 2 vols. Paris: Quarto Gallimard, 2001.

—— *Psychiatric Power: Lectures at the Collège de France, 1973–1974*. Trans. Graham Burchell. New York: Palgrave Macmillan, 2006.

—— "Qu'est-ce qu'un auteur?" (1969). In *Dits et écrits*, 1:817–849. 2 vols. Paris: Quarto Gallimard, 2001.

—— "Qui êtes-vous, professeur Foucault?" (1967). In *Dits et écrits*, 1:629–648. 2 vols. Paris: Quarto Gallimard, 2001.

—— "'Se débarrasser de la philosophie': A propos de la littérature." In Roger-Pol Droit, *Michel Foucault, entretiens*, pp. 75–88. Paris: Odile Jacob, 2004.

—— "Sexuality and Solitude." In Paul Rabinow, ed., *Essential Works of Foucault, 1954–1984*, 1:175–184. 3 vols. New York: New Press, 1997.

—— *Society Must Be Defended: Lectures at the Collège de France, 1975–1976*. Trans. David Macey. New York: Picador, 2003.

—— "Structuralism and Post-structuralism." In Paul Rabinow, ed., *Essential Works of Foucault, 1954–1984*, 2:433–458. 3 vols. New York: New Press, 1998.

—— "Structuralisme et poststructuralisme" (1983). In *Dits et écrits*, 2:1250–1276. 2 vols. Paris: Quarto Gallimard, 2001.

—— "Sur les façons d'écrire l'histoire" (1967). In *Dits et écrits*, 1:613–628. 2 vols. Paris: Quarto Gallimard, 2001.

—— *Surveiller et punir: Naissance de la prison*. Paris: Gallimard, 1975.

—— "The Confession of the Flesh." In Colin Gordon, ed., *Power/Knowledge: Selected Interviews and Other Writings 1972–1977*, pp. 194–228. New York: Pantheon, 1980.

—— "The Death of Lacan." In Tim Dean and Christopher Lane, eds., *Homosexuality and Psychoanalysis*, pp. 57–58. Chicago: University of Chicago Press, 2001.

—— "The Discourse on Language." In *The Archeology of Knowledge and the Discourse on Language*, pp. 215–237. Trans. A. M. Sheridan Smith. New York: Random House, 1972.

—— "The Ethics of the Concern for Self as a Practice of Freedom." In Paul Rabinow, ed., *Essential Works of Foucault, 1954–1984*, 1:281–302. 3 vols. New York: New Press, 1997.

—— *The Hermeneutics of the Subject: Lectures at the Collège de France, 1981–1982.* Trans. Graham Burchell. New York: Palgrave Macmillan, 2005.

—— *The History of Sexuality*, vol. 1: *An Introduction.* Trans. Robert Hurley. 3 vols. New York: Vintage, 1978.

—— *The History of Sexuality*, vol. 2: *The Use of Pleasure.* Trans. Robert Hurley. 3 vols. New York: Random House, 1985.

—— *The History of Sexuality*, vol. 3: *The Care of the Self.* Trans. Robert Hurley. 3 vols. New York: Random House, 1986.

—— "The Masked Philosopher." In Paul Rabinow, ed., *Essential Works of Foucault, 1954–1984*, 1:321–328. 3 vols. New York: New Press, 1997.

—— *The Order of Things: An Archeology of the Human Sciences.* New York: Random House, 1970.

—— "The Thought of the Outside." In Paul Rabinow, ed., *Essential Works of Foucault, 1954–1984*, 2:147–170. 3 vols. New York: New Press, 1998.

—— "What Is an Author?" In Paul Rabinow, ed., *Essential Works of Foucault, 1954–1984*, 2:207–222. 3 vols. New York: New Press, 1998.

—— "What Is Enlightenment?" In Paul Rabinow, ed., *Essential Works of Foucault, 1954–1984*, 1:303–320. 3 vols. New York: New Press, 1997.

Foucault, Michel, and Ludwig Binswanger. *Dream and Existence.* Ed. Keith Hoeller. Trans. Forrest Williams. Atlantic Highlands, NJ: Humanities, 1993.

Freeman, Elizabeth. "Time Binds, or Erotohistoriography." *Social Text* 84–85 (Fall/Winter 2005): 57–68.

Garber, Linda. *Identity Poetics: Race, Class, and the Lesbian-Feminist Roots of Queer Theory.* New York: Columbia University Press, 2001.

Gearhart, Suzanne. "The Dialectic and Its Aesthetic Other: Hegel and Diderot." *Modern Language Notes* 101, no. 5 (December 1986): 1042–1066.

—— *The Interrupted Dialectic: Philosophy, Psychoanalysis, and their Tragic Other* Baltimore: Johns Hopkins University Press, 1992.

Goldstein, Jan. *Console and Classify: The French Psychiatric Profession in the Nineteenth Century.* Cambridge: Cambridge University Press, 1987.

Gordon, Colin. "Extreme Prejudice: Note on Andrew Scull's *TLS* review of Foucault's *History of Madness*," May 20, 2007. http://foucaultblog.wordpress.com/2007/05/20/extreme-prejudice/; accessed 13 September 2008.

—— "*Histoire de la folie*: An Unknown Book by Michel Foucault." *History of the Human Sciences* 3, no. 1 (1990): 3–26.

—— "History, Madness, and Other Errors: A Response." *History of the Human Sciences* 3, no. 3 (1990): 381–396.

—— Review of *History of Madness*. *Notre Dame Philosophical Reviews*, February 23, 2007. http://ndpr.nd.edu/review.cfm?id=8904; accessed 13 September 2008.

Griffiths, Paul. *The Sea on Fire: Jean Barraqué*. Rochester: University of Rochester Press, 2003.

Grimshaw, Jean. "Practices of Freedom." In Caroline Ramazanoglu, ed., *Up Against Foucault: Explorations of Some Tensions Between Foucault and Feminism*, pp. 51–72. London: Routledge, 1993.

Gros, Frédéric. "De Borges à Magritte." In Philippe Artières, ed., *Michel Foucault: La Littérature et les arts*, pp. 15–22. Paris: Kimé, 2004.

Gutting, Gary. "Foucault and the History of Madness." In Gary Gutting, ed., *The Cambridge Companion to Foucault*, pp. 47–70. New York: Cambridge University Press, 1995.

—— "Introduction, Michel Foucault: A User's Manual." In Gary Gutting, ed., *The Cambridge Companion to Foucault*, pp. 1–27. New York: Cambridge University Press, 1995.

Habermas, Jürgen. "The Critique of Reason as an Unmasking of the Human Sciences: Michel Foucault." In *The Philosophical Discourse of Modernity: Twelve Lectures*, pp. 238–265. Trans. Frederick G. Lawrence. Cambridge: MIT Press, 1995.

Halberstam, Judith. *Female Masculinity*. Durham: Duke University Press, 1998.

Halley, Ian. "Queer Theory by Men." *Duke Journal of Gender, Law, and Policy* 11 (2004): 7–53.

Halley, Janet. *Split Decisions: How and Why to Take a Break from Feminism*. Princeton: Princeton University Press, 2006.

Halley, Janet, and Andrew Parker, eds. "After Sex? On Writing Since Queer Theory." *South Atlantic Quarterly* 106, no. 3 (Summer 2007).

Hallward, Peter. "The Limits of Individuation; or, How to Distinguish Deleuze and Foucault." *Angelaki: Journal of the Theoretical Humanities* 5, no. 3 (August 2000): 93–111.

Halperin, David M. *Saint Foucault: Towards a Gay Hagiography*. New York: Oxford University Press, 1995.

Hayman, Ronald. *Nietzsche: A Critical Life*. New York: Oxford University Press, 1980.

Hegel, G. W. F. *Phenomenology of Spirit*. Trans. A. V. Miller. Oxford: Oxford University Press, 1977.

Hirschmann, Nancy. *The Subject of Liberty: Toward a Feminist Theory of Freedom*. Princeton: Princeton University Press, 2003.

Howe, Susan. *My Emily Dickinson*. Berkeley: North Atlantic, 1985.

—— *The Europe of Trusts*. Los Angeles: Sun and Moon, 1990.

Hulbert, James. "Diderot in the Text of Hegel: A Question of Intertextuality." *Studies in Romanticism* 22 (1983): 267–291.

Hutcheon, Linda. *Irony's Edge: The Theory and Politics of Irony*. New York: Routledge, 1995.

Hyppolite, Jean. *Génèse et structure de la Phénoménologie de l'esprit de Hegel*. 2 vols. Paris: Aubier, 1946.

Irigaray, Luce. *Speculum de l'autre femme*. Paris: Minuit, 1974.

—— *Speculum of the Other Woman*. Trans. Gillian Gill. Ithaca: Cornell University Press, 1985.

Jagose, Annamarie. *Queer Theory: An Introduction*. New York: New York University Press, 1996.

Jamison, Kay Redfield. *An Unquiet Mind: A Memoir of Moods and Madness*. New York: Random House, 1995.

Jauss, Hans Robert. "The Dialogical and the Dialectical *Neveu de Rameau*; or, The Reciprocity Between Diderot and Socrates, Hegel and Diderot." In *Question and Answer: Forms of Dialogic Understanding*, pp. 118–147. Trans. Michael Hays. Minneapolis: University of Minnesota Press, 1989.

Kaufman, Eleanor. *The Delirium of Praise: Bataille, Blanchot, Deleuze, Foucault, Klossowski*. Baltimore: Johns Hopkins University Press, 2001.

Kirby, Vicki. *Judith Butler: Live Theory*. London: Continuum, 2006.

Kristeva, Julia. "La Musique parlée, ou remarques sur la subjectivité dans la fiction à propos du *Neveu de Rameau*." In Michèle Duchet and Michèle Jalley, eds., *Langues et Langages de Leibniz à l' Encyclopédie*, pp. 153–224. Paris: Union générale d'éditions, 1977.

Lacoue-Labarthe, Philippe. "L'Imprésentable." *Poétique* 21 (1975): 53–95.

Laplanche, Jean, and Jean-Bertrand Pontalis. *Le Vocabulaire de la psychanalyse*. Paris: PUF, 1967.

Lorde, Audre. "Uses of the Erotic: The Erotic as Power." In *Sister Outsider: Essays and Speeches*, pp. 53–59. Trumansburg, New York: Crossing, 1984.

Macey, David. *The Lives of Michel Foucault*. London: Hutchinson, 1993.

MacKinnon, Catherine. *Feminism Unmodified: Discourses on Life and Law*. Cambridge: Harvard University Press, 1987.

—— *Toward a Feminist Theory of the State*. Cambridge: Harvard University Press, 1989.

McNay, Lois. *Foucault: A Critical Introduction*. New York: Continuum, 1994.

Mandrou, Robert. "Trois clés pour comprendre l'Histoire de la folie à l'époque classique." *Annales: Economie, Sociétés, Civilisation* 17 (July-August 1962): 761–771.

Marcuse, Herbert. *Eros and Civilization: A Philosophical Inquiry Into Freud*. Boston: Beacon, 1955.

Martin, Biddy. "Feminism, Criticism, and Foucault." *New German Critique* 27 (1982): 3–30.

Mbembe, Achille. "Necropolitics." Trans. Libby Meintjes. *Public Culture* 15, no. 1 (Winter 2003): 11–40.

Megill, Allen. "Foucault, Ambiguity, and the Rhetoric of Historiography." *History of the Human Sciences* 3 (1990): 343–361.

—— "The Reception of Foucault by Historians." *Journal of the History of Ideas* 48 (1987): 117–141.

Mercier, Louis-Sébastien. *Le Tableau de Paris*. Paris: Gallimard, 1998.

Midelfort, H. C. Erik. "Madness and Civilisation in Early Modern Europe: A Reappraisal of Michel Foucault." In Barbara C. Malament, ed., *After the Reformation: Essays in Honor of J. H. Hexter*, pp. 247–265. Philadelphia: University of Pennsylvania Press, 1980.

Miller, James. *The Passion of Michel Foucault*. New York: Simon and Schuster, 1993.

Moreno Pestaña, José Luis. *En devenant Foucault: Sociogénèse d'un grand philosophe*. Trans. Philippe Hunt. Broissieux: Croquant, 2006.

Muñoz, José. *Disidentifications: Queers of Color and the Performance of Politics*. Minneapolis: University of Minnesota Press, 1999.

Nancy, Jean-Luc. *Being-Singular-Plural*. Trans. Robert Richardson and Anne O'Byrne. Stanford: Stanford University Press, 2000.

Nealon, Jeffrey. *Foucault Beyond Foucault: Power and Its Intensifications Since 1984*. Stanford: Stanford University Press, 2008.

Nietzsche, Friedrich. *Beyond Good and Evil: Prelude to a Philosophy of the Future*. Trans. R. J. Hollingdale. New York: Penguin, 1973.

—— *Daybreak: Thoughts on the Prejudices of Morality*. Trans. R. J. Hollingdale. Cambridge: Cambridge University Press, 1997.

—— *On the Genealogy of Morals*. Trans. Walter Kaufmann. New York: Vintage, 1969.

—— *The Gay Science*. Trans. Walter Kaufman. New York: Random House, 1974.

Nigro, Robert. "Foucault lecteur critique de Bataille et de Blanchot." In Philippe Artières, ed., *Michel Foucault, la littérature et les arts*, pp. 23–43. Paris: Kimé, 2004.

Norton, Rictor. "A Critique of Social Constructionism and Postmodern Queer Theory: A False 'Birth.'" June 1, 2002. http://www.infopt.demon.co.uk/social15.htm; accessed 20 September 2008.

O'Grady, Helen. "An Ethics of the Self." In Dianna Taylor and Karen Vintges, eds., *Feminism and the Final Foucault*, pp. 91–117. Urbana: University of Illinois Press, 2004.

Oksala, Johanna. *Foucault on Freedom*. Cambridge: Cambridge University Press, 2005.

O'Leary, Timothy. *Foucault and the Art of Ethics*. London: Continuum, 2002.

—— "Foucault, Literature, Experience. " *Foucault Studies* 5 (2008): 5–25.

Parker, Andrew. "Foucault's Tongues," *Mediations* 18, no. 2 (1994): 80–88.

Perez, Hiram. "You Can Have My Brown Body and Eat It, Too!" *Social Text* 84–85 (Fall/Winter 2005): 171–192.

Philo, Chris. *A Geographical History of Institutional Provision for the Insane from Medieval Times to the 1860s in England and Wales: The Space Reserved for Insanity*. Lewiston: Mellon, 2004.

Plaza, Monique. "Our Damages and Their Compensation—Rape: The 'Will Not to Know' of Michel Foucault." *Feminist Issues* 1 (Summer 1981): 25–35.

Porter, Roy. *A Social History of Madness: Stories of the Insane*. London: Weidenfeld and Nicolson, 1987.

Poulet, Georges. "Phenomenology of Reading." *New Literary History* 1, no. 1 (October 1969): 53–68.

Price, David W. "Hegel's Intertextual Dialectic: Diderot's *Le Neveu de Rameau* in *The Phenomenology of Spirit*." *Clio* 20 (1991): 223–233.

Puar, Jasbir K. *Terrorist Assemblages: Homonationalism in Queer Times*. Durham: Duke University Press, 2007.

Quétel, Claude. "Faut-il critiquer Foucault?" In *Penser la folie: Essais sur Michel Foucault*, pp. 79–105. Paris: Galilée, 1992.

Racevskis, Karlis. "Michel Foucault, Rameau's Nephew, and the Question of Identity." In James Bernauer and David Rasmussen, eds., *The Final Foucault*, pp. 21–33. Cambridge: MIT Press, 1987.

Rajchman, John. *Truth and Eros: Foucault, Lacan, and the Question of Ethics*. New York: Routledge, 1991.

Ray, Janisse. *Ecology of a Cracker Childhood*. Minneapolis: Milkweed, 1999.

Reich, Wilhelm. *The Sexual Revolution: Toward a Self-Governing Character Structure.* Trans. Theodore P. Wolfe. New York: Farrar, Straus, and Giroux, 1971.

Richlin, Amy. "Foucault's History of Sexuality: A Useful Theory for Women?" In David H. J. Larmour, Paul Allen Miller, and Charles Platter, eds., *Rethinking Sexuality: Foucault and Classical Antiquity*, pp. 138–170. Princeton: Princeton University Press, 1997.

Rose, Jacqueline. "Femininity and Its Discontents." In *Sexuality in the Field of Vision*, pp. 83–103. London: Verso, 1986.

Rose, Nikolas. *The Politics of Life Itself: Biomedicine, Power, and Subjectivity in the Twenty-First Century.* Princeton: Princeton University Press, 2007.

Rubin, Gayle. "Catacombs: A Temple of the Butthole." In Mark Thompson, ed., *Leatherfolk: Radical Sex, People, Politics, and Practice*, pp. 119–141. Los Angeles: Alyson, 1992.

—— "Thinking Sex: Notes for a Radical Theory of the Politics of Sexuality." In Henry Abelove, Michèle Aina Barale, and David M. Halperin, eds., *The Lesbian and Gay Studies Reader*, pp. 1–44. New York: Routledge, 1993.

Rubin, Gayle, and Judith Butler. *Marché au sexe*. Trans. Eliane Sokol and Flora Bolton. Paris: Epel, 2002.

Rubin, Gayle, with Judith Butler. "Sexual Traffic: Interview." In Elizabeth Weed and Naomi Schor, eds., *Feminism Meets Queer Theory*, pp. 68–108. Bloomington: Indiana University Press, 1997.

Sawicki, Jana. "Foucault's Pleasures: Desexualizing Queer Politics." In Dianna Taylor and Karen Vintges, eds., *Feminism and the Final Foucault*, pp. 163–182. Urbana: University of Illinois Press, 2004.

Schmidt, James. "The Fool's Truth: Diderot, Goethe, Hegel." *Journal of the History of Ideas* 57, no. 4 (October 1996): 625–644.

Scott, Charles E. *The Question of Ethics: Nietzsche, Foucault, Heidegger.* Bloomington: Indiana University Press, 1990.

Scott, Joan Wallach. "The Evidence of Experience." In Henry Abelove, Michèle Aina Barale, and David M. Halperin, eds., *Lesbian and Gay Studies Reader*, pp. 397–415. New York: Routledge, 1993.

Scull, Andrew. "Michel Foucault's *History of Madness*." *History of the Human Sciences* 3, no. 3 (1990): 57–67.

—— "The Fictions of Foucault's Scholarship." *Times Literary Supplement*, March 21, 2007. http://tls.timesonline.co.uk/article/0,,25347-2626687,00.html; accessed 13 September 2008.

Sedgwick, Eve Kosofsky. *A Dialogue on Love*. Boston: Beacon, 1999.

—— *Between Men: English Literature and Male Homosocial Desire*. New York: Columbia University Press, 1985.

—— *Epistémologie du placard*. Trans. Maxime Cervulle. Paris: Amsterdam, 2008.

—— *Epistemology of the Closet*. Berkeley: University of California Press, 1990.

—— "Privilege of Unknowing: Diderot's *The Nun*." In *Tendencies*, pp. 23–51. Durham: Duke University Press, 1993.

—— *Tendencies*. Durham: Duke University Press, 1993.

—— *The Coherence of Gothic Conventions.* New York: Methuen, 1986.

—— *Touching Feeling: Affect, Pedagogy, Performativity.* Durham: Duke University Press, 2003.

Sedgwick, Eve Kosofsky, and Adam Frank. *Shame and Its Sisters: A Silvan Tomkins Reader.* Durham: Duke University Press, 1995.

Sedgwick, Peter. *Psycho Politics.* New York: Harper and Row, 1982.

Shea, Louisa. *The Cynic Enlightenment; or, Diogenes in the Salon.* Baltimore: Johns Hopkins University Press, 2009.

Sloterdijk, Peter. *Critique of Cynical Reason.* Trans. Michael Eldred. Minneapolis: University of Minnesota Press, 1987.

Soper, Kate. "Productive Contradictions." In Caroline Ramazanoglu, ed., *Up Against Foucault: Explorations of Some Tensions between Foucault and Feminism,* pp. 29–50. London: Routledge, 1993.

Spargo, Tamsin. *Foucault and Queer Theory.* Cambridge: Icon, 1999.

Stoler, Laura Ann. *Race and the Education of Desire: Foucault's History of Sexuality and the Colonial Order of Things.* Durham: Duke University Press, 1995.

Stone, Lawrence. "Madness." *New York Review of Books.* December 16, 1982, pp. 28–36.

Swain, Gladys. *Dialogue avec l'insensé: Essais d'histoire de la psychiatrie.* Paris: Gallimard, 1994.

Taylor, Dianna, and Karen Vintges, eds. *Feminism and the Final Foucault.* Urbana: University of Illinois Press, 2004.

Turner, William. *A Genealogy of Queer Theory.* Philadelphia: Temple University Press, 2000.

Veyne, Paul. *Foucault: Sa pensée, sa personne.* Paris: Albin Michel, 2008.

Villarejo, Amy. "Tarrying with the Normative: Queer Theory and Black History." *Social Text* 84–85 (Fall/Winter 2005): 69–84.

Weed, Elizabeth. "The More Things Change." In Naomi Schor and Elizabeth Weed, eds., *Feminism Meets Queer Theory,* pp. 266–291. Bloomington: Indiana Univesity Press, 1997.

Weiss, Peter. *The Persecution and Assassination of Jean-Paul Marat as Performed by the Inmates of the Asylum of Charenton Under the Direction of the Marquis de Sade.* Long Grove, IL: Waveland, 1981.

Wiegman, Robyn. "Dear Ian." *Duke Journal of Gender, Law, and Policy* 11 (2004): 93–120.

—— "Heteronormativity and the Desire for Gender." *Feminist Theory* 7 (2006): 89–103.

Willett, Cynthia. "This Poem That Is My Body: Irigaray." In *The Soul of Justice: Social Bonds and Racial Hubris,* pp. 123–156. Ithaca: Cornell University Press, 2001.

Wing, J. K. *Reasoning About Madness.* Oxford: Oxford University Press, 1978.

Winnubst, Shannon. *Queering Freedom.* Bloomington: Indiana University Press, 2006.

Index

Abnormal (Foucault), 5, 23, 36, 38, 210, 288*n*55, 298*n*57
abnormals, xiv, 23, 60, 114, 153, 247
abnormality, xiv, 23, 37, 40, 49, 60, 72, 108, 114, 145, 151, 153, 235, 247
abortion, 97
"About the Beginning of the Hermeneutics of the Self" (Foucault), 310*n*74
acts (versus identities), 49, 62, 67–79, 108, 113–14, 129, 174, 198, 265,
Aesthetics (Hegel), 213
aesthetic practice, 194, 209, 214–15, 258, 277
affect, 167, 169, 172, 202, 203, 206, 226, 270, 273
"Against Proper Objects" (Butler), 46
Age of Reason, 26, 32, 41, 48–59, 61–3, 66, 73, 79, 103–5, 108, 153, 195–96, 207, 221, 226, 230, 291*n*41; *see also* Enlightenment
agency, 119, 136–37, 165, 173–75, 177
alcoholism, 189, 190
Allen, Amy, 290*n*29

alterity: archival, 43, 274; and divergentism, 82; erotic, 79; ethical, 101–2, 118, 168, 175–76, 185, 197, 224, 227, 229, 247, 249, 261, 273, 275; experience of, 27; historical, 96, 198, 226, 229, 248, 253, 268, 276–277; in Levinas, 247; madness as 144–45, 176, 243; as objectification, 138, 145; and psychoanalysis, 160–61, 164, 175–76; sexual, xiv, 74–75, 89, 161; of subject, 51–54, 61, 145, 168, 261, 273; *see also* other; othering; otherness
AIDS, 135, 255, 279
Althusser, Louis, 15, 32, 170–71, 188, 218, 281*n*1
anal pleasure, 115, 135, 184, 230, 304*n*104, 311*n*100
ancient Greece, 79, 259, 261; *see also* Greco-Roman world
animality, 88, 105, 115, 205–6, 230, 233–34
Annales School, 25
anonymity, 32, 98, 117, 121
Antigone's Claim (Butler), 185

265–67; *see also assujettissement*;
subject; subjectivation
Birth of the Clinic (Foucault), 27, 123
Birth of Tragedy (Nietzsche), 29, 87,
236
Black Power movement (U.S.), 6
Blanchot, Maurice, 31, 50, 76, 79, 89,
91, 99, 120, 293*n*79
Blasius, Mark, 264, 265, 310*n*74
bodies and pleasures, 48, 95, 125
Bodies That Matter (Butler), 172
body: archival, 250–51, 270; erotic,
xvi, 71, 77, 94, 180, 220, 230, 266,
268, 271–73, 275; individual, 256,
309*n*59; as part of psyche, 297–
98*n*53; sexual, 133, 271–72; species,
256, 309*n*59; *see also* mind-body
split
book: as explosive, ix–xii, xvii, 34, 37,
210, 164, 239–40; as object-event,
x–xii, 17, 20, 24, 37; as tool, 34, 39,
164, 240
Borges, Jorge Luis, 208, 210, 279
Bosch, Hieronymus, 55, 57, 71, 146
Boulez, Pierre, 14
Bourdieu, Pierre, 218, 303*n*74
bourgeois morality, 58–59, 72, 75–76,
80, 243; *see also* bad conscience;
conscience
bourgeois order, 58, 63, 105, 107, 146–
48, 153
bourgeois values, 58, 80; *see also* family
values
Boyne, Roy, 286–87*n*19
Brandt, Sebastian, 57, 71
Braudel, Fernand, 25
Bray, Alan, 135
Brook, Peter, 189
Brown, Wendy, 177
Butler, Judith: on biopower, 255–56,
308–309*n*48n; on confession in
Foucault, 23; dialectic in, 112–13;
on ethics in Foucault, 275; and
feminist-queer split, 46; and
performativity, 41, 113–15, 122, 165,
230–31; and psychoanalysis, 42, 136,
165–78, 184–85; and queer theory,

8–9, 69, 255; reception in France,
282*n*12, 286*n*10
——Works: "Against Proper Objects,"
46; *Antigone's Claim*, 185; *Bodies
That Matter*, 172; *Gender Trouble*, 9,
23, 70, 113–14, 136, 165, 167–69, 172,
174, 185, 255; *Giving an Account of
Oneself*, 185; "Imitation and Gender
Insubordination," 115; *Precarious
Life*, 185; *Psychic Life of Power*, 42,
163, 165–76, 178, 184, 185, 298*n*65;
"Sexual Inversions," 255; *Undoing
Gender*, 114, 119, 185

caged freedom (psychoanalysis as), 148,
153–54, 163, 206, 248, 263, 269, 271;
see also freedom; liberation
Canguilhem, Georges, xi, 15, 90, 218
Caputo, John, 29, 60, 63–64, 80, 102,
284*n*52, 287*n*34, 287–288*n*36
care of the other, 118, 228, 248, 275,
277, 306*n*129
care of the self, 118, 182, 228, 234, 258–
59, 264, 275, 277, 278, 309*n*61
Care of the Self, see *History of Sexuality
Volume Three* (Foucault)
Cartesian: cogito, 50, 74, 94, 107, 109,
219, 222; coup, 74, 77, 93, 100, 141,
153, 160–61; doubt, 110, 143, 227,
291*n*41; error, 143, 291*n*41; method,
110, 143, 227, 291*n*41, 296–97*n*38;
mind-body split, xvi, 16, 77, 79, 105,
121, 188, 205, 229, 272; moment,
107, 128, 195, 221, 257, 259–60,
265, 267–68; orgasm, 125–26;
rationalism, 37, 55, 60, 76, 93,
100, 133, 153, 160, 195, 228, 291*n*41;
rejection of madness, 58, 125, 147,
198, 205, 222, 257, 261, 296–97*n*38;
subjectivity, 58, 88, 93, 222, 258,
269; *see also* Descartes, René
Cartesianism, 50, 126, 194, 215
"Catacombs" (Rubin), 311*nn*100, 104
Catherine the Great, 210–11
Catherine wheel, 124, 191–92
cause and effect logic, critique of, 88,
91, 108–9, 112–13

Simone de Beauvoir, Philosophy, and
Feminism
NANCY BAUER

Pursuing Privacy in Cold War America
DEBORAH NELSON

But Enough About Me: Why We Read Other
People's Lives
NANCY K. MILLER

Palatable Poison: Critical Perspectives on
The Well of Loneliness
EDITED BY LAURA DOAN
AND JAY PROSSER

Cool Men and the Second Sex
SUSAN FRAIMAN

Modernism and the Architecture of
Private Life
VICTORIA ROSNER

Virginia Woolf and the Bloomsbury Avant-
Garde: War, Civilization, Modernity
CHRISTINE FROULA

GENDER AND CULTURE
READERS

Modern Feminisms: Political, Literary,
Cultural
EDITED BY MAGGIE HUMM

Feminism and Sexuality: A Reader
EDITED BY STEVI JACKSON
AND SUE SCOTT

Writing on the Body: Female Embodiment
and Feminist Theory
EDITED BY KATIE CONBOY,
NADIA MEDINA, AND SARAH STANBURY

The Scandal of Susan Sontag: Private and
Public Affairs
EDITED BY BARBARA CHING
AND JENNIFER A. WAGNER-LAWLOR